JAMES A. MICHENER

A BIOGRAPHY

# JAMES A. MICHENER

## A BIOGRAPHY

### By
### JOHN P. HAYES

W.H. ALLEN · LONDON

COMET

Printed and bound in Great Britain by
Mackays of Chatham Ltd, Kent
for the Publishers, W.H. Allen & Co. PLC
44 Hill Street, London W1X 8LB

ISBN 0 491 03474 1 (W.H. Allen hardcover edition)
ISBN 0 86379 024 0 (Comet Books softcover edition)

# Contents

Preface      ix

Acknowledgments      xiii

Chapter One: *"A Great Citizen of All Mankind"*      1

Chapter Two: *The Fires of Youth*      11

Chapter Three: *The Road Out of Doylestown*      20

Chapter Four: *The Swarthmore Experience*      31

Chapter Five: *The Journey Begins*      45

Chapter Six: *Epiphany*      59

Chapter Seven: *Just a "Johnny One-Note"?*      72

Chapter Eight: *The Right Place, The Right Time*      89

Chapter Nine: *Dateline: Asia*      105

Chapter Ten: *Private Affairs*      119

Chapter Eleven: *Teller of Epic Tales*      133

Chapter Twelve: *A Nation To Be Won*      151

Chapter Thirteen: *Barnstorming*      164

Chapter Fourteen: *Writing Again*      179

Chapter Fifteen: *Youth, Rebellion, and Michener*      195

Chapter Sixteen: *A Gift for America*      212

Chapter Seventeen: *A Place in the World*      231

Notes      241

Index      267

# Preface

I met Jim Michener in the summer of 1970 when the Cleveland *Plain Dealer* assigned me to interview him in Kent, Ohio, where he was preparing to write a book about the tragedy that had occurred at Kent State University on May 4. I was a senior journalism major at Kent State at the time and had been an eyewitness to the horrible weekend confrontation that had ended in bloodshed and the deaths of four students.

To interview Michener was a rare opportunity. He was one of the world's best-known writers, author of *Hawaii, Iberia, The Source,* and at least a dozen other books. I found him in his motel room one morning in August, shortly after his daily jog. He had changed from his sweat suit and was dressed casually in shorts, sneakers, and a loose-fitting shirt that he did not bother to tuck in at the waist. Except for his attire, he resembled any one of several reserved humanities professors. At sixty-three, he was impressive looking, tall and firmly built. His hair was turning gray and thinning, making his high forehead and large facial features all the more striking. He wore glasses, and he spoke slowly in a deep voice that sometimes rose to a high pitch when he wanted to make a point. It was easy to listen to him, and to like him, and for several hours we got to know each other, although he was much more successful at getting me to talk about myself than I was in learning anything new about him.

At the end of our discussion, Michener asked if I would like to work for him. He had already hired several journalism students to do some research and writing for his book, which was sponsored by *Reader's Digest,* and he thought I might be able to assist, too. On the spot I accepted the offer, which was a promise of several hundred dollars in exchange for two or three interviews and a written account of what I had seen at Kent State that first weekend in May. The money was important to me, since I was working my way through college, but not nearly as important as the opportunity to assist a professional writer, particularly one who had worked in many parts of the world.

For the rest of the summer and into the fall, I had several more meetings with Michener, and on each occasion I found him congenial, but always surprising, if not mysterious. Sometimes he asked questions that had nothing to do with our immediate topic of conversation: For example, once as I was leaving his motel room and had already said good-bye, he shouted down the driveway, "How do you get along with your parents?" On another occasion he had just ended an interview, which he had allowed me to observe, and he decided that we should all go outside and play a round of Frisbee. Something in him wanted to be a part of the gang, yet he always maintained a distance. He drank beer with a group of us one night, but he hardly said a word, and afterward he disappeared.

He did not want to be recognized as a celebrity or a famous author. One morning after I had known him for a while, he said, "I don't think of myself as famous, *ever*, and I am constantly amazed when other people do. I've had some very wonderful things happen to me, and it [recognition] disarms me. I often think it's misguided. I don't think of writing as a particularly meritorious career. I have a very prosaic view of that, partly because I've seen so many people make complete horses' asses of themselves. It just goes against my grain. I shouldn't get any more points for being a writer than for being a damned good dentist. That's the kind of person I am."

I thought his ideas were admirable, although unusual. Who *was* this man? What *did* he consider meritorious? And how had he become so famous without seeking fame? For the next couple of years I sought answers to these and other questions while interviewing Michener for several magazines. Then, still struck by his modesty in light of his phenomenal popularity, and certainly in awe of him, I requested permission to write his biography. I hoped to tell the story of how he had become one of America's, and indeed the world's, most cherished authors in the post–World War II era. On July 10, 1974, he replied:

> "I have noted carefully your interest in writing my biography, and I do not know how to respond at this time . . . but legally there is absolutely nothing to halt you from pursuing the project and I want you to understand very clearly that you have every right to do so. The degree that I would want to cooperate or provide additional materials is uncertain at this point, and I do not know when my attitude would clarify."

He added, "there is a collection of my papers in the Library of Congress and these could occupy a researcher for a long time. There is also a collection under way at the University of Northern Colorado . . . which will have some excellent material, and finally the library at Swarthmore College has a copy of almost everything that I have written."

He then provided letters of permission granting me access to these various collections.

During the next couple of years, as I visited Michener about once a year at his home in Bucks County, Pennsylvania, it became obvious that he was willing both to cooperate and to provide additional information for my project. On several occasions he talked with me for hours at a time about his life, his work, the people he has known, and the times in which he has lived. He spoke freely during long walks on his hilltop estate, lush in the spring and snow-covered in the winter. He was always relaxed and revealing, sometimes alarmingly so. One day he dropped at my feet a cardboard box full of the mail he had received that week and invited me to pore over it. When his wife Mari spotted me, she cried, "Cookie, *what* is he doing?" Michener assured her that I had his permission, and our discussion continued, although Mari was still annoyed.

In all, I recorded more than twenty-five hours of interviews with Michener, and gradually, while my respect for him remained intact, my awe disappeared. He was no longer larger than life, although I always felt there was something about him that I could not reach, a part of him that perhaps no one could reach. Sometimes, when his wife or a friend joined us at dinner or in conversation, Michener sat among us, but he was not *with* us. He read a magazine or he stared blankly, gazing out across his hillside as though he were thinking about an idea or a character. All at once his focus returned to his company, and he was amiable again and responsive to every question.

On occasions when his travel or writing assignments left no time for interviews, he invited me to send him a set of questions, which he then promptly answered. Through the years there were a half-dozen of these exchanges. In addition, much to my delight, every so often I received an unexpected letter from him, mailed from some part of the United States or a foreign continent. For example, from St. Michaels, Maryland, in 1977 he wrote, "I greet you on Shakespeare's birthday, an anniversary all writers should honor." He then went on to advise me of two people who he thought might tell me more about his childhood. On other occasions he introduced me to his friends and acquaintances, both social and professional.

At all times he was encouraging, particularly after I entered a Ph.D. program at Temple University, where I intended to write my dissertation about him. In 1980, however, he advised me that I was not alone in my pursuit. He sent me a letter that began with the salutation "Gentlemen." In it he explained that four people were currently writing about him, "and each of you had better be aware of the activity of the others." Two of us were writing biographies, and two were producing illustrated books based on Michener's travels.

"All this adds up to rather more activity than common sense would dictate, but the work is under way," he explained. "None of these arrangements is or can be exclusive. I have *authorized* none of them, in the old sense. I am writing no copy for any of them. . . . I am distributing this letter merely to keep the record straight and the air cleared. You all have my earnest good wishes."

With somewhat more speed my work progressed. I conducted more than one hundred interviews across the country and corresponded with a score of Michener's former classmates, colleagues, and associates, most of whom would not cooperate with me without first getting Michener's approval. I studied the various Michener collections, spending three days in Greeley, Colorado, two days at Swarthmore College, and thirty-five days in the Manuscript Reading Room at the Library of Congress. During several weeks I conducted additional research in Michener's hometown, Doylestown,

Pennsylvania, where the Mercer Museum Library, the Bucks County Free Library, the Melinda Cox Library, and the morgue of the *Doylestown Intelligencer* provided much useful information.

I read twenty-seven of Michener's books and more than five hundred magazine articles, speeches, and essays, plus countless critiques and reviews. I also discussed his articles and books with critics, as well as many of Michener's fans. The numerous secondary sources I consulted included the literary studies, *James A. Michener*, by George J. Becker (1983), and *James A. Michener*, by A. Grove Day (1966 and 1972); *James A. Michener's USA*, edited by Peter Chaitin (1981); *A Talent for Luck*, by Helen M. Strauss, Michener's agent (1979); *In Search of Centennial*, by John Kings (1978); and *At Random*, by Bennett Cerf, Michener's publisher (1977).

All the while Michener and I continued to exchange questions and answers. Finally, in July 1982, he decided that we had "reached a logical halting spot." I had sent him several questions, these somewhat more sensitive than those I had asked previously, and he replied, "After careful consideration I've decided not to respond to your new list of interrogations." He gave me four reasons for his decision: (1) he had cooperated with me for many years, answering all my questions "forthrightly, promptly and with good spirit"; (2) the decision "cannot harm you because you already know more than anyone else on earth about your chosen subject matter"; (3) "Were I to die tomorrow you would be totally competent to publish what you already have and to make shrewd, intelligent guesses about the rest; I feel confident your guesses would be close to the mark. . . . Well, you should proceed now as if I were gone, and in doing so I feel reassured that you will make few errors"; and (4) "Most important, I have never cared much one way or another as to what anyone wrote or said about me. . . . So you will have now and in the future my fullest support in whatever you care to write."

That said, only the writing remained.

John P. Hayes
North Hills, Pennsylvania
1984

# Acknowledgments

During the past ten years, more than one hundred individuals contributed to this biography. Most of these people set aside time to grant me interviews, write me letters, or speak with me by telephone. To each one I am indebted for helping make this a more substantial and revealing book. I especially want to thank those whose names follow:

John M. Allen, Clark Allison, Milton Berkes, Ben Bestler, Richard C. Bond, Art Buchwald, Philip E. Coleman, Walter Conti, Walter Cronkite, Professor Emeritus A. Grove Day, John DeGroot, Barbara Pearson Lange Godfrey, H. Thomas Hallowell, Jr., Marion Holland, Mayre Kagohara, Richard M. Kain, Jonathan H. Kistler, Leslie Laird Kruhly, Kathleen Landes, Charles P. Larkin, Jr., Owen Laster of the William Morris Agency, Hobart Lewis, Hugh McDiarmid, Robert "Peg" McNealy, Hanna Kirk Mathews, David G. Michener, Harry Ralph Michener, Mari Yoriko Sabusawa Michener, Marie Michener, Patti Koon Michener, Judge Harriet M. Mims, Osmond Molarsky, Neil Morgan, Wilbur Murra, Ann Kagohara Nakata, Peter Nehemkis, Nadia Orapchuck, Fulton Oursler, Jr., Edward J. Piszek, William Poole, Robert T. Porter, M.D., Dickson Preston, Professor Emeritus Edith M. Selberg, Wilmer Shaw, Mrs. Joseph (Terry) Shane, Herman and Ann Silverman, Professor Emeritus Robert E. Spiller, Helen M. Strauss, James H. Taylor, Edward T. Thompson, W. Lester Trauch, Ed Twining, Errol Uys, Eleanor Van Sant, William V. Vitarelli, Ph.D., John T. Welsh, Howard C. Westwood, Ruth Wilson, and Stow L. Witwer.

My thanks also go to Bill Nash, who first suggested that I write this biography; Allen F. Davis, Ph.D., David M. Jacobs, Ph.D., both of the History Department, and Maurice Beebe, Ph.D. of the English Department, all Temple University; magazine editors Kirk Polking, Mel Shestack, James Spada, and John Taylor, who through the years provided assignments for me to interview Michener; book editor Fred Kerner, who had worked at *Reader's Digest;* literary agent Ray Lincoln, who provided early editorial advice; Bob Roberts of the Blitman Communications Library, Temple University; George Brightbill of the Paley Library, Temple University; Margaret Triplett of the Bucks County Free Library, Doylestown, Pennsylvania; Catherine Vorndran of the James A. Michener Branch of the Bucks County Free Library, Quakertown, Pennsylvania; Gil Hause of the James A. Michener Library at the University of Northern Colorado; Charles Kelly and staff of the manuscript reading room at the Library of Congress; Terry A. McNealy of the Bucks County Historical Society, Doylestown, Pennsylvania; the Philadelphia Free Library; Martha and Alice Edgar of the Melinda Cox Library, Doylestown, Pennsylvania; Ed Fuller of the Special Collections Department at the Swarthmore College library; Joyce Baur of the Elkins Park Free Library.

Also, photographer Keith Myers; Herbert Mitgang of the *New York Times;* the Rev. Kenneth A. Moe, who began but did not complete a biography of Michener and then shared some of his research with me; Jon Ford, at the time he was press secretary to former Texas Governor William P. Clements, Jr.; Robin Kuzen of the Pulitzer Prize Committee office at Columbia University; Ted and Dorothy Princiotto, who shared their home with me while I was doing research at the Library of Congress; Bob and Anna Marie Clayton, and Gene Kennish, all of whom helped with my research in Colorado; historian Margaret Bacon of the Religious Society of Friends Center; Professor Emeritus George J. Becker, who wrote a literary study of Michener for the Frederick Ungar Literature and Life Series; Peter L. Brill, M.D., director of the Center for the Study of Adult Development; Lila Finck and John Grant, who assisted with my research; authors John Jakes and Curtis W. Casewit; several writers who critiqued portions of the manuscript: Bruce Beans, Jack DeWitt, Phil Goldberg, Barbara Holland, Ralph Keyes, Tom Maeder, Margaret Robinson, Arthur Sabatini, Harriet May Savitz, who was also a constant source of encouragement, Mike Schwartz, and Robin Warshaw; my agents, Virginia Barber and Mary Evans; my editor, Stefanie Woodbridge, and editorial assistant, Amy Reyelt, at The Bobbs-Merrill Publishing Company, Inc. I am also grateful for the support of my wife, JoAnn, and daughters, Holly and Elizabeth, the three people who made the most sacrifices.

Finally, I thank James A. Michener, without whom all of this would have been so much more difficult to complete.

FOR JO ANN

## BOOKS BY JAMES A. MICHENER

(All published by Random House unless otherwise noted)

TALES OF THE SOUTH PACIFIC, Macmillan, 1947
THE FIRES OF SPRING, 1949
RETURN TO PARADISE, 1951
THE VOICE OF ASIA, 1951
THE BRIDGES AT TOKO-RI, 1953
SAYONARA, 1954
THE FLOATING WORLD, 1955
THE BRIDGE AT ANDAU, 1957
RASCALS IN PARADISE (with A. Grove Day), 1957
SELECTED WRITINGS OF JAMES A. MICHENER, 1957
THE HOKUSAI SKETCHBOOKS, Selections from the Manga, Charles
    E. Tuttle, 1958
JAPANESE PRINTS: From the Early Masters to the Modern, Charles E.
    Tuttle, 1959
HAWAII, 1959
REPORT OF THE COUNTY CHAIRMAN, 1961
THE MODERN JAPANESE PRINT, Charles E. Tuttle, 1962
CARAVANS, 1963
THE SOURCE, 1965
ADICKES: A Portfolio with Critique, DuBose Gallery, 1968
IBERIA, 1968
AMERICA VS. AMERICA: The Revolution in Middle-Class Values, New
    American Library, 1969
PRESIDENTIAL LOTTERY, 1969
THE QUALITY OF LIFE, 1970
FACING EAST, Maecenas Press, 1970
KENT STATE—WHAT HAPPENED AND WHY, 1971
THE DRIFTERS, 1971
A MICHENER MISCELLANY: 1950–1970, 1973
CENTENNIAL, 1974
ABOUT CENTENNIAL: Some Notes on the Novel, 1974
SPORTS IN AMERICA, 1976
CHESAPEAKE, 1978
THE WATERMEN, Selections from CHESAPEAKE, 1979
THE COVENANT, 1980
SPACE, 1982

JAMES A. MICHENER

A BIOGRAPHY

# CHAPTER ONE

# "A Great Citizen of All Mankind"

Men are not born citizens of the
countries they inhabit. They are like
wanderers on whom fall the ashes of
many places, and some men live forever
in countries they never even dimly
understand. No! Men grow to
citizenship. They earn it. How do they
earn it? By love, work, a passion for
things better than they are, or by flashes
at night when all the vast land from New
York to California stands illuminated.
That is how men gradually come to
know where they live and why.

JAMES A. MICHENER
THE FIRES OF SPRING, 1949

JIM MICHENER MUST have been very angry the morning he found a subscription request from *Newsweek* magazine in his mail. "Gentlemen," he responded,

> For you to send me a cheap promotion letter so soon after you
> maliciously and rather boorishly clobbered my latest novel, both
> in your columns and over the radio, bespeaks either a collossal
> [sic] ignorance or an arrogance of majestic proportions.
> However, it was obvious to me at the time that you were
> reviewing not me but your major competitor, Time-Life Inc. and
> I can understand your bias, since they do things so much more
> capably than you are able to do with your more limited staff and
> subscription list.

Therefore as a bow to your arrogance, as a forgivenness [sic] of your ignorance, and as a help to your subscription list, herewith my card.

In many ways that letter epitomizes James Albert Michener, America's favorite twentieth-century storyteller. He is unpredictable. He is insecure. He is a gentleman even in anger. He is sure the American literary establishment rarely evaluates his work fairly. And he is a survivor.

Since *Tales of the South Pacific* was published in 1947, no author in America has been more "beloved" by readers, according to one bookseller, than James A. Michener. In 1983 the nation's newspaper editors, responding to a survey conducted by the Sunday supplement, *Family Weekly* magazine, voted Michener one of America's living national treasures. Wherever he appears in the United States the public's response to him is always overwhelming. In Philadelphia during one Christmas season, for example, an autograph party at John Wanamaker's huge department store was scheduled to last for two hours beginning at 1:00 P.M., but at noon the line stretched three hours deep from the center of the store out to Chestnut Street and wrapped partway around one side of the block-long building. In the store's history no author had ever drawn a larger crowd than the one already gathered for Michener, and the book manager began to worry that his supply of *Chesapeake* would be depleted before the line ended. By 4:30, when the last person asked for an autograph and a thousand copies of the novel had been sold, Michener stood up, straightened his back, and said to no one in particular, "Where do they all come from?"

Booksellers across the United States ask that same question every time a new Michener title appears, and no one is less prepared to answer the question than Michener himself. At home one afternoon in Pipersville, Pennsylvania, about an hour's drive north of Philadelphia, he propped up his feet in his living room and explained,

A fundamental fact about me is that I came along in the age of television when it was predicted that the novel was dead. So why my novels go on selling I don't know. There must be some need for the reading experience. I can't imagine there are millions of people who want to read my books, but it has happened, and I'm at a loss to explain it. . . . All I know is that I'm a very lucky guy. I have such a good time doing whatever I want to do, whenever I want to do it, and enjoy it so thoroughly, that it's disgraceful to get paid for it.

There has never been an author in America quite so elusive and yet so popular as Michener. He began writing at the age of forty in 1947, when writers truly mattered in the United States, when Fitzgerald, Hemingway, Dos Passos, Lewis, Faulkner, and Steinbeck defined an era through their work in the mid-twentieth century. That era came to an end in the 1950s as the communications and travel industries expanded America's horizons and created an appetite for excitement, adventure, and knowledge.

Soon Norman Mailer, Truman Capote, Gore Vidal, and Tom Wolfe arrived as the new literary personalities—somewhat more interesting than authors—and a smaller, more refined class of writers including John Cheever, John Updike, James Gould Cozzens, and Joyce Carol Oates surfaced as the new stylists. Off to one side working quietly alone, more social journalist than novelist, more craftsman than writer, was Michener. Better than any contemporary writer he mirrored mainstream America. Like Norman Rockwell, Michener showed readers much about themselves, their ideals, morality, values, fears, and aspirations. His sociohistorical literature filled a gigantic void for readers who wanted to know more about history, art, science, technology, geology, and the peoples of the world. Thus, Michener's career coincided with the awakening of a nation. Unlike his predecessors who created an era, Michener was created by an era. His popularity was the result of timing and talent, a coincidence that permitted him to capture a special spirit in America.

Through four decades Michener has appealed primarily to what is known as Middle America—the God-fearing, optimistic, morally conscious, center-of-the-road citizens whom Richard M. Nixon identified as the silent majority. Trying to improve themselves, if even painlessly, Middle Americans have likened Michener's books to a seminar, and read them as a way of continuing their education. In turn, Michener has become one of the most cherished teacher-authors of all time.

Something else must be said about Michener's success. Timing and talent may account for his popularity, but the motivation behind his career is deeply rooted in his own need to be accepted. More than anything, Jim Michener writes as a means of attaining immortality. The money and the fame mean little to him. He wants to be assured that he belongs to a certain people and a specific place, for he is haunted by the feeling that he may become dispossessed. "I'm afraid that life has passed me by," he confided late in his career to John DeGroot, a former college classmate, while the two of them sat in the shade of a sprawling oak tree on a farm in Michener's native Bucks County. "I've worked too hard, paid too high of a price, and some days I look at my life and I get the feeling that it's bankrupt."

Literary critics have contributed to Michener's moments of desolation. A few critics, however, think Michener has been too harshly judged simply because he is so popular; he is, in other words, a victim of the success-is-suspect syndrome. But the fraternity of eastern critics, whose appraisals weigh most heavily, claim that Michener is overrated. They say that, instead of writing literature, he compiles money-generating yarns that appeal only to middlebrows. They argue that his characters are one-dimensional and unremarkable; that his plots are contrived and superficial; that his research, while exhaustive, is inaccurate and misleading; and that his books are too long.

Quipped one critic about a Michener tome: "My best advice is don't read it; my second best is don't drop it on your foot."

Michener likes the public to believe that he never worries about critics. He says that their opinions are not germane so long as his popularity endures—and critics don't determine which authors endure. But on one occasion Michener listed all the books the Sunday *New York Times* and *Time* magazine reviewers regarded as superb in years when those same periodicals said his books were not. He explained:

> Years later no one had heard of any of [the authors who had written the superb books], not even literary quarterlies. They had made no contribution. I stopped reading reviews. If you know you are going to reach ten or fifteen or twenty million people—you can afford to be magnanimous. . . .
>
> I have no complaints against critics. As my wife will tell you, I never read criticism, good or bad. If they are good they inflate me, and if they're bad they deflate, and I am not a balloon. My wife reads them and makes a list of names into which she sticks pins. . . . I shouldn't be disarmed or have my creative attention blunted by what critics say.

Michener has never written to please the critics. Early in his career, as a writer of short novels and reportorial books about the Far East, he merited at least the respect of critics, but after the success of *Hawaii,* his first epic novel, his reviews soured. Complaining to a sympathetic book editor at the *Philadelphia Inquirer,* he said,

> It's not fair. I am not a formula novelist. I do not play according to the rules. I break them. I'm a serious writer. I think I have something to say. If some critics find me deficient in literary skill, the readers still get the message. My books last . . . and that's the important thing.

Like the critics, academics also have mixed opinions of Michener. "It bothers Jimbo that he's a teacher and the universities ignore his work," says Edward J. Piszek, a Michener acquaintance and Philadelphia entrepreneur. "So I told him we'd make educational films around the world and get them into the schools. That way he can make his points, and I think he liked that."

Mass appeal renders Michener unacceptable by the standards of most college literature programs, and yet Michener wrote,

> I am more academic than almost any successful writer. My college grades and various tests would, I am confident, stand way at the top. I was summa cum laude wherever I went and didn't get anything but A's. I am a damned good writer with a strong classical background and a staggering knowledge of European novelists. . . .

I'm probably more academic than any of my critics.

Academicians, however, contend that Michener is "unscholarly," that his research methods are "unreliable," and that his books are "unworthy" of the classroom. For his part, Michener says he excuses the academic critics because there are many writing tastes, and some of them are conflicting, but all the while he enjoys the irony of being a perennial choice to speak at college commencements. By 1977, and by his own count, twenty-four colleges and universities had granted him honorary degrees in the fields of "science, humanities, writing [and] general citizenship." Michener values those degrees and uses them to gauge his acceptance. In 1973 he noted in his personal papers:

> One of the most reassuring things about working hard for three or four decades is that at the conclusion one has acquired a reputation for better or worse that stays with him the rest of his life and upon which he can, in a sense, depend in the years ahead. Thus, many universities wish to confer degrees upon him for his body of work. And after those number in the dozens he can look back upon a lifetime of work that others have at least paid attention to.

For this same reason he treasures awards. He frequently points out that he has received three of the most coveted: the Pulitzer Prize for fiction, granted for his first book, *Tales of the South Pacific;* the Navy Gold Cross, the highest military award bestowed on civilians for distinguished public service in the areas of morale, recruiting, and public information; and the President's Medal of Freedom, reserved for America's most outstanding citizens and presented to Michener by President Gerald R. Ford. Conspicuously absent from this list, however, are the American Book Award, bestowed annually by the National Institute of Arts and Letters advised by a panel of "distinguished authors and critics"; the National Medal for Literature, granted annually to "an American writer for a distinguished past and continuing contribution to American letters"; and the Nobel Prize for Literature, awarded to those who confer "the greatest benefit on mankind." Unhappily, Michener is not a likely candidate for these honors, and he knows it:

> I have a form letter that I send to people who write to me about the fact that I have not received a Nobel Prize. It begins: "When I think of the great men of my generation who did not get the prize — Proust, Henry James, Conrad, Tolstoy—and compare them with some of the clowns who did, I would much rather stand with the former than with the latter."

Michener's scorn is sour grapes. The guiding spirit of his life is Kant's "categorical imperative": "So live that you would be willing to posit every act that you do as a law universal." Nothing would please Michener more than the Nobel Prize, the one relevant honor that confirms Kant's ethical theory of duty to mankind. In fact, in a postscript to his form letter he contradicts himself by adding that in considering some of the people who have won the Nobel Prize, "anybody would be very proud to be with them."

Countless Michener fans have offered his name for the Nobel Prize, claiming that he is "a great citizen of all mankind." Shortly after Ernest Hemingway won the Nobel Prize for "technological contributions" in 1954, Michener wrote an essay that fell just shy of suggesting that his war novel, *The Bridges of Toko-ri,* which echoed Hemingway's style, also merited the world's highest literary honor. But by passing over Michener every year thereafter, the Swedish Academy has chosen not to acknowledge Michener's international message of brotherhood and peace, his theme in more than two dozen books since 1947.

In spite of these disappointments, Michener thinks of himself

> as a hell of a good pro. I obviously am. And when that's the case, nothing else matters. It's a justification and it's gratifying. . . . Almost every morning of my life I receive letters from all over the world, including some from the greatest minds, saying that I'm the best writer in the world. I live in a total environment of acceptance. I need two secretaries just to say no to my mail. I live in this constantly and I have to be careful not to take it [the environment of acceptance] too seriously.

Perhaps if he had taken this environment more seriously he might have avoided a life of conflict and contradiction—one that seems less appropriate for him than for the tormented protagonist of one of his epic tales. However, Michener appears to thrive on personal complications, and he never plans to stop working long enough to unravel either the truth about himself or the meaning of his life. Perhaps he fears wanting something more, or something that he cannot achieve. To protect himself, he seems to have created an embellished image of simplicity to cover up his inner complexities and to conceal himself from himself, and from his friends and admirers as well. Among writers this is not unusual. Henry James, Willa Cather, Zane Grey, Mark Twain, Walt Whitman, and many others went to the trouble of changing their names to conceal their true identities. Few of them were as honest about their lack of self-knowledge as Michener, though. As late as 1981 he told a national audience:

> There is a great deal about me that I don't want to know. I have stabilized my life. I get by. I have no belief at all that it is as good as it could be, but I sure as hell don't want somebody messing around with it when I am reaching a kind of stabilization, pitiful as it is. . . . It is better to be philosophical about life than to actually analyze what has occurred. You've got to take life in stride.

There are advantages to an insulated life. It limits vulnerability. It confuses facts with irony and exaggeration. It leaves a person free to work and to resist temptation. But it also keeps Michener at a distance from people, even from friends. John DeGroot, the former college classmate who heard Michener say his life was bankrupt, understood what had gone wrong: "Jim has money and fame, but nothing right under his nose. He has no hometown, no family, no real friends. He threw away everything so that he could achieve, and sometimes he can't even see that he's done that."

Michener's friends include Walter Cronkite and Art Buchwald, but no one knows him well. His "dearest friends," he says, are Herman and Ann Silverman who live not far from his home in Pipersville and whom he met at about the time he wrote *Tales of the South Pacific*. But even the Silvermans disagree about Michener's personality. "Jim is strange," says the handsome and rugged-looking Herman Silverman. "It's tough to have a friendship with him because he's so secretive." Contrary to her husband's opinions, Ann Silverman, pert and vibrant, characterizes Michener as being insensitive at times: "He is not interested in most things that other people have to say. He's been to our home a thousand times with a houseful of people, but if he's not comfortable with people he doesn't converse in day-to-day terms. Ask him a question and you'll get a one- or two-word answer, provided he hasn't already walked into the next room and turned on the TV. . . . I admire Jim's strength of character and will. He came from the bottom of the barrel to the top, and that takes determination. But I don't hang on every word Jim says because I know he exaggerates. His wife will often disagree with him about something he says is fact."

A good part of the Michener–Silverman friendship centers on politics and current events. All four are Democrats and as such, oddities in Bucks County. Their liveliest arguments occurred during the Vietnam era. "Jim thought the involvement of the United States in smaller countries was necessary to keep out the communists," revealed Ann Silverman. "We had to remain the dominant world power, according to Jim, because that was part of our sphere of influence to fight these little wars so as to prevent a third world war. We would always have the little wars, he said. How ridiculous! We were imperialists with no business in Vietnam. . . . Eventually, after the peace movement grew so strong Jim said, 'I think it's time to get out.' He had not changed his position, but the war's unpopularity far outweighed our government's reasons for being there."

Ann Silverman, bold enough to challenge Michener face to face, gets aggravated when Michener fails to stand behind his principles: "He was all for the Great Society, but what did he support? He's anti-abortion and he's *for* censorship in Pennsylvania. Why? Because abortion leads to promiscuity. In Denver [where Michener lived in the early 1970s while writing *Centennial*] he was not far from a noisy, 'bad' area with several pornographic movie houses. We've had heated arguments about this, and at least he changed his mind about testifying in favor of censorship once he thought about the ramifications."

Herman Silverman tries to overlook much of what annoys his wife about Michener. "We are Jim's closest friends," he says. "We forgive him for all his nonsense. We enjoy him. He's complicated, and we don't really know him. He's a raconteur; he gets on a subject and embellishes it, and Ann objects to that. But that's what a writer does."

The Silvermans and other friends balance Michener's idiosyncracies against his "good citizenship," which they consider his most admirable quality, and which is enhanced by his Quaker beliefs. Driven by duty, Michener is forever repaying society for his success. Quietly he has given away up to $14 million of the royalties earned by his books. He has contributed most of the money to universities (a $3 million American art collection to the University of Texas at Austin; $2.1 million to Swarthmore College and $100,000 to Kent State University); museums ($80,000 to the Honolulu Academy of Arts); and students (a $500,000 fellowship endowment to the Writers' Workshop at the University of Iowa, and five scholarships annually for children of newspapermen who served in World War II or the Korean War).

Michener is probably the writing profession's greatest benefactor. It is his belief that "Everybody who works in the arts is a brother to everyone else who works in the arts. I feel a deep commitment to helping talented people and a keen sense of responsibility to the new generations, so I have plowed my money into these various channels."

While it is true that the philanthropy eases Michener's tax burden, a point overworked by those who portray him as a "cheapskate," his motives are not selfish. "Jim takes no advantage of his money," says Silverman, himself a wealthy man. "He doesn't know the cost of living, and he never changes his spending habits. I don't understand this. He says he lives the way he would if he were on Social Security, and he means it!"

Indeed it is sometimes difficult for Michener to part with money. His friend Edward Piszek recalled an incident in Frankfurt, Germany, when Michener gave a cashier one dollar for an out-of-town newspaper that on page one carried a price of sixty-five cents. While the cashier jammed the dollar into the register, Michener held out his hand for change. The cashier looked at him and explained that the price of the newspaper was a dollar.

"It says sixty-five cents," Michener protested.

"It's a dollar."

"I don't want it then. I'm not paying a dollar for a sixty-five-cent paper," Michener argued. "Give me back the dollar."

When the cashier explained that the register could not be opened until another customer made a purchase, Michener planted himself at the newsstand to wait. Finally the cashier handed him his money, and he returned the newspaper.

"Atta boy, Jimmy," Piszek shouted from the background. "That's the way to give it to 'em."

Similar scenes have occurred throughout Michener's life and he accounts for them by saying that as a Quaker he cannot easily spend money on himself. Asked if he had ever splurged on anything, he replied with a straight face, "Pineapple juice." Nobody could tell Michener that money was not important:

> I am a depression Quaker who has seen the terror that a lack of money can evoke, and for this I make no apology. . . . I have lived my life as if it were all going to fall apart two weeks from now. The urgency stems from some devastating experiences in child- hood. . . . So money remains one more life problem which I have not been able to solve with any distinction.

He maintains a nearly threadbare existence that amuses his friends and associates. In New York one winter he reported to Random House for several days of editing a book manuscript; arriving from a warm climate without a coat, gloves, or scarf, he was unprepared for New York's bitter weather. With his hands turning blue walking along Sixth Avenue to a Chinese restaurant for lunch, one of his companions suggested they stop and buy a pair of gloves.

"I have gloves at home," Michener snapped, and he continued walking at a brisk pace. This same companion was sure that Michener held on to the first suit he ever bought and that he wore it to work at Random House.

The inheritor of the Protestant ethic and Victorian morality, Michener is a man of old-fashioned values. In retrospect he thinks his rigid background has been more harmful than helpful in his career, but the Puritan ethic has provided a structure for his life. As a result of it, he has sought excellence through education; he remains optimistic in times of adversity; he organizes his work habits and focuses his attention on significant world problems. And most important, he has developed a social conscience that is admired by millions of readers who have responded enthusiastically to the stories and articles Michener has contributed to *Reader's Digest, Life, Look, Collier's,* the *Saturday Evening Post,* and *Holiday,* over the years, and to his books, which include *The Voice of Asia, Sayonara, The Bridge at Andau, Caravans, The Drifters,* and *Kent State—What Happened and Why.*

Some sophisticated readers and critics, however, think Michener's social conscience is a weakness as well as a strength: it has helped attract readers, but it is otherwise ineffective except as "educational entertainment." As Ann Silverman explained, "Jim makes people aware of issues, but he avoids controversy. In *Iberia,* for example, he avoided any analysis of Franco, and in other books he skirted the really important problems. He'd be effective if only he took a stand."

It seems impossible for Michener to take a stand unless he knows he is on solid ground—in opposition to bigotry, for example, or to hatred, war, the loss of basic freedoms, and other generally unpopular abstractions. Michener is not a risk taker. It is his job to probe for solutions, not necessarily provide them, and he does so with striking compassion while exploring world vistas in dramatic, descriptive, painfully informative narratives that incorporate new ideas and lay raw feelings bare. His fiction and nonfiction bolster the soul, and that is Michener's gift. He is neither stylist nor scholar. He is less thinker than craftsman, perhaps, but he is a storyteller most of all. In works that are both boundless and luminous, he entertains and edifies with words.

Unfortunately, at times this is not good enough for Michener. He hates being regarded as a popular writer. That distinction, he believes, belongs to the Irving Wallaces, the Harold Robbinses, and the Jacqueline Susanns of the world—the purveyors of sex and sensationalism. Michener insists that he is several notches above them, a "serious writer" who addresses the world's professional readers, and his best efforts go into maintaining this image of himself. For example, at his autograph party at Wanamaker's in Philadelphia, most of the people who waited in line to meet him were middle-aged women carrying three and four copies of his novels. Afterward, basking in the approbation, Michener said, "I'm amazed that there were so many people. And did you notice that most of them were men in business suits? Who were they? Lawyers, doctors, professionals. . . . Some even came in from the suburbs."

At that moment, Michener, the survivor, was satisfied—for all the wrong reasons. He has never been able to accept himself. This is the tragedy of James Albert Michener. Although he is an enigma to everyone who knows him, he is especially an enigma to himself. He was born an enigma, and any understanding of him begins there.

# CHAPTER TWO

# *The Fires of Youth*

> When you grow up at the bottom of the
> totem pole, you see things from a
> different perspective, and with me there's
> always the circumstances of my birth. If I
> really don't know who I am, I can hardly
> look down on anyone. I seem to have a
> Germanic turn of mind, but I may be
> Jewish or Lithuanian or part black. With
> the uncertain background, one's attitude
> becomes quite liberal.
> JAMES A. MICHENER, 1977

MUCH SPECULATION SURROUNDS the facts of James Michener's parentage, and the truth of the matter may never be known. *Who's Who In America* says he was the son of Edwin and Mabel Michener, of Doylestown, Pennsylvania, but this cannot be accurate because Edwin Michener had died in 1902, and James was born five years later, on or about February 3, 1907; the exact day was not recorded. When asked to clarify the story, Michener revealed that he never knew his parents and that he was a foundling saved from an orphanage by Mabel Michener, a loving, penniless widow. Evidence suggests, however, that this explanation also contains more fiction than fact. Members of the Michener family and many lifelong residents of Doylestown are certain that James was the son of Mabel, born to her during her widowhood.

Until he was nineteen years old and a freshman in college, Michener had every reason to believe he was the son of Edwin and Mabel Michener. He never knew a father, but he was told that Edwin had died shortly before his birth, leaving his mother to rear him and his older brother, Robert, who *was* born to Edwin and Mabel in 1901. But then, in a moment of truth, prompted by reasons unknown, Edwin's brother Louis told James the correct year of Edwin's death. Since Edwin Michener's relatives had always mistreated him, Jim at first refused to believe Louis. But curiosity naturally led him to seek the truth from his mother.

Mabel Michener was the saving grace of James Michener's childhood, but pride must have prevented her from telling the truth about his birth. When Louis revealed her secret about Edwin, she twisted the facts even more by denying that she was James's mother. He was a foundling, she said, delivered to her as an infant without a name or even a birth certificate. Someone—she said she could not remember who—told her James had been born in Mount Vernon, New York, several days before she claimed him, but she knew nothing more. She insisted that she had "adopted" him—though never officially—named him James Albert after a favorite uncle, and loved him like her own son.

There had been many crises in James Michener's childhood, but none could have troubled him more than Louis's and Mabel's revelations. After nineteen years of believing he was the child of a father he never knew and a mother he cherished, he was suddenly no one. Now he wanted answers. For weeks he asked questions and searched for information. Who was he? What was his nationality? Were his parents still alive? Was he abandoned? Should he feel ashamed or betrayed? He asked Mabel's two sisters to help him, but they volunteered nothing, saying they did not know the circumstances of his birth. He looked for a birth certificate, but found none. Finally, convinced that he could learn nothing more about his birth, he vowed to accept Mabel's upsetting story. "I decided 'to hell with it,'" he explained years later. "I was never going to know what had really happened, and I wasn't going to worry about it again. I put it out of my mind when I was nineteen."

It was not that simple to forget, however. Shortly after college graduation, Michener had an opportunity to study abroad, but without proof of citizenship he risked losing his scholarship. When Mabel heard of this, she marched him into the office of an attorney in Doylestown and swore that he was her son, fathered by Edwin Michener. The attorney knew this was not true, but he used the testimony anyway to secure James's passport. For years thereafter, Michener claimed to be the son of Edwin and Mabel Michener. Even his hometown newspaper, the Doylestown *Daily Intelligencer,* out of respect for his mother, no doubt, referred to him as Edwin's son.

Until Mabel Michener was an elderly woman, however, respect was rarely shown to her. She had arrived in Bucks County as a teenager, the oldest daughter of Robert and Kate Haddock, who bought a farm near Doylestown in the late 1800s. At the Quaker meetinghouse one night Mabel met Edwin Michener, son of Ezra, a lineal descendant of John and Mary Michener, who had carried a certificate from Friends in England to Philadelphia Monthly Meeting about 1687. Ezra was a grandson of Isaiah Michener, a prominent Bucks County veterinary surgeon.

Everyone in the Doylestown area knew the Micheners, farmers who also served as postmasters, township trustees, school board chairmen, and Republican committeemen. Ezra, who had seven children, raised Guernsey cattle and attracted much attention to his farm in Carversville. "He has bred many famous cows," wrote local historian William W. H. Davis in 1905, "and always has a fine herd on his farm, in which he takes great pride."

The Haddocks also farmed in Carversville, but nothing they accomplished ever merited mention in Bucks County history books. Thus, the Micheners frowned on the romance between Edwin and Mabel, who met at Buckingham Meeting and married in 1900. The young couple moved in with Edwin's parents, who needed his help on the farm. The next year Mabel bore a son and named him Robert Ezra, in honor of the two grandfathers. Tragedy struck the family when Edwin developed bone cancer and died in early 1902. Mabel and her infant were then forced off the farm.

Little is known about Mabel's life immediately following her husband's death. Supposedly she returned to her parents' home and was later courted by several men, including a Doylestown physician who eventually moved abroad, and Edwin's younger brother Louis, who apparently thought it was his duty to look after his brothers' widows. In fact, in 1908 Louis married the widow of his brother Isaiah, who had died in 1906.

It is known that, in early 1907, pregnant and apparently unwed, Mabel traveled to her brother's home in Mount Vernon, near New York City, with one of her sisters and five-year-old Robert. There she gave birth to her second son, James Albert. Years later, shortly before his death in California, Robert recalled the event:

> Strange how vivid this one memory is. . . . I remember Hannah Haddock, mother's youngest sister, a young nurse in training, doing all the chores for mother—alone. I remember lying on a cot in the same room with Arthur Haddock, mother's youngest brother, lying on his side and shielding me from any view of the proceedings. Also trying to quiet me. It was thus that James Albert entered this world, so help me God.

Soon after James's birth Mabel moved to the outskirts of Doylestown where she began the sweatshop existence of taking in laundry, sewing buttonholes, and mending clothes. Apparently, the birth of her second son alienated her from the community as well as from her own parents and left her in even deeper disfavor with the Michener family. But in spite of what must have been her shame and the added frustration of her indigence, Mabel intended to survive, supporting and protecting her sons at all costs.

"Survival" was often a generous description of James Michener's childhood. He recalled,

> There were almost weekly crises and we never had a cent. What money we could earn had to be used for food and rent, but we

were evicted six times because my mother couldn't pay the land-
lord. I remember standing out on the road at dusk wondering
where we would find a place to sleep. For a child, that was pretty
frightening.

A meal, Michener remembered, often consisted of tomato gravy over
pork fat, or potatoes and green vegetables from the garden, or a bowl of soup
and a chunk of bread, or a mustard sandwich. Mabel rarely managed to buy
meat. Every so often she prepared a delicacy—homemade sauerkraut, for
example, or dandelion greens soaked in vinegar and sprinkled with salt—but
there was seldom anything more. "On many nights we went to bed without
eating at all," Michener recalled. "As a result of our poor diet, some of my
bones never developed properly, and my mother was frequently too sick to
get out of bed."

The worst days occurred during Mabel's illnesses when she sent Jimmy to
her sister Hannah Pollock, whose husband was the caretaker at the local
poorhouse. In that depressing environment, where even the people reeked of
insecticide, and many of them cried all through the night, the young James
Michener began to think seriously about his destiny.

The Pollocks lived comfortably in a stone farmhouse and never wanted for
food, but across the field from them, in two red brick buildings—one for
men, the other for women—several dozen desolate people waited out their
final years. Most of them had been overpowered by circumstance and were
now abandoned, hopeless souls. "If only . . ." they used to begin and end
their stories as they strolled around the poorhouse grounds or mumbled to
themselves from the dark corners of their rooms. On good days some of
them babbled unwittingly when they spotted Jimmy. They pulled him into
their wrinkled lives with hugs and kisses, but at other times they flinched if he
walked near them, screamed and poked at him as they would an intruder. As a
result, Jimmy never knew whether to feel sorry for these old people or to
blame them for their own desolation.

One summer, while living with the Pollocks, Jimmy became friendly with
several old men, who must have seen him as a second chance in life. On many
days Jimmy listened for hours as the old men talked about life and love and
hope, and what might have been. One man recited poems to make his points,
while others drew from their knowledge of literature, nature, and science.
Everyone expressed a different opinion, but from each man's message Jimmy
sifted a common theme: Education, hard work, and a little luck could save a
man from the obscurity of a poorhouse. In reflective moments Jimmy
thought about the old men and worried that he might be headed for the same
dead end.

One morning they found one of the old men hanging from the rafters in
the barn. It was then, at the age of nine or ten, that Jim Michener decided
what he must do. Years later he explained, "I made up my mind in that
poorhouse that I would do anything, *anything* to keep myself out of there.

These were pathetic people whose lives had soured, and I was not going to end up on the same ash heap." Consequently, before he was a teenager, it was clear to Jim Michener that, regardless of what he chose to do in life, he had to work at it zealously, like a man running from certain doom.

Life improved slightly for Mabel and her boys after they moved into the borough of Doylestown, although no one there particularly welcomed them. As soon as people knew about Mabel's second child—and in Doylestown such news traveled fast—she was sneered at publicly for having blemished a good family's name.

Like other rural towns in early twentieth-century America, Doylestown was charming, but its residents were narrow-minded God-fearing people who moved in cliques. Built on a hilltop in a historic area—George Washington really did sleep in many Bucks County homes—this quaint borough was founded by men and women of foresight. The name originated with the town's first innkeeper, William Doyle, who in 1745 obtained a license to "keep a publick house" at the intersection of two stagecoach lines in southeastern Pennsylvania. Doylestown became a popular rest station for travelers between Washington, D.C., and New York, Philadelphia, and the Pocono Mountains.

In the early 1800s, fewer than one hundred people called Doylestown home, but in 1813 an event occurred that assured Doylestown's prosperity and helped make the borough one of the eastern seaboard's most desirable communities. That year Doylestown became the county seat, thus attracting doctors, lawyers, real estate agents, and many enthusiastic merchants who created a vigorous community with the courthouse as the focal point of their activities. By midcentury the railroad improved transportation between Philadelphia and the mountain resort towns, and a real estate boom soon followed. Suddenly, city dwellers transformed the quiet farmland of Bucks County into a resort, and by the turn of the century Doylestown's population had jumped to thirty-five hundred people.

When Jim Michener moved into town with his mother, Doylestown was a friendly borough, but a borough where social status counted. While farmers, mostly Mennonites and Quakers, surrounded the village and stimulated the local economy, their significance ranked second in importance to the professionals who set the standards in Doylestown. From their impressive stone homes and their private lodgings and clubs, Doylestown's elite, most of them Presbyterians and Baptists, watched over their community with a critical eye. Anyone who dared to be different, or was rendered different by circumstance, found it difficult to get along in this village. Catholics, blacks, the impoverished, the eccentric, and anyone of inordinate talent or wealth could expect to be snubbed by the self-righteous citizens of Doylestown, Pennsylvania.

Soon after she rented an old frame house in the heart of the borough, probably in 1917, Mabel Michener became one of Doylestown's least favorite people. Not only was she a poor woman with a tainted reputation, but she also defied her neighbors by opening a boardinghouse for children who needed temporary shelter. Scornful looks and wagging tongues followed Mabel in Doylestown, but her stubborn determination gave her the courage to walk proudly and confidently and to smile under the worst of circumstances. She set this same example for her children, including those whom she took off the streets. During a ten-year period in the middle years of Mabel's life, she devoted herself to caring for other people's children. In all, more than thirty youngsters, most of them under the age of ten, called her Mama. Four of these children arrived at Mabel's as infants, born to unwed mothers in Philadelphia and New York City. The others came for weekends when it was "inconvenient" for their parents to keep them at home, or for summer vacations while their parents traveled abroad.

One of the infants was Eleanor Van Sant, born to a teenage mother in Philadelphia General Hospital and delivered to Mabel within hours of her birth. In 1980 Eleanor reminisced about the first eight years of her life, those spent with Mabel Michener.

"She was a strict mother but, oh, so loving, and she made time for all of us. There was always something going on in her house—lots of confusion but never any men. We were just a bunch of happy little kids. I think there were seven of us, and we all got along. We all thought we were brothers and sisters and that Mabel was our mother.

"I remember she punished us one day for bickering, and Mary Smith and I had to sit in the kitchen on a stool. Mary blamed me for getting us into trouble and I blamed her, and all of a sudden she grabbed a butcher knife and threw it at me. I've got the scar to remember her by. . . .

"Mabel used to take us to the movies and read to us all the time. She was soft and cuddly. I can't really see her face but I remember she was so warm. She was concerned that we'd get lost coming home from school, and I recall how she used to drill us.

"'What's your name?' she asked each one of us in the mornings.

"'Eleanor Van Sant.'

"'Where do you live?'

"'Thirty-one North Clinton Street, Doylestown, P.A.'

"A long time ago, after my real mother's sister came to get me at the Micheners', I went back to Doylestown and tried to find Clinton Street, but I couldn't. I'll never forget the house on Clinton Street, though. I slept on the third floor with several other girls, and we loved it. . . . I really am very grateful to Mabel because she gave me a wonderful life."

Eleanor Van Sant was separated from the Micheners in the mid-1920s when Mabel closed her boardinghouse, but fifty years later she found her "brother" Jimmy. "When I saw the movie version of *Hawaii* I wondered if that James A. Michener could be my older brother, but I didn't do anything about it. Then finally after many years I wrote to him, and he wrote back that he remembered me. What a coincidence. We were together early in our lives, and here we are late in life, together again."

At a reunion one weekend in the late 1970s, Eleanor and Jim remembered how their lives in Doylestown centered around a compassionate Mabel. Every evening "Mama" gathered her "children" around a rocking chair and read to them. The smallest children, dressed in pajamas, cuddled close to her bosom, while the older children, including Jimmy, sat at her feet.

With a bent for dramatization, Mabel favored tales of romance and adventure, and epic poems like the *Iliad*. She especially enjoyed the stories of Charles Dickens and Mark Twain, and by reading such works to the children Mabel introduced her son to the narrative technique he later adapted to his own writings. At the time, of course, Jim Michener cared less about style than he did about his mother's performance, and his imagination ran wild during each reading.

Sometimes the stories—Dickens's *Oliver Twist,* perhaps, or Twain's *Huckleberry Finn*—rang with familiar echoes: Jimmy knew about loneliness in a poorhouse and nights with nothing to eat; he had learned about the freedom and danger of rafting on a river, for he had floated down the Delaware, just a few miles from home. The verisimilitude of these stories impressed him and made him long for new experiences. And whenever Mabel read, Jimmy was content to sit and listen, and to dream.

On nights when Mabel was too busy or too sick to read she cranked up an old Victrola, a Christmas gift from her brother, and filled the house with music. She then commanded the children to listen to the rhythms and melodies that she thought rivaled the most beautiful lines of literature. Despite her lack of resources, this penniless widow, who had little formal education and never enough money to buy herself a new dress or a winter coat, shared some of the world's greatest books and music with children. As people knew in Doylestown, Mabel's home was not at all typical.

One Christmas Eve, Mabel's neighbors discovered there were no limits to her determination. Birthdays and most holidays passed without notice, because Mabel had no money for gifts or parties. But Christmas was especially for children, she said, and she liked to celebrate it in the fashion of Dickens. Aside from its religious significance, Christmas meant bright packages and stockings full of candy, and a huge evergreen tree decorated with homemade ornaments and ribbons. However, one year there was no money for even a tree, and Mabel's home looked dismal. It was a cold night, and a heavy snow had fallen, Michener recalled:

> I was surprised to see the wintry days speed by with no sign of secret boxes or red wrapping paper. . . . On Christmas eve my mother was strangely silent. She put the five younger children to bed and then sat in her chair, rocking back and forth furiously. She would not look at me, and I was afraid to speak, for I had never seen her this way before. Suddenly she said, "Get out all the decorations!" Joyfully I pulled down the boxes of old tinsel and

bright stars. We placed them on the empty kitchen table and then she said: "Go to bed! At least we'll have a tree."

Wrapping a shawl around her shoulders, Mabel then left by the back door. Tracking through ankle-deep snow, she marched into the shopping district where a man was selling evergreen trees. She did not ask, and she refused to beg. Instead, she grabbed a tree and shouted in the salesman's direction, "You can arrest me tomorrow if you want, but a home with six kids has got to have a tree." She dragged the tree home and began to decorate it in preparation for Christmas morning.

Later that night, the Christmas tree salesman helped a few other men gather a basket of food and toys, which they took to the boardinghouse on Clinton Street. Mabel greeted them from her rocking chair. "I expected you to come," she said defiantly. "God couldn't miss Christmas in a house where there are six children."

For all of her life, Mabel Michener maintained an almost Pollyannaish optimism. No matter what went wrong she believed she could make it right, and her children thought she always succeeded. There was one crisis, however, that even Mabel could not control. She set it in motion herself, breaking her heart in the process.

As a middle-aged woman, Mabel lacked the energy to mother a houseful of children, many of whom required constant attention. She worried most, however, about keeping the children healthy and paying for their educations. She expected each child to go to college, but even with support money from their biological families, who did not always cooperate, Mabel could not manage. Finally, she decided to close the boardinghouse and make other arrangements for the children.

Eleanor Van Sant remembered the day her aunt came to take her away from Mabel's. "I was only eight," she explained. "I couldn't understand what was happening." Mabel packed Eleanor's clothes and gave her a school transfer card that proved she was in the second grade. Then two tall, stern-looking women arrived at the door. One of them was Eleanor's aunt. Eleanor screamed to Mabel, "Don't let them take me. You are my mama, you are my mama," but the women took the youngster to a bus and then to their home. "I was frightened and confused," Eleanor remembered, "but everything turned out fine. My aunt's family loved me, and they gave me a very nice life."

No matter how much her children admired her, Mabel Michener remained an outcast in the eyes of Doylestown's citizens, and her sons never adjusted to the way their mother was treated. Why people denigrated their mother they never knew, for this was not a topic that children discussed. They saw in Mabel a generous, loving woman who worked hard and enjoyed few of life's pleasures. She had not prospered as had other parents in Doylestown. She could never buy bicycles or roller skates or baseball mitts, and her children wore sneakers year round with the broken laces tied together in several knots. But how, they wondered, had she offended the people of Doylestown?

Jim Michener must have always known something was amiss in his life. The feelings began even before Mabel moved into the borough. Occasionally Edwin's brothers and sisters visited Robert with candy, but refused to share it with Jimmy: ·

> They fed him right in front of me, and if I asked for candy, too, they shoved me aside and told me, "Get away, you're a bad boy who doesn't deserve candy." I hadn't a clue as to what they were talking about, but right then I wrote them out of my life. They were miserable people.

Compensating for her in-laws' behavior, Mabel protected James, perhaps to Robert's irritation, and the two brothers never got along. After Robert graduated from a trade school, he ran away from home, rejecting Mabel and their life in Doylestown. "I tried to correspond with Robert. He never wanted anything to do with me," Michener said. "I really don't know what to make of that." But Jim Michener never considered abandoning his mother. He had seen abandonment dozens of times at the poorhouse, and he could never forget those days. He loved Mabel, in spite of Doylestown, and in his mind he remained her adopted son. In his heart, however, he must have known the truth.

## CHAPTER THREE

# The Road Out of Doylestown

I think an essential fact about me is that
I've always known people can end on the
ash heap.

JAMES A. MICHENER, 1976

WHEN MABEL MOVED into Doylestown and created what neighbors called "a madhouse, with children running everywhere," young Jim Michener became a vagabond, seeking his peace of mind outdoors. At ten, his distinguishing characteristics included curly, reddish-brown hair, a pair of practically toeless sneakers, with the laces knotted together, and an insatiable curiosity that wore out his welcome in many parts of town.

He managed to sneak through the side door of the courthouse one morning and eavesdrop during a murder trial. He was so impressed by the attorneys' arguments that he tried to make the courthouse visit a weekly ritual. Invariably someone spotted him in a dark corner, however, and the bailiff chased him away. Undaunted, Jim found something else to do.

Many mornings he greeted the farmers at the train station, south of town, and in exchange for a boxcar ride he helped them load their milk and vegetables for the Philadelphia market. On summer days he swam in Deep Forge Creek, and when he could hitch a ride out to the Delaware River, several miles from home, he hopped a barge for New Hope or Washington's Crossing and met the "river families" along the way. More than anything, he seemed to enjoy meeting different people and learning about their work.

Frequently, against Mabel's better judgment, Jim explored the controversial construction site at the edge of town where Dr. Henry Mercer was building a grand museum using only rods of iron and concrete. Most people in the borough thought Mercer was a fool, in spite of his wealth and Ivy League education. No one could erect a building without a hammer and nails and expect it to stand, they claimed, and furthermore, anyone who went near Mercer's museum of reinforced concrete was endangering his life. Parents warned their children to stay away from the site and, for that matter, from Mercer, too. He wore a shiny black cape and rode a bicycle all over town, followed by a noisy little dog. At night he inspired fear, particularly when he suddenly emerged from a dark alley. Mercer had little time for the people of Doylestown, but he was no fool. After he and his small band of laborers completed the museum, they used reinforced concrete to build Fonthill, Mercer's palatial home, and a sprawling tile factory, too. These buildings became landmarks, and as a child, Jim Michener could explain in detail how they had been constructed. Once or twice he even managed to strike up a conversation with Mercer.

As a teenager Jim strayed farther from home. With spending money that he earned by mowing lawns and delivering newspapers, he rode the streetcar to the Willow Grove Amusement Park, one of the Philadelphia area's major summer attractions, frequented by the orchestra of Victor Herbert and the band of John Philip Sousa. One summer he worked at the park as a cashier and practiced the art of shortchanging, accepting a two dollar bill and claiming it was a one. The streetcar also delivered him to Philadelphia where he visited museums and attended the theater. Eventually, the chance of greater adventures lured him to the open road, and he claims to have visited all but two or three states before he reached the age of eighteen.

On several of these occasions he visited his mother's sister, Laura Haddock, a Detroit teacher, who cherished a collection of Honoré de Balzac's novels. En route to Detroit he spent a week, sometimes longer, hitchhiking and hopping freight cars, observing local customs along the way, and trying not to travel the same roads twice. "It was very leisurely," Michener recalled:

> People who owned some of the earliest automobiles were eager to show off their possessions, so it was not difficult to get a ride. The next thing you knew they offered to take you home and feed you, plus give you a place to sleep. These were absolute strangers, but I thought they were the greatest people in the world. For $1.35 I went from Doylestown to the Mississippi several times, and it never hurt me a bit. Bakers gave me stale bread and bologna; farmers gave me vegetables and chores to do in exchange for

pocket money. You didn't meet brutal types unless you sought
them out, and I was never courageous in that respect.

Occasionally he did run into trouble, however. Once, a "knight of the
road" assaulted him in a boxcar and stole his money and food; and several
times local authorities carried him off park benches in the middle of the night
and detained him while they checked his identity. But Jim was resourceful,
and he survived without any ill effects.

In fact, these trips across America accounted for the most important
experiences of his childhood. They made him an incurable optimist, much
like his mother. At his aunt's home he spent most of his time reading Balzac,
escaping in the *Comédie Humaine.* He later said, "I am as indebted to [Balzac]
as I am to any living human being who ever touched me because his books
were so . . . filled with violence and compassion and sex and religion and the
business of earning a living. He was precisely the kind of person I missed in
real life and whom I needed so desperately."

The great French master and the goodwill of more than fifty American
families gave Michener a reason to feel hopeful about his own future for the
first time in his life. Mabel, and the old men in the poorhouse, had told him
about the American ethic—trust in equality, hard work, and education—but
what had they to show for it? Until he met these strangers, he had no proof
that an American dream existed. Now, however, he had experienced life
beyond Doylestown, and he found it so stunning that he began to pursue that
dream single-mindedly.

More than anything else in childhood, Jim Michener missed having a
father, but he was grateful to one man who shared an interest in his adolescence. George C. Murray—Uncle George to all the boys of Doylestown—
was slender, soft-featured, and remarkably patient. In his prime he looked
like a Norman Rockwell portrait: mustache, wire-rimmed glasses, and bald-
ing head. He was a bachelor and a tinsmith, and the boys thought him a man
of infinite knowledge. He spent the last twenty-five years of his life showing
more than 450 Doylestown boys how to become "good American citizens."

"As a result of his efforts," Jim Michener reminded an audience of Murray
admirers in 1957, "hundreds of us were kept from developing into tough
young punks."

Following the Spanish American War, Murray purchased a load of army
fatigues and dress blues and a crate of rifles from the government. He altered
the uniforms and polished the rifles, and then, one day in 1906, he invited
George Baxter, of John Wanamaker's Drill Corps in Philadelphia, to teach the
boys of Doylestown how to march. Later that year he and Baxter formed a
Doylestown chapter of the United Boys' Brigade of America, a national
organization with a scintilla of military fol-de-rol and a tenuous allegiance to
the Presbyterian church.

Any boy ten years or older qualified for membership in the Boys' Brigade,
and every boy hoped to belong, at least until the Boy Scouts of America

formed a local troop. Many parents said that Murray had formed the brigade only for Doylestown's disadvantaged boys, and Catholic parents objected to Murray's Sunday school lessons, so many youngsters' parents forbade them to join. These boys later became Boy Scouts, but the brigade members looked down on them because the scouts did not march and tote rifles.

Every Friday evening, sporting their khakis—or dress blues during winter—brigade members reported to their social center, an old building that Murray had renovated with his own money. Upon arrival, each boy paid dues of ten cents and presented himself to a stone-faced senior officer whose immaculate dress, including white gloves and shiny boots, impressed even the veterans in town. Standing erect, with a rifle slung over his shoulder, the officer handed each comrade the evening's Bible verse. After a moment of study the underling felt a nudge toward the second floor, where he met an equally polished officer who demanded that he recite the passage. If the youngster repeated the verse without error, he entered the meeting room; if not, he walked to the foot of the stairs and tried again.

Commander Murray opened every brigade meeting with a prayer and roll call. Youngsters who had attended Sunday school earlier in the week, answered "Present" when Uncle George shouted their names; those who had missed Sunday school were admonished to say "Here."

The highlight of the evening occurred when the boys marched two abreast in drills with the bugle and drum corps, trained by Baxter. Each drill was a contest to see who could follow the commander's directions without missing a beat, and the marching continued until only one boy remained on the floor. Commander Murray then awarded the winner a medal and gave the boy who had placed second a fifty cent piece. Thus, without realizing it, he encouraged certain boys to settle for second best. Once a boy had won a medal, he did not need another, but every boy wanted fifty cents, and there was always a brawl to claim it!

Following the presentation of awards and a few obligatory words about sportsmanship, Murray introduced the next Sunday's Bible lesson, then concluded the meeting with his favorite prayer,

> Let the words of my mouth, and the meditation of my heart,
> be accepted in Thy sight, O Lord, my strength and my redeemer.
> (Psalms 18:15)

Members of the Boys' Brigade became officers only if they participated in weekly meetings, attended Sunday school, and learned how to drill flawlessly at least some of the time. Jim Michener was not among the officers, because his mother, who grew up a Quaker, disapproved of rifles and war games. Becoming an officer was of no consequence to Jim, however; he was happy as long as he could participate in brigade basketball, the activity he preferred over all the others.

Murray had built a basketball court on the second floor of the social center, and Jim played there year round several times a week. "The court had every conceivable deficiency," he recalled.

> The baskets were hung flat against the end walls, which meant that those of us accustomed to using them mastered the art of dashing headlong at the wall, planting our right foot against the planking, and vaulting upward toward the basket, ending high above the rim so that we could then dunk the ball downward. . . . The ceiling was unusually low, with a wide, heavy rafter right above the basket, and we became expert in speeding down the floor, and with maximum force slamming the ball vertically upward, so that it caromed back down through the basket. . . . On this bizarre floor the Doylestown Boys' Brigade fielded teams with far more than normal skills . . . and never lost a home game in three years!

For hours at a stretch, especially during weekends, Jim practiced basketball. On Saturday mornings he scrimmaged with several companions, including Bob McNealy and Ed Twining, but by noon everyone except Jim wanted to play baseball or go fishing or swimming. Waving away his friends, in spite of their prolonged coaxing to join them, Jim continued to shoot baskets.

"A quirk in Jim's character" made him want "to be the best in whatever he was doing," remembered Lester Trauch, a childhood friend who later became a writer for the Doylestown *Daily Intelligencer.* "He was not one for hunting and fishing, although he had a lot of interests and when he felt like it he could make us all laugh. But he was not one of the gang. He liked to walk along the canal and be by himself, don't you know? He was obsessed with basketball, though. He had to excel at it. It was his relief from the kind of life he faced at home." As a result, when Jim Michener insisted, friends let him live in a world all his own.

On the day he entered Doylestown High School and refused to sit in the B class in 1921, Jim Michener let everyone know that he was a serious student who intended to make the most of his education. The B class was for students who had not attended kindergarten—the A class, of course, included those who had—and teachers favored the A class because those students were supposedly brighter. Mabel Michener's indigence had prevented her from sending Jim to kindergarten, but he was as bright as the best A student, and he knew it. Rather than sit with the B students he voiced his displeasure in the superintendent's office—and was quickly transferred into the A class. As a consequence, however, he became one of the superintendent's pet peeves.

It must have surprised the superintendent, Dr. Carmon Ross, when Jim Michener earned excellent grades and led his class scholastically. He was a model student, with a photographic memory. Since he read incessantly about most topics that his teachers introduced, he was the one student who could be counted on to do extra work.

A legend in Doylestown says that Margaret Mead, who later became the world-famous anthropologist, and Jim Michener owned the first library cards at the Melinda Cox Library, a narrow repository housing several hundred volumes across from the school and courthouse. It may have been so, for Michener claimed that he read every book at Melinda Cox prior to his high school graduation and that he sent the librarians out for additional titles. Childhood friends said that he haunted the library and gave reading preference over all his other interests, including basketball. He used to sit in a corner and page through stacks of *National Geographic,* depending on the magazine's editors to show him the exotic countries of the world. China became his first love; the Pacific his second. Supposedly he read everything the librarians could find about Asia.

"One thing we knew about Jim was that he never wasted a minute," said Trauch. "He walked to school reading his lessons, and he read in the halls between classes. While the rest of us acted like a bunch of noisy chickens, Jim was studying. And then we'd get to history class and the teacher would ask some damn thing about the Versailles Treaty, and Michener was the only one to know. He knew it all, and he'd rattle off the answers, or he'd stand up and deliver a report on Lafayette, for example, because he had done all this extra research. The teacher was fascinated, but we all just laughed like hell."

The tauntings bruised Jim's ego—"To be a bright child in America is a dreadful handicap because everyone makes fun of it," he said later—but he continued working hard nonetheless. By the time he graduated, the effort had begun to produce results.

During his first two years at Doylestown High School, Jim clashed with older students, and with several teachers, too. Every boy in high school wore a jacket and tie, and Jim's were noticeably secondhand, although Mabel kept them mended. One clique of students constantly tormented him about his clothing, and even a teacher added to the insults. A former classmate reminded Michener in 1963 that one of their teachers had subjected them "to the most sadistic treatment ever accorded a student" for wearing trousers that had not been pressed. The slightest remark rankled Jim, aggravating his shame and insecurity, and since he did not fight back, he was an easy target. Even if he wanted to fight, his mother forbade any form of violence.

In time, the jeering abated, particularly when Jim led the Doylestown basketball team to numerous victories. In his senior year, he was elected class president and appointed editor-in-chief of *The Torch,* the school's magazine. Earlier, an article in *The Torch* had described Jim as "the most talkative . . . most prompt . . . most original" student in the school.

Dr. Ross was not as quick to appreciate Jim, in spite of his qualities. Ross had earned the respect of Doylestown parents, who regarded him as an educator ahead of his times, but most of them never knew about the superintendent's crude principles. He had a Machiavellian method for discovering whom to punish for any wrongdoing that occurred in Doylestown High. When he heard about a violation, he immediately suspected the same bunch of boys, which included Jim Michener.

Ross's method of ferreting out the guilty student began when he met privately with each boy. "I know who did this," he shouted, "and if you don't tell me his name I'll punish you along with him. Now is your only chance to save yourself." The tactic was distasteful, but it worked—at least until the boys caught on.

Despite frequent grillings, Jim never capitulated to the superintendent's rantings, but he never forgot the day that Ross embarrassed him in front of the entire student body. The superintendent had intercepted a love note that Jim had intended for a female classmate, and he later berated both Jim and the girl at a school assembly. He shamed the youngsters for their "silly sentimentalities," and he warned the school that he planned to punish any student caught sending or receiving similar notes.

Jim sat among his classmates, downcast and humiliated, but he was not about to let the matter drop. He could make words work to his advantage, and in the next issue of *The Torch* he wrote an editorial entitled "Silly Sentimentalities." A more biting satire had never appeared in the school magazine:

> At last the authorities of our high school have hit upon a most distressing evil that is abounding in our school. I refer to the "silly sentimentalities" that are so prominent of late.
>
> I entertain the same opinions as do the faculty. Why should there be so much valuable time wasted on the absolutely foolish attachments, which invariably end in nothingness, at the most, and not infrequently in quarrels? Why should the big red blooded boys and girls of this school find amusement in making themselves conspicuous by casting their affections on one certain person?
>
> It annoys me, and many others also, to see some lovesick swain cast languishing glances upon some flower of his heart, and become insensible with ecstasy if she even so much as deigns to smile at him.
>
> It may be as some of the advocates of these "sentimentalities" claim, that they are not silly, but natural. However, the thinkers and well wishers of the school will not pay much attention to these thrusts by those who are foolish enough to think that they are capable of true affections at the tender age of fifteen or sixteen.
>
> One of the boys who is proud to be classed as a "sentimentalist," has the open effrontery to inquire whether or not the people who are continually knocking him, and his associates, would have different opinions if they had had the opportunities to be "silly sentimentalists" in their high school days. Such deliberate

insults as these will not be tolerated much longer, and if that inquisitive boy must know, it is said, on good authority, that not a few of the people who are opposing this ultra-modern movement in our high school, had to fight off their admirers of the opposite sex in their younger days.

I may as well add, now that I am assured that my readers understand my ideas on this subject, that it is not a case of sour grapes with me, although I wouldn't exactly be against a mild sort of friendship were my face to warrant it, but that I honestly believe that it should be abolished in this school. All those having the same trend of thought can join our society, The Society for the Abolishment of Silly Sentimentalists, by paying the yearly dues, $1.00, to me.

No one paid dues to Jim's society, but the editorial remained the final word in the "silly sentimentalities" episode. The essay displayed Jim's flair for writing, and it also proved that he could laugh at himself, a quality that his friends had thought he lacked. However, he never forgave Ross for embarrassing him. Fifty years after his high school graduation, Michener said, "Ross was a miserable son of a bitch. No one in my crowd liked him, and . . . he gave me some real problems. Although I must say that later in my academic career he came forward wanting to be helpful, but by then the damage was done."

In spite of Ross, Jim never lost enthusiasm for Doylestown High School, and during his final two years there he was the school's most ardent promoter. His sports column appeared in the local newspaper and he spent late nights editing *The Torch* and writing about the opportunities at DHS. He always praised the progressive ideas of the faculty, particularly those of Miss Kirk, the short, fiery English teacher who occasionally tangled with the superintendent. And he persuaded many of his classmates to support the school and participate in extracurricular activities. In an editorial entitled "An Old, Old Theme," he wrote that "school is probably the biggest thing in life right now." The subject was school spirit, which he defined as "respect and love combined." He wrote, "School may be very matter-of-fact, and often it is the little things that make it interesting. The more interesting it can be made, the better we like it, and the better we like it, the more we get out of attending it."

It may seem strange for a free-spirited youngster to have written with such feeling about his school, but this merely proved that Jim Michener, like most teenagers, sought acceptance and admiration. For him, it was easy to win accolades through school-related activities, and none gave him more triumphs than the basketball squad. During his junior and senior years, he was one of Doylestown's star players.

When Jim tried out for the basketball team, he had already played the sport for six years in the Boys' Brigade, and his long hours of practice paid off. By the time he graduated in 1925, his athletic prowess was legendary, but an examination of the record book shows that he ranked among the most talented athletes in Bucks County. With the guidance of his coach, Allen Gardy, he became an adept player, handling the ball well, shooting with one hand, when it was still the custom to shoot with two, and running the full length of the court with enviable speed. He and his teammates, still including McNealy and Twining, captured the 1923–24 Bux-Mont Cup, then the basketball crown of neighboring Bucks and Montgomery counties.

Allen Gardy—printer, publisher, and part-time coach—followed George Murray as the second most significant man in Jim Michener's adolescence. "At a time when my personal life was chaotic and required a firm hand, [Gardy] was there, a surrogate father, a stern counselor, a man who never doubted that good things lay ahead for me," Michener explained years later. Unlike Uncle George, however, Gardy was not blessed with patience. Every boy who played for Gardy remembered him as the "benevolent dictator."

One day, recalling Gardy, Michener said, "He subscribed to the highest possible standards and observed them himself. You could go to him with any problem and get an immediate clear-cut decision. . . . He was a simplistic man to whom everything was either good or bad."

Gardy made a lasting impression. Democrats, labor union leaders, troublemakers, radicals, and college professors were all bad, he said. His list also included fried foods, alcohol, cigarette smoking, and dating girls. "Girls are *very* bad for athletes," he claimed, and he expected his boys to be as chaste as they were skilled. Said Michener, "The psychological costs were extreme when you played for Gardy, but we were champions. And to Gardy, *that* was good."

Basketball practice began early each fall in Doylestown. The school had temporarily banned football, because a coach in a neighboring community objected to pitting his charges against a black athlete on the Doylestown squad. That ended football at DHS for the first half of the 1920s, but it gave Coach Gardy an advantage: several extra weeks of practice before the start of the basketball season.

As soon as Gardy closed the local fairgrounds, where he administered the county's annual fair each September, he started basketball practice for the "D-Men." Having been a good athlete in his youth, and crediting his accomplishments to his discipline, Gardy was a taskmaster. His teams, whether they played at home or away, were generally favored to win.

At the forward posts in 1923, Gardy played Harry Bigley and Jim Michener, Doylestown's leading scorers. Bob McNealy and Jack Waddington covered the guard positions, and Ed Twining alternated with "Doc" Tomlinson at center. These boys, dressed in gold and white shorts and jerseys, each with a capital D across his meager chest, formed a memorable squad.

Prior to the 1923–24 season, there had never been a more exciting basketball squad in Doylestown's history. The D-Men set their pace in the first outing, shaming Langhorne, 82–5. Bigley scored thirteen field goals and "Noisy" Michener followed with ten. "He doesn't know what it means to miss a field goal," reported *Torch* sports editor Joseph Van Pelt. "He is all over the floor. If he had been in the game all night we might have lost count of the score."

The D-Men won all but a few of twenty-five games that season, but Langhorne fell easiest of all. They clinched several last-minute victories and played their two most critical contests against Perkasie. Early in the season they eked out a 14–11 decision on Perkasie's court by getting ahead and then stalling most of the game. That night, ball handling was the decisive factor. Gardy's lads dribbled close to the floor, passed cautiously, and wasted the time that Perkasie could have used to score.

Later in the season, to decide the Bux-Mont title, the Perkasie team traveled to Doylestown, and against a home-court advantage the visitors kept the score tied most of the night. With the game locked at 36–36, and only seconds remaining to play, "Doc" Tomlinson, "the class of the Bux-Mont circuit," according to *The Torch,* tossed a two-handed wild shot from mid-court. For a moment the crowd hushed in one long gasp, but then the excitement exploded when the officials signaled that the basket was good and that Doylestown had won. Fans rushed to the court, hoisted the champions to their shoulders, and paraded around the gymnasium. The victory triggered a month-long celebration during which time Doylestown's merchants treated the champions to banquets, ice cream sundaes, and a half-dozen social affairs. Everyone in town saluted the athletes, and nothing less than a Republican landslide could have made the residents happier.

For the first time in Jim Michener's life he was a champion, and he savored every moment. Interestingly, many years later, he embellished his memory of this triumph. In his own nostalgia for the victory, he reported that he, and not Tomlinson, had scored the winning points.

> In the last moments of the game I had thrown the ball a disgraceful distance with no hope of scoring, and somehow the ball had dropped into the net. . . . That Saturday I had to explain to the men of our town how I had made that last, unbelievable shot, and the men said, "The whole town is proud of you."

After the basketball triumph, everyone Jim met extended a congratulatory hand or kissed his cheek. Suddenly he knew what it meant to belong, and he liked the feeling. Nothing so wonderful had ever occurred in his life:

> In our little world we were champions, and from that simple fact radiated an inner confidence that has never left me. I could never become a bum, because I was a champion. . . . I came to regard myself as a champion. I carried myself a little taller, worked a little harder in school, built a confidence that was crucial. I drew away from the boys who were headed for reform school and patterned myself after those who were headed for college."

No other experience—not school, the library, or religion—had ever made young Jim Michener feel like a champion, and he hoped to remain a champion forever. Long before he expected to, he had experienced the rewards of hard work, team play, dedication, and loyalty—the most earnest of American values.

In his final year of high school, all but one of Jim's teammates returned to defend the Bux-Mont crown, and when the D-Men embarrassed Sellersville 64–2, it looked as if the cup belonged to Doylestown for another year. But when Gardy's lads traveled to Perkasie, last year's runners-up had improved, and with a home court advantage beat the D-Men 16–8. Four other losses left Doylestown out of the championship campaign of 1925, and Perkasie captured the title. The D-Men had won twenty of twenty-five games, but without the championship it was a disappointing year.

Even so, Jim Michener benefited from that final season. "It's a funny thing," he said later, "but if a child is good at sports, all is forgiven . . . and after those high school victories, and the pats on the back that I received from my mother and some others, I knew I had a chance in life."

Still, he was stunned at graduation when Swarthmore College offered him a four-year scholarship, one of five awarded annually. He had hoped to attend college, and Mabel had vowed to send him, but it was only Swarthmore's scholarship that made their plans financially feasible. Now Dr. Ross congratulated him and urged him to major in history, as he had, and then return to Doylestown High School to teach. Jim made no promises. Leaving Doylestown was a significant step. Of itself this meant he had overcome life as he knew it best and feared it most. The future he had already surrendered to Swarthmore and to fate. He was almost certain, though, that he could never return home. "It's a terrible thing," he said later, after years had blurred the memories, "but during all my life in Doylestown, as a child who was difficult but exceptional in many ways, I never had a person give me help, no recognition or encouragement, or even used clothes. Nothing. *Ever.*"

The words rang hollow. Not even Uncle George, Coach Gardy, the championship season, or Mabel, had erased the shame and rejection of Jim Michener's childhood. When he left high school, diploma and scholarship in hand, he took with him many memories, but he never looked back. All that mattered in 1925 lay beyond the boundaries of his hometown.

## CHAPTER FOUR

# The Swarthmore Experience

> Ask anyone who knew me and they'll tell
> you I never had any goals or
> ambitions. . . . I had no burning desire
> to be a great writer, a great politician, or
> a great anything. But I wanted to be a
> good citizen.
>
> JAMES A. MICHENER, 1980

A MORE INTENSE student than Jim Michener was nowhere to be found on a college campus in the frivolous 1920s. He arrived at Swarthmore College determined to earn what he called his "passport to civilization," and thus he planned to analyze and test his education, but never take it for granted. "For this is the journey that men make: to find themselves," he wrote later in his partly autobiographical novel, *The Fires of Spring*. "If they fail at this, it doesn't matter much what else they find. Money, position, fame, many loves, revenge are all of little consequence, and when the tickets are collected at the end of the ride they are tossed into the bin marked FAILURE."

Fear of failure, of "ending on the ash heap," motivated Michener at Swarthmore College, forcing him to apply himself at every opportunity. He had left Doylestown a champion, having pulled himself up from the bottom rung of society, but now, on a campus where almost every student boasted some familial tie to the institution, he was an outsider once more. Again, he had to prove himself, and keeping his head above the crowd was not always easy. Like his alter ego David Harper in *The Fires of Spring,* he withdrew "into a shell of quiet learning," often secluding himself from campus activity. At the end of four years, he graduated with perhaps the highest honors in nearly half a century of Swarthmore's history, and he had won the respect of his fellow students. But in spite of these accomplishments, he later exaggerated the story of his life at college, no doubt compensating for continued insecurity and rejection.

From its inception in 1864, Swarthmore College maintained academic standards equal to those of the best colleges. The founding fathers had been liberal Quakers who sought to provide a "guarded education" for men and women "far from the evils and temptations of city life." Established twelve miles southwest of Philadelphia, not far from the prosperous Main Line, the campus became a "garden enclosed," a shelter from the world that existed beyond the circle of Quakerism. At first, values and ideas overshadowed social causes. The administration banned novels from the library and barred pianos from the parlors. The faculty taught a curriculum devoid of literature, poetry, art, and music. Changes were made cautiously and slowly—not until the early twentieth century.

In the fall of 1925, when Jim Michener entered this idyllic environment, complete with ivy-covered stone buildings, a meandering creek, intermittent gardens, and five hundred bright students, the "ideal Swarthmore experience" was now less "guarded"; it promised "service to society with education for successful living." Structured "more to the world of living than to the life of the Society of Friends," an expanded curriculum offered limited courses in the arts, literature, and languages, including Russian. Women majored in these subjects; men continued to pursue degrees in engineering, history, and social science.

Public transportation delivered Michener to the campus just ahead of his roommate, George Hay Kain, who arrived with his father in a chauffeured black Cadillac. The senior Kain was an attorney for the Pennsylvania Railroad; after Swarthmore he had studied at Harvard Law School. Now he advised his son, and his son's gangling roommate, that if they applied themselves, remained in the good graces of the faculty and attended Quaker Meeting regularly, they also might get to Harvard Law School and become counselors for the Pennsylvania Railroad. Young George marked every word of his father's lecture, but having just survived the snobbery of Doylestown, Michener resented Mr. Kain's condescending tone. After one semester he moved out of the dormitory to "flee the contamination," as the Quakers had taught him to say.

Coincidentally, Swarthmore was renovating a Victorian farmhouse at the edge of the campus. It had been bequeathed to the college by a former board director and named in memory of the itinerant Quaker preacher, John Woolman. Michener claimed the third floor of Woolman House and began a Bohemian life-style that raised the eyebrows of more than a few people around the campus. "I think he just moved in without asking anyone," recalled a former professor. "The place was huge with a sprawling porch that wrapped around three sides, and Michener decided he wanted to live there, even though it was supposed to house upperclassmen. I remember him walking across campus with his cot propped on his head and a big Victrola in one arm. Next thing we knew, he was blasting classical music at full volume."

With several roommates who also resisted dormitory life, Michener created a zany existence at Woolman House, sleeping all day and studying at night, permitting only the interruptions of classical music and a game of bridge. A former classmate who frequently visited Woolman House remembered that the ramshackle environment included cats and dogs and stacks of borrowed library books and magazines. A chemistry major brewed beer in a closet, and another roommate set all the radiators in the house at right angles, calling this "dynamic asymmetry."

The most sophisticated member of the house was the charismatic Evaristo de Montalvo Murray, scion of the New York Murrays who hailed from Greenwich Village. Full of ideas, but unwilling to join any campus group, "Risto", a devoted reader of the *New Yorker,* then a new magazine, epitomized intellectualism at Swarthmore. Michener liked him from the start, and together they outlined a book about social attitudes, which they never wrote. They remained good friends, however, even while maintaining an unspoken rivalry.

Murray told his friends that Michener was a "special case" who had won a phony scholarship to play on Swarthmore's college basketball team. He said that a group of Doylestown businessmen had underwritten Michener's scholarship with the idea of doing something good for a poor but deserving local boy who could also bring attention to the borough as a college athlete. By Murray's account, when Michener arrived on campus to compete for a spot on the Swarthmore squad, he realized he was neither tall enough nor fast enough for the college game, and he promptly decided to become an intellectual instead. Murray claimed that Michener never went near the gymnasium thereafter, and he said that Swarthmore, fuming over the incident, could not revoke the scholarship without admitting that it had been awarded surreptitiously. Sports scholarships were not awarded at colleges like Swarthmore. Michener, meanwhile, according to Murray, enjoyed getting the best of both Swarthmore and the smug businessmen of his hometown.

Murray's story was almost entirely fabricated, but Michener must have encouraged it; indeed he reiterated portions of it during his lifetime. In 1976 he wrote that his former high school basketball coach "was helpful in getting me an athletic scholarship to Swarthmore." And in 1981 he reportedly said, "My success on the basketball court won me a full scholarship to Swarthmore College." Later he admitted privately that his high school Latin teacher had recommended him for one of Swarthmore's "open scholarships," established in 1922 by President Frank Aydelotte in the fashion of the Rhodes Scholarships. In the September 15, 1925, edition of *The Phoenix,* an article introducing the freshman class explained that Michener had won the scholarship because he was "a high academic leader in Doylestown High School."

It was true that he had hoped to play basketball at Swarthmore, even though he later explained that "by the time I got to college I decided to play only intramural basketball . . . primarily because I had things on my mind of a much different type." Actually, it seems he could not make the team. Like David Harper in *The Fires of Spring,* a character Michener probably began to develop in a Swarthmore English class, he found "the college game was too fast for him, and with many tall, aggressive players available the coach would have been foolish to waste his time with a dead-eye forward who hogged the ball and held back when the game got rough. David was eleventh man on the freshman team, but did not even make the squad in his sophomore year."

Michener tried several times to make Swarthmore's varsity team and succeeded only in his senior year, when, he claimed, "I was needed." Until then he played with a "jayvee" team, and a community league where teammates nicknamed him "the Gunner." Swarthmore's former basketball coach recalled in 1982 that while Michener finally made the team, he rarely played. Part-time jobs and other interests frequently kept Michener from practice sessions, where he at least demonstrated a good eye for sinking long shots.

"Once at the Palestra in Philadelphia," recalled Coach Charles P. Larkin, Jr., "I substituted Michener for the first team forward who was ill. I told Jim to shoot whenever he got near the foul circle. He did, and he missed every time. He was just too busy to be a good basketball player. We all liked him, though, and he was amusing." One night on a road tour Larkin ordered the team to bed by midnight, but during a room check he found Michener in a tub of hot water reading Shakespeare. "After a game he used to beat us all back to the hotel so he could resume reading."

As the fraternities quickly discovered, Michener was a social misfit at Swarthmore College. Tall and slim, with hazel eyes and a broad smile, he was handsome enough, but in other ways he resembled his soon-to-be-created David Harper. As a fraternity scout said of David "He's got no money. Not a cent. How could he pay dues, let alone dance fees? . . . he was all-county for three years (in high school basketball). But you know the small-town athletes. They bloom in the bushes but they bust in college. . . . Another brain trust. Probably wind up a radical. Hands off! We've got our share of headaches as is."

No student attended Swarthmore in the mid-1920s without pledging to a fraternity, however, for around them evolved all campus social activities. Even women joined fraternities in the twenties, as sororities had not yet arrived. The "frats" sponsored parties, dances, informal dinners with the faculty, hayrides, and intramural athletics, the social events that made college memorable. Michener pledged to Phi Delta Theta, one of the quieter fraternities known for scholarship rather than parties or athletics. But for several reasons the fraternity circuit made him uncomfortable: he could not afford it, he could not relate to the revelry, and he found it discriminating. Finally, he bolted out of Phi Delta Theta to spearhead a revolt against the existence of all similar organizations on campus. "I saw them as doomed and brought down a storm on my head," he explained later: "in a democratic, academic situation it was criminal to turn the social life of the college over to organizations that did not admit Negroes or Jews and weren't very happy with Catholics. I didn't have to be too bright to figure that out, but I did have to have a certain amount of guts to act on it."

Former "big man on campus," Thomas Hallowell, who in three years missed only six minutes of playing time on Swarthmore's football team and served as class president and fraternity president, remembered debating the fraternity issue with Michener: "Everyone knew Jim, and we all admired him, even though we didn't always agree with him. Overall there was nothing wrong with the fraternities. We had a great time. I for one despised the academic life. I wouldn't have been caught dead studying, and I never cracked a book. To a certain extent Jim was right about the discrimination, but we were bound by our charters. Some of us appealed to the national headquarters for changes, but that wasn't successful. I think Jim's protest convinced a few people to drop their memberships, but a lot of students shied away from the fraternities anyway. Nothing drastic occurred, and the fraternities survived."

Nonetheless, Michener saw himself as a "campus radical" in the fight against fraternities at Swarthmore. Interestingly, he portrays David Harper as a troublemaker at the fictitious Dedham College in *The Fires of Spring*. One night, to protest a fraternity-sponsored May Queen event, Harper and a friend storm the dormitories, breaking eggs in the bureau drawer of the student body president, wrecking furniture, and mixing hair tonic and shaving cream in piles of fresh shirts. Michener's real life protest was not that obstreperous, however, and in his earnest way he could not have been a campus radical. In fact, aside from his temperament, the way in which he differed most radically from the average Swarthmore student was in his life-style. "He might have owned a coat and tie, but I never saw him in anything except army surplus pants and gray, baggy sweat shirts," recalled a former classmate.

Michener enjoyed the thought that he was a troublemaker at Swarthmore because it gave him an identity all his own. On numerous occasions he claimed that Swarthmore had expelled him more than once for disorderly conduct:

> I was a difficult young man and Swarthmore had every right to expel me . . . for breaking rules that were not very important. Once it was for breaking dating rules [he sneaked into a dormitory and dropped ice cubes into a coed's bed] and for some student disturbances that stemmed from my absolute refusal to be pushed around by anyone. The consensus of the faculty and the people who knew me was that I wouldn't amount to much, even though they knew that I was probably the brightest kid on the block . . .

I think Swarthmore deserves a tremendous amount of credit for not having taken away my scholarship but I was so straight A that it was shocking and so it was easy, perhaps, for them to make this concession. Two faculty meetings were convened to discuss tossing me out, but I was saved by the defense of my English professor who said the college could not afford to lose a student who writes his term papers in Elizabethan blank verse.

There is more fiction than truth to Michener's memory. His transcripts prove that he earned almost as many C's and B's as A's during his first two years in college. And his former English professor, Dr. Robert Spiller, who became a distinguished scholar in American literature, said there were never any meetings to discuss dismissing him. Furthermore, Swarthmore College has no record of Michener's expulsions, or of any campus infractions committed by him. He may have been "campused," a common disciplinary action for rule violators, but few students escaped this punishment. He was not expelled. In fact, there were no expulsions at Swarthmore in the mid-1920s. Neither were there campus radicals.

One gray-bearded professor from Iowa embraced socialism, however, and tarnished Swarthmore's image in the process. From beneath his black sweeping cape, Professor Jesse "Ducky" Holmes, a Johns Hopkins Ph.D., introduced his students to progressive ideas, attacked the Bible, and supported Social Security, the nationalization of the railroad, and desegregation. As a result, Holmes helped create the unfounded fear that Swarthmore was a spawning ground for communists and other undesirables.

For thirty-four years, beginning in 1900, Holmes was Swarthmore's self-appointed gadfly. He was officially professor of philosophy and the history of religion, and even his most liberal colleagues tagged him a radical and, later, a communist. "Ducky" endeared himself to the student body, though, particularly once it became known that in his basement, awaiting his need, he stored a coffin purchased at a bargain price!

During the presidential campaign of 1928 Holmes brought Socialist party candidate Norman Thomas to the campus and created one of the most embarrassing incidents in Swarthmore's history. The city of Philadelphia had lent its new voting machines to local colleges so that they could hold mock elections in October. Swarthmore's students upset the status quo with an overwhelming 90 percent majority for Thomas. "Some Philadelphia newspaper got wind of the results and ran a headline—something like 'Quakers Go Socialist,'" remembered one Swarthmore alumnus. "Well. By 10:00 A.M. the big cars were pulling onto the campus as outraged members of the Union League [the oldest Republican organization in America] arrived to accuse the college of brainwashing their offspring."

Swarthmore College could not have survived another Holmes, but Michener thought he was the highlight of an otherwise formal education:

What we got at Swarthmore was really pretty drab. We had to go out and get what we wanted, and it was a kind of distillation of the artistic spirit. I studied "after hours" with part-time faculty in art and music. There was no emphasis on current events, though. In four years of college on the very edge of the depression, I never heard one warning note. *Not one!* When the economy collapsed, the most surprised educated man on the eastern seaboard was me. But those of us who persevered had that Quaker determination which was very powerful.

For someone who sought independence as Michener did, Swarthmore's system of education was ideal, particularly during Michener's last two years. During his junior year he qualified for Swarthmore's Honors program, instituted in 1921 by President Aydelotte, under whose leadership the college began to earn national recognition in the mid-1920s. A Rhodes Scholar and Oxford graduate, Aydelotte believed that colleges wasted more talent than they developed, and he planned to make Swarthmore a more efficient academic institution. One of his first directives established the Honors system in which self-direction ultimately made the difference between a college graduate and an educated person.

With the distant guidance of a faculty adviser, Honors students chartered their own education by reading selected books and articles and writing weekly papers. There were no lectures and no schedule of classes. Instead, Honors students studied two subjects each semester for two years. Then, a team of outside examiners, scholars from other colleges, tested the students orally and decided who among them deserved a Swarthmore Honors diploma.

For Michener, the Honors challenge began in 1927. "Life does not consist of taking courses in small segments," he recalled the words of his faculty adviser.

A productive life consists of finding huge tasks and mastering them with whatever tools of intelligence and energy we have. We are going to turn you loose on some huge tasks. Let's see what you can do with them. . . . Pick out three fields that interest you. [Each student selected a major field and two minor fields. Michener chose English literature, history, and philosophy, respectively.] Go to the library and learn what you can about your fields. At the end of two years we'll bring in some experts from Harvard and Yale whom you've never seen, and they will determine whether you have educated yourself."

The primary requisite of the Honors program was discipline, a quality that Michener had acquired in childhood.

Without discipline, our "brotherhood of learning" was impossible, but I never wasted a moment. I read everything that was any

good by American writers and eighty percent of all the good
European novels then in translation. I formed opinions about
what was important in the world, and learned to defend these
opinions. It was a marvelous experience without which I would
have become a rather stuffy dolt. It was the Honors program that
showed me how to become an educated man.

Consequently, he wrote to another Honors graduate in 1976, Honors
students performed rather better in public service and good deeds than the
generality. With self-direction, Honors students left college better prepared
to plot their own lives. And Michener, more than any Honors graduate,
made a career of the system. All through life he conducted seminars in his
own behalf, writing books about those topics that interested him most.

Free to study what and when he chose, Michener's scholastic performance
improved during his last two years at Swarthmore. In 1929, after he was
tested and the faculty posted the Honors rankings on the meetinghouse door
— where many a quaking senior sent a friend to scan the list and report back
in privacy—his name appeared first, summa cum laude. In *The Fires of Spring,*
after two years in a Readings program at Dedham, David Harper ranks
equally high.

Although the Honors program helped Michener academically, he continued to flounder socially. Insecurity forced him to overachieve at every
opportunity, alienating him at times from his classmates. In geometry, when
asked to work twenty theorems, he fanatically turned in one hundred and
basked in his teacher's praise "for the most beautiful work" she had ever seen.
Meanwhile his friends wondered why he worked so hard.

David Harper endures a similar problem at Dedham. He is so entangled in
personal problems—anguish for his mother and bitterness about his
impoverished childhood—that he buries himself in course work. His friend
Joe Vaux, a wiry Boston Irishman, tries to convince David to thresh out his
personal problems. "If you carry a thing like that around with you long
enough it'll eat away your mind. You must get it out of your system."

In an English course, Michener found his Joe Vaux.

Professor Spiller was ten years Michener's senior, recently out of graduate
school and just beginning his academic career. He would spend a quarter of a
century at Swarthmore, and almost a quarter of a century more at the
University of Pennsylvania, where he helped establish the American Civilization program and led the American Studies Association. At Swarthmore
in the mid-1920s, he became Michener's mentor.

As a student of T. S. Eliot, Professor Spiller believed in the poet's idea of
the objective correlative, a literary device for channeling emotion in art. Eliot
had recently published his best-known essay, "Tradition and the Individual
Talent," in which he posed the major points of his later criticism: the
significance of literary history and tradition, and the belief that poetry lies not
in a controlled expression of emotion but in an escape from emotion. Spiller

encouraged his students to heed Eliot's advice. "In my writing workshops," he remembered years after the fact, "I asked my students to focus on penetrating questions that made them experience raw feelings. I told them not to get lost in their own problems, but to write about what they knew. I said a writer must have courage to analyze his own life and write a story about it. This fires him so that from there he can go into the world and write." Without this psychological exercise, Spiller thought a writer risked becoming too reflective, and second-guessing himself to a point of immobility.

Former classmates said Michener never talked about wanting to be a writer at Swarthmore, but Spiller's workshops must have triggered his desire to write. Otherwise, Michener would not have attempted his mentor's painful method of self-analysis—what David Harper calls thrusting himself into "the seat of sickness." Every week Michener appeared in Spiller's class eager to read his prose and poetry, often to the chagrin of his class. "Jim had no sense of humor," recalled one class member. "He could not laugh at himself. Whatever subject came up in a seminar he attacked it earnestly. Interminably. I remember when he discovered the word 'bespoke' . . . from there on something always 'bespoke' to Jim. And he wrote with a 'gee whiz' air. 'Gee whiz, look what I discovered!'"

Even this early critic, however, found Michener's prose "interesting at times." It never delved too deeply into his personal thoughts and problems, but "there was a special quality to Jim's work. . . . It ran deeper than the usual excitement of small-town teenagers who encounter their first real ideas in college, with critical teachers and unlimited reading."

During an annual Hamburg Show, a vaudeville of college talent that celebrated the end of the football season, Michener presented a sample of his work to the student body. He created and performed a pantomime, to which a classmate contributed piano accompaniment. Reportedly, the pantomime concerned the career of a soldier, and it was most poignant and effective, while also showing a good sense of scene and drama. On many other occasions, Michener's work appeared in the *Portfolio,* a campus literary magazine that included essays, stories, and poetry. He wrote about a Spanish legend in his poem, "Dos Sabios"; the impoverishment of an English nobleman in a one-act play, "Gold," for which he received second prize in the Curtain Theatre competition; and love, lost love, and lovers in search of love in "Spring Virtue":

> Love, come out into the moonlight,
> For the entire world is mating;
> And I stand here in the starlight,
>         Waiting, waiting.
>
> Sleep has come to all but lovers
> And the night is waiting for you—
> One sad message near you hovers:
>         "I adore you."

Come, for Springtime knows no virtue,
Spring is an eternity—
Love, I could not harm or hurt you.
      Do not fear me.

Love, come out into the moonlight
Where a lover waits for you,
Swearing, in a flood of starlight:
      "I adore you."

This lyric fell in the middle of a story that explained how "Springtime caused these things to happen; Springtime brought him to her window with his mind filled with the visions and his asking heart articulate with song."

Professor Spiller sensed nothing spectacular in Michener's lines of melodrama, but he saw no harm in them either. If they unburdened the man who expressed them, Spiller deemed them worthwhile. Twenty years later, after reading Michener's diffuse novel, *The Fires of Spring,* Spiller knew "the writing was bad," but still that did not matter. The book, he predicted, was the beginning of "a very worthy writing career," the groundwork for which had been laid in his workshops.

Michener never bared his soul in Spiller's classes, of course, for he had already decided to block out the ambiguous and painful truths about himself. It was in college, after Louis Michener had told him the truth about Edwin Michener, that he gave up searching for his ancestry, darkening forever that corner of his life, and hardening his masked identity at the age of nineteen. At the same time he also quit seeking answers about the existence of God and the universe, deciding never to bother about anything that he could not experience.

Spiller's exercises may have contributed another dimension to Michener's life at Swarthmore, particularly as his prose and poetry revolved around the subject of love. Many of Michener's classmates, who had no way of knowing that he was inhibited by a rigid Victorian morality, speculated about his love life, but as a former roommate recalled, Michener had earned a Sir Galahad reputation for leaving the coeds untouched. However, he was not without opportunities.

"My own principal impression of Michener," remembered Osmond Molarsky, an underclassman who felt privileged to live at Woolman House, "was that he was a 'great lover,' as we said in those days. This was because he frequently would dash in from the night, where I presumed a young lady was waiting impatiently for him, grab an armload of blankets from my bed, together with my prized terry-cloth bathrobe, disappear back into the night and in due time return, in a euphoric state, each time with the bathrobe more completely unraveled by what I could only conclude was an encounter with a briar patch. I was disenchanted, however, by assurances from [Evaristo] Murray [and Bill Rice, another roommate] that in these encounters Michener remained persistently chaste. I supposed they knew this not through any disclaimer or protestation by Michener, but from reports by their own girlfriends, who knew the girls that Michener was dating."

By graduation, Michener had fallen in love with a junior who became his inspiration for Marcia Paxson, David Harper's elusive Quaker girlfriend in *The Fires of Spring*. Michener had hoped to marry Ruth Jackson—"no one," he told Molarsky, "is as beautiful as Ruth Jackson in love"—but something foiled his plans.

Molarsky said he understood that Ruth Jackson's parents objected to their daughter's relationship with Michener. "Swarthmore, though founded by Friends and supposedly following the humanistic traditions of Friends, managed to nurture strong class distinctions between students . . . and through the sway of middle-class values, which put a high price on having legitimate family ties, Michener was rejected." Molarsky was sure the repudiation wounded a lovesick Michener and that it pushed him all the harder to prove himself.

With few exceptions, it was difficult for Swarthmore students to penetrate Michener's shell of protection. Everyone knew who he was and admired his scholarly aptitude and determination, but his moody disposition kept most students at a distance. One former classmate thought that Michener got along only because "Everyone took him at his own evaluation. This made him a different kind of college landmark, or big man on campus."

A baffling personality was part of Michener's defense mechanism. In the event of failure, it kept him from falling too far. He was a bundle of personal contradictions, always confounding his friends. He participated in numerous campus events, including theatrical productions and pep rallies, but he refused to be photographed for the yearbook. While he was sometimes shy, he was also enterprising and inventive. For example, when he heard about the eccentric collector of Impressionist and Post-Impressionist paintings, Dr. Albert C. Barnes, who hoarded his prized collection in his house on the outskirts of Philadelphia, Michener managed to get a private viewing by posing as "a poor steelworker" who wanted to see the "nice pictures," a ploy he must have guessed would appeal to Barnes, who sympathized with "plain people." On another occasion, while traveling one summer with Swarthmore's Chautauqua, one of several educational tent shows that crisscrossed the country in the 1920s, Michener went for a haircut and forgot to return in time for that evening's performance. He apologized later to the leading lady, explaining that he went home with the barber, who had invited him to dinner.

His singularity also surfaced at pep rallies, where he looked out of place leading cheers, and during orations that he frequently delivered to the student body in Collection Hall. His topics ranged widely, from school spirit to presidential candidates, but he approached each speech analytically, as though his future depended on its sedate delivery.

In 1927 he won first place in Swarthmore's Extemporaneous Speaking Contest, expounding for three minutes about the importance of college grades. Ironically, no one in the Honors program believed in grades! Given a choice, he preferred to talk about politics, although once this topic embarrassed him in front of a packed auditorium. During the presidential campaign of 1928 he delivered an impassioned plea in support of the Catholic Al Smith, apparently overlooking his Quaker audience's obvious preference for the Friend, Herbert Hoover. These and similar incidents made Michener an oddity on the Swarthmore campus.

The two experiences that affected Michener more than any others at Swarthmore stemmed from his membership in the Society of Friends and from a summer spent touring with Swarthmore's Chautauqua troupe. Both events directed his future.

It was merely a matter of time until Michener became a "convinced" Quaker, for he was a ripe prospect for the Society of Friends, a group that was neither doctrinaire nor ecclesiastical, neither hierarchical nor inclined toward leadership. Swarthmore Quakers were Hicksites, representing the liberal branch of Quakerism. Hicksites denied the divinity of Christ, followed no scripture, sponsored no formal creed, and convened without the benefit of ministers. A fluid group of Elders sat, but did not necessarily speak, at Meetings, and Swarthmore students frequently joined them, because they liked the serene atmosphere.

There was no proselytizing at Swarthmore, and even with the town's meetinghouse on the campus, students were not obliged to attend. Of course there were obvious reminders that Swarthmore was affiliated with the Society of Friends—daily collection (chapel), for example, and the use of "thee" and "thou" by some faculty and students—but Quaker values were not imposed on anyone. Friends believed in independence and abhorred an imposed morality.

"The hazard of attending Meeting," recalled one graduate, "was that *anyone* could arise and speak at length, as the spirit moved. A centenarian in black bombazine might creak to her feet, fumble in her reticule for her glasses and a newspaper clipping, read the clipping aloud, and then share her thoughts on its inspirational message for a long, long time."

The religious and theological aspects of Quakerism never loomed large in Michener's mind. "I respect the religious teachings; I see them as part of the great Judeo-Christian ethic; and I certainly think they are valid for all who seek religious guidance," he explained many years after his Swarthmore graduation, ". . . but I have never felt any strong pull toward theology."

Instead, Michener valued the personal interaction that occurred during the Quaker Meeting, regarding it as an example of democracy through argument and persuasion. He deferred to the attitude of Saint James who taught that religion should be tested primarily by works rather than faith:

> When one has sat in Meeting for a long time listening to leaders
> of the community discuss the political, social and economic prob-
> lems of the day, it is extraordinarily refreshing to hear some older

mystic rise to remind the meeting that concern over [these] problems is meaningful only when exercised in relation to the overall
problems of the religious life."

In that context Michener preferred the Society of Friends, whose efforts
historically embraced social, political, and economic reforms, and whose
members considered experience their final authority. For these reasons, Jim
Michener found peace with them, and after four years at Swarthmore, he
defined his personal creed by Quaker values:

"That the fate of all men is inextricably interrelated, that,
ultimately, no man is free so long as one person remains in
bondage; that no man is secure so long as one man lives in fear;
that no man is virtuous so long as one person is lacking in virtue;
that no man is wealthy while another lives in poverty; and that
God may make truth available through anyone, not only through
an intellectual, political or religious aristocracy."

Through their examples of hard work, perseverance, honor, fairness,
devotion to America, and through their sense of destiny, the Quakers inspired
Michener. However, their quiet and unfanatical determination also thickened
his protective shell.

Balancing that effect, and drawing him out into the world, was
Swarthmore's traveling Chautauqua, organized in 1909 by Professor Paul
Pearson, whose son, Drew Pearson, was a controversial political columnist
during the mid-twentieth century. In the early 1900s, Professor Pearson
visited Chautauqua Lake in New York State where a minister and an Ohio
industrialist had formed the Chautauqua Assembly at a Methodist summer
camp in 1874. The founders had shared the same dream: "That every man has
a right to be all that he can be, to know all that he can know, to do all that he
pleases to do." They developed a mildly civilizing program that evolved from
a semi-religious, semi-intellectual regional gathering to a national movement
of education and inspiration.

At the turn of the century, people from all parts of the country crowded
into southwestern New York to attend the Chautauqua, with its peculiar
blend of edifying lectures, theater, and religion. Later, someone formed a
traveling company in the Midwest, and then Professor Pearson planned a
circuit on the Atlantic seaboard. The traveling companies were not formally
linked to the Chautauqua Assembly, but during the 1920s, the Chautauqua
movement touched perhaps a third of the United States population:

"The Swarthmore Chautauqua traveled from town to town, from Vermont to Virginia and as far west as Pittsburgh, stopping for a day to offer each
little community our cultural program," explained Barbara Pearson, the
professor's daughter. "Our circuit included a trained dog, but that was as
'carnivalish' as we got. Every evening we had lectures by eminent theologians
and politicians, including the outspoken Senator Robert M. La Follette, Sr.

We performed operas and plays—*Robin Hood,* for example—and always one classic; and there were lectures about different artists and recitations from their works."

At $41 a week, Michener joined the Swarthmore company the summer before his senior year. Molarsky hired him to work the afternoon marionette shows and to act in several of the evening stage performances. By Michener's own evaluation, he was a "frightfully bad" actor. "Irritating," was Miss Pearson's appraisal. "I was serious about a career in the theater, but Jimmy was there only because it was a job. Once, playing my boyfriend, he fell asleep backstage on a pile of curtains and missed his cue, leaving me stranded for what seemed an eternity. They had to bring down the curtain until they found him."

While the work was hectic and tiring, the Chautauqua was a meaningful experience for Michener, as it was for most of the young performers. He enjoyed setting up a show in some little town, striking the show that evening, and driving, sometimes through the night with Molarsky, to the next stop to begin all over again. As often as possible along the way he met strangers and introduced himself to new ideas and customs, just as he had done earlier during his summer jaunts across the country. All the while he was gaining confidence. Here he was, like David Harper, also to become a Chautauqua puppeteer, "a poorhouse crum pulled from impossible surroundings and offered the world, if he wanted it." All he had to do now was reach out and grab his share of prosperity.

## CHAPTER FIVE

# The Journey Begins

I doubt that a young man can waste time,
regardless of what he does. I believe you
have till age thirty-five to decide finally
on what you are going to do.

JAMES A. MICHENER
CAMPUS COLLOQUY, 1974

ON BACCALAUREATE SUNDAY in June 1929, a confident Jim Michener delivered Swarthmore's Ivy oration and advised his fellow graduates to "look for the last time across the campus where we have enjoyed ourselves, and . . . dedicate ourselves silently to the task before us, saying, with a happy smile, 'On, and ever on!'"

October 1929 was about to deliver the most devastating financial crisis in the nation's history, but Michener could not have anticipated that in June. Along with most Americans, he believed in Coolidge-Hoover prosperity, and he did not doubt that a high standard of living awaited the members of his graduating class. "We have been well prepared for what is to follow," he told his classmates, "and if we are no more capable of earning than we were when we entered, we are at least better qualified to spend what we do earn, and in that lies the secret of happiness." The onslaught of a Great Depression never entered his mind.

Years later, recounting his teeming optimism, Michener blushed with embarrassment: "We really did believe we were a fortress at Swarthmore. We thought all we had to do was let the world know we had arrived, and we would be protected."

For him, it actually happened that way, and when the bottom fell out of the economy, he was not affected. Upon graduation, a prep school in Pottstown, Pennsylvania, offered him a teaching job at a salary of $2,100, which was $100 above the average American income for 1929. He had applied for a Rhodes Scholarship, hoping to study overseas, but when denied the honor, he accepted the Hill School's offer, although with reluctance to begin teaching so soon after college.

Founded in 1851 as a family-style boarding school for boys in grades eight through twelve, the Hill School espoused one primary aim: to transmit to students those basic principles that men in all times have found to be of permanent value. By the turn of the century, the school's academic reputation was preeminent. Modeled in the European tradition, with a solid liberal arts curriculum and an emphasis on Christian living, the Hill sent most of its graduates to Harvard, Princeton, and Yale.

When Master Michener arrived to teach English, "posing to look intelligent," he remembered, the department chairman informed him that "We place great emphasis here on diagramming the sentence. It teaches the student how to think, how to keep his ideas in line."

Youngest among the faculty, and distinguished by a full head of curly reddish hair, Michener protested that he knew nothing about diagramming.

"Learn," he was told.

So "for half a year I stayed one lesson ahead of my class, but in the second half I became a tiger in the field. In fact, I became one of the great diagrammers of that period." As a result, he later wrote in the Hill School *Bulletin,* he acquired a feeling "for the majesty of the English sentence." However, he was sure he had taught his students less than they taught him.

In many respects, Michener was perfectly suited for the Hill, an isolated country school about thirty miles northwest of Philadelphia. Rich in ornate buildings that exemplified the mastery of American craftsmen in woodcarving, stonecutting, and stained-glass windows, the campus was aesthetically pleasing but void of social opportunities for young masters. All of this suited Michener's quiet personality. Every so often another master arranged a date for him to go dancing at the nearby Sunnybrook Ballroom, but for two years Michener rarely left the Hill. Six nights a week he served as a hall monitor and actually enjoyed the assignment. It forced him to save money, he recalled, and "it kept me indoors, kept me at attention, and provided me with the time to read most of the great books, which were to dominate my later life."

Balzac, Dostoyevsky, and Tolstoy still ranked among his literary favorites, and now he added Zola, Nexö, Reymont, and Björnson. As for American writers he warmed slowly to Ernest Hemingway, but he found Theodore Dreiser's *An American Tragedy* "soul shattering" and wished he had written it.

On occasion, in those evening hours of hall duty, with his faithful Victrola softly playing Caruso, Martinelli, and Tetrazzini, Michener was also writing. He gave up, however, after reading *Huntsman in the Sky,* by Granville E. Toogood. The quality of this first novel, by one of Michener's contemporaries, convinced him that he could not write professionally, "at least not at the moment." He thought he lacked both "the imagination and the technique" to write anything of significance, but there was no doubt that he wanted to write.

*Huntsman in the Sky* explored social responsibility on Philadelphia's Main Line, a familiar setting to a Swarthmore graduate. The novel followed the life of Bertrand Garrison, member of an aristocratic family and a useless, selfish sort of fellow, until he buckled down in a career. He then became a successful composer.

Michener read the novel as both a model and a challenge: "It came along at precisely the time I needed it." Garrison's example goaded him into thinking about life beyond the Hill, and shortly thereafter he visited the headmaster and resigned. He had to move on, he said, "to find out what in life was of value."

Clinching his decision was news that Swarthmore College had awarded him the Joshua Lippincott Fellowship, an annual prize that entitled the recipient to study and travel abroad. (It was at this time, when Michener needed a passport, that his mother provided the apocryphal account of his birth to officials in Bucks County.)

There could hardly have been a better time to flee America than the period between 1931 and 1933, when the darkest clouds of the depression hung over the country. Michener spent most of two years alone in Europe—studying, thinking, drifting, challenging ideas, and occasionally working at odd jobs to supplement his stipend. No experience in the States impressed him more deeply. He discovered in Europe his Walden Pond and he matured intellectually.

His stint began at St. Andrews University in Scotland where he teamed up with "a mathematical genius" to win the university's bridge championship. In more serious matters, he twice debated his Nazi roommate, whom he found pitiful, slovenly, and impossible to befriend. "Herr Wagner was phenomenal," Michener recalled. "He supported total revolution along the Nazi lines and I didn't agree with him at all. He was overwhelming, though. It was shattering to think that he was from the best educated nation on earth, and that his profound philosophical and cultural leadership was going beserk."

Communism also piqued his curiosity abroad and when his studies freed him to travel he sought out Europe's "trouble spots" where communist youth groups touted revolution. He attended seminars in London, Glasgow, Amsterdam, and Brussels, but walked away from every meeting shaking his head, unconvinced by the communists' dogmatism. He denounced their radical ideas, opposed their last-resort ferocity and brutality, and satisfied himself that he preferred a strong democracy instead. "Luckily I found out what I needed to know away from home," he later explained. "If I had associated with these same groups in my own country I would have been blackballed [during the age of suspicion]."

Fear and poverty marred Michener's travels in Europe, itself a continent of dismal ruin. Temporarily, he found solace in London's cultural scene. From there he sent a somber letter to his former mentor, Professor Spiller:

> I am settled here in the revered shades of Russell Square, pegging away at the endlessness of the British Museum. . . . London so far has been devoid of rain—and Americans . . . [but] on the whole I find Britain delightful. It agrees with my blood, and I like the people, but I should feel intellectually and spiritually amputated if I were faced with the prospect of spending the rest of my life away from America.

His daily routine began at 9:00 A.M. with a visit to the museum library; then to the National Gallery at 11:30 "for a lecture on some phase of the old masters therein"; lunch at 1:00; the museum for several hours in the afternoon; a walk to Hyde Park, the river, Burlington House, Wallace House, or the zoo; a bedroom dinner of his own preparation at 7:00; and the theater or a novel in the evening. "I find it delightful and instructive," he assured Spiller.

He was writing again, although without success. He outlined a novel, *Passage to Vyborg,* but could not complete the manuscript. Instead, he returned to studying the novel form. He told Spiller that Upton Sinclair's *Oil,* was "strong in conception," yet "weak in execution." He thought the story "always promised to become something, but never quite did. Its internal construction failed to hold together." Later, Spiller recalled with interest that Michener had studied Sinclair, who used the novel as a forum for social ideas, just as Michener began to do after World War II.

Rounding out his interests abroad, Michener researched the Renaissance in Spain and, prefiguring Ernest Hemingway's interest, joined a touring troupe of bullfighters. He moved to Italy and studied the Sienese school of painting, and then to France to examine the Honfleur and the work of Eugene Boudin. He daydreamed about investing in the works of the great French masters. He planned to begin with Renoir and "work down" to Derain and Vlaminck.

One summer, for a change of pace and a few shillings, he enlisted in the British Merchant Marine. He served as chart boy on a collier bound for Mediterranean and Baltic ports, and by duty's end claimed to have memorized the entire coast of the Mediterranean Sea. Whether or not that was true, he at least fell spellbound to the ocean's grandeur, mesmerized by winds slapping at his face and waves bouncing his ship from port to port. That summer he formed a bond with the sea. Eventually, he sailed all but a few of the world's great waterways.

Independence marked Michener's tour of Europe, and solitude consoled him at all times. One winter, with native Celtics who spoke no English, he lived on the island of Barra in the Hebrides, and never saw the sun during the first twenty-nine days. He went there to collect old songs. The Reformation had missed Barra; while Scotland turned Protestant, the island remained Catholic and retained the Hebridean chants, considered by some the richest musical heritage in Europe. "The setting was heavenly," in spite of the clannish and introspective natives, Michener remembered. "It was a formative experience away from books, movies, and newspapers and it awakened my love of islands and travel." More important, Barra aroused his interests in people and traditions, two subjects that later became grist for his storytelling.

Having arrived at St. Andrews an "academic bum," Michener left Europe a changed man in the summer of 1933. He was sure the experience had saved his life: "Knocking around Europe threw me into the radical movements of Nazism and communism, and put me in a new ball game. It shot me way ahead of my contemporaries. While they were working hard at their first jobs, I was laying the groundwork for a long, productive life." In the final analysis, like Toogood's Bertrand Garrison, Michener had joined the middle class. It was time now to begin repaying what he always thought of as his "debt to society."

Apple sellers and soup lines greeted his arrival in New York, yet the worst of America's depression was history. The "Roosevelt Revolution" had gained a toehold in the country, and the general mood was optimistic. Americans seemed to have accepted the fact that nine to ten million of them could not find work. Luckily, a small Quaker boarding school in Bucks County offered Michener a teaching job. The salary was $1,200, about half of what he had earned at the Hill, but he grabbed the opportunity.

During the next three years he devoted himself to teaching at George School, a private secondary institution in Newtown, not far from Doylestown. Whereas in 1929 he had stumbled into the classroom, in 1933 he arrived self-confident and eager to share his recent experiences. Now, in between lessons on punctuation and sentence analysis, he introduced his students to "sensible idealism" and "sensible optimism." In a speech he explained his intentions to the National Council of Teachers of English:

> I believe that brightness of vision is better than brightness of rifle barrels; and I believe without question that young people must be instructed in the principles of idealism. . . . I cannot admit that I am a sentimentalist about this. In the hard facts of national existence, idealism pays. . . . Let students meet in their teachers people who are not afraid to affirm the great humanist values, for I believe that it is upon these values that we build a strong society. . . . It is dignity we must show our students lest they fall into the sinful indignity of thinking their world to be a gruesome and lost place.

It was the English teacher's role, he said, to lead students through the "dark night of failing idealism," and this he proposed to accomplish through the classic works of literature. He required his students to read books that demonstrated the supremacy of people. "People are the aim and end of life," he argued. "People are the focus of our interest, our only hope." To emphasize his point he included on his reading list: *David Copperfield*, *Great Expectations*, *Vanity Fair*, *Babbitt*, *Hamlet*, *Ethan Frome*, and a dozen other books, as well as poems. His students read and discussed six books per semester, and he selected titles that illuminated the ideas he believed needed to be stressed.

Students welcomed his ideas, although his command of literature overwhelmed them. A former student remembered how Michener propped boards across his bathtub in Drayton Hall and stacked dozens of books on them. "He was brilliant," remembered James H. Taylor, who also lived in Drayton, "and we all respected him. He never shouted, never made hasty judgments, and he was always willing to help, whether with studies or a personal matter. Every once in a while he brought a carton of ice cream into the dormitory and shared it with us."

Colleagues, on the other hand, viewed Michener from a distance. The George School faculty was a society unto itself, frequently sponsoring teas and bridge parties. Members and spouses socialized daily, particularly after dinner when they convened informally to discuss school projects and current events.

"During these get-togethers," recalled Terry Shane, whose husband Joseph was a faculty member, "Jim had two habits that raised eyebrows among our more reserved faculty. If he did not like the dessert served in Temperance House, the dining hall, he walked to the local bakery and bought something else to eat. And then, depending upon our topic of conversation, if he was not interested he sat in a corner and read a magazine or book. Some of the faculty thought he was rude; others called him a maverick."

In spite of his unsociable ways, when Michener felt like talking he was an enthusiastic participant in faculty discussions. "He was thought-provoking," remembered Mrs. Shane, "and he had something to say about everything. His ideas were vivid, particularly since he had traveled throughout Europe, and we all enjoyed listening to him."

Michener argued conservatively about matters of economics, education, and war and peace, but he invariably proved to be the most politically liberal member of the campus. Of course, Bucks County was still a Republican stronghold, and few of George School's faculty thought much of FDR. Michener favored New Deal legislation, so long as it was temporary. Later he explained, "I liked seeing FDR introduce some radical reform only to have the Supreme Court cancel his plans two years down the road. That way we got the advantage of a revolutionary reform solution without getting strapped to it."

While several George School faculty thought Michener was their most promising member, no one knew him intimately. Free-spirited William Vitarelli, who taught art and rode a motorcycle, knew him best, but their friendship revolved around the campus marionette shows they produced, and exhaustive games of basketball and table tennis. Even in his leisure Michener was "all business," Vitarelli discovered. He was not inclined to talk about himself. "Jim had a keen competitive spirit and concentration," emphasizing his will to get ahead.

Women found Michener particularly annoying because nothing seemed important to him unless it promoted his career. On the other hand, friends observed that since the unhappy end of his relationship with Ruth Jackson, women had intimidated him. He was no longer the romantic of the Swarthmore Campus. Courting was now a ritual that seemingly left him uncomfortable. Occasionally he dated a George School secretary who had the unfortunate nickname of "Bouncing Betsy," but they argued intensely about inconsequential matters, and their relationship ended. For months after that he did not date at all.

Apparently he wanted a wife more than anyone realized, however, for he suddenly married during the summer of 1935. The campus was shocked when he returned with a bride. In June he had left George School to enroll in a summer program at the University of Virginia. There he met Patti Koon, daughter, granddaughter, and sister of Lutheran ministers. In July they won a doubles championship in tennis, and on July 27 they were married.

Nicknamed Butch, Patti Koon has been described as an unlikely wife for James Michener. She spoke in a raspy southern drawl and dressed like a character out of *Tobacco Road*. She "looked like a boy," according to Mrs. Shane, and was sometimes mistaken for a boy. "One night a group of us went out to a movie, and the ticket seller told Jim, 'It'll be a quarter for you and ten cents for the little guy.' Several people snickered, but Jim clenched his teeth. 'This is my wife,' he said, as he plopped down fifty cents."

Short, stocky, and muscular, Patti seemed more at ease playing touch football than attending the faculty's social gatherings. Ostentatiously unfeminine, she scorned women who discussed clothing, makeup, cooking, and housekeeping. She wore pants and shirts at a time when few women did so, and she kept her hair cut short. "Patti was actually a very dear person," recalled Mrs. Shane. "She just had no feminine ways. She was happy-go-lucky and full of fun. She and Jim got along fine, although they were not what you would call close."

From the outset the marriage was unconventional, but Michener seemed content to have it that way. He probably married Patti because she posed no threat to him, and because he needed a wife to fulfill his role as a member of the American middle class. Patti enjoyed sports, particularly tennis, and she liked collecting and mounting prints of the old masters. These activities interested Michener, and so long as Patti remained in the background of his life, their relationship worked.

By the end of the 1936 academic year, Michener had tired of teaching English, although not of the profession itself:

> I had moderately large classes which I taught with all the vigor
> I could command. I took my responsibilities seriously, reading an

infinite amount of world literature to prepare myself. . . . I used
to correct themes until I thought that I had read every possible
way of putting together inadequate sentences. . . . I was, to put it
simply, caught up in the awful drudgery of teaching gram-
mar. . . . It was hard work, and as I looked about me I perceived
that teachers in other subjects did not have to work so diligently.

When the Colorado State College of Education in Greeley, later to become
the University of Northern Colorado, invited him to pursue a master's
degree and teach social studies in its laboratory school, he and Patti made
plans to move west. Colleagues advised Michener not to go. The West, they
said, was a dead end in education. "The sands of the desert are white with the
bones of young men who went west and are trying to get back east," intoned
one associate. Michener hoped for the best and departed "with practically no
regrets."

En route to Colorado he spent part of the summer preparing at Ohio State
University, and shortly after he arrived in Greeley at summer's end, he
discovered that good social studies teachers worked just as hard as good
English teachers. But he never once regretted his decision. In fact, his move to
the West became a turning point in his career. In Europe he had matured
intellectually; in the West he was about to grow up professionally.

Colorado was progressive in the field of education, and the environment
made all the difference for Michener. At twenty-nine he was the youngest
member of the College High School faculty, an associate professor of social
studies, and his twenty-three colleagues included some of the brightest
people in education. Many of them earned national reputations while working in Greeley, then a backwoods country town of 13,000 residents, located
approximately fifty miles north of Denver, with a view of the snow-capped
Rocky Mountains.

One renowned faculty member was Dr. William Wrinkle, director of
College High School and the man who hired Michener. He was a leader in the
modernization of secondary education and during the middle and late 1930s
he experimented with a new curriculum at College High School. Dr. Wrinkle
faulted the traditional secondary school curriculum for requiring "hundreds
of thousands of boys and girls . . . to undertake work in mathematics, in
foreign languages, and in highly differentiated sciences in which they have
little interest and in which there is little expectation that they can find utility
or satisfaction." With the guidance of his faculty, he planned to reorganize
traditional subjects so that they emphasized "meaningful experience" rather
than the "accumulation of knowledge."

The College High School faculty believed that students should be prepared
first for their obligations as citizens—education leading to a "rich and satisfying personal life"—and second for occupations—education for "participation
in some special calling." Therefore, they built a curriculum around broad
fields of experience involving nature, communications, the arts, vocations,

and people. They were among the nation's first secondary school faculty to abandon requirements for ancient history, economics, chemistry, and other "narrow, highly specialized courses."

Michener, the idealist, quickly found his niche on the Colorado faculty. Behind him were the days of teaching students to diagram sentences, even though he still thought that such exercises taught orderliness. Now he wanted his students to resolve "to work for a better world." Each graduate, he explained in *The New High School in the Making,* a book produced by the College High School faculty, "should be concerned with just laws, decency in public life, economic justice, the dignity of work, and the welfare of the community." He continued:

> The social studies teacher has a right to believe in deferred payment; the final evaluation of his work this year will come in ten or fifteen years. Then his students will either be voting wisely, paying their taxes, entering into community life, living happily with their families, and taking upon themselves the full obliga-tions of citizenship, or they will be ignoring public welfare, fighting through divorce courts, dodging taxes, denying demo-cratic procedures, and living unhappy, useless, ignorant lives.

If Michener's expectations seemed harsh, he knew of no greater calling than citizenship. He never underestimated his responsibility to Greeley's students, and he became one of the faculty's prized members. In addition to teaching the Growth of American Democracy, his course load included Great Music, Motion Pictures, and Family Relations.

Not all of Michener's colleagues appreciated his approach to teaching, but "He was *one* of the most dynamic educators I have known," remembered Edith M. Selberg, a former Greeley faculty member. "He stimulated youth to comprehend interrelationship among all fields of knowledge. . . . He taught his students how to create ways to learn and use their knowledge, to use research methods and compile data useful for community action and for democratic participation. His former students still relate to me the conceptual schemes and new avenues of knowledge [that he taught them]."

Michener's classroom operated like a "functioning democracy" where he introduced topics of discussion, and the students, acting as citizens, estab-lished policies and enforced standards of behavior. As a result, Michener speculated, by teaching "ideals, ways of thinking, attitudes toward continu-ous problems, good social habits, and immunity to fraud and deception," his students learned "moral leadership" and "constructive thinking."

His assignments incorporated several innovative approaches to teaching. For example, he asked his students to select a problem—one class chose the social and economic concerns in the field of nursing—and then investigate the problem in the library, as well as through local, state, and federal agencies. In a second assignment his students studied life in a different part of the country. By throwing a dart at a map of the United States one student selected a city.

Michener then subscribed to the city's newspaper, and the members of his class wrote to students in that city's high school.

His major accomplishment, however, as Edith Selberg pointed out, was interrelating disciplines, a practice that he later adapted in his writing. He rarely taught a social studies lesson without referring to literature or music. In a journal article entitled "Bach and Sugar Beets," he explained,

> In the social studies I am supposed to teach of man's great experiences, and to me there has never been a worthy human experience that has not been put into immortal music. Almost any subject that I elect to teach in the field of history or human relations has been discussed by the great musicians, and I would be foolish not to utilize their works in the same way that I use textbooks and magazines.

Each semester he used Bach to teach his students about the sugar beet industry, an important lesson in Greeley, where the economy depended on the harvesting of beets. He began with a discussion of sugar and progressed naturally to a survey of farm life. "And that's where Bach comes in," Michener explained to his students.

"Was he a farmer?" they asked.

"No," Michener replied, "he was a musician, and he was like most other musicians. He liked the country. You've been studying about farmers and farm life. So did Bach. You write creative papers about it. He wrote some great music."

Crowding around Michener's phonograph the students then listened to a medley of classical compositions, beginning with Charpentier's "À Mules" from the *Italian Suite,* and incorporating parts of Beethoven's *Pastoral Symphony,* Germont's aria from *La Traviata,* and the Kermesse scene from Gounod's *Faust.* The medley concluded with Bach's "Shepherd's Christmas Music," which evoked a group of country people sitting on the ground watching the heavens, much like the young Colorado and Wyoming sheep men of the 1930s.

"I told my students this and they understood," Michener continued in his article. "They knew why sugar beets and Johann Sebastian Bach had some slight strain in common. Each dealt with man's unending battle with the soil and with things of the spirit."

Using the same approach, he taught the Renaissance and Reformation, relying on Purcell's operas and Martin Luther's hymns. He encouraged other teachers to follow his lead: "I believe that social studies . . . and music need to cooperate on this problem of training the imaginations of our school children . . . music is perhaps the finest single instrument we have by which to achieve the development of fine, sensitive, perceptive imaginations."

Greeley's students appreciated Michener's approach to teaching. "We respected all our faculty members because they were excellent teachers, but we especially learned a lot from James Michener," remembered Mayre

Kagohara, daughter of a beet farmer and a College High School graduate of 1937. "He knew how to get his points across in an interesting way, and he was very intelligent. We expected him to become a great philosopher and a legend of our time."

It never occurred to Michener to become either a philosopher or a legend. Good citizenship remained his personal quest, and he devoted himself to that goal in Greeley. Shortly after he and Patti settled in a basement apartment not far from campus, they looked for opportunities to participate in the life of their community. They joined the First Congregational Church where Jim offered his Family Relations class in the evenings. They patronized a Works Progress Administration repertory company at the Baker Federal Theater in Denver. They played tennis regularly with Patti competing in regional matches and winning a championship. And they frequently entertained students, sharing their music and literature and slides of their cross-country travels.

The most rewarding of these community activities was the Angell's Club, a discussion group that Michener organized with the help of Floyd Merrill, a Greeley newspaper editor. Members included local bankers, ministers, doctors, professors, and farmers who met informally twice a month to talk about current events. During a return trip to Greeley in 1973, Michener remembered that the Angell's Club "was the best thing that happened to me in Colorado. We were working far from New York and Washington and at that time we didn't have the communications which we have now, so about fifteen of us got together at the Tea Room run by Mrs. [Nellie] Angell on a street over beyond the university, and we would just sit there and talk and exchange ideas."

As secretary, Michener organized the meetings and invited guest speakers. Discussion topics ran the gamut of current events, but in this borderline Democratic state, politics riled the members more than anything else. Michener enjoyed this early exercise of seeking out experts, learning from them, debating with them, and forming his own opinions as a result. In time he used the same process to research articles and books.

No one in Greeley encouraged Michener more than Floyd Merrill, the forty-year-old editor of the local *Tribune,* and a man of fierce partisanship and profound commitment to American traditions, particularly those of the West. In Michener's view, Merrill epitomized the western editor: "opinionated and tough-minded," the "archetypal man with a universe of interests" and "a good prose style."

Eager to share his knowledge with anyone who showed an interest, Merrill became Michener's "cicerone to Colorado." He introduced the young teacher to the state's legislators, to businessmen, and community leaders; he conducted numerous field trips on Michener's behalf, taking him across Colorado and as far west as California; and he taught Michener to use a camera, and to capture many of the West's most vivid scenes on slides.

"At least three times each month," Michener recalled in 1974, "Merrill and I went on excursions out of Greeley, sometimes to the intricate irrigation systems which made our part of the desert a garden of melons, sometimes to glens far above the timberline, from which we would look down into valleys crowded with blue spruce and aspen, and quite often out onto the prairie east of town where majestic buttes rose starkly from the barren waste." At each stop Merrill knew which problems required attention. In the meadowlands, for example, he contrasted the merits of the Hereford bull with the Angus. And along the South Platte River he examined every facet of the system used to make water work to enhance the quality of life in Colorado. Michener found each of Merrill's lessons a revelation. "They knocked some sense into me," he said, "and saved me from becoming an Atlantic seaboard type."

Merrill's knowledge of the West transcended his technical expertise. He talked incessantly about western literature, most of which Michener was reading as a graduate student in history, and analyzed the many treatments of western themes. Once while exploring the cliff dwellings at Mesa Verde, Merrill gave Michener a copy of *The Delight Makers,* a sensitive Indian story by a Swiss immigrant of the nineteenth century. He dreamed of a similar book about Colorado, Merrill said, and perhaps he even planned to write it, although this he did not confess. Maybe he saw in Michener a young man who could write the book, but again, he did not say so. And Michener, now devoted to a university career, never suggested that he should write the story, yet the thought must have crossed his mind. In fact, the groundwork was being laid for him to do just that—thirty-five years later.

He had begun writing again in Greeley. A colleague from the English department helped him revise part of a novel, but his only published work was scholarly. Between 1936 and 1941, when he resigned from Colorado State, he contributed fifteen articles to journals, edited *The Future of the Social Studies* (1939) for the National Council for the Social Studies (NCSS) and co-authored *The Unit in the Social Studies* (1940) for Harvard University Press. He felt proudest of his essay, "The Beginning Teacher," chosen by the NCSS in 1939 to introduce the organization's tenth yearbook, but he won notoriety with a short story called "Who Is Virgil T. Fry?" published by *Clearing House* in 1941 and reprinted a half-dozen times.

"Who Is Virgil T. Fry?" unraveled the plight of a mysterious high school teacher who was condemned by his colleagues and discharged by the school board but loved by his students because he inspired them to learn. This entertaining story, Michener's first successful work of fiction, demonstrated his skill at making a point in popular literature as well as his desire to reach both general and academic audiences.

These publications, plus involvement in several professional organiza-tions, advanced Michener's reputation in higher education and led to the offer of a visiting lectureship from Harvard University in 1939. If, as his former colleagues had claimed, the West was a dead end for young teachers, Michener was the exception. He requested a year's leave of absence from

Colorado State and returned east that summer with Patti to begin teaching in Harvard's School of Education where he also worked toward a Ph.D., which he never completed.

That fall, reporting to Professor Spiller, he said,

> I find myself irrevocably committed to [social studies] as my future job. [I am] in charge of the students at Harvard who wish to become teachers of the social studies. . . . I certainly don't regret my work in English, for it has given me a warmth and an understanding that many of the people I work with in education lack. On the other hand . . . [I am] miles removed from what I ever foresaw in Swarthmore.

Still, he had not given up writing. "In between the classes and the journals and the editorials and the attacks on pedagogical reaction, I think of an epic or two in iambic pentameters," he continued. And in a final paragraph he revealed he was writing a novel about the Mexican Revolution—"something closer to [the] nature of what I envisioned in the earlier days"—although without any success.

When Spiller read the letter he knew that his former student was still the frustrated writer whom he had taught at Swarthmore. "What impressed me was that he really wanted to write, more so than he wanted to teach," Spiller recalled in 1981. "He hadn't found the courage yet. He was floundering, running away from writing, but always coming back to it." Spiller was not surprised, therefore, when Michener resigned from teaching in 1941 to become an editor, a job that took him one step closer to the writing profession, where he really wanted to be.

However, his departure from the teaching profession was abrupt, and not without ill feelings. When the Harvard assignment ended in August, 1940, Michener visited his mother in Doylestown, returning to Colorado State that fall for the next academic year. During this time, he decided to leave teaching when a colleague inadvertently informed him that his application had never been seriously considered for a much sought after faculty position at a prestigious university—simply because he did not have a Ph.D. Immediately Michener concluded "that if my profession enforced such criteria, I had no future in it and no further interest."

In spite of other offers from universities, Michener's career remained in limbo until P.A. Knowlton of the Macmillan Publishing Company visited Greeley in the spring of 1941. Publishers and editors frequently visited Colorado State in search of talent, and Knowlton needed an editor for Macmillan's high school text division.

"He didn't need me," a modest Michener explained as he later recalled the visit, "but he needed someone like me, about thirty-five, who could fill the gap in Macmillan's chain of command. I was available."

Friends, including Floyd Merrill, advised Michener to turn down the offer. "We thought he had too much talent for a publishing house," remembered Dr. Robert Porter, a Greeley physician who belonged to the Angell's Club. "We told him to finish his Ph.D. and go with Stanford or Chicago, who both wanted him."

Intuitively, Michener spurned the advice. "If I had listened to friends," he remembered, "I would not have moved to Colorado in the first place, and the time I spent there was not insignificant. A much freer society existed out west than in Pennsylvania, where I had become a semi-sophisticated easterner, politically and socially. The West really helped to make me."

That was true, but teaching deserved most of the credit. Social studies led Michener into several other disciplines, satisfied his natural curiosity, tested his ideas and his ability to gather information, forced him to interrelate with colleagues, and broadened his base of knowledge. Teaching had served its purpose, and then the challenge disappeared. Macmillan's offer intrigued him, and so he resigned from Colorado State and reported to work in New York City.

## CHAPTER SIX

# Epiphany

> I was always a diffident, free-spirited
> don't-give-a-damn sort of guy. I've never
> had any ambition to be anyone. In fact,
> friends used to assume I would be a
> professional bum.
>
> JAMES A. MICHENER
> PHILADELPHIA EVENING BULLETIN, 1974

JIM MICHENER'S IMMEDIATE concern as he began editing textbooks for Macmillan in 1941 was not his transition into publishing, but the question of his responsibility if America entered World War II. Editing was every bit the challenge that he expected, and full of surprises, too, as he discovered after he selected a photograph of Errol Flynn to demonstrate the quintessence of manhood in a high school textbook. Two weeks after the text appeared in classrooms, Flynn was charged with statutory rape, leaving Michener and his publisher slightly embarrassed. Everything about publishing palled, however, next to the likelihood of President Roosevelt leading the nation into war.

Unlike many Americans who argued for isolation, Michener was resigned to intervention. "War was inevitable, and inevitable for America," he had informed his students the spring before in Colorado. He was certain that few Americans understood why the United States was irretrievably committed to the defeat of Nazi Germany, and in the November 1941 issue of *Progressive*

*Education* he clarified his position in an article entitled "What Are We Fighting For?" He outlined six reasons for American intervention:

> I.   Decency: "Is Solomon Cohen living a more decent life in New York City than Abraham Levitski is living in Warsaw? There is a difference."
>
> II.   Economics: "Much of our confusion springs from the fact that capitalists hope to salvage a capitalist economy from this war and socialists a socialist economy. Many conservative Americans dread the thought of strengthening communist Russia."
>
> III.   Social issues: "Our nation is now and probably always will be struggling to preserve the essential services, rights and freedoms, upon which we have flourished in the past."
>
> IV.   Government: "We are fighting for a representative government which serves the wishes of most of the people most of the time."
>
> V.   Self-interest: "We are fighting to preserve ourselves, both as individuals and as a nation. . . . Our continuing unselfish ideals will be betrayed if we supinely surrender one idea after another."
>
> VI.   The democratic spirit: "America is fighting for the preservation and the extension of its spirit."

America's international prestige, its supremacy, and its cherished ideals depended on defeating "a dedicated group of convinced Germans," Michener concluded in an article that demonstrated his ability to simplify complex issues. That said, and providing that America declared war, all that remained for him to decide was whether he should join the battle.

At thirty-five, Michener was among the oldest men called by the United States draft. "The people on the draft board," he said later, "were out to get me"—but that was his fantasy. Macmillan's P. A. Knowlton told Wilbur Murra that for most of a year an agonized Michener vacillated between joining the service or registering as a conscientious objector, which was expected of a Quaker. His indecision continued until the Japanese bombed Pearl Harbor, the turning point for all of America.

"After war broke out," remembered Wilbur Murra, who knew Michener through the National Council of Social Studies, "[Jim] became an ardent advocate of the war as a moral imperative to stop Hitler and the Japanese aggressors; and he was determined to have a part in it himself."

Michener later explained that "What I saw and heard in Europe as a student convinced me that I had to join the service." He was so determined, in fact, that friends overheard him persuading Patti to join the Women's Army Corps. In the summer of 1942 she reported to Louisiana for basic training.

On several occasions during 1942 Michener traveled to Washington, D.C., in hope of landing a commission in the armed forces. Murra was now living in the nation's capital, and Michener frequently visited him. "[Jim] was disappointed with not getting what he wanted, with delays, et cetera," Murra recalled. Due to poor eyesight, there was some doubt that he could pass a physical examination. He finally joined the navy in October as an enlisted man. Then, in early 1943, a commission came through.

Michener's disappointment continued, though, for the U.S. Navy did not know what to do with a thirty-six-year-old lieutenant. He requested an assignment in Mexico City, where he had once thought about writing a book, but because of his experience in the British merchant fleet, his superiors selected him for Mediterranean duty. Pleased with that decision, he completed special training at Dartmouth. Just as he was about to leave for the Mediterranean, however, the navy scuttled his plans and sent him to Washington, D.C., where the Bureau of Aeronautics needed a publications editor. Michener hated the job and for several months pleaded for an overseas assignment. Meanwhile, he spent his leisure time in the National Gallery of Art trying to forget navy life.

In November 1943, Lieutenant Michener was transferred to Philadelphia's Aviation Supply Depot as publications and personnel officer. Overqualified for this job, too, he was just as annoyed by it until a labor dispute gave him a chance to bargain for a better assignment. He petitioned his superiors in Washington, stipulating that upon resolving the problems at the navy warehouse, he expected to be sent overseas. The request was granted. He went to work as a mediator, and four months later, in April 1944, he sailed for the South Pacific. Late that month he arrived on Espíritu Santo in the New Hebrides, south of Guadalcanal.

By this time American forces had secured Guadalcanal and were moving north to Munda in the Solomons. Michener followed the action "as a kind of superclerk for the naval air forces." For eight months he traveled from island to island inspecting ground installations, delivering messages, replenishing supplies, and reassuring servicemen and natives alike. The job was relatively safe. "I usually got to the islands three days after the fighting was over," he explained. "It was like going to a Sunday picnic when I landed, and we just walked ashore. I had occasion to visit most of the islands where the action was going on. . . . I never did anything that a good woman secretary could not have done better."

The navy provided Michener with a life of leisure in the South Pacific as publications officer for the Solomon Islands. It put a Quonset hut, a jeep, and two corpsman at his disposal and gave him ready access to several craft for traveling among the many islands. Michener enjoyed another advantage in that certain officers assumed he was related to the powerful Vice Admiral Marc A. Mitscher.

Michener's tour of duty resembled his earlier *wanderjahr* abroad, but instead of immersing himself in European culture, he steeped himself in South Pacific lore. Everything that he had read as a teenager about the South Sea Islands came alive for him between the spring of 1944 and the fall of 1945 when he served on forty-nine islands and traveled approximately 150,000 miles on assignment in the Pacific. During this experience he finally decided to begin a career in writing, but the moment of decision was still in the offing.

For several months Michener had all he could do to explore the exotic South Pacific islands, many with glowing red hills that rose spectacularly from green valleys, and volcanoes that pierced the empty loneliness. Connecting everything was a deep blue Pacific, stretching from one atoll to the next. "On most of my assignments," Michener reminisced in 1981, "the time came when there was nothing to do but wait for a plane going somewhere. At such times I managed to take long trips through the jungle or to the more remote islands. I got to know natives, their dialects, something of their history, and the ways in which they lived." He was forever studying customs, ideas, and life-styles.

A typical assignment sent him to one island in search of a village that had rescued American fliers during the early days of the war. On behalf of the U.S. government, it was Michener's privilege to thank the natives with gifts of clothing and food. "A French planter took me to the island in his small boat," Michener recalled. "We coasted along the forbidding island for two days. At night we lay off the fever-ridden shore and listened to the soft jungle sounds. Early in the third day we went ashore. . . . We walked through dense jungle for about an hour and came finally upon a clearing. An astonishing sight greeted us."

Seventy black Melanesian girls between the ages of ten and eighteen ran up to them, laughing melodiously and dressed only in brief red and white gingham kilts. Behind them stood five bamboo buildings that looked to Michener like a school. Fields of corn, yams, watermelon, pineapple, and taro surrounded the buildings and flourished in the tropical soil. The entire scene had been chopped out of the jungle, and as Michener admired it, he wondered about the farmer who must have made it all possible. Just then, the girls parted, and from behind them entered a gray-haired white woman of fifty.

"She was as stately as a queen," Michener later described her. "Nobility spoke in every motion she made. She was barefoot. Her feet were splayed and hard. She wore a kind of sacking for a dress. . . . Her hands were rough from heavy work, and her handsome face was weatherbeaten."

At once the girls introduced her in English. "This is Mother Margaret!" they cried, and they watched her with affection.

Michener displayed his gifts and explained that he was looking for the brave men who had saved the Americans from the Japanese.

Mother Margaret laughed and pointed to one of the older girls. "There's your man!" she said. "Yes, that girl saved the Americans. When their planes went down offshore, she paddled out and dragged them into her canoe."

Michener rewarded the youngster whose friends circled to watch, and then he turned to learn more about Mother Margaret. Who was she, and what was she doing in the jungle?

Surprisingly, she had been a first honors student at St. Leonard's School for Girls, where Michener, as a student at nearby St. Andrews, had once spent an uncomfortable afternoon attending a stuffy faculty tea. She was on Tulagi when the Japanese invaded and destroyed her school, along with all her valuable books. She hid in the jungle and watched and then, in a small boat, fled six hundred miles south to this dismal island where she built a mission with the help of village girls whose ancestors had been cannibals. She had mastered jungle agriculture, and she taught the girls how to grow crops and how to fish. They then taught the entire island how to grow and cook corn, how to weave, how to build better houses, how to control mosquitoes. She worked ten to fourteen hours a day, striding over her budding farm with bare feet hardened by rocks and jungle briars.

Every night, with her work in the fields completed, Mother Margaret settled in a barren room and wrote in Matu a textbook for her girls. By the time of Michener's visit, she had written nineteen textbooks. As soon as she finished one, each girl who could read made a copy of it, and in turn taught another child to read and write.

Michener could hardly believe that such a mission existed, let alone the woman who inspired it, but he spent a day getting acquainted with Mother Margaret and her girls. "Here was teaching that I had never known before," he later wrote. "Here was the very essence of all that education stands for: a dedicated human being tearing the lessons from the world's past experience and sharing it with . . . children."

Michener was deeply affected by his visit to Tulagi, and he promised Mother Margaret a favor. "As soon as I get back to Guadalcanal," he said, "I'm going to cable for a complete library. You'll have so many beautiful books . . . well, you won't have room for them all!"

True to his word, Michener relayed Mother Margaret's story to his superiors at Macmillan, and soon afterward the publishing company shipped her more than two hundred American schoolbooks.

On another assignment, Michener flew to Bora-Bora—"the most beautiful island in the world," he said—to investigate an extraordinary situation. American soldiers and sailors who had served overseas for two years were now being welcomed at home as heroes. "They had been fighting in malarial islands, beset by jungle, a fearful enemy, and terrible loneliness, with never a woman in sight," Michener explained. But the men who served on Bora-Bora refused to go home. Some threatened mutiny if anyone dared to separate them from the island. It was Michener's job to find out why.

After two weeks on Bora-Bora Michener also dreamed about staying forever. "It was as close to paradise as men in this world ever get," he thought. The island was void of disease, war, and bitterness, and inhabited by beautiful Polynesian girls who lived among the Americans. "There was a party every night of the week. There was dancing till dawn. There was good island food and a regular supply ship from the States once a month," Michener discovered. Eventually he returned to Guadalcanal to file a report, but the sweet attractions of Bora-Bora lingered in his memory.

Between assignments Michener frequently had little to do, and to help pass the time he read voraciously. In December 1944, he wrote another long letter to Professor Spiller at Swarthmore to let him know what "the well dressed naval officer is reading these days." The letter confirmed his continued interest in literature and history.

His reading list included John Marquand's *The Late George Apley*, which he found "very thin and not quite worth the praise lavished upon it," and the Latin American prize-winning novel, *Broad and Alien Is the World*, which he said "held me closely. . . . Some of the scenes depicted were immense . . . none of the characters in the book impressed me much, but the total picture, hackneyed as it was, was damned fine reading." (Ironically, the criticism later leveled at Michener's books echoed these same sentiments.)

He also enjoyed Guedalla's *The Duke*, a biography of the Duke of Wellington: "staunch reading for these times," he told Spiller. "The problems of the Congress of Vienna are so similar to the problems of today, that I repeatedly found myself reading long quotations [from Guedalla's biography of Wellington] as if they applied to Hitler (Napolean), Russia (the French Revolutionists), British Labor (the Whigs), and the repatriation of worn-out royalists (Spain and France)."

*A Tree Grows in Brooklyn* impressed him as "one of the most deftly and obviously artistic books I've read in a long time," but *The Land below the Wind* seemed "terribly trivial." Resinberg's *The Pacific* disappointed him even though the author wrote "with a touch of Conrad . . . the epic of the Pacific has never yet been touched, I am afraid," he said.

He "grew tired" of Harvey Smith's *The Gang's All Here*, and he could not get through *The Travels of Marco Polo*, *The Apostle*, Maugham's *Ashenden*, or Shelley's *Life of Lord Nelson*. Hemingway's *Men at War* was "rewarding" because it contained "about 98% of material that was new to me," but he considered Stalling's *The Vale of Tears* "the best war story I've read . . . it could be duplicated a dozen times." He said nothing, however, about trying to duplicate it himself.

There was much more that he had read, "and most officers and men read more than I do," he continued. "Believe me, the literary fare served up by Uncle Sam for his distant nephews is excellent. . . . It's so very good that I think civilians must have decided what books to send out here. No army could be so intelligent."

Relieved of pressure, the other officers and men of the South Pacific fleet had almost as much free time as Michener, and many of them used it to educate themselves. One carrier admiral studied tank warfare, and the head of Michener's outfit spent six hours a day learning French.

To take advantage of this accumulated knowledge and to make better use of his free time, Michener formed an officers' discussion group, similar to the Angell's Club in Colorado. On Espíritu Santo he met a former member of that club, Dr. Robert Porter, now a major assigned to the army's 31st General Hospital, and the two of them invited others to join their round table.

Without knowing it, this group became the catalyst that caused Michener to begin his writing career in the South Pacific.

During most of one year the officers met weekly to share information about whatever subjects they had been studying. One night a member asked Michener, "By the way, Jim, what are you studying?" The question stunned him. Suddenly Michener realized, "I had been studying exactly nothing." That night he walked back to his quarters, and in a lantern-lit, mosquito-filled tin shack, he began writing *Tales of the South Pacific,* his first novel.

Something else had happened finally to force him into writing, although the full effect had been postponed until now. Weeks earlier he had almost died in a plane crash on New Caledonia. He had been on a routine mission flying out to one of the islands when his plane sputtered in darkness over the Pacific. Miraculously, the pilot nursed the aircraft to the New Caledonia airstrip, and then, plunging to the ground, he leveled the plane at the last moment. It crashed in a belly-up landing. There were no serious injuries, but everyone was badly shaken. Michener stumbled away from the wreckage frightened and numbed. For a moment he must have assumed the worst: he was going to die. But walking along the airfield in the thick Pacific humidity, he later recalled, death meant nothing at all. Then and there he saw the unimportance of his life, and it made no difference if he lived or died. He feared nothing ahead of him; and he left nothing behind. "That discovery, which many young men never make," he wrote later in *The Fires of Spring,* "was the threshold by which David [Harper] passed from callow youth to manhood. He was unimportant; therefore he was free."

Some internal voice that night told Michener he was a better man than the navy or the publishing business or the universities had ever known, and all at once he wanted so much more. He had nothing to prove to anyone but himself, and he wanted to prove himself as a writer. In the final analysis, he did not want to fail for having never tried.

Forever after New Caledonia, Michener thought of the crash as his epiphany, the manifestation of all that he knew to be true about himself. "I was as good a man as I would ever be the moment after that decision on the airstrip," he wrote to a friend in 1973, "and all that happened subsequently merely reflected the change."

Dr. Porter found out almost immediately that Michener had changed: "One Sunday Jim asked me and a couple of the other doctors to go along with him on a field trip. We were on the east side of Espíritu Santo, which is shaped something like Idaho, and Jim wanted to cross a body of water for about a mile over to the island of Malekula. There was an Englishman over there who had a plantation that Jim said he wanted to visit because one day he might write the story of planters in the South Pacific. . . . This was the first I had ever heard of his interest in writing."

For a while, all Michener could do was collect notes, but once he started writing, motivated by that innocent question, "By the way, Jim, what are you studying?" he worked on his manuscript day and night. Each afternoon, beginning sometime during the late fall of 1944 and continuing through the spring of 1945, he escaped to a deep cacao plantation where he drafted outlines of several stories about the men and women of the South Pacific. At seven o'clock each night he and everyone else on the base saw a movie, and then, at about nine, he gathered several mosquito bombs and a stack of photographs that he used for describing people and places, and returned to the plantation. In one corner of a big empty warehouse he pecked at a typewriter with his index fingers and wrote the stories that he had outlined earlier in the day. He worked until two o'clock in the morning, seven nights a week.

Strangely, he felt no great ambition for his work, intimidated perhaps by the long literary tradition already inspired by the South Pacific. It had begun with Melville and continued with Charles Warren Stoddard, Joseph Conrad, Robert Louis Stevenson, and W. Somerset Maugham. None of these writers, however, had studied the archipelago as carefully as James Michener had. He delivered an unusual perspective to each of his tales, and he began to realize that as he turned several of his stories over to two navy men for their opinions:

> One was a brilliant, acidulous officer who always said, "Christ, Michener, this stinks! Why don't you change it here and there?" He depressed me so much that if I ever own a bulldog I shall call it after him.
>
> The other critic was an enlisted man who would . . . take the manuscript pages and go to his Quonset hut where he and five other men would read them aloud. Each morning he would bring them back and say, "It's wonderful. I wouldn't change a word of it!"
>
> Between them they saw me through. Whenever I worked on a long story the word would pass that, "This one is about our own rock," and half a dozen men would apply for permission to criticize it for me.

As he continued writing he saw that his stories had begun to serve a purpose, and when the war was won, he thought, his book would be even more valuable. Many men and women would want to look back and remember the South Pacific campaign as one of the crucial experiences of their lives:

> I wanted them to have a record of what it was really like. It became my job to counteract much of the crybaby nonsense that was going on at the time. If America was committed to the retention of bases in the Pacific, then many Americans would have to live in that region, and living there would not be as bad if silly preconceptions were not allowed to prejudice first judgments.

It was true that life on Guadalcanal was oppressive and most unpleasant. But there were many islands where living was good. The natural beauty was abundant. In some of the islands standards of living and enjoyment were greater than comparable standards in many parts of the States. I wanted to protect this memory and describe how different the war in the Pacific was from any other war of which I had read. The fighting wasn't actually so tough. It was worse in Europe where the Germans had great artillery barrages."

And so Michener's manuscript began with a yearning:

I wish I could tell you about the South Pacific. The way it actually was. The endless ocean. The infinite specks of coral we called islands. Coconut palms nodding gracefully toward the ocean. Reefs upon which waves broke into spray, and inner lagoons, lovely beyond description. I wish I could tell you about the sweating jungle, the full moon rising behind the volcanoes, and the waiting. The waiting. The timeless, repetitive waiting. But whenever I start to talk about the South Pacific, people intervene.

The people were his characters: Bus Adams, Bloody Mary, Atabrine Benny, Tony Fry, Nellie Forbush, Luther Billis, Joe Cable, and the beautiful Liat of Bali Ha'i. They were not people he knew, although each, including the sentimental line officer who inspected all the islands on routine assignments and narrated the tales, resembled someone he knew. "One might say my manuscript is a memorial to the bull sessions at the Hotel De Gink in Guadalacanal," he wrote to an editor at the *Saturday Evening Post*. "Therefore nothing in the manuscript is entirely fictitious."

As critics later discovered, *Tales of the South Pacific* contained four distinct levels of experience and observation: (1) navy life, with its boredom and comedy, its jealousies and antagonisms; (2) a romantic desire for beauty, love, tranquillity; (3) the granite facts of military struggle; and (4) the impact of two alien cultures on each other—of airplanes, jeeps, bulldozers, marines, and canned goods superimposed on a simple, natural life on the most peaceful, most beautiful islands in the world.

Beneath their seeming simplicity, several of Michener's tales rang with symbolism. The best example was "The Cave," which introduced the raffish Tony Fry and the enigmatic Remittance Man:

Each man I knew had a cave somewhere, a hidden refuge from war. For some it was love for wives and kids back home. . . . For others the cave consisted of jobs waiting, a farm to run, a business to establish, a tavern on the corner of Eighth and Vine. . . . For still others the cave was whiskey, or wild nights in the Pink House at Noumea, or heroism beyond the call of valor. When war became too terrible, or too lonely, or too bitter, men fled into their caves, sweated it out, and came back ready for another day or another battle.

When Michener finished writing his eighteenth story, "A Cemetery at Hoga Point"—where three hundred good men lay buried, among them Lieutenants Cable and Fry—he packaged his manuscript and mailed it to Macmillan in New York. There it was opened by George P. Brett, Jr., Macmillan's chief executive, a man who was most eager to see Michener back at work in New York City where a job as senior editor awaited him.

As early as January 1944, prior to Michener's transfer to the South Pacific, Brett had tried to coax him into leaving the navy:

> Now, I know you have done an amazingly good job, and I know that you are as anxious to continue serving your country as you ever were and that probably because of your efficiency and your ability you will be one of the last ones who will be asked to "retire." However, there is a big job to be done [at Macmillan]. I am satisfied that you have a good future with this company, and I am hoping to persuade you to take advantage of the first opportunity that comes along to come on back. You are needed here, and if it will save face with you at all, let me assure you that there can be no doubt that contributing to the education of the youth of America is an important part of winning the peace, and that there is no use in winning the war unless we can win the peace.

Convincing though it was, Brett's letter arrived two days late. Michener had already requested an overseas assignment. "I am thirty-seven years old and am qualified for sea duty," he informed his commanding officer. "With your permission I should like to stop by your office . . . to see about more active duty."

To Brett, Michener responded at the end of January:

> You know well how my affections and hopes turn toward your company. Your letter was one of the best bits of news I could have received. My whole desire is to rejoin you as soon as I can. But I have worked hard to be sprung for sea duty. . . . I simply can't ask for my release right now.

The next year, when he turned thirty-eight, he guessed the navy would want to retire him.

> If you are still of the opinion that I can help at Macmillan, I'll put in for my release at that time. In the meantime I know that some of the work you brought me into the company to do is being unavoidably postponed. I am aware of this and it disturbs me [but] if I'm worth a damn, there will be something I can do when I get back.

It was risky for Michener to turn down Brett's offer in 1944, but he was resolved to serve overseas. A year later, when Brett received *Tales of the South Pacific,* the publisher must have thought the wait had been worthwhile. He liked the stories, and in May he wrote enthusiastically to Michener: "I didn't know, although I certainly held the young man in very high esteem, that one James A. Michener was really a potential author in the trade field."

He did not, however, use the manuscript to further induce Michener to come home. In fact, he submitted the book to three outside readers and asked for their appraisals. But he also removed Michener's name from the title page because, he explained, "Long experience has taught me that where a Macmillanite becomes involved in authorship it is far better not to let anyone know anything about it until after a decision has been made with reference to publication."

That spring, Michener had every intention of returning to the States, discharged from the navy. But just as he was preparing to leave Guadalcanal, his superiors offered him the job of naval historian for the South Pacific territory, covering all the islands from New Zealand to Tarawa, and from Australia to Tahiti. Ironically, this was the job held by the narrator of *Tales of the South Pacific.*

The opportunity to visit another two dozen islands and to see part of China as well was more than Michener could resist. He canceled his return passage and began documenting the story of the U.S. Navy in the South Pacific. He wrote extensive critical histories of naval operations at Bora-Bora and Tangatabu, and he supervised the writing of twelve other histories, including those of Espíritu Santo, Fiji, New Caledonia, Aitutaki, Upolu, Wallis, and Guadalcanal.

"All in all, I judge that in eight months I caused to be written well over a million and a half words and that in the same time I myself wrote 791 pages of history." The reports, along with charts and photographs, were mailed to Washington, D.C., where they were to be reviewed by the House Naval Affairs Committee. "Long after I'm dead," chided Michener, "somebody will find [the reports] gathering dust . . . and they'll be published as affectionate little records of the absurd."

While Michener's duties continued overseas, Macmillan continued its evaluation of his book manuscript. In June, Brett reported that "There is a lot of work ahead for you, my lad, if the book is to be made as good as it ought to be, as good as you can make it. But I am only the president around here and not an editor. I have turned the whole file over to Harold Latham, vice president in charge of trade editorial."

Two outside readers had now evaluated the manuscript, both favorably. One found "some mighty fine stuff in *Tales of the South Pacific.*" There was a feeling that several of the stories were so "tall" that Michener had imagined much of them and that some of the stories were too "thin" and had to be eliminated. Overall, however, the good qualities offset the bad and "the writer's own attitude is interesting . . . the book is interesting for its wealth of details and sidelights. . . . One gets the impression that this book lets the reader behind the scenes more than the average war book does."

In July, Michener received two pages of criticism from Latham. "All of us agree that there is much interesting and valuable material in your book," he wrote. "However, it is fairly obvious that it is your first book, and that there are certain faults."

The chief criticism was directed at Michener's characterization. "You have imagined your characters indistinctly, with the result that in their various appearances they seem to be different people," Latham reported.

He complained of several melodramatic scenes, as well as Michener's humor, which he said did not work, and he also objected when Michener wrote philosophically: "you have not yet acquired the skill to do this sort of thing and write this kind of conversation without becoming stilted and self-conscious."

In conclusion, Latham asked, "Does this all sound too harsh, as though there were little left worth keeping? I don't mean to say so, because I think a great deal of the book is excellent," and he encouraged Michener to do some additional work on the manuscript.

Either Michener was discouraged by Latham's criticism, or the mail was delayed between New York and Guadalcanal, for he did not respond until late November. By then he agreed with "almost all of your criticisms" and he was willing to revise the book:

> My recent experiences in [the South Pacific] have somewhat enlarged my perspective from what it was when I wrote the manuscript. . . . I have lived with as lusty and hell-raising a bunch of old salts as live today, and studied the most intimate records of about thirty of the islands. . . . At this late date I realize that my original manuscript has lost much of its forcefulness and that your interest may have waned considerably. I hope that is not the case.

He promised to begin rewriting the stories as soon as he arrived in the States, probably in January.

However, Brett wanted him back immediately, and this time he meant immediately. Macmillan could not hold open his job indefinitely. "We need you and need you now," Brett demanded. Prior to the war Macmillan had been grooming Michener for "an important editorial post":

> we have been marking time ever since because your service with us before the war clearly indicated that you were well qualified for this job, and we wanted you. But . . . things are moving rapidly. We have a world-wide educational program, we are cooperating with our government in its program in the "liberated" countries. . . . I hope that I may persuade you to present your case as vigorously as possible with a view to getting released.

Brett had already discussed Michener's future with the navy and had learned that Michener could appropriately request preferential consideration because of his accumulated points, his many months of foreign service, "and the fact that this job is a golden opportunity for you if you can get it."

Michener appreciated Brett's frankness and immediately requested his discharge. The navy cooperated, commissioned him a lieutenant commander, and sent him home on the U.S.S. *Kwajalein*. In mid-December he reported to Macmillan prepared to resume his responsibilities and possibly to get a book published as well.

## CHAPTER SEVEN

# Just a "Johnny One-Note"?

The ages of twenty-three to forty-two
will be the tough years for you.
Sometime at about the age of forty-three
you will find that if you are one of the
good ones, you have no competition.
You will stand on a plateau and you will
be able to pick the things you want to do.

JAMES A. MICHENER TO THE GRADUATING
CLASS OF ALBRIGHT COLLEGE, 1968

WAR HAD FORCED many changes by the time Michener returned to the States at the end of 1945. A folksy Harry S Truman had inherited the White House upon President Roosevelt's death. The New Deal was practically at a standstill. War financing had inflated the national debt to $250 billion, up from less than $49 billion in 1941. Taxes had jumped to a new high. Delegates from fifty nations had attended the San Francisco Conference and formed the United Nations. "Demobilization" of forces and "reconversion" to a peacetime economy dominated the national news.

Enormous social changes had resulted, too. Millions of men and women in uniform had traveled from coast to coast and then to battlefields scattered from Europe and Africa to the far reaches of the Pacific. Never had the nation been more mobile. Marriages were on the increase, and the birthrate had risen sharply as a result of the nation's prosperity. At the same time, the divorce rate had nearly doubled since 1941.

Michener had also changed. Not only did he want to write, but having seen so much of the world he was now a confirmed traveler. Doubtful that he could combine these interests and also earn a living, he returned to Macmillan prepared to accept the editorship Brett had offered him. "I figured costs to the hundredth of a cent and loved it," he later explained, and for a while he settled into the New York publishing scene.

Patti had already returned from Europe after serving as a sergeant in General Eisenhower's command. War had changed her, too, particularly in regard to her marriage. She had given Jim a wedding band just before he sailed overseas, and asked him not to forget her, but now in New York she had apparently forgotten him. No one knew what had happened for sure, and Michener said only that Patti was "a war casualty."

Patti and Jim never lived together after the war, but they saw each other socially until Patti returned to her hometown in South Carolina. Michener never saw her thereafter.

Almost immediately Michener began looking for another wife, but without success. His friend from college days, Osmond Molarsky, who lived near Michener and became an author of books for young people, remembered that "Jim was secure at Macmillan, no doubt had saved some money and surely must have been lonely. He knew a number of attractive, accomplished young women, including an editor at a major publisher, an elegant little blonde with a doctorate from Radcliffe or Barnard, a widely published short story writer, and a girl who ran her own publicity agency. Any one of them would have filled the bill as the second Mrs. Michener. But all had a high sense of women's liberation, even by present day standards, and two of them expressed to me some dismay at [Jim's] failure or reluctance to meet them on that level, an ambivalent position, considering what he admired in a woman." By patronizing women, Michener discouraged those he liked the most.

As always, Michener shied away from intimacy, preferring instead to entertain groups of friends at his West Twelfth Street apartment or at a restaurant. Molarsky recalled several "generous dinners" for as many as ten guests, with Michener the congenial host. Entertaining in his one-room apartment without a kitchen was a notable accomplishment. He managed with a portable oven and grill set on a shelf in his bathroom. He was known for serving a mixed grill—a combination of pork tenderloin, steak, sausage, and green peppers. For dessert he favored macaroons from a local bakery, and Drambuie or Cointreau, although with the exception of an occasional beer he abstained from alchohol.

While living well, Michener was also working hard. Every morning before reporting to Macmillan he awakened before dawn to rewrite *Tales of the South Pacific*, sometimes playing Brahms's Symphony No. 1 in C Minor to remind him of the swelling Pacific.

In mid-February, a final reader's review from Granville Hicks contained further suggestions for revision. Macmillan then offered Michener a contract to publish the book, granting him a $500 advance against royalties, plus serialization rights, so that he could sell spin-offs from the manuscript to magazines, as well as theatrical and motion picture rights. Michener received the contract from Harold Latham and responded that "You have no doubt heard *ad nauseam* that this or that author felt 'that if Macmillan's publishes it, it will really be a book.' I can't say it in any new or striking way, but believe me, I mean it." From Michener, *that* was enthusiasm.

With *Tales of the South Pacific* finally finished, almost two years after Michener began writing the book, publication was further delayed, although happily, when the *Saturday Evening Post* offered Michener $4,000 to serialize two of the book's short stories. The payment was a huge sum for a man who never expected to own a savings account, and who until recently had never earned a nickel from his writing.

In December 1946, to a readership of more than three million, the *Post* introduced James A. Michener as the author of an "extraordinary book," one that the editors believed "brought home more of the what-it-was-really-like flavor of the war in [the South Pacific] than anything" previously written. Included was a photograph of Michener, now with a deeply receding hairline, a full, puffy face, protruding nose, and thoughtful eyes behind wire-rimmed glasses. His face looked resolute; and was easily forgotten, but as soon as the *Post*'s loyal audience read his stories, full of action and friendly characters, the name James A. Michener was etched in their memories.

December's installment of "Remittance Man" was followed in January with "Best Man in de Navy." The first was the story of an island beach-comber who helped save Guadalcanal, and the second, the tale of Commander Hoag and the 144th Sea Bees who had fifteen days to build an airstrip on Konora so that American forces could capture the island of Kuralei. Both selections, full of colorful characters and told in Michener's strong, first-person narrative, led thousands of readers to wonder whether the author was writing fact or fiction. Either way, they enjoyed the stories, and they inundated the *Post* with letters of inquiry about and congratulations to Michener.

"I wonder," wrote a former serviceman, "whether the author in portraying the Commander [Hoag] was referring to an officer who later became Captain McCarthy." And another said, "You put in words what it was like out there even in the good days when I was there . . . you really have it, that indefinable 'feel' of the situations and the people, especially the people."

Michener answered every letter. He hoped *Tales of the South Pacific* would become a best-seller, but when Macmillan released the book in February, Michener thought it looked "awful" and "sleazy." There was no great celebration. The "crucial event was marked by few people other than the author," wrote A. Grove Day, a Michener friend and early biographer:

> The rare first edition of the *Tales* makes an odd item for collectors. . . . The book was considered to have such slight hopes that the publisher used up an overstock of chalky paper

whose surface was different on either side, and these pages were draped in a shoddy binding. New chapters were started right under the last line of the previous ones, and "Fo' Dolla," which was to inspire one of the most successful musical comedies of our generation, began six lines from the bottom in order to conserve paper, thus saving a few dollars.

When the readers of the *Post* began responding enthusiastically to Michener's stories, Macmillan ordered a second printing. Still, there was little urgency about upgrading the product. Several editors believed that the popularity of *Tales* was destined to fade as quickly as it had appeared. Tom Heggen's *Mister Roberts* had already satisfied the public's appetite for stories about the navy, they believed. Now the country wanted to "get out of uniform" and forget the war and everything connected with it.

The opinions were not entirely wrong. Readers bought out the first edition of *Tales of the South Pacific* even before publication date, and forced two additional printings almost immediately. Still the book never became a best-seller. Its shabby appearance and untouted launch may have discouraged the most important reviewers from considering it. The news weeklies and the *Saturday Review of Literature* ignored the book altogether. "The book isn't going to create a big stir," Michener assured a *Post* editor. But "it is going to do better than we thought a war book would do."

Several critics acclaimed Michener's first novel a success. Orville Prescott, who reviewed for the *New York Times,* was most encouraging:

> This long book of eighteen loosely linked short stories is, I am convinced, a substantial achievement which will make Mr. Michener famous. If it doesn't there is no such thing as literary justice. It is original in its material and point of view, fresh, simple and expert in its presentation, humorous, engrossing and surprisingly moving. *Tales of the South Pacific* is not quite as funny as *Mister Roberts.* But it is twice as long and just as good reading. It ought to be at least as popular.

John Cournos of the New York *Sun* found *Tales* "a pleasure as well as an education," since it combined readability and excitement with "a general picture of war as it was fought in the South Pacific." He said Michener was "above all, adept at describing character."

And in a Sunday *New York Times* review, David Dempsey thought some of Michener's stories ran too long, but he rated *Tales* as "truly one of the most remarkable books to come out of the war in a long time."

Readers' praises continued and many asked for more stories.

> My dear Mr. Michener . . . the *Tales* are fine yarns. . . . I have an idea that there are many more observations whirling around in your mind. I hope you keep writing them down. Since these seem to have come off so well, how about some more about our

currently peaceful (?) life? If you will use a pen, I'll be around for
more inscriptions. You've created a fan.

Every so often a negative letter appeared among the fan mail. "Michener's
trash nauseated me," wrote Commander C. A. Whyte to the editors of the
*Saturday Evening Post.* Whyte had served in the South Pacific, and he thought
Michener's book was "about as far from a true story as anything I have ever
read, and I may add, experienced."

Michener could not resist answering criticism, and the harsher the words,
the longer his replies, even late in his career. He responded to Whyte in five
single spaced pages, politely defending himself and his book. The stories
were fictitious, he said, but based on fact.

The mail also included a scattering of letters from people who hoped to
take advantage of a suddenly famous author. The executive director of the
National Father's Day Committee wanted Michener to address the organization's annual meeting and accept the Literary Father of the Year award.

"The purpose of these awards," explained the director, "is to give substance to our program of inculcating true democratic ideals into American
youth through the family head, the Father."

Michener laughed when he read the request. He responded,

> As soon as I got your letter this morning, I jumped on the
> telephone and called my wife just about as quickly as a man could.
> The purpose of the phone call was to ask her whether in the course
> of the morning anything had happened which might qualify me
> to accept the generous offer of your committee. Somewhat dejec-
> tedly she had to inform me that I was still not a father.

A similar sort of letter came from Mary Smith, one of the children whom
Mabel Michener had reared "till I got foolish and wild." She was now living
in Corpus Christi, Texas, divorced from a sailor, and in need of money. When
Michener contacted her, he told her that Mabel had died in March 1946.
"When I got home from the war she was senile and never knew who I was, or
that I became a writer."

Several literary agents, recognizing Michener's potential, also wrote to ask
if they could represent him. He was flattered, but he considered their requests
premature. He did not think he could earn a living as a writer. The profits
from *Tales* were "substantial, but not extraordinary," he told one agent, and
until he finished a second novel, he would not know if the first had been little
more than luck.

That spring and summer Michener polished a second novel, *The Fields of
Troy,* about a boy growing up near Doylestown, Pennsylvania, and all the
while his mail showed him that perhaps he could succeed as a writer. His fan
mail had dwindled to a few pieces every week, but interest in *Tales of the South
Pacific* and its author never died completely. Donald Friede of MGM wrote to
say that he was endorsing *Tales* for the MGM Prize, and he mentioned the

possibility of a movie. The editors of *Good Housekeeping, Ladies' Home Journal,* and the *Saturday Evening Post* bargained for his next piece of fiction. He favored *Ladies' Home Journal* where two of his short stories, "The Empty Room," and "Yancy and the Blue Fish," each earned $1,000 in the fall of 1947. Both stories were war related.

In November 1947 Latham sent Michener's first royalty check, the best proof of his popularity. "It is not often that a publisher has the privilege of writing to one of his own staff to congratulate him on the success of a book," said Latham. "We are all distinctly proud of *Tales of the South Pacific,* and of the fact that you are its author, and at the same time a Macmillan man." Shortly thereafter, as further evidence of Macmillan's contentment, Latham sent Michener a $1,000 advance and a contract for his new novel, retitled *The Homeward Journey.*

Even better news arrived in early 1948. By now *Tales of the South Pacific* had sold approximately 25,000 copies in hardcover and Pocket Books decided to issue 150,000 copies of a twenty-five-cent paperback edition. The most promising news, however, came from composers Richard Rodgers and Oscar Hammerstein II, who wanted to buy the dramatic rights to *Tales* for a Broadway show.

When MGM turned down a movie option—"No one could make a movie from this," said one studio executive—stage designer Joe Mielziner carried the book to Rodgers and Hammerstein. Almost simultaneously, director Joshua Logan, upon the recommendation of Henry Fonda, who studied *Tales* for his role in *Mister Roberts,* also sent the book to the musical collaborators. Rodgers and Hammerstein wanted to write a play based on one or two of the stories in *Tales.* They advanced Michener $500 against royalties and scheduled their production to open during the spring theater season of 1949. Thus, Michener had all the more reason to believe he could succeed as a writer.

Still, he was cautious. He continued writing in the early mornings and working full-time at Macmillan. However, problems developed there. George Brett, Jr., apparently thought Michener was wasting his time trying to write. He called Michener into his office one afternoon and revealed a plan for him to succeed P. A. Knowlton, who was about to retire. Michener was interested, but as a prerequisite for the job, Brett wanted him to quit writing. No one, Brett maintained, could become a successful novelist while also managing one of the publishing world's major educational departments. Michener had to choose one career or the other.

Faced with this ultimatum, Michener left New York in March to sort out his feelings at a mountain lodge in Colorado. For two weeks he considered Brett's offer. He remembered a letter that Orville Prescott had written to him a year earlier, right after Prescott had enthusiastically reviewed *Tales.*

> I flinch a little at the thought that anything I might have written might have persuaded you to take any specific action in your own life. Supposing that next book of yours does not turn out well,

will you blame me because you turned down the wonderful non-writing job? I will try not to lose any sleep over this and can always comfort myself with the thought that my occasional literary enthusiasms are really intended for prospective buyers and readers of books and not for their authors.

Prescott's words registered forcefully now. Never for a moment did Michener fool himself about the odds against the budding writer. At the time, he knew that one in 400 novels was accepted for publication, and that only one of every 2,450 magazine articles found an editor willing to purchase it. The average novelist earned about $1,800 a year, and there were at any one moment at least 250,000 people trying to write the great American novel.

All of this Michener weighed against Brett's advice, but when the internal voice that he had first heard on the airstrip at New Caledonia returned to remind him that he was as talented as many of the writers he edited, he knew exactly what he had to do:

> After your first book everyone has to ask himself that frightening question, "Am I a Johnny One-Note?" Real writers establish themselves as non-quitters. It is the three-book, four-, five-, and six-book writers, men and women like Moss Hart and Pearl Buck, who are the real writers. I knew then that I had many more books to write and stories to tell.

From Colorado he wrote to Brett and turned down Knowlton's job. Expecting to be fired, he said "[I] shall harbor no ill feeling at all if that's your decision." Furthermore, he thought "it would be embarrassing for Macmillan to publish *[The Homeward Journey]*. I believe the contract should be voided, and I accordingly return herewith the $1,000 advance . . . . Since reaching this decision, and entirely on my own initiative, I've approached a neighbor of mine, Saxe Commins of Random House, [with hope that he might publish the book]."

In spite of his determination to write, Michener was never more unsure of himself. He expected to regret his decision, he told Brett, and he asked to remain at Macmillan as long as possible, "regardless of condition or salary." In a rare touch of sentiment he also informed Brett that "one of the worst things that could come out of this, would be for me to lose your friendship. I hope that won't happen."

Few people meant more to Michener than Brett, and the feeling was mutual as Michener discovered when he read Brett's gracious response of March 18:

> Dear Jim Michener . . . the most important part of [your letter] is reference to our friendship and your continued interest in The Macmillan Company. . . . We shall now, of course, have to go out and try to find the fellow to succeed Knowlton. . . . But I do hope I may persuade you to carry on with the department

along the lines of the divided interest, you to work for us three
days a week and for yourself the other four. This means your
workload will have to be lightened somewhat, but your salary
will be increased to $7,500 per annum.

Brett also asked Michener to resurrect the contract for *The Homeward
Journey*. He doubted that Commins, who edited such literary greats as
Eugene O'Neill and William Faulkner, had the time to edit Michener. "I have
a strong conviction that unless a lot of work is done on that manuscript before
it is published you will be doing yourself a great injustice."

Appreciatively, Michener accepted all of Brett's terms, with the exception
of giving back *The Homeward Journey*. Random House, at the time one of
New York's elite publishing houses, was set to publish the novel. Now,
Michener thought he had the best of two worlds: the security of the part-time
job at Macmillan's, with its generous salary, and the opportunity to free-lance
in his spare time.

When he returned to New York at the end of March, Michener wrote to
Macmillan editor Cecil Scott, whom Latham had assigned the task of editing
*The Homeward Journey*:

> I feel a much older man than when I left New York. It's as if the
> pleasant dream world in which I lived had been pretty roughly
> banged about. But Oliver Allston has a remarkable passage in
> which Brooks speaks of the men who try to live with one foot in
> business and one in art. He says that when the pinch comes, they
> always cling to business. I did my damnedest to be the one who
> knew where his feet, and his heart were.

Scott was angry that Michener had left Macmillan, although it must have
perturbed him even more to see Commins, a competitor, get *The Homeward
Journey*. Michener hoped to make amends:

> The rupture that this causes in our personal relations is difficult
> for me to believe. I'm terribly sorry, Cecil. . . . I know I'm going
> to regret my decision. I could have been quite happy as an execu-
> tive, playing bridge with the gentry. . . . But it didn't work out
> that way. Ten years from now I may kick hell out of myself. . . .
> But I shall have given a few things a fling in the intervening years.

By the time Michener returned to New York, he must have felt better
about his decisions. Commins had wired him in Colorado to say he was
"wildly enthusiastic" about the manuscript, although not about the title. He
compared Michener to Dickens, a compliment that Michener cherished and
hoped was true. Commins wrote, "you have the Dickens feel for people and
story. . . . [The] quality [of the manuscript] is always exciting, penetrating
and compassionate . . . completely honest and so radiant with character."
Commins said Michener's strength, like that of Dickens, was in narration.

The manuscript required some work, Commins thought, but nothing more than editing. The story had to be reduced from 300,000 words to a more manageable length: "I have many ideas on the subject that we can discuss, sitting side by side . . . what is important now is the first glow of enthusiasm for the book itself. It is that, above everything else, which helps to determine the fate of a book in a publishing house."

In closing, Commins asked if Michener preferred a fall or spring publication date, and "what sort of contract would you want? Any advance?"

Near the end of April Michener signed a Random House contract specifying a spring 1949 release for his new book to be titled, *The Fires of Spring*. He accepted a "small advance"—probably $1,000—and relaxed knowing that one of Bennett Cerf's prized editors was shepherding his manuscript through publishing channels.

Meanwhile he spent three days a week at Macmillan and on his own time struggled with the rough drafts of two new novels, one set in Mexico and the other in an imaginary state near Colorado. He had written his first two books with ease, compared to the difficulties he was having now, and neither manuscript developed beyond the preliminary stages. Writer's block stopped his progress for several months, even after he received what might have been the most encouraging news of his career.

P. A. Knowlton was with him on May 3, 1948, editing a geography text when the telephone rang in Michener's office at Macmillan. Annoyed by the interruption, Knowlton grabbed the receiver and listened quietly for several seconds as Michener continued working. Without expression Knowlton quickly said, "Thank you for the information" and hung up the phone. Continuing in the same matter-of-fact tone, Knowlton looked at Michener and said, "That was the Associated Press. *Tales of the South Pacific* just won the Pulitzer Prize for fiction." And without skipping a beat, as though they had anticipated this news—when in fact no one had dreamed it was possible—they returned to their work.

At first it seemed to Michener that there had been a mistake. A second call to retract the announcement would not have surprised him. He had had no idea that *Tales* was in the running for a Pulitzer Prize; he did not even realize that a collection of short stories was eligible for the fiction award, although he always considered *Tales* a novel. As the news spread throughout Macmillan, colleagues congratulated him, but Michener did not seem to share their excitement. That afternoon he continued working, and then in the early evening he walked to the YMCA, where he was known as "the Spiker," and played several games of volleyball.

The next morning he returned to Macmillan, still wondering why the Pulitzer advisory board had awarded the fiction prize—intended for "a distinguished novel, preferably dealing with American life"—to his collection of semifictional short stories about life overseas. It had seemed to him, and to many others, that the top contenders for the 1947 prize were *The Big Sky,* by

A. B. Guthrie, Jr., Willard Motley's *Knock on Any Door,* and Saul Bellow's *The Victim.*

By midmorning, with the *New Yorker* and other magazines calling for his reactions, he realized that he had won one of literature's coveted awards. In a brief note to Dean Carl Ackerman at Columbia University, he relayed his happiness:

> With the deepest of pleasure I accept the award of your Advisory Board of the Graduate School of Journalism of the Pulitzer Fiction Prize for the year 1947. It would be difficult to express my deep appreciation.

Aside from the $500 that accompanied the award, Michener could only guess what the Pulitzer Prize meant to his career. Pocket Books immediately increased its press run to 250,000 copies of *Tales,* and letters from fans and editors once again flooded his mailbox. Any expectations must have abated, however, when a barrage of critical comments came from book editors who doubted that *Tales of the South Pacific* merited a Pulitzer Prize.

"For the life of me I cannot understand how [*Tales*] won any prizes," wrote Victor P. Haas, book editor of the Sunday *World Herald.* "Mr. Michener's 'novel' is, in reality, a collection of 19 [sic] short stories. . . . Don't misunderstand me—Mr. Michener has written some good short stories, but I do not find them 'distinguished.'"

Across the country, other critics echoed similar sentiments. They questioned the contributions of a writer who so obviously combined fact with fiction—indeed, many critics never forgave Michener for what some of them eventually called a "faction" style of writing—and they attacked the advisory board's judgment for awarding the fiction prize to a book that was not a novel.

The Pulitzer Prize controversy continued for many years. In 1966, long after Michener had won the prize, W. J. Stuckey claimed in *The Pulitzer Prize Novels* that the advisory board had apparently lifted its ban on short story collections just to recognize Michener. "Only by a liberal stretch of one's definition can [*Tales*] be called distinguished fiction," Stuckey wrote. "It is simply a collection of descriptions, character sketches, unconnected incidents, anecdotes, off-color jokes, patriotic editorials, all loosely held together by a central narrator who can see into the minds of other people and report what is happening in places miles away. Michener's characters are wholly improbable."

That same year, a writer for *McCall's* magazine explained how *New York Times* correspondent Arthur Krock, prompted by Alice Roosevelt Longworth, daughter of Theodore Roosevelt and widow of the Speaker of the House of Representatives, coerced the advisory board into selecting *Tales.* According to Robert Bendiner, Krock "tended to dominate" the advisory board, which had supposedly decided against awarding a fiction prize for 1947. But at the last minute Krock received a telephone recommendation for

*Tales* from Mrs. Longworth, and he "forcefully relayed the opinion" to the board.

Actually, as explained by John Hohenberg in *The Pulitzer Prizes,* a redrafting of the Pulitzer Prize Plan of Award occurred in 1947 and made collections of short stories eligible. The revised formula was in no way linked to Michener, but it did invite the nomination of *Tales* by Orville Prescott, the *Times* critic who had raved about the book. Prescott was one of three jurists who read fiction for the Pulitzer Advisory Board. The other judges—Maxwell Geismar, literary critic and writer, and John R. Chamberlain of *Time* magazine—thought less of *Tales* than did Prescott, and when they tallied their combined ratings of a dozen potential prize winners, *Tales* ranked fifth, behind *The Big Sky, Knock on Any Door, The Garretson Chronicle,* and *The Stoic.*

Then on April 23 the Advisory Board considered the jurists' recommendations and made their final decisions regarding the awards. At that time, Krock nominated Michener's book. "I gave my reasons and the Board accepted them," he later explained. "That prize initiated the public and critical awareness of Michener that assured his subsequent literary prominence and success."

True enough, although at the time Michener was not so sure that his book deserved the award. During the controversy that followed the awarding of the Pulitzer Prize, Michener agreed with the critics that he was not a part of the literary renaissance of Hemingway, Faulkner, Eliot, O'Neill, and Dos Passos. *Tales of the South Pacific* was of no great significance, Michener told novelist John P. Marquand. At most, he admitted, the book was a faithful chronicle of the war in the South Pacific. He did not regard it as Pulitzer Prize material, and the award distracted him. Like Norman Mailer—whose early celebrity for *The Naked and the Dead* haunted him and caused him to say, "Look, I know I don't belong"—Michener suffered a crisis of confidence. Many years later he recalled:

> There was a flurry of interest in me following the Pulitzer Prize and a lot of invitations resulted, but I didn't have the skill to fill them. As a result I wasted a lot of time and heartache. I've *never* had that confidence many [writers] seem to possess. I have a sense of competence—I'm a competent workman—but maybe it's best one doesn't have that confidence; makes you cautious; keeps you from making a damn fool of yourself.

Except for his second novel, nothing hovered on Michener's literary horizon in 1948, and for about a year it looked as though he had lost interest in a literary career. He was busy, but not writing. Macmillan sent him across the country searching for high school textbook writers at several universities, including Colorado State. On weekends he visited friends in Bucks County, not far from where Oscar Hammerstein was writing the libretto for *South Pacific.* And when possible he courted Vange Nord. Her full name was

Evangeline Nowdoworski, and she was a tall, attractive honey blonde whom he had fallen in love with during a party in New York City. After several months and a quick trip to Reno to divorce Patti Koon, he married twenty-five-year-old Vange, an aspiring writer who had studied architecture in Michigan and worked as a researcher in New York.

While a second marriage fulfilled Michener's personal life, his writing career remained in limbo until the spring of 1949 when Random House published *The Fires of Spring* and *South Pacific* opened on Broadway. His landlady, Nancy Shores—who was also a writer—and her literary agent, Helen Strauss, finally persuaded him that the Pulitzer Prize ensured his place in the American literary tradition. But, they warned, if he did not rise to the occasion he would forfeit many opportunities—and perhaps his writing career. His only alternative, they insisted, was to quit Macmillan and write full-time.

The moment of decision could not have occurred during a more hectic year. It began sourly when Random House released *The Fires of Spring* to a field of critics who hungrily awaited another novel from the questionable winner of a Pulitzer Prize. No reviewer found any redeeming value in what Michener described as a "somewhat autobiographical" novel that attempted "to get at the growth of a very ordinary American boy into the full stream of American life . . . in the years between the richness of the 1920s and the despair of the early 1930s."

The book is a character study of David Harper who spends his boyhood in a Bucks County poorhouse where his aunt is the superintendent, then attends a Quaker college near Philadelphia, works in a summer amusement park where he meets John Philip Sousa, travels with a Chautauqua company, and eventually migrates to New York City to become a writer. It is exactly the sort of cleansing experience that Professor Spiller prescribed for fledgling writers in his classes at Swarthmore. Critics immediately spotted a "first time" novel and accused Michener of turning over to his publisher a "discarded manuscript." Michener denied the allegations, even after telling two reporters that he had begun writing the book prior to joining the navy, but by publication date it was a moot point. Critics demanded more from a Pulitzer Prize winner.

"*The Fires of Spring* is full of grotesques," complained William DuBois in the *New York Times*. "One suffers as Mr. Michener warms up his opinions of literature, music, art—and offers them in page-long monologues. One suffers most of all when Love pants in on cue, every twenty pages or so."

J. H. Burns in the *Saturday Review of Literature* said "Most of the writing is brilliant high school stuff . . . soggy prose . . . [and] embarrassing dialogue." "*The Fires of Spring* is flawed by sentimentality and naiveté," blasted C. J. Rolo in the *Atlantic*. A reviewer for *Catholic World* assured readers that "the book is quite without value."

The most thoughtful criticism came from G. D. McDonald writing for *Library Journal* "[The] basic weakness," he said, "is probably the lack of

definition of the central character." Like Pip in *Great Expectations,* David
Harper, as a central character, was not as strong as the novel's supporting
characters, but Dickens knew better than Michener how to create such a
character and then depend on him to carry the story. This was an ambitious
literary technique that required much skill. George Brett, Jr., had warned
Michener about the problem, but unfortunately Saxe Commins overlooked
it. Michener's rigid, nineteenth-century prose glossed over both characterization and plot, and from an academic viewpoint his novel was unsatisfying.

His narrative style, however, was rapid and exciting, and readers enjoyed
*The Fires of Spring* and made it a best-seller in defiance of the critics. Young
men particularly identified with the romantic David Harper, and with
Michener they shared their unabashed enthusiasm. "The things which both-
ered David . . . seem to be tripping me up right now," confided a college
sophomore who wrote from the Midwest. Nearly every fan who read the
book recalled the passage that began, "For this is the journey that men make:
to find themselves." Many readers copied the words on a separate sheet of
paper and asked Michener to autograph it. He was overwhelmed by the
response.

"If I had written only one book and if each year I were to receive only one
letter about it like the ones I receive almost every week about *The Fires of
Spring,*" Michener commented in 1965, "my life as a writer would have been a
success." Even so, he sometimes wished he had not written the book. "When
I read letters from fans who can't spell, and others who are barely literate, I
wonder about my audience." In time, he satisfied himself that *The Fires of
Spring* was "a good book for people who do not regularly read literature."

While critics picked over Michener's second novel and stripped his confidence bare, Rodgers and Hammerstein rewarded him on Broadway. Two
nights before the opening of *South Pacific,* the collaborators offered Michener
a financial deal the likes of which has never been heard of since.

Hammerstein telephoned Michener and encouraged him to invest in *South
Pacific* as a backer. He and Rodgers were confident that the musical would be a
long-running hit, and they wanted Michener to share in their windfall. As the
author of the book, Michener was entitled to a small royalty, but Hammerstein said it was a pittance compared to what he could earn as an "angel."
Michener said he did not have the capital to invest, as he and Vange were
building a home in Bucks County. So Rodgers and Hammerstein offered him
$4,500 to buy 6 percent of the property. An astonished Michener accepted the
loan and, without realizing it, secured his financial future. At that moment,
with *South Pacific* about to begin a New York stage run of 1,925 performances
and with the film rights still up for auction, James A. Michener became a
wealthy man.

Until he struck this deal with Rodgers and Hammerstein, Michener had
shown little interest in *South Pacific.* He had kept a distance from the production, preferring to leave the script in the hands of the men who owned the
dramatic rights, and he never regretted his decision to put his book in the care

of Rodgers and Hammerstein. "The script was finished without mussing an eyebrow on one of my characters," he believed. He did contribute the title "Bali Ha'i" for the song that Hammerstein said would epitomize the haunting quality of the South Pacific islands, but otherwise he remained in the background.

One night he and Vange rode the train to Connecticut where the play was in rehearsal. Afterward, in a long letter, he offered his opinions to several friends, including Lester Trauch, who followed the theater scene from Bucks County.

> The whole tenor of the show is superb. . . . The thing that impressed me was the warmth and right-heartedness of the whole damned thing. . . . Pinza is terrific [and] Mary Martin is given everything to do . . . she'll be the talk of the town. . . . A wonderful Negro woman is the Tonk, and she very nearly steals the show. . . . Her daughter is unbelievably beautiful and ought to win the heart (or other extremities) of every man in the audience. Some dish!
>
> The songs ought to be the talk of the town. "Some Enchanting Evening" should be a hit-parade item. "Honey Talk" [sic] is simply superb. . . . "Dames" [sic] will surely stop the show. . . . "I'm In Love" is a Mary Martin song that may or may not do well on records. . . . "You've Got To Learn To Hate" [sic]—I'll let you wait to hear that one yourself."

On another evening, during a final dress rehearsal, Michener saw Mary Martin, for twenty years one of the world's most cherished theatrical stars, take a dangerous fall. As Nellie Forbush, the "cock-eyed optimist" navy nurse, Miss Martin was turning cartwheels across the apron of the stage when she became disoriented and fell into the orchestra pit. She knocked over the conductor and a pianist before she fainted, and everyone in the theater thought she had died when she hit the floor. Fortunately she suffered only bruises, but she played the next two performances shot full of novocain. Later, she presented Michener a photograph of herself, inscribed, "To James Michener—that wonderful guy, father of us all."

In a nutshell, Michener was "very bullish on this musical. Everyone in show business who sees it in rehearsal says Rodgers and Hammerstein have hit their stride. It should run for two years," he told his friends.

His prediction fell three years short. American audiences loved war-inspired drama, particularly as musical comedy. Following the Spanish American War of 1898, Broadway's sensational shows included *The Sultan of Sulu* and *Floradora*. After World War I, audiences flocked to see *Journey's End* and *What Price Glory?*. *South Pacific* and *Mister Roberts* delighted playgoers in the aftermath of World War II. Of course, Rodgers and Hammerstein, who had given audiences the celebrated wartime hit, *Oklahoma!*, helped seal the fate of *South Pacific*. Critics said the show was "a magnificent musical drama."

The year after its debut the play won the Pulitzer Prize, and ever since, it has been performed at least once a week somewhere in the United States.

The importance of *South Pacific* to Michener's writing career cannot be underestimated. The show's proceeds guaranteed him a base income for life. "It never amounts now to more than $10,000 annually, but it's enough to cover our necessities," he explained in 1971. This income minimized his financial risks as a free-lance writer.

Even so, he moved slowly toward giving up his position at Macmillan. Something more than flagging confidence kept him behind an editor's desk. Two recent suicides by talented young authors had shown him the tragedy of what William James called the American bitch-goddess—success. Ross Lockridge, who had written *Raintree County,* and Tom Heggen, creator of *Mister Roberts,* committed suicide after allowing early success to possess them. Lockridge was in his early thirties when he took his life in 1948; Heggen was twenty-nine at his death the next year.

"In many ways my life resembled the lives of those two fellows," Michener later explained, "and I could have easily fallen into the same trap as victim number three." The blight of success troubled him more than the comments of critics or the lack of money or confidence.

Nancy Shores, another writer who died tragically in the late 1950s, and Helen Strauss, an agent who recognized Michener's literary potential, came to his rescue in the spring of 1949. Shores was one of Strauss's first clients, an eccentric woman whom Strauss said was "constantly the victim in troubles of her own making," but a prolific short story writer for *Ladies' Home Journal, McCall's, Collier's* and the *Saturday Evening Post.* Early in Shores's career, writing about "clean, upright, foursquare American families," she earned enough money to buy a brownstone in a good section of Greenwich Village. Near the end of World War II she converted the house into apartments, and when Michener returned from the service he became one of her tenants. As fellow writers, the two developed a continuing friendship, with Shores constantly encouraging Michener to strike out on his own, and Michener forever saving Shores from her own bouts with alchoholism.

Shores was determined to introduce Michener to Strauss. "I've never really been certain whether or not Nancy thought I'd be a good candidate as Jim's next wife, or whether she thought I should become his literary agent," Strauss wrote in her 1979 autobiography, *A Talent for Luck.*

One day in 1946, Strauss recounted, two years before meeting Vange, Michener telephoned Strauss and asked to see her at the William Morris Agency in Rockefeller Center. Strauss nervously wondered what Shores had told Michener about her, but Michener was more interested in finding a date to accompany him to the Metropolitan Opera than he was in signing with an agent, so nothing definitive occurred. Their meeting ended when Strauss, who was not an opera lover, declined Michener's invitation.

Later that same year Michener again called Strauss and asked her to dinner. This time she accepted, but he was still not interested in her professional services. Strauss did not push, particularly since she knew nothing of Michener's writing talent back in those days, for he had not yet completed *Tales of the South Pacific*. When they finished dinner early Michener mentioned playing handball at the YMCA, and "being an accommodating young woman who would never think of interfering with a good game of handball" Strauss excused herself and took a cab home alone.

Strauss considered Michener a gentleman, although she knew he was not an easy person to understand: "One must always remember that he is a man of many moods and a loner, and his interests are varied. One might be put off by his reticence, but his modesty and humility are genuine."

During the next two years Michener and Strauss saw little of each other, but with Nancy Shores as a go-between they remained in touch. When Michener won the Pulitzer Prize, Strauss telephoned *him* for lunch, and at Sardi's she laid the groundwork for becoming his agent several months later. Their relationship was not formed immediately because Michener's only interest was in an agent who could represent him for the moment at the bargaining table with Rodgers and Hammerstein. Strauss, shrewd though she was, felt she was not a match for the famous collaborators. Wary of bungling the negotiation and losing Michener for good, she recommended a veteran agent. As it turned out, she regretted giving that advice. The other agent sold Rodgers and Hammerstein all rights to *Tales* and prevented Michener from selling any future spin-offs from the book.

Strauss had a bigger challenge in store for herself, however. Somehow she had to prove to Michener that he could earn a living without working at Macmillan. He was mature enough, she knew, to manage in the curse of fame should he become as successful as she predicted. But until he began writing full-time she doubted that he could capitalize on his budding reputation.

During a second lunch at Sardi's, awaiting the fate of *South Pacific,* Strauss told Michener he could earn more money writing nonfiction for magazines than working as an editor. (Following the war, nonfiction became more popular than fiction and commanded a better rate of pay.) Strauss asked if Michener was willing to return to the South Pacific and write an article.

"He looked at me rather incredulously," she remembered, "and said it was most unlikely a magazine would send him there!"

She promised to see what she could do, and for the next twenty years, until she left the business to work in the film industry, Strauss was Michener's agent. Her subtle pursuit of him presumably netted millions of dollars for the William Morris agency, and probably made a fortune for her as well.

Michener also fared handsomely. Strauss was one of the most aggressive literary agents in New York, and no writer could ask for better representation. As soon as she left Sardi's and returned to her office, she called *Holiday* magazine and convinced the editors to send Michener to the South Pacific to write a series of articles. Then she offered Bennett Cerf the opportunity to publish the series in book form, as *Return to Paradise*. Cerf told her she knew nothing about publishing and virtually threw her out of his office. Insulted, she marched over to Doubleday and offered an editor there the chance to pick up a Pulitzer Prize winner. Doubleday offered a contract and an advance, but when Cerf found out that he might lose Michener, he reciprocated with a better offer.

By summer 1949, the package now complete, Strauss reported to Michener. Since their last lunch he had thought of little more than what he would do if Strauss kept her promise. "It's a major decision for a man to say, 'I'm going to become a free-lance,'" he reminisced long after he had made the decision. "It's a very difficult way to earn a living." He had not yet realized that the stage production of "South Pacific" was about to deliver a windfall.

In preparation for meeting Strauss again, he had presented his work to the critic John Mason Brown and asked for his opinion. "You can make it, Michener," Brown told him. "Take the risk." That encouragement made the difference. In June Michener resigned from Macmillan and at forty-two years of age, he was finally on his own.

## CHAPTER EIGHT

# The Right Place, The Right Time

> World War II and the airplane opened the
> horizons and Americans suddenly
> wanted to read about the rest of the
> world. I came along and wrote books
> that satisfied the reading experience.
> Since then I guess I've had a very good
> track record.
>
> JAMES A. MICHENER, 1971

AFTER MICHENER PROPOSED to Vange Nord in the summer of 1948, he sent her to Bucks County with earnings from his Pulitzer Prize–winning novel to find a piece of land so they could build a house. He had looked for land in Connecticut and New Jersey, closer to New York, but having reacquainted himself with friends in Doylestown during the preceding two years, he decided that Bucks County was home.

At this time, a year before *South Pacific* opened on Broadway, he had no intention of quitting his three-day-a-week job at Macmillan. Like other Bucks County residents who had business ties in the city, about ninety minutes away by car, he planned to commute. The county was already an artist's hideaway. In addition to Oscar Hammerstein II, the most famous residents included Pearl Buck, S. J. Perelman, John Wexley, Moss Hart, James Gould Cozzens, and Budd Schulberg. Michener never thought of himself as "one of them," but he was the only member of this literary group to have grown up in Bucks County. He was also the last to buy his property at the bargain price of sixty dollars an acre!

With the assistance of Herman Silverman, a landscaper and contractor who knew most of the properties in Bucks County, Vange found a seventy-acre tract in Pipersville on a densely wooded hillside that was perfect for a home and would give them a chance to enjoy nature. Michener walked the land during his honeymoon weekend and decided to build a home at the summit of the property, from which he could look out over Bucks County. Vange drew plans for a ranch-style frame dwelling with a flat roof, six rooms, a bath, and numerous picture windows through which to enjoy the rustic view. She also added a guest apartment to the back of the house. Michener asked Silverman to build the home, but to conserve costs, he and Vange planned to do most of the finishing work themselves during long weekends. To work with Silverman, Michener also hired his former George School colleague, William Vitarelli.

Construction got under way at about the time Michener saw *South Pacific* in dress rehearsals, and as his enthusiasm mounted with each performance, he sent modified plans to Silverman. "Go ahead and put in the [second] bathroom," he wrote after watching a rehearsal in Connecticut. Then, after Rodgers and Hammerstein made their generous offer, he could afford to add a garage, and "plant some pine and spruce, plus shrubs and rhododendron; grade the land and drain it, put in some lawn, etc."

There was little time for the Micheners to help with this work before Helen Strauss arranged Jim's return trip to the South Pacific in the summer of 1949. Once Michener accepted *Holiday*'s assignment, he was busy making preparations. Vange planned to accompany him on the trip as his "Man Friday," and in July she informed friends of their itinerary:

> About August 7 we move to Greeley, Colorado, where my husband will lecture at the Colorado State College of Education. August 25 sees us off for Australia from San Francisco, by plane, it seems, for there isn't a chance of sailing. Of course excitement runs in my veins in lieu of blood these days at the thought of tromping about the Solomons, Tahiti, Fiji, the New Hebrides, New Caledonia and many other islands.

Michener was equally excited, and before departing New York he sent a short note to columnist Walter Winchell:

> Some time ago you said that if I ever had any news to pass it along. . . . I am leaving shortly for an extended revisit to the South Pacific. . . . If one wanted an explanation it would be that I am going . . . where nobody will want tickets for *South Pacific*.

In a sense, Michener's return to the South Pacific was a case of life imitating art, a phenomenon that he later remarked often occurred in his lifetime. In his original version of *Tales of the South Pacific* he had included a story about a

Professor Lobeck from the University of Virginia. Lobeck was an anthropologist with "a hankering suspicion that perhaps the white man, after all, had not been destined by God to rule all colored races." This opinion, of course, Lobeck kept to himself, but gradually his mind drifted into "a monomania, out of which he developed the idea that America's destiny would not be determined by her relations with Europe, as he had always taken for granted, but rather in Asia."

Early reviewers of *Tales* told Michener's editors that "Lobeck, the Asiatic" was a humorless, poorly written story based on a ridiculous idea. They wanted it eliminated. Against his better judgment, Michener acquiesced, but instantly he regretted it. As a penance, he later admitted, he adopted Lobeck's monomania. "The destiny of the United States will be determined in large part by the decisions we make regarding our relations with Asia," he predicted. Then he waited for the opportunity to return and write about the people and their continent.

Now as he departed, he thought:

> There is only one sensible way to think of the Pacific Ocean today. It is the highway between Asia and America, and whether we wish it or not, from now on there will be immense traffic along that highway. If we know what we want, if we have patience and determination, if above all we have understanding, we may insure that the traffic will be peaceful. . . .
>
> But if we are not intelligent, or if we cannot cultivate understanding in Asia, then the traffic will be armed planes, battleships, submarines and death. In either alternative we may be absolutely certain that from now on the Pacific traffic will be a two-way affair.
>
> I can foresee the day when the passage of goods and people and ideas across the Pacific will be of far greater importance to America than the similar exchange across the Atlantic. Asia must inevitably become more important to the United States than Europe. That is why we must all do all that we can to understand Asia. . . . It has become, especially as it leads to New Zealand and Australia, one of our highways to the future.

On the heels of World War II, few Americans would have agreed with Michener's monomania. Except for following the adventures of General Douglas MacArthur in Japan, Americans expressed little interest or hope in Asia. Books set in Asia by Pearl Buck and John Gunther, and several leading magazine articles by a young Irving Wallace, had attracted masses of readers early in the decade, but by the mid-1940s the popular press practically ignored the continent. What little material appeared often failed to promote understanding and, instead, fostered several generally accepted clichés about Asia, including the notion that Asia's people are ignorant and backward and will never build first-rate, modern countries. When a Gallup poll asked Americans where they wanted to travel after World War II, Great Britain and France received the majority of votes; Asia did not even make the list.

Late in the 1940s, however, during the expansion that followed peace, U.S. foreign policy called for "a more intensive exchange of information and [the] establishment of more numerous and broader contacts" with the people of Asia to overcome the "deficiency of knowledge and understanding" that existed between the continents. American minds awakened to the world abroad as the dawning of the jet age stimulated foreign travel, and many U.S. companies opened offices overseas. Almost overnight people wanted to know more about the world, both the East and the West, and Michener's timing—he called it luck—was perfect. Ten years earlier or later, he would have missed capturing a gigantic audience. As it was, he spent the next several years as a roving ambassador and introduced the trans-Pacific world into almost every American home through magazines articles, books, and lectures.

*Holiday* introduced Michener's year-long series in May 1950, the first major treatment of "the cockiest continent on earth" to appear in a general-interest publication. Each article was primarily a travel piece, as assigned. Noncontroversial and unpoetic, but teeming with personal observations about race, religion, trade, primitive culture, social and economic tensions, the articles, written in Michener's breezy, didactic style, fostered understanding.

For example, the series began with this observation of Fiji:

> Imagine a group of islands blessed by heaven, rich in all things needed to build a good life, plus an ideal climate—and even gold mines. Picture a native population carefree, delightful and happy. Add a white government that works overtime to give honest service. Top it all off with a democracy that enables dozens of different levels of society—from Oxford graduates to bush dwellers—to have a fine time. That makes the Fiji Islands seem like a pretty wonderful colony, doesn't it? But there's something wrong with the picture.

It continued with an article about Australia:

> Today Australia faces the challenge of an unknown future. She stands, like a bewildered woman, at the schizophrenic moment, bedazzled by flattering choices, frightened by oppressive dilemmas. She has no clear idea of what she wants to become.

And this analysis of life in New Zealand:

> the relationship between brown and white is far superior to that between black and white in America . . . the Maori-Pakeha relationship is not all sweetness. A good deal of hypocrisy

obscures realities. Many Maori villages are in fact slums. Sensitive
Maoris confide that they never really feel at ease among whites,
who shout public acceptance, but practice private ostracism.

Readers eagerly anticipated each installment, all the while congratulating
*Holiday* and Michener for the series. Critics added their approval, too. One
said that after reading Michener's article about New Zealand, he was sure he
knew more about that country than most of its residents. Another added,
"The essays are superb, [Michener] does it all with unfailing zest, sympathy,
and discernment."

In the spring of 1950, after eight months of traveling and reporting, the
Micheners returned to Bucks County, but for Jim the homecoming was brief.
He had mailed the last of his installments to *Holiday* and was polishing *Return
to Paradise* when Strauss contacted him with additional assignments. While he
was abroad she had sold several of his short stories, all with tropical backgrounds, for sums of $1,500 to $2,000, to *Collier's, Esquire, Reader's Digest,*
and *Today's Woman,* and she negotiated with foreign magazines for the rights
to his *Holiday* series. By late summer she had packaged another trip to Asia,
this one for *Life* magazine and the New York *Herald Tribune*. Michener
departed for Japan in September, leaving Vange at home; he did not return
until January 1951.

Events in Asia concerned him now more than ever as turmoil erupted
throughout the East. General MacArthur's plan for the United States to
dominate the air and sea powers of Asia worried him. The forced formaliza-
tion of an American-Asiatic coalition was not in either continent's best
interest, Michener argued. He supported American assistance in Asia, but
believed that, ideally, the continent had to develop its own strength to work
out its destiny. Americans had nothing to fear from a secure and prosperous
Asia, he insisted, but a weak Asia could cause the continent to fall prey to
"some European adventurer."

"If we are resolutely determined to oppose Asia's self-determination,"
Michener insisted, "then the Asia-Europe-Africa coalition will become a
reality, possibly led by Russia, but just as possibly by some Asiatic power in
the 1980s or 1990s." Such a coalition would threaten not only American lives,
but the entire free world. He concluded that "life as we know it would
vanish."

*Life* gave him the opportunity to share these and similar opinions in his
article "Blunt Truths about Asia," in June 1951. "Asia [has] exploded into the
center of American life. Now it will stay there forever. What we do about the
fact can make or crush us as a nation," Michener asserted. "For whatever help
it may be, I offer a handful of plain and important facts."

To everyone who read Michener's views, he imparted a thoughtful,
friendly outlook toward Asia, one based on historical perspective and his
own sensible analysis. Asia was not made in America's image, he said.
Americans had to accept that the continent was run by oligarchs. "Whether

or not the idea is congenial to our predispositions, we must deal with [the oligarchs], with all their prejudices and limitations," he believed. Even accepting this, "we must not think we have found some permanent formula for political action, for this continent and its oligarchs are going to keep on changing with sometimes bewildering speed. And we will have to change with them."

Michener's anxiety about future relations with Asia was equally evident in the New York *Herald Tribune,* which gave his news feature series, "Tales of South Asia," front-page prominence for fifteen days in early 1951 and syndicated the articles to newspapers across America. Michener created the impression of a dissolving continent, one where the combined forces of war and conquest, the breakdown of colonialism, the impact of Western ideas, and steady fermentations within the inherited cultures had pushed people to the frontiers of existence. Each article introduced an Asian who had a story to tell. Included was Mansor Adabi, a young Moslem teacher whose thirteen-year-old Dutch-Moslem bride set off the Singapore riots; a Siamese boy, who transported passengers on his samlor, a three-wheel bicycle; and Par Anake, a Buddhist monk, who guided the author through Bangkok.

"Mr. Michener's articles emphasize how vitally important it is for us to understand the Asiatic in today's world. In his opinion, it is these people whose lives and thoughts we must know if we are to defeat Communism in Asia," touted a *Herald Tribune* promotion for the series.

When Michener returned from Asia in January 1951, having logged 21,000 miles, Random House released *Return to Paradise,* an unusual book of fact and fiction. It became a Book of the Month Club selection and one of the year's top ten best-sellers, and it resulted in two movies: "Return to Paradise," with Gary Cooper and "Until They Sail," with Paul Newman.

Unwilling to let the book become a collection of his *Holiday* articles, as planned, Michener used portions of the published material to introduce short stories that he had written about each of the islands he revisited: "it occurred to me that the trip would be justified if I attempted to write a kind of book that—so far as I knew—had never been tried before. Such an adventure would make the return to the Pacific intellectually honorable." (What he really meant was that he wanted to be a novelist, not a writer of nonfiction.)

However, when the book appeared, major reviewers praised the essays and faulted the fiction. "With *Return to Paradise* Mr. Michener puts away childish things," said Robert Payne in the *Saturday Review of Literature.* "The passage from childhood to maturity has not been painless. . . . Some vestiges of childhood remain, for the stories are bunk. It is when Mr. Michener describes his travels that he is most convincing."

By now, although he had not given up the idea of being a novelist, he was convinced that he should produce a book of nonfiction. Strauss negotiated a contract for a book called *The Voice of Asia,* an expanded version of his *Herald Tribune* series. Random House issued a $6,000 advance and published the book in late 1951. It was immediately well received, selected by the Literary Guild in 1952, and translated into fifty-three languages.

In its time, *The Voice of Asia* represented the most logical, and popular plea for a cooperative Asiatic policy. Some reviewers complained that Michener oversimplified America's relationship with Asia, but in general critics agreed with his position. "America has an honorable place in Asia," he reported, "not as the new imperialist, for Asia will not tolerate that; nor as the perpetual Santa Claus, for the American taxpayer will not condone that; but as a cooperating friend working on problems of mutual concern and no doubt mutual profit."

Michener begged Americans to keep "normal wits" about Asia, which "is not a continent of barbarian hordes or inscrutable evil," and to keep in mind that "we [Americans] are fighting for the understanding of a very few people. If we could convince this handful that our way is better than the Russians', we would win Asia."

The "very few" included Nehru, Sukarno, Liaquat Ali Khan, Chou En-lai (who had already been lost to the Russians), members of the media in Asia, industrial leaders, college professors, small businessmen and farmers, and college graduates. "In this sweeping, swirling world what people think still determines history," Michener reasoned. Therefore, the United States had no choice but to support substantial governments in Asia, and to "back forever and forever the ultimate masses of the people as they grow toward responsibility and the control of their own political existence."

By the end of 1951, no American writer had contributed more to America's knowledge of Asia than James A. Michener, whose name was practically a household word. His fame interested him less than the fact that he wanted to write fiction, however, and he promised himself to begin writing a collection of five Asiatic novels following *The Voice of Asia*.

Earlier in the year he had made known his plan to Helen Strauss who responded enthusiastically on behalf of her agency:

> For the life of us we see no reason why you shouldn't have alternate or succeeding books of fiction or non-fiction. Our point of view is that you must write what you want, when you want to write it and on a subject of your own choosing, and in the manner that suits your mood and your need. Most writers fear being typecast and seek to diversify their work. You, on the contrary, seem to worry about spreading yourself. Put your mind at ease about that and let your fancy dictate whatever you want to do. Our confidence in you is supreme.

But finding the time to write these novels was another matter, for neither Strauss nor Michener saw any logic in discouraging the line of magazine editors who craved only his nonfiction. *Holiday* was ready to send him overseas again, this time for articles about Hawaii, Japan, and Siam, and a short piece about Angkor. He accepted the assignment and spent the first half of 1952 in Asia, again without Vange.

He returned that summer just in time for a meeting at the *Reader's Digest,* which published only nonfiction. DeWitt Wallace, the founder of *Reader's Digest,* had been following Michener's career ever since *Tales of the South Pacific,* and in June he asked Michener to lunch with several editors. "I'm sure that we should become acquainted," he said. "Although we haven't any assignment in mind, it should be possible to cook up a project, now or later."

Michener was interested, but not enthusiastic. He still wanted to write fiction. However, there was no harm in agreeing to lunch, particularly since the *Digest* offered him the munificent sum of $2,500 just for the honor. What he did not know was that if Wallace's plans for him developed satisfactorily, the publisher intended to offer him an unusual financial arrangement, surpassing the generosity of Rodgers and Hammerstein, and making him independent and free to follow the life of a free-lance writer.

The story of the *Reader's Digest* has been used frequently to demonstrate what can be accomplished by the entrepreneur in America. As a young college graduate working for a printer in St. Paul prior to World War I, Wallace discovered that the U.S. government published dozens of excellent pamphlets, free to anyone who knew they were available. He gathered a host of those pamphlets, which he thought might be of value to farmers, and he packaged them in a booklet entitled *Getting the Most Out of Farming.* Almost immediately he sold 100,000 copies of the booklet to banks, which imprinted their names on the covers and distributed them free to their farm customers.

World War I interrupted the publication of a second booklet, but in the fall of 1918, as a wounded soldier in the army general hospital at Aix-les-Bains, a long convalescence gave Wallace an opportunity to broaden his plans. Now he was reading dozens of consumer publications and clipping articles that seemed to him of *lasting value.* After he was discharged from the service, he selected thirty-one of these articles, condensed them to readable, salient versions, and published them under the title, *Reader's Digest.* The articles included: "How to Regulate Your Weight," "What People Laugh At," "Is Honesty the Best Policy?" and "Men vs. Women as an Audience." He had selected them from the *Saturday Evening Post, McClure's, Ladies' Home Journal,* the *New Republic, Vanity Fair, American Magazine,* and others. The *Digest* was "the one magazine containing articles only of such *permanent* and *popular interest* that each issue will be of as great value a year or two hence as on the date of publication," promised the publisher. It was "the magazine of 100% Educational *Interest* . . . no articles on purely transient topics and no articles of limited or specialized appeal."

Wallace was elated with the first issue but hardly anyone else noticed. Publishers, including William Randolph Hearst, rejected Wallace's proposal to buy the magazine and to retain him as editor. One publisher called the idea ridiculous. Bitterly discouraged, and having gambled all his savings, Wallace shelved his magazine and went to work in the international publicity department of the Westinghouse Electric and Manufacturing Company in Pittsburgh. However, during the depression of 1921, he was the first man let go, and while he could not have guessed it at the time, the discharge was the turning point of his life. Thereafter he worked full-time on the *Reader's Digest*.

In the fall of 1921 Wallace married Lila Bell Acheson, who became not only his bride but his partner as well. On the day they were married, they used borrowed capital to mail several thousand circulars soliciting subscriptions to the *Reader's Digest*. Then they left for their honeymoon in the Pocono Mountains, and when they returned to their Greenwich Village apartment they found waiting for them 1,500 charter subscriptions, each worth $3. Beginning in February 1922, the enterprising couple began monthly publication of their magazine.

From that time forward, *Reader's Digest* became one of the world's favorite periodicals, a lesson in itself, teaching faith in God, family unity, the work ethic, and participation in government. The magazine offered every reader spiritual and moral guidance while also making the world seem less complicated. In the 1950s, when Michener began contributing to it, the *Digest* claimed the world's largest circulation with thirty-seven foreign editions in thirteen languages.

In the United States alone the magazine climbed to a circulation of twelve million by the mid-1950s, almost twice that of its nearest competitor. On average, one month's issue of *Reader's Digest* was read 168 million times, reaching one in every four adults in the nation. No other magazine offered a writer the oportunity to address such a cross section of the country. The average *Digest* reader was thirty-eight, and had a higher income and level of education than the median for all magazines.

Primarily, the readership was middle class. "The ultra-sophisticated, literary types and intellectuals are not interested and do not read the magazine, although some do," explained Hobart Lewis, who began editing the *Digest* in the 1950s and continued into the 1970s. "People who pride themselves on their education don't read it, but the *Reader's Digest* is not for them. It's for busy people who don't have lots of books and access to education. The *Digest* is written for everyone, from the non–high school educated person to someone with a Ph.D., but by and large it is for Middle America."

Part of the reason for the Wallaces' success was that they never deviated from their original formula. Their magazine offered an article a day, each condensed from a leading magazine. Every article, however, had to satisfy three criteria: applicability, lasting interest, and constructiveness. The first two were not unique to the *Digest*. When Benjamin Franklin and Andrew Bradford published America's earliest magazines in the 1740s, they aimed to include articles that were practical ("applicable") and worth reading a year after publication (Wallace's definition of "lasting interest"). But the magazine's third criterion was different, and meaningful in the post–World War I era. Constructiveness, in Wallace's view, meant optimism, the key element in the philosophy of the American middle class. The *Digest* saw "sermons in trees, books in the running brooks and good in everything." As Wallace explained, the magazine was intended "to promote a Better America, with capital letters, with a fuller life for all, and with a place for the United States of increasing influence and respect in world affairs."

When Michener was invited to lunch in 1952, the *Digest* was already operating out of a mansion in Pleasantville, New York. Wallace greeted the author by saying that he and Mrs. Wallace had loved *South Pacific*. Their favorite song was "You've Got to Be Taught," which showed how racial prejudice was taught by bad example. Michener commented that during tryouts Rodgers and Hammerstein had been pressured to strike the song, but they had fought to keep it. "This is what the play is all about," said Michener. "People are born good and have to be taught to act bad." Wallace agreed, and then introduced Michener to several editors, including Hobart Lewis.

At lunch, hearing that Michener had recently spent some time with a U.S. Marine division on the front line in Korea, one of the editors asked the author to elaborate on what he saw. Up to this time, most of the reporting from Korea had centered on Panmunjom and the air battles, and little of it had come from the front lines. For the next two hours Michener offered his observations of two armies deadlocked in trench warfare along a 140-mile front. The editors and Wallace were impressed. Michener had not only entertained them, he had also demonstrated maturity and confidence, and most appealingly, a quiet reserve.

Finally, Wallace asked Michener to write for the magazine. Hobart Lewis recalled hearing the publisher's words: "Mr. Michener, do you have some project that you have a burning desire to write about for us?"

With a blank expression, Michener responded flatly, "Mr. Wallace, I have never had a burning desire to do *anything* in my life."

No writer in Lewis's memory had ever spoken so bluntly to a group of *Digest* editors. "Another writer would have come up with a roomful of ideas, and maybe one of ten would have been good," Lewis later commented. "Not Michener. He was a man of few words and, like Wallace, a terrific listener." His honesty was appreciated, and if he did not have ideas for the *Digest,* then the *Digest's* editors, with Wallace's blessings, intended to develop some for him.

If ever a magazine was designed for a writer, the *Reader's Digest* was designed for James A. Michener: teacher, patriot, student of the world, and optimist. The combination of magazine and writer was a perfect fit; one that has been rarely repeated in the history of publishing.

The winning combination had much to do with the genuine respect and admiration that developed between Wallace and Michener. The publisher and author shared many qualities and goals: they believed in the Protestant ethic, they were devoted to their jobs, generous with their thoughts and money, and committed to international friendship. From the outset they liked each other, and they remained close friends until Wallace's death in 1981. In 1973, thinking of their friendship, Michener explained:

> For some reason I have yet to discover, Mr. Wallace agreed with my approaches to problems; he liked the manner in which I expressed myself; and he found me congenial. . . . I liked [him] immensely; indeed, I felt toward him as a son feels toward an understanding father. I found him easy to talk with and filled with ideas. Nor was I ever afraid to rebut him in argument. . . . He adored my wife and we were the only Democrats he knew. He may have felt that out of decency he should have a guy like me around.

Soon after the luncheon in Pleasantville, Lewis asked Michener to explain what was happening in Korea to the *Digest's* audience. "All of us here understand the problem better than we did before, and now we would like to find a way to share with the American people some of the things you told us. Would you have time to cast it all up in an article?"

Lewis left the article's point of view to Michener's discretion: "whether you tell it as a personal experience of a day you spent at the front, or whether you tell it objectively, you will want to include human details to bring it all to life." He then posed a page of questions that the article should address:

> How long do men stay [on the front line]? What are the eating and sleeping facilities? Are the men equipped with antishrapnel vests? Is most of the terrain ideal from a defensive standpoint? And what is our defense in depth [i.e., how many men support the front line]? How good is enemy marksmanship with rifles, with artillery? Which appeals (of psychological warfare) are most effective?

In a postscript, Lewis offered $2,500 for the article, and a $500 kill fee, explaining that "if for any reason we are not able to publish the article, we will . . . return the manuscript to your possession."

Michener accepted the assignment, wrote the article that summer, and mailed it to Lewis in September.

"Your picture of the way it is in Korea is magnificent," Hobart Lewis responded on September 30. "Nothing like it has come from the front, and it surpasses our expectations, which were set very high. . . . I very much hope you will keep us in mind for your future work. It will be a great service to the American people to publish your account of the facts of life and death in Korea."

Wallace was in Europe when the article arrived, but when he returned and reviewed it, he immediately wrote to Michener: "Your classic on Korea is rightly scheduled as the lead article in our January issue. . . . What are your present plans and future projects? I hope you are keeping us in mind, for there is no one whose work we value more highly."

After Michener contributed several additional articles, Wallace asked for an exclusive relationship to prevent competing magazines from benefiting from Michener's talent. But Helen Strauss objected. "A writer of Jim's talents must at all times be completely free," she informed him. Wallace then responded with what may well have been one of the most generous offers in publishing history:

> You can go anywhere in the world you want to go. You can write anything you want to write. I don't care what it covers or if it's something we couldn't conceivably be interested in. We'll pay all your expenses, no matter where you go or what you do. All that's required is that you let us have first shot at what you've written. If we can't use it, you can sell it elsewhere and you won't owe us a penny.

That offer made Michener one of the most financially secure writers in America. It freed him, he said, to take risks that other writers could not afford in the early years of a writing career.

Michener now had nothing to lose. He could write fiction if he wanted to, and even if he did not succeed, the *Digest's* income was guaranteed. The magazine paid him between $3,500 and $5,000 per two-thousand-word article, and for long pieces, including book excerpts, Strauss negotiated fees that ranged between $10,000 and $30,000. In one month during 1965, the *Digest* paid Michener $85,000!

During the next eighteen years, with Lewis as editor-in-chief, Michener was a *Digest* roving editor. As such, he contributed more than sixty articles to the magazine, and no other free-lancer rivaled his insatiable curiosity and kaleidoscopic interests. He wrote about Japan, housewives, rock music, Afghanistan, Indonesia, religion, Australia, Nehru, Hawaii, art museums, Mexico, political campaigning, pornography, Italian designers, and much more.

Among the *Digest's* editors in the States and abroad, Michener developed a reputation for dependability. More important, he worked quickly and accurately, and always maintained an optimistic point of view. "Middle America demanded this," said Lewis "and Michener had the technique for supplying exactly what we ordered: a compelling, easy-to-read narrative, with lots of facts, plus drama and color."

Michener's two shortcomings as a *Digest* writer were his inability to master the magazine's trademark, the anecdotal lead that introduced most articles, and his tendency to write pieces that were too long for the *Digest*. Lewis told him not to worry about it and to continue writing: "Cutters and lead-writers we have."

Michener liked this arrangement and was sure it benefited his work. Surprisingly, it never resulted in a moment's dissatisfaction. Many other writers objected when the *Digest* edited their material, but Michener rarely questioned Lewis's editorial judgment. "Once a piece of mine might have been purposely postponed because it would have helped the Democrats, and an article that I wrote about Mexico was rejected probably because the *Digest* disagreed with my analysis, but I have no complaints," he said.

No one at the *Digest* complained either. Lewis and Wallace valued Michener more than any writer working at the time. "There is no name that we can think of that we would rather see in the magazine," Lewis frequently reminded Michener. Wallace agreed, and every so often, as token of his appreciation, he sent Michener a bonus check amounting to several thousand dollars.

In contrast to this professional relationship, which helped Michener amass both a fortune and an audience, he was caught in a painful alliance with a lecture agency that sent him across the country twice a year on tours. Right after winning the Pulitzer Prize he had signed a contract with W. Colston Leigh, president of the country's most aggressive booking agency, with offices in New York, Chicago, and San Francisco. While the lecture circuit was good publicity for Michener, he knew he had made a mistake after his first outing. However, he was under contract for five years. In 1971 he recalled:

> I have many scars from those days. Public speaking is the hardest way in the world to earn a buck. It was brutal making train connections, or driving all night to be on time for a speech. But for a writer trying to earn a decent living, it was honest, dependable work, and I recommend it highly.

In the late 1940s, Michener received at least one request a week from organizations whose members wanted to hear him talk about the South Pacific or Asia. By advertising Michener's availability to his clients, Leigh increased the number of requests, coordinated Michener's calendar, negotiated his fees, and paid him 65 percent of the proceeds. He never really needed the money, though, particularly after he became a client of the William Morris Agency. In fact, the lecture circuit became a nuisance to him. It interfered with his travel plans and drained him of energy that he should have devoted to his writing. Since he did not enjoy either the speaking or the attention that resulted from it, he began to resent both Leigh and his audiences.

He was sure that among the PTAs, the charities, clubs, civic organizations, and college groups that invited him to speak, few people listened to what he had to say. He thought a lecture should be educational first and entertaining second, but unfortunately, members of his audiences were often more interested in his personal life than in America's relationship with Asia. Their questions frequently disappointed, and even annoyed him. The most insulting one, he said, came from a fashionably dressed woman in the Midwest.

"Mr. Michener," she began, "as you spoke, one question kept going over and over in my mind. Where did you get that suit made? I want one exactly like it for my husband."

He must have been equally offended by unprepared newspaper reporters who asked inexcusable questions such as "How old are you?" "Are you married?" and "What are the titles of your books?" One reporter indicated she was inconvenienced by having to consult *Who's Who* "to learn that the famous author had studied at four American colleges," when indeed it was her responsibility to know something about him in advance of the interview. Michener told her that anything he said about himself was "entirely irrelevant."

Nothing seemed to make him angrier than a letter from Leigh's treasurer, chastising him for an uncooperative attitude. The letter tactfully stressed the importance of client–agency relationships, but Michener read it and exploded.

He replied, "I'm warning you and your whole office that if I ever get another letter from any of you like yours of November 3, I'll damned well never get up on another platform for you." The letter covered a full page and in essence he claimed he always cooperated with clients. "I even answer their silly stupid letters about dinner here and lunch there," and he had never missed a speaking engagement in his life. "Let's not get confused as to who's lecturing whom, for the next time I hear a peep from your outfit on manners this whole goddamned contract goes up in smoke." In an otherwise serene career, those were probably Michener's harshest words.

Leigh treated Michener like any another temperamental client and apologized for the letter, but their relationship never improved. In November 1952 Michener advised Leigh:

> I must seriously consider whether or not I can risk my reputation by appearing under your management. While in West Virginia I was told of a college in Ohio that had to close down its lecture series because the first two speakers you provided were charged by the American Legion with being communist. I must be careful to avoid such associations and am consulting my lawyer.

Of course, no one was going to label the author of *Tales of the South Pacific* and *The Voice of Asia* a communist, and Leigh ignored the threat. But following each touring season Michener decreased his time commitment and limited the distance he was willing to travel to present a speech. Finally, in 1953, he fulfilled his obligations and informed Leigh that he could not conceivably "conduct any kind of business" with him in the future. Undaunted, Leigh offered Michener $500 per speech in 1954, a large sum at the time for speaking engagements, and extended similar offers in 1959 and 1965. Michener never signed again, and in the years thereafter he accepted few speaking invitations.

Accolades and money did not affect Michener's personality. Fame did not change him in the 1950s, or ever, as evidenced by a letter he received in 1966 from Wilbur Murra, his former social studies colleague. Murra explained that when he joined the faculty at the University of Hawaii, Grove Day invited him to lunch. "It was a foregone conclusion," he said later, "that our conversation would focus on someone called James Michener. Before we met, however, I wondered if we'd be talking perhaps about two different persons: I about Michener 1938–46; Day about Michener 1950–66. Our conversation hadn't proceeded very far, however, until it became apparent that we were talking about the same man—even though Murra kept referring to him as Jim and Day kept referring to him as Mitch."

Even Michener's life-style remained the same, except that, beginning in the 1950s, he traveled extensively, and he suddenly needed a part-time secretary and professional help to manage his income.

In 1950, not knowing whom to consult about his finances, he wrote to money columnist Sylvia Porter and asked for advice. She sent him to a brokerage firm where he began a stock portfolio. Later, on his own, he became a client of Julius Lefkowitz and Company, an accounting firm in New York City.

He opened his portfolio with stocks worth $10,000, most of them in Kennecott Copper. Every six months, when he received royalty payments, he purchased additional stocks and reinvested his dividends in the oil, chemical, metal, utility, food, and communications industries. By the fall of 1952, Merrill Lynch valued his portfolio at $107,428.

In 1951, with four books in print, a hit show on Broadway, and two movies in production, he earned slightly more than $100,000 in royalties and fees. That figure was small in comparison to future earnings, but Michener never lost sight of a dollar's value. He fretted over the cost of living, and with the exception of his home in Bucks County, he spent very little money for possessions or pleasure. In 1951 Vange recorded an inventory of their household goods, valued at $38,882.20. In addition to four hundred record albums, assorted clothing, and two automobiles, this included a library worth $4,573, and living room furnishings valued at $3,887.

How he spent his money was his own business, he advised anyone who asked. "The struggle of my life," he said many times during the 1950s, "is how to adjust to acceptance without allowing it to color my behavior or contaminate my writing." He succeeded at not allowing it to do either, but success did not necessarily make him happy.

He was still moody and distant, often to the embarrassment of his friends. Frequently he did not speak during luncheons or parties. "He had that ability to close out and concentrate, no matter who was around him," reminisced Hobart Lewis. "Once Jim and his wife were at our home for dinner and he picked up a book, sat at one end of the couch and read. Even when people were introduced to him he continued reading. That was just his way."

His way was that of a man who feared his own psyche. At one dinner he attended, the other guests were comparing their analysts. Michener commented that he could never delve into his own life history; it was bound to be too painful, he said, even if he could learn from it. Apparently, he thought it was safer to bury himself in work, to research in depth, and to write about other people and problems larger than life. Unlike his contemporaries, Ross Lockridge and Tom Heggen, he was protected by his moody spells, which provided distance, insulating him and granting him a narrow perspective. He was unimportant, he said humbly; as a result, he spared himself many problems, not only in the 1950s, but throughout his career. He was famous, but he was not a celebrity. He had no extraordinary talent, and no exceptional skills as a writer, he claimed. Nor, he thought, did he have ambitions or expectations.

Like most serious writers, however, Michener cared about literary immortality, and he began laying the groundwork for his own in the early 1950s. "I want to write books that people will read fifty and one hundred years after I'm gone," he often told interviewers. Nothing was more important to him, and for the rest of his life he worked toward that one goal.

## CHAPTER NINE

# Dateline: Asia

> The luckiest aspect of my life as a writer
> has been the opportunity it has given me
> to live part of each year in Asia. It has
> been my good fortune to know Asia in a
> time of great flux. . . . America and
> Asia, from here on out, are indissolubly
> linked insofar as interest, development
> and history are concerned. That the
> people of these lands are so easy to know
> and to love makes our job easier. That
> the world has grown so small makes the
> work imperative.
>
> JAMES A. MICHENER
> SELECTED WRITINGS OF JAMES A. MICHENER, 1957

IN THE EARLY 1950s, having arrived as the sole literary proprietor of the vast territory west of San Francisco, Michener intended to begin writing the five Asiatic novels he had mentioned earlier to his agent. *The Americans*—a story about his own countrymen traveling through Asia—was to introduce the series.

However, as "the sort of guy who feels committed to write about the events of my time," he was diverted by the Korean War. On five occasions during the unpopular conflict, Michener returned to the front lines for *Reader's Digest* and other periodicals. It troubled him that while the fight had generated little sympathy in the States, American troops fought "a tremendous war on a shoestring." He wrote to Herman Silverman:

> Don't let me hear any complaints against taxes! . . . I was in Korea at Christmas when we were getting our worst beating. Our men behaved admirably. Although they often had inadequate protection from the cold, and although they had fought in the last

war and had been yanked back into service, few of them whimpered. I was impressed by their courage and ability to absorb very rough treatment.

Several times in 1952, with the war practically stalemated, newspapers throughout the United States splashed Michener's observations across their front pages. The headlines, "Brave Men Write a Korea Saga: They Lose—But How They Lose!" and "Night Riders Blast the Daylights Out of Foe," ran above two of his articles in the New York *World-Telegram and Sun*.

From the U.S. carrier *Essex* off Korea, Michener hitched a ride with a bombing mission and later wrote the story of Felix Bertogna, a thirty-six-year-old pilot, and his wingman, Red Stillwell, who roared their bombers up the coast at 300 miles an hour and, in total darkness, blasted a large munitions plant.

Then, with U.S. Task Force 77, he watched a desperate effort to save an American flyer. Young Ensign Norman Broomhead of Salt Lake City took off from the aircraft carrier *Valley Forge*. Moments later, while he attempted to bomb a bridge in North Korea, enemy fire disabled his plane. In a crash landing Broomhead was severely injured, but for several hours through the night his buddies attempted to rescue him. Heavy volleys of enemy fire prevented their success.

"Here was complete failure," Michener wrote in an agonizing account. "But as you watched it you did not know that it was a failure. For there was a spirit of exaltation among the flyers involved. . . . 'We don't desert our men,' they said. . . . Sometimes defeat—like the Alamo or Dunkerque—does actually mean more to a democracy than victory."

Broomhead's story inspired Michener to write *The Bridges at Toko-ri*, a bitter novel that defends America's presence in Korea. In Michener's re-creation of Broomhead's experience, Lieutenant Harry Brubaker, USNR, becomes "one of the voluntary men who save the world." At twenty-nine, Brubaker has a good job in Denver, a devoted wife and two lovely daughters. He is minding his own business when the Korean War erupts and the navy orders him back into uniform.

Without knowing why, Brubaker suddenly finds himself aboard the carrier *Savo*, where his thundering ninety-ton jet awaits the night it must destroy four vital communist bridges at Toko-ri. The mission, directed by a salty old admiral named Tarrant—pronounced "tyrant"—is nearly impossible, because Toko-ri sits in the bottom of a narrow valley around which the enemy has packed the hillsides with batteries. Even a 550-mile-an-hour jet is a sitting duck.

Brubaker haltingly tells his heartsick wife, who has joined him on liberty in Japan, that "the communists know where you have to come in . . . and where you have to go out. So they sit and wait for you." Like other American wives who think the war is "stupid," she wonders if those bridges are worth

American blood. The admiral, and possibly Brubaker, too, believes that indeed they are, for their destruction protects America's freedom.

*Life* magazine originally commissioned *The Bridges at Toko-ri,* and Random House, calling the book a "masterpiece," published it concurrently in July 1953, the same month the war in Korea ended. Everyone who read the story gained a clearer perspective on the official reasons for America's intervention in Korea, and hundreds of readers agreed wholeheartedly with Michener's message. Novelist Herman Wouk read the galleys and called the book "A battle hymn of the republic in fiction! God bless Michener for telling his yarn so well. His eyes have seen the glory!"

Book critics expressed less enthusiasm than Wouk, although none disputed Michener's implied conclusions. "With Mr. Michener's point I agree fully," commented H. C. Webster in the *New Republic.* "With his art I do not." Webster complained that while Michener's pilots were "good Americans and two-dimensional . . . what they do and feel and say sounds too frequently more like the Voice of America than fine art." A reviewer in the *New Yorker* expressed a similar opinion: "[Michener's] theme is admirable, but his treatment of it is thin and facile, and he contents himself time and again with situations so trite that we weary of them even before they begin to be resolved."

Other critics disagreed and hailed *The Bridges at Toko-ri* as the best of Michener's five books. "He has not written the novel of Korea we are all waiting for, but he has entered more compassionate depths than ever before," commented Robert Payne in the *New York Times.* James Kelley added in the *Saturday Review* that the book was "a honed-down story of action, ideas, and civilization's responsibilities, [and] moves forward with the inevitability of literature."

In Michener's opinion, *The Bridges at Toko-ri,* which Frederic March and William Holden brought to life on the screen, was his best effort to date, and in time he thought it represented his finest contribution to the traditional English novel. Long after it was published he explained,

> I wrote it just to see if I could do it. I satisfied myself that I could. I could have written one of those books every year for the remainder of my life, but I took no great pride in it and I would have been ashamed of myself. It wasn't big enough; it didn't have the complexity I wanted. I might have a better reputation in the long run if I had written more of my books in this style, but it showed me nothing. I have a great respect for Dashiell Hammett and Raymond Chandler and I think I could have moved into their field.

Most critics in 1953 doubted that Michener was another Hammett or Chandler, but one who read *The Bridges at Toko-ri* called him the successor to Hemingway. That was a predictable, though unsupportable comparison, regardless of the praise for this latest novel. Michener the patriot and Hemingway the expatriate were contemporaries, novelists, and sometimes journalists who wrote about man's courage under increasing external pressures, but their literary similarities ended there. Michener was developing a distinctive style and a feeling for character, but he never achieved the rhythmic prose and intense characterization that distinguished Hemingway's works. Hemingway's readers were thought to be "sophisticated," while Michener's were "middlebrow." However, Michener's prose frequently struck forcefully, and his popularity rivaled Hemingway's.

The publication of *The Bridges at Toko-ri* and several articles in leading periodicals set Michener in the foreground of American journalism during an era of cold war politics and military "containment." As a result, the U.S. government—particularly the State Department, which frequently sought the assistance of a sympathetic and respected author—closely followed Michener's career.

His official introduction to Washington occurred shortly after *Reader's Digest* accepted his first article about Korea. Hobart Lewis had sent the piece to the Department of Defense for a reading, and—although the word was never spoken—approval. After some "concern" that the article revealed the vulnerability of American forces and that it might adversely affect the morale of Americans at home and at war, the Pentagon supported the article's publication with minor revisions.

"I think they did not relish the idea of asking you to unsay the things that they knew you had a right to say and that the American people have a right to know," Lewis told Michener. But the Magazine and Book Branch of the Defense Department wanted Michener to rewrite the final paragraph of his nineteen-page article to make, in Lewis's words, "the case for the war as strong as, in all conscience, possible." Lewis said this was a reasonable request and hoped that Michener agreed: "If you will send along a revised final page we will then proceed to get your valued report before the public."

If there was irony, not to mention danger, in a major American magazine asking a government that had not declared war to approve an article about the Korean War prior to publication, Michener apparently did not object. He seemed to welcome the government's perusal, and accepted it as a final verification of the facts. Having already written in the first paragraph of his article that there was "little hope for victory," he rephrased the last paragraph to assure the *Digest*'s readers that the bloodshed was not in vain:

> The war has been wearisome, the outcome frustrating, but, now that we are in it, there seems to be no reasonable alternative. We can take comfort from the fact that the things we have gained were worth fighting for.

Michener's cooperative spirit and mainstream ideology pleased the *Digest* and earned him respect in the nation's capital. Thereafter, he was repeatedly asked to serve the government in one civilian capacity after another. For example, in 1952 the Department of State, which had monitored Michener's travels overseas, asked him to narrate "Appointment in Asia," a series of weekly half-hour television shows presenting Asian countries to American audiences. But his greatest challenge began in 1953 when the government sought his help to save the Asia Foundation, a San Francisco–based nonprofit and supposedly apolitical organization that the communists relentlessly tried to infiltrate.

Citizens for Free Asia, later to become the Asia Foundation, was formed in 1951 by a group of San Francisco citizens under the leadership of businessman Brayton Wilbur. The committee shared the goal of promoting the manifold aspects—spiritual, civic, economic, artistic, social, and educational—of the Asian renaissance. According to its preamble, the organization used private funds to encourage voluntary activity, "believing that action by individuals working as private citizens is a fundamental requisite of democratic societies."

Initially, the committee collected and distributed vegetable seeds to farmers in the Philippines. As its interests escalated, it began to sponsor scholarships and fellowships, teacher-training institutions, debate clubs, Radio Free Asia, student magazines, book publishing ventures, and various civic organizations that spawned participation in programs that helped build a communist-proof society. For example, foundation money sent the NBC Symphony Orchestra on a tour of Japan. Concert receipts were donated to the Japanese chapters of the World University Service. In addition to stimulating Japanese interest in orchestras and other musical groups, the purpose was to show Japanese students that non-communist nations shared an interest in their welfare.

The committee's threefold direction was formally established in its Articles of Incorporation, filed at the time it became the Asia Foundation:

> To make private American support available to individuals and groups in Asia who are working for the attainment of peace, independence, personal liberty, and social programs.
>
> To encourage and strengthen active cooperation, founded on mutual respect and understanding, among voluntary organizations—Asian, American and international—with similar aims and ideals.
>
> To work with other American individuals and organizations for a better understanding in the United States of the people of Asia, their histories, cultures and values.

Michener was not originally a member of this committee, but he endorsed it, contributed to it, and finally spearheaded a campaign to save it from the communists. In 1980 he recalled:

> The foundation was a marvelous showcase. It was very prestigious and provided many entrees, so naturally the communists

wanted control. I stepped in to help save it from evil times and we
had a hell of a fight.

Michener's campaign began with a letter to "every distinguished citizen"
of his acquaintance, asking for financial support:

> A group of Americans . . . have determined to advance a
> concept called "Our Asian Interest" for the consideration of the
> American people. We believe that one of the great problems, if not
> the greatest, which confronts the American people in the second
> half of the Twentieth Century is that of our relationship to Asia.

To help shape the future work of the foundation, Michener traveled abroad
as an observer and periodically reported his findings to the executive committee. For example, he delivered these observations in 1955:

> In Ceylon, the recent change in government has given rise to
> renewed demands by communists and their sympathizers that the
> Foundation be expelled. The new government will, in one form
> or another, undoubtedly wish to exercise some supervision over
> our work. . . .
> In Indonesia where we have been received with exceptional
> warmth . . . there has unexpectedly developed an attitude of
> unfriendliness on the part of Prime Minister Ali. . . .
> We have not realized the extent to which our work would
> attract attention and give rise to controversy or suspicion, most of
> which might be quite undeserved. The flexibility of our pro-
> cedures and the diversity of our activities make it difficult for
> outsiders, particularly Asians, to identify just who we are and
> what we do.

To the committee's and the government's satisfaction, Michener continued
in this capacity for several years, but when he discovered that the CIA had
secretly provided operating funds for many of the foundation's programs, he
quickly resigned. He explained that it was a conflict of interest for him to
work abroad in any capacity for the government, and he gracefully bowed
out. His work had not been fruitless, though, for by now the foundation's
leadership was sufficiently strong to protect its programs from communist
manipulation.

In spite of this resignation, politicians never forgot that one of Michener's
"most solid contributions . . . was as a guiding light and intimate adviser to
the powerful Asia Foundation," as Senator Daniel K. Inouye, then a representative from Hawaii, reminded the House in 1962. Michener's social and
political ideology had pleased the American political establishment. Consequently, it was difficult at times to separate Washington's interests from
Michener's work abroad. Throughout the 1950s, countless State Department
officials, ambassadors, and members of foreign governments asked

Michener to visit Korea, Japan, Thailand, or some other Southeast Asian country and write about a specific concern there. Michener accepted many of these invitations.

Because Michener commanded the attention and respect of a huge audience throughout the world, the staffs of many American embassies eagerly courted him by offering to organize state affairs in his honor, arrange interviews for him with foreign dignitaries, and provide other services, including research support. To his credit, Michener shied away from embassy invitations—he was rarely a houseguest at an embassy, for example, although he usually had that option—but since he occasionally accepted an embassy's privileges, and because he supported the consensus ideology, critics some-times dismissed his work as propaganda for the American government. This was unfair because Michener was generally responsible for his own research. Working alone, he personally verified research to the best of his abilities through libraries, independent sources, and "man on the street" interviews. In most instances he "went into a nation, sat quiet, listened, and in time found that all sorts of people wanted to talk with me."

Michener was as much a loner abroad as he was in the States. Vange rarely traveled with him anymore—she was at home pursuing her own writing career, unsuccessfully—and he often worked for months at a time without seeing a familiar face. An occasional letter to his wife or Herman Silverman provided a glimpse of how he spent his days.

The most fascinating of these letters was five pages long and written to Silverman in July 1955 from the Majestic Hotel in Saigon. Most of the letter concerned a real estate venture he and Silverman had begun in Bucks County. Each paragraph carried a one- or two-word caption. The captions included Profits, Figures, Caution, Extra Land, Policy, and—interestingly—Riots:

> If this letter becomes a bit confused it's because there's a riot on outside and all of us are staying indoors for the time being. Nothing serious but it makes a hell of a lot of racket. Seems the local people hate the Indians and the Poles on the international commission . . . feel they are too pro-communist. Nehru, the leader of Asia, should hear what some of his supposed followers are shouting right now!

On this particular day, Michener discovered what it meant to be an American in Saigon. Rioters had stormed his hotel:

> It was (and is) pretty horrible. At least I found out whether or not I had guts. I stayed here in the Majestic and listened to them coming down my hall. They completely annihilated the room next door and then started in on mine. I thought the lock would hold, but it didn't, so when the door crashed in I stood with my typewriter and said, "I'm an American writer. Behave or I'll write

bad things about you." They stood there for a second and then we all laughed.

As I write this, quite shaken up, a little boy stands guard at my door and says, "An American friend.". . . Whether anyone has been killed I can't say, but this has really been a jolt. All the rooms around me have gone now, and I've been standing in the doorway smiling limply and saying in as firm a voice as my quaking knees and throbbing heart would permit, "American." Today it's been a damned good word.

The army had arrived with machine guns and occupied the Majestic, sending "a heavy rain of small bombs" into the streets:

Brother Herman, if I sound casual about this, I ain't. Only my determination not to let the gang in after the door went down saved things here and if one of those wild men with the clubs had said "Boo" I'd have fainted.

For two more hours the riot continued while Michener watched from his window. Finally, he wrote,

The machine gun fire has stopped, the bombs have stopped and things seem reasonably well settled for the time being. . . . This my my [sic] one riot, I hope. I couldn't stand another. . . . I have often been kidded about having a bland, preacher's smile. Jesus, I'm glad I had one today because it got me home free this time.

In addition to those in his letters, the best descriptions of Michener's activities abroad appeared in the *Reader's Digest,* which published the bulk of his magazine work. Nine times in 1955, the *Digest* carried Michener's byline. No other author contributed as frequently. Each of his articles read in a simple, familiar tone, distinctly that of a professional globetrotter who wrote with authority and purpose. Encyclopedic, colorful, and full of human interest, the articles included:

*Afghanistan: Domain of the Fierce and the Free*—Beyond the storied Khyber Pass lies a high wild land of extraordinary people. Geographically close to Russia, the Afghans look to America for friendship.

*The Riddle of Pandit Nehru*—India's Prime Minister has few kind words for America, yet his policies may be our greatest source of strength in Asia.

*Why I Like Japan*—The hidden secret is known to millions of Americans whose wartime hatred has turned to deep affection for a strange and charming people.

*Today's Wild West: The Great Australian North*—There remains nowhere in the world a frontier existence to compare with the challenging life on Australia's vast cattle stations.

Collectively, these articles addressed three separate issues. The most obvious was the fight for a free Asia, a concern of every politically conscious American during the cold war era. Michener's articles never included exaggerated denunciations of communism. He never tried to infect the reader with fear, but he made it clear that communism was the ultimate enemy. He supported a "tough stand" against the communists and called for military aid to Pakistan, "so long as it is not used aggressively," and Indonesia where it was needed to save Southeast Asia and Australia.

Second of these issues was Michener's determination to help Asians build self-sustaining societies. The Afghan man, for example, seemed to him an ideal worth preserving:

> It is great to be an Afghan man. You are tall, spare, tough. You wear a beard and carry a gun. You don't pay too much attention to what the government says and you are one of the most hospitable men on earth. The minute a stranger crosses your threshold you order a sheep killed for celebration, and between fights you sing and dance and travel the high mountain passes. It's a rare, free life.

The Afghan woman was less glamorous, but in Japan, young women set an example for the Eastern world. Prior to World War II the Japanese woman was "the world's loveliest gift to man," according to Michener. Then, through a series of dramatic laws in 1945, General MacArthur decreed her freedom and left her bolder, if not lovelier. "The results shook Japan worse than the 1923 earthquake and the islands have not yet recovered," Michener explained. However, Michener supported the revolution, and expected it to save Japan from communism:

> Throughout Asia many countries have either fallen to communism or seem about to do so partly because the women of those countries could see in old patterns absolutely no hope for a decent life. . . . Across Asia, communists are whispering, "When we take over your country, things will be better.". . . But in Japan this whispering campaign has no appeal.

Michener's third issue, and the theme that appeared in most of his writing, whether for periodicals or books, was the optimistic belief that peoples of the world could live together in peace:

> I really believe that every man on this earth is my brother. He has a soul like mine, the ability to understand friendship, the capacity to create beauty. In all the continents of this world I have met such men.

There were few lectures, no harsh criticism, and no prophecies of dooms-
day in Michener's articles. In a decade dominated by fear and dull politicians,
his words rang louder than despair and cynicism. He was, as British journalist Peter Lewis said of men and women in the fifties, "young enough to feel
concerned, mildly rebellious and naively optimistic that solutions could be
found." In this context, millions of Americans, and foreign residents, too,
responded to his work.

Perhaps Michener's most utopian and naive belief was that men and
women of different nationalities could live together harmoniously, in spite of
widespread social prejudice, and that this harmony would evolve naturally:

> I do not believe it is my duty to preach to other people and
> insist that they also accept all men as their true and immediate
> brothers. These things come slow. . . . I had to learn gradually, as
> I believe the world will one day learn.

He used his next novel to promote the idea, however, and unwittingly
created a battle among movie and play producers. *Sayonara,* a timely and
dramatic story about the love of an American serviceman and a Japanese
woman, resulted from Michener's own love affair with Japan between 1949
and 1954. More than any other novel of its time, *Sayonara* brought the
problem of interracial marriage into focus.

Interest in the story mounted even before it was written. Movie producer
David O. Selznick cabled Michener in Rome to ask if his next novel might be
adaptable to the screen. Michener was genuinely surprised when producers
inquired about his work because he never wrote with movie or play adaptations in mind. He preferred to leave such matters to his agent's discretion,
without becoming involved in them. This time, though, the producer was
married to actress Jennifer Jones, whom Michener admired, and his next
novel just happened to be a perfect vehicle for her, although he was not so
bold as to say so. That decision he left to Selznick, to whom he sent "in
strictest confidence and against my agent's wishes and my own better judgment," a brief synopsis of his next book:

> A twenty-eight-year-old major in the United States Air
> Force . . . is asked by his chaplain to dissuade a dead-end enlisted
> man from marrying a Japanese girl. When the two men get to
> Japan the dead-end character goes ahead with the marriage to a
> most unprepossessing young woman, while the major checks in
> with the American commanding general of the area whose attrac-
> tive daughter he is about to marry. Because the general's wife
> promises to be an extraordinarily tough mother-in-law, and
> because the general's daughter shows some signs of becoming a
> standard domineering American wife, the major shies away. At
> this moment, through the enlisted man and his wife, the major
> meets a remarkable twenty-nine-year-old Japanese actress from

the Takarazuka Girls Opera (a theatrical troupe composed exclusively of girls . . . the prima donnas of Japan).

The central portion of the book is a deeply emotional love affair between the major and Takarazuka girl. . . . They move in with the enlisted man and his wife, and the story becomes one of discovery and appreciation for the strange Japanese way of life. The subplot concerns the enlisted man who by the law then in effect . . . is forbidden to bring his Japanese wife into the United States. At the same time, a tough Army lieutenant colonel, who hates the Japanese, is sending the kid home.

The story ends on a definite down beat, for the enlisted man and his wife commit suicide—as so many Americans have done under these or related circumstances. The actress . . . remains at Takarazuka, and the major, who was most eager to marry her . . . is sent back to duty at Randolph Field and the likelihood of swift promotion for his unusual performance in Korea to one of the youngest generals in the Air Force and a reasonably satisfactory position as the husband of the commanding general's daughter.

"There it is," Michener told Selznick. "I have no knowledge of what could be done with it. In fact, I do not know whether it is even going to make a good book. I do know that it is colorful and, in parts, moving."

Selznick knew at once that he wanted the story, if not for its intrinsic value, then because Miss Jones expressed a "fervent ambition to play the lead." He was willing to make a "generous offer" for the film rights if Michener refrained from inviting bids for the property. But Helen Strauss immediately dashed those hopes and opened the bidding. She had already stirred up interest in Hollywood and had promised Metro-Goldwyn-Mayer an early look at the book. According to *Variety,* the asking price for the adaptation rights to *Sayonara* was a $150,000 first payment and an unusual (at that time) escalation agreement that could earn royalties up to $250,000 for Michener. Within several weeks Strauss received qualified offers from MGM, 20th Century Fox, and William Goetz, an independent producer.

Selznick, who thought bidding was demeaning, reluctantly joined in the activity, and for a while it looked as though he might get the property, particularly because Michener favored his approach to moviemaking. But then one evening after seeing a Broadway play, Michener met Joshua Logan at Sardi's and their discussion led to one of the most unlikely episodes of Michener's career.

Logan and Michener had continued their friendship ever since *South Pacific,* and when Michener divulged the story line of his soon-to-be-published novel, Logan said he wanted *Sayonara* for the Broadway stage; to get it he was willing to buy both screen and dramatic rights. The more they talked about it, the better Michener liked the idea of another play. Strauss was about to conclude the negotiations for the film adaptation, thus forestalling a stage production, but Michener called her at home that night and told her to sell *Sayonara* to Logan. She said that was impossible because Logan had not submitted a qualified bid. Michener insisted, however, and the next morning Logan's offer was accepted.

This news distressed the other bidders. Selznick quietly dropped out of the competition, deeply disappointed. MGM, 20th Century Fox, and Goetz filed a joint lawsuit to stop the transaction. In an unprecedented suit, the plaintiffs insisted that Michener sell the rights to one of them, and for the next several years the fate of *Sayonara* as a dramatic property remained in the New York courts. The case eventually reached the state's supreme court, and as Helen Strauss revealed in her book,

> Jim Michener received $250,000 instead of $150,000, but no percentage. Bill Goetz was awarded *Sayonara,* which Warner Brothers released. In one of those settlements in which everyone seems to win and everyone owes something to someone, Josh Logan directed the picture for Goetz, agreed to direct *Bus Stop* for 20th and tentatively agreed to do penance on the Metro lot.

Selznick, unfortunately, walked away with nothing. And Strauss implored Michener not to get involved in future negotiations.

There was no need for Michener to do anything except write so long as Helen Strauss represented him, and he finally realized that when she forced Random House to assign him a new editor beginning with *Sayonara*. Saxe Commins's enthusiasm for Michener's talent had been flattering, but Michener felt he needed intensive editorial guidance to make his books truly works of literature rather than merely reportage. Commins had frequently irritated John O'Hara and William Faulkner by being overly intrusive in his editing of their manuscripts, but he went too far the other way when editing Michener's material. For example, after reading the first fifty-six pages of *The Voice of Asia,* Commins wrote to Michener with a few reassuring comments, but little that was editorially beneficial:

> —The pattern is more than okay, it has order, sequence, conviction.
> —Pages 38 to 50 will be deleted over my dead body. This is one of the fairest and best balanced commentaries in so brief a compass that I have ever seen on the character and contribution of MacArthur. . . .
> —Page 39, seventh line from bottom, instead of "had grown into" I would say "I had developed."
> —Where do you get the idea that Conclusions (pages 51–56) is "the heaviest writing"? I disagree completely.

Since *The Voice of Asia* was nonfiction, Commins may have devoted less time to it than he might have spent on a novel, but when Michener turned in the complete manuscript of *Sayonara,* Commins disappointed him a final time. Michener knew that *Sayonara* needed revision, and when Strauss read the manuscript she agreed. She sent the book to Commins and explained that, with editorial guidance, Michener planned to rewrite the manuscript. However, when Commins read *Sayonara*—still untitled at the time—he decided to title it *Japanese Idyl,* and then he sent it to the printer and scheduled it for early publication! As an afterthought he telephoned Strauss and said that no revision was necessary. To him, the book read well.

"This was very upsetting," Strauss later revealed, since "most writers need editorial help, and frequently a good book can be hurt by careless editing and a good book can become a much better one if the author and editor work together."

By now Michener was frustrated. He objected to Commins's title because the word "idyl" had nineteenth-century connotations. Furthermore, he had lost faith in the editor who had once promised to help him develop his writing talent. "I needed an educated man with a good eye to edit my work," Michener later recalled, "and if I couldn't find him at Random House then I was ready to look someplace else."

Strauss suggested that Commins "was on in years" and perhaps too busy to help Michener, so with her client's approval, she insisted that Random House assign him a new editor. She confronted Bennett Cerf and, as she later explained, triggered a "palace revolution" because she "touched on just about the most delicate nerve in publishing. Even lesser editors become prima donnas at the very thought that one of their authors would want to change his editor. Furthermore, I was only an agent, and I had the effrontery to be critical of Saxe, who was *the* great editor!"

Nonetheless, Strauss pushed doggedly ahead and suggested that Albert Erskine, who edited Moss Hart and Robert Penn Warren, work with Michener. "Bennett figuratively hit the ceiling. . . . I threatened to have Jim's contract canceled . . . [and] it was finally agreed to make the switch."

Commins retrieved Michener's latest manuscript from the printer and turned it over to Erskine, who retitled it *Sayonara.* From that book forward, Erskine and Michener worked together. The arrangement, Strauss believed, was "probably the best thing I did for his career, because with Albert and, later, Bert Krantz, his copy editor, Jim got the editorial help he always wanted."

In the meantime, *McCall's* magazine, which had asked Michener for a love story in 1951, paid $35,000 for the serialization rights to *Sayonara.* Random House released the book in January 1954. By then, in spite of a new editor, Michener knew exactly what to expect from critics.

"In *Sayonara* Michener mounts a soap opera on a soapbox," said the reviewer for *Time* magazine. Michener "falls into errors which rob his creation of some of its effectiveness," offered Bradford Smith in the *New York Herald Tribune.* And, "one can only wish that the author had revised his script a few more times," opined Vern Sneider in the *New York Times.*

But there was merit in *Sayonara,* and reviewers who overlooked the technical imperfections discovered the book was Michener's most expressive and accomplished writing to date.

"[He] has fallen in love with big chunks of Japan and its people and is feeling more deeply and truly for them than he ever felt for aircraft carriers or platoons," commented John Metcalf in the *Spectator.* Fanny Butcher praised Michener's sensitivity in the Chicago Sunday *Tribune* and said that *Sayonara* included a quality rarely found in modern fiction—moral conviction. And in what was the most authoritative evaluation of the book, Pearl Buck, who had introduced Asia to Americans long before Michener, said that *Sayonara* was an unusual gift, strikingly clear and compact, fresh in its point of view, and filled with accurate impressions. In the Book of the Month Club *Bulletin* she explained:

> [Michener] writes as a man seeing countries and peoples with an open mind and a receptive heart. He has no preconceived notions about people and places which hitherto he has not known. Wherever he is, he is there as himself, seeing what he sees and making his own discoveries and sharing all with his readers.

In these few lines, Pearl Buck explained the talent of James A. Michener, the author, in the mid-1950s. There was nothing magical about his work, and very little that was unusual about his talent. His prose was not good writing; it was often stilted and awkward; and he had not produced "great literature." But critics tended to overlook one compelling truth about Michener as a writer: his strength lay in his conviction and in his commitment to his subject. His storytelling was authentic, openhearted, and always unpretentious, and readers were attracted to his refreshing—if sometimes trite and melodramatic—tales. By the time *Sayonara* was published, Michener's book sales had surpassed all expectations: *Tales of the South Pacific* had topped 2 million; *Return to Paradise,* 703,000; *The Fires of Spring,* 472,500; *The Voice of Asia,* 236,000; and *The Bridges at Toko-ri,* 38,000. So long as Michener's stories remained unpretentious, so long as he wrote with passion about other cultures and people and problems, he satisfied a ravenous craving among the world's readers.

CHAPTER TEN

# Private Affairs

> Marriage is a social and psychological
> jungle in which only the eternally
> vigilant can find their way.
> JAMES A. MICHENER, 1981

WHILE MICHENER'S ROMANCE with Asia continued, problems developed at home in Bucks County. Vange must have begun to think of him as an occasional guest instead of a husband. During some years he spent fewer than three months in Pipersville, and even then, between speaking engagements and government obligations, he was rarely home.

Still, he savored the homespun quality of life "on the hill," where he drove a jeep, wore dungarees and kept two mutts from the local pound. He enjoyed nothing more than clearing a walking path across his acreage, or planting evergreens to give away at Christmas, or reading by the light of a blazing fire on a snowy night. In every respect he was the country gentleman.

He liked his neighbors, too, and he participated in community events. He dressed as garish "Mich the Witch" to read fortunes at a township arts festival, which raised money for the community's Improvement Association, and at least once a year he shared his latest travelogue with the Bucks County

Friends of the Free Library. When possible, he attended the memorial breakfast sponsored every spring in Doylestown to honor George Murray and the Boys' Brigade.

People were not bashful about seeking his attention, either, except in his hometown where some residents refused to let go of his past. A bank officer, for example, convinced that a poor boy from Doylestown was too much of a financial risk, refused to give him a $10,000 mortgage loan in 1948. Around Pipersville, however, with its many artists and professionals, most people were friendly, and some were curious as well.

For many years the Micheners shared a telephone line with eighteen other families, some of whom liked to eavesdrop. Once, Michener recalled, Bennett Cerf telephoned to discuss selling the rights to a book. The financial terms of the contract were puzzling, and Cerf repeatedly tried to clarify every point before finally requesting a decision. When Michener paused to think, a third party whispered into the phone, "Michener, you'd be a dope not to accept." Michener laughed, but later he requested a private line and an unlisted number. The latter was made necessary by the many callers who asked for literary advice, and the name of Michener's agent.

Except in winter, when Michener's hill was usually snowbound, an unlisted number did not stop strangers from reaching him and asking for favors. Whenever the local press announced that Michener was home, visitors arrived at his front door at any time of day and night. On one occasion, at midnight, the pastor of a local church walked into his study and enlisted support for the family of a girl who needed surgery after she had been thrown from a horse and severely injured. Michener knew neither the pastor nor the family, but he reached for his checkbook and said, "I will be happy to give you five hundred dollars. I think this is the type of concern a community must have for its members."

The minister had something else in mind, however, and he stopped Michener from writing the check. The surgery was expensive, and he was looking for a page-one story for the Doylestown *Daily Intelligencer*—a tale that would inspire others to contribute money. "A story by you will give me that spot," said the minister.

Michener explained that he was leaving early the next morning on an overseas assignment and that he was short of time. Again he reached for his checkbook, but the pastor refused the money. "I know you are a busy man," he told Michener. "I also know your talent is worth much more than five hundred dollars. [That] would be the cheapest thing you could give. It wouldn't represent a sacrifice. . . . I'm asking you to give your time and talent."

The pastor had made his point, and Michener told him to look in his mailbox the next morning for the story, which he would deliver en route to the airport. The *Daily Intelligencer* printed the piece a few days later, at about the time Michener landed in Japan, and the injured girl's family received almost $5,000 in contributions as a result.

From behind countless scenes, Michener was a philanthropist even though many people thought otherwise. When he refused to buy coffee for newspapermen in Hawaii, reporters there branded him a "skinflint," promoting the notion that he was slow to reach for a check. Perhaps these reporters did not know that Michener had established a scholarship fund for the children of newspapermen who had served in World War II and the Korean War. Other people, friends included, also said Michener was stingy, when in fact he was not. True, he never spent money carelessly, and he rarely indulged in luxuries or even conveniences, but this was a residual psychological effect of an impoverished childhood. Financial insecurity haunted Michener even after he became a millionaire. As a result, he always worked too hard and never learned to enjoy his wealth. He admitted this on many occasions:

> Money is a factor that has to be grappled with in every human life and most of us don't do it very well. I have not handled it well, but remember, my success came very late. . . . Money was absolutely all important when I was young simply because we never had any. My mother did back breaking labor, but still many times we were down to absolutely nothing. This tightens you inside, and it's not something that you forget.

Michener invested his money, but he did not hoard it. Quietly he gave away large sums—by 1977 he estimated he had donated $4 million—most of it to universities and museums. In addition to providing scholarships, he commissioned young painters, established awards for poets, donated entire collections of art to museums, and, late in his career, contributed half a million dollars to the Writers Program at the University of Iowa.

With his time, Michener was equally unselfish, and he did not limit himself to what he considered civic responsibilities. In hours of need, friends depended on Michener's support, and in several instances he helped them save their jobs and their reputations. No one knew that better than William Vitarelli, a former George School colleague, who joined the faculty at Columbia University in the 1930s and then fell victim to Senator Joseph McCarthy's warriors in the mid-1950s.

Vitarelli had been employed by the U.S. Department of Interior as education administrator in the Western Caroline Islands of the Pacific, a job Michener helped him get, and for which he was well qualified. Suddenly, in February 1954, a Security Board investigation of government employees said Vitarelli was a security risk, and he was promptly dismissed. The board's finding was based on several undeniable charges: Vitarelli had associated with communists, had read the *Daily Worker* and *New Masses,* and had registered as a member of the American Labor party.

Of course, at Columbia University, many of Vitarelli's students were communists, as well as technocrats, fascists, Trotskyites, and soapbox orators of all sorts. To keep abreast of the times, he used communist-inspired publications, as well as the *Wall Street Journal* and the *Christian Science Monitor,* to teach his classes. It was true he had belonged to the American Labor party, but not when the organization was communist-dominated. "My being a professed and registered pacifist did not help the accusers to see that I could not rationally be a communist and be a pacifist," Vitarelli recalled while discussing his case in 1980. In fact, no explanation interested his accusers, and in the midst of McCarthy hysteria, Vitarelli became one of many similar government statistics.

Vitarelli informed Michener of his problem and asked for a loan—the government refused to authorize his travel expenses and he had to return to the States from Koro with his family—and for a notarized statement that he was neither a communist nor a security risk. Michener provided both, and for the next several years helped Vitarelli and his attorneys mount a persuasive defense by writing telegrams and letters and by personally intervening when he could help Vitarelli by doing so. In Washington, for example, Michener testified for one hour before an investigating committee, but without any noticeable effect. He then petitioned the secretary of the interior to review the case personally, assuring him that the charges were "trumped up and without foundation." And he advised Congressman Douglas McKay that "a grave injustice was inadvertently done [in the Vitarelli case] but can quietly be corrected."

While an unemployed Vitarelli and his family remained in Bucks County, the case continued through 1957 before it reached the U.S. Supreme Court. There, in a final argument, Vitarelli was cleared and reinstated to employment with back pay. After the victory, Michener wrote to congratulate him and said, "you marked the last of my friends whom I spoke out for to be returned to full and active respectability."

Reports of Michener's generosity, civic involvement, and participation in community events sometimes led people to make demands on his time that must have irritated his wife. Vange saw him so infrequently, particularly after she stopped traveling overseas with him, that when Michener was home, she wanted him to spend more time on the hill.

Originally, judging from several enthusiastic letters to the Silvermans, Vange had enjoyed traveling with Michener and exploring different countries and cultures. From Java in 1951 she wrote that Michener was hard at work on a *Life* assignment and that she was "hard at work on him to allow me to buy more and more batik. Beautiful stuff indeed." And from Japan that same year, she described a Japanese household where she and Michener had lived for several days in Morioka:

> The obedient mama-san seemed to be frozen in a perpetual kowtow while papa-san played the master of the household to the hilt. Very reminiscent of the back woods of [Bucks County]! . . . We've been spending much time at the kabuki-za and yakking with Japanese and collecting Japanese art and it's a great life. In the next life we want to be born Asians!

All was not so wonderful, though. Before the trip ended, Vange suffered from exhaustion, according to Michener, and he left her in Rome to recuperate while he continued his journey. "I expect to join her later," he informed the Silvermans on Valentine's Day 1952, "and hope that I will find her in good condition. This travel can be hard work sometimes, although now that I have recovered from a bad case of Korean flu, I myself feel pretty delighted with it." Thereafter, however, Vange rarely accompanied Michener when he was working overseas. The pace was too fast and tiring, and besides, Vange said she wanted to develop a writing career of her own, and she could not do it while traveling abroad.

Almost everyone who knew Jim and Vange said they were a mismatch, but her letters to him in the early years of their marriage indicate that she loved him. They had been married for two years in October 1950, when Michener was alone on assignment in Asia and Vange wrote to him from Pipersville:

> Dearest Dear,
>     This morning is bursting with sunlight and color and there's a nice clip of wind thru the north woodlot. Wish you were here to see our arrogant rascal of g-hog meandering around the grounds with his meanest swagger. He's a real comedian.
>     This is to tell you I love you and that it's a day to review and sum our life together and that I'm humble in the face of your great gifts and grace and your love. Long time between love notes, Jimmy, and may they never stop stirring an enormous heart for you within me. I do love you so very much.

She then asked about his trip, relayed messages from his mail, accounted for his recent income, and spent a lengthy paragraph complaining about an editor who had lost some of her manuscripts. She wanted to "explode," she said. "Please bring home a durable Jungle Gym Punching Bag. I shall have punched thru all available walls by midweek!"

From the beginning of the Micheners' life together in Pipersville there was tension between them. It was partly due to Jim's hectic schedule, but more so to Vange's frustration as a fledgling writer. Being married to a man who had agents, editors, and publishers constantly awaiting his next manuscript, regardless of the subject, must have been discouraging, to say the least. Surely Vange was happy for Jim, but she yearned for the limelight, too, and on her own terms. However, Vange may have created many of her own problems. Different people described her as "superficial," "flighty," "immature," and "a dilettante." Perhaps she was also envious of her husband's success. She told the Silvermans that she was a better writer than Jim, but that publishers refused to give her a chance.

Regardless of what her acquaintances said about her, Vange was a proud, determined woman, never willing to surrender her life to her husband. That created almost as many problems for him as it did for her. She insisted on using her maiden name as a writer, and Jim took that as a personal affront. He knew better than to argue about it, though.

Unfortunately, Vange's writing career never progressed beyond a few published pieces, and with her husband away from home most of the time, her main concern seemed to be bringing him back to Pipersville more frequently and for longer periods of time. A baby, she hoped, might help, but Jim thought he was sterile, the result, perhaps, of a savage case of mumps during childhood, and they had been unable to begin a family. Vange suggested they adopt an Amerasian infant from Pearl Buck's Welcome House, and Jim agreed.

How appropriate for James A. Michener, who now said that he had begun life as an orphan, to repay a debt to society for Mabel Michener's unselfishness in the early part of the century. It was a grand moment for international friendship, too. "The song, 'You've Got to Be Taught' is working out in practice, and that is fine," Floyd Merrill wrote in a note of congratulations from Colorado. "There's no finer thing than giving a home to a homeless tot."

As ideal as this adoption seemed, it turned out to be a mistake for the Micheners and a misadventure for the infant Japanese-American son whom they named Mark. "Vange was not interested in being a mother," remembered Ann Silverman, who at the time worked as a volunteer at Welcome House. "Vange wanted a career, and a husband to foster it." Unfortunately, that was not immediately obvious to Pearl Buck, who approved of two-week-old Mark's adoption with enthusiasm.

For a while during 1953, Mark brought so much happiness into the Michener home that Vange asked Welcome House for a second son and Jim wrote to the Child and Family Service of Honolulu to inquire about adopting a Chinese-Caucasian child. Meanwhile, he established a $10,000 trust fund in Mark's name. Soon, Welcome House sent another boy, this one nineteen months old. The Micheners named him Brook, and Vange made arrangements to spend the next summer in Europe with Jim and both boys.

By early winter, however, when Michener departed for Asia, it must have been clear to Vange that her plan had failed. The presence of two sons at home did not inspire her husband to travel less or to reduce his work load. His career still came first, or so it seemed. And with each passing day, Vange must have found it more difficult to be a single parent. Finally, in early 1954, she decided that she wanted a divorce. By this time, before the second adoption was final, she had already returned Brook to Welcome House.

In February, after four months abroad, Michener arrived in New York. Vange met him at the airport and told him she was filing for a divorce. She explained the grounds: "indignities to person," meaning he was never at home.

Michener was dumbfounded, a sign, perhaps, of the poor communication between him and Vange. Several days later, in a letter to Vitarelli, who had just been fired, he expressed his confusion:

my own affairs are in such chaos that I am wondering about my own job. When I got home from Korea the other day Vange told me that she wanted a divorce and was leaving with the little boy. What it's all about I don't fully understand but you have seen my wife in these devastating moods and you . . . know there is no hope of arguing with her.

Vange immediately left Pipersville and moved to Philadelphia with Mark while the divorce action continued through January 1955. Neither of the Micheners discussed the settlement publicly, but the press learned that Jim paid Vange one-quarter of a million dollars, a substantial sum, which in the 1980s would equal roughly one million dollars. In addition, she won custody of Mark. In pre-court hearings Jim also sought Mark's custody. He argued that the child would be happier with him. But his attorney, Harriet Mims, advised him that a court would not permit a father to take a child from his mother. Of course, unless Michener planned to limit his travel abroad, which was not likely, a court might also have decided that he was not a suitable father for a toddler.

The collapse of this second marriage barely interrupted Michener's work. He was seen in New York in the company of Dorothy Sarnoff, who played a featured role in *The King and I,* and with the actress-singer Janis Paige, who played the lead in the hit musical, *Pajama Game.* Once his divorce from Vange was final, he had to be notified of the decree by registered mail in San Francisco, where he was about to depart for nine months in India, Pakistan, Afghanistan, and Indonesia. After Vange left Pipersville, Michener most likely never intended to see her again. As if she had been a footnote in his life, he lost track of her whereabouts several years later, just as he had forgotten Patti Koon. He harbored no bitterness toward either of his ex-wives.

"War played havoc with my marriages," Michener said in 1971. "World War II and then Korea kept me away from home." In retrospect the justification probably sounded logical to him, but the fact remained that, if there had been no wars, something else related to Michener's career would have kept him away from home. Short of serious illness, nothing in his personal life *ever* interfered with his career. His friends understood that, and if Michener hoped to make a marriage succeed, he had to find a wife who accepted it, too.

Ironically, in 1954 *Life* magazine asked him to write an article about the pursuit of happiness in a marriage. He chose to write about the marriage of a former American GI and a Japanese "war bride." Following the release of *Sayonara,* Michener had received a flood of mail from American servicemen who sought his advice about marrying Japanese girls. Invariably he advised against it, citing the cultural gap as too wide to be bridged in a marriage. "Wonderful as they are," Michener once wrote to Silverman, "[Japanese women] seem to get a man softened up for American marriage."

However, in the home of Frank Pfeiffer, a commercial movie cameraman, and his Tokyo-born wife, Sachiko Sekiyas, Michener discovered that at least one interracial marriage had bridged the cultural gap. The Pfeiffers were among the nearly 20,000 American-Japanese couples who had married shortly after World War II. Occupation authorities forbade their relationship at the time, but eventually the rules were relaxed and the Pfeiffers moved from Japan to Chicago and began a lively, though frightening, life in America.

Neighbors called Sachiko "that dirty Jap" and threatened to have the couple evicted. The prejudice became so fierce that the couple voluntarily fled the city and moved to suburban Melrose Park, a community populated by many World War II veterans. There the neighbors welcomed them, and when Michener met them and their two children, they were a secure Japanese-American family.

To facilitate Michener's research in Chicago, *Life* organized a luncheon in his behalf, and along with friends of the Pfeiffers, the magazine invited experts on Japanese-American marriages. Among the guests was Mari Yoriko Sabusawa, an editor of the American Library Association's *Bulletin,* a candid Japanese-American woman who thought the suicide scene in *Sayonara* was misleading, and who seized the opportunity to so inform Michener. Japanese-American marriages did not always end in tragedy, she maintained, and as one who had been helping Japanese war brides become accustomed to life in the United States, she could prove her point.

So, for the next ten days, while Michener worked in Chicago, Mari Yoriko Sabusawa, a second generation Japanese-American and a graduate of Antioch College, assisted with his research. In the process Michener interviewed her, and fell in love again.

Mari was born in Colorado in 1920. Her father was a melon farmer who had migrated from Japan to Colorado at the turn of the century, hoping to make a fortune. Her mother, a "picture bride," was an eighty-year-old widow, planning her first return trip to Japan. In spite of hard work, Mr. Subusawa's fortune had remained only a dream, and in 1925, he had moved his family to southern California. They remained there until the Japanese attacked Pearl Harbor. Then, along with 110,000 other Americans of Japanese ancestry, they were confined in internment camps on the West Coast. At age twenty-one, Mari was interned at the Santa Anita Race Track, where she occupied the stable made famous by Equipoise. The treatment was abominable—"thrown into stables fifteen to a room"—and she watched helplessly as her people lost their dignity, their freedom, and most of their possessions. After four months, she was transferred to a "relocation center" in Granada, Colorado. Near the camp lived several friends with whom she had grown up. She remained in "protective custody" behind barbed wire.

The American Baptist Home Mission Society rescued her from internment through the National Japanese-American Student Relocation Council, an experiment begun by Quaker Clarence Pickett and endorsed by several faiths. The program placed relocated Japanese-Americans in college communities. Mari was sent to Antioch College where she spent two years studying political science and international relations and participating in student activities. Through Antioch's cooperative job program, she moved to Washington to analyze Japanese propaganda for the Foreign Broadcast Intelligence service. In just a few years, with the war yet to be won, Mari progressed from internee to employee of a secret agency of the U.S. government.

Later she enrolled in a graduate sociology program at the University of Chicago. She specialized in race relations and went to work for the American Council on Race Relations. Eventually she landed an assistant editorship with the American Library Association, and that led her to the *Life* magazine luncheon. She almost missed meeting Michener, though. Friends had to coax her to accept the invitation. She was not a Michener fan, but she knew his work.

At five feet and 100 pounds, with brown eyes and black hair, Mari was not the sleek Hana-ogi of *Sayonara,* but Michener thought she was "heavenly." She had more acquaintances in all walks of life, and of all races and creeds, than anyone Michener knew in America or Asia. She was an extrovert, a comic, a Dodger fan, and she had a fiery temperament that excited her famous friend, who was thirteen years her senior.

Mari fell in love with Michener, too. He was a "man of the world," she informed a friend, distinguished, yet shy, gentle, soft-spoken, and obviously in love with her. There were a few differences between them, but the worst of these Mari quickly settled. For example, Michener was in the habit of saying "Jap" for "Japanese." As he later explained, he thought the abbreviation was "a splendid invention. It's short, it's accurate, it takes up little space in a headline, it's . . . definitive. It seems an ideal word to me."

"We don't like that word because of the way William Randolph Hearst used it to crucify us," Mari explained the first time she heard Michener say "Jap."

He used it a second time, and she said, "We don't like that word because it was used pejoratively throughout California to throw us in jail."

When Michener ignored her pleas and used "Jap" a third time, she bristled. "If you ever use that word again, I'm going to take a catsup bottle and knock out the rest of your teeth." Then Michener understood, and thereafter he used the word "Japanese."

When Michener finished his work in Chicago, he informed Mari that he was leaving for a ten-month assignment overseas. He promised to write, and to return. He kept his word, and at the end of a second ten-day trip to Chicago in the fall of 1955, he married Mari in the University of Chicago Chapel. The Reverend Jitsuo Morkawa, pastor of Chicago's First Baptist Church, performed the ceremony. It was an international marriage in every respect.

Several dozen former servicemen must have read about the wedding in *Life* magazine and wondered how Michener could justify his own interracial marriage after advising them against it. "Experience shows that it is better for human beings to marry within the group," Michener responded to one correspondent in 1955,

> but there are many men who are adventurers, or [who] find the mores of the group tedious, and are willing to step outside it. While I would not recommend to anyone that he go outside the group, I believe we are all indebted to the men who do. I think a great deal of good is accomplished for society in general by the infusion of new blood.

Although he regarded himself as an adventurer who was bored by American women, Michener risked a third marriage. But this marriage was different, he said later in *Good Housekeeping,* for it required a greater commitment than the first two:

> People need to have a stake in marriage for it to endure. Friends, children, possessions, interests are all to the good, but are not as effective as community pressure and established pattern. . . . If [Mari and I] were to get a divorce, people would say that Japanese-American marriages never work. We're committed to proving that they do.

After a small wedding party in Chicago, the Micheners departed for an around-the-world honeymoon. "It's much less expensive to go all the way around than to go to Asia and back," Michener told the press, in his practical, no-nonsense way. Of course, it was going to be a "working honeymoon," financed by *Reader's Digest,* but Mari understood that. She did not intend to reform Michener or to compete with him, she said, but to serve him. At last, Michener had found the perfect wife for him.

The honeymoon began in November 1955 in Australia, where several years earlier the second Mrs. Michener had charmed the foreign press corps. A third, Japanese Mrs. Michener risked a less friendly reception, but Michener informed the Silvermans,

> My lady has been a sensation in Australia where they hate the Japanese, and with some reason. She has wonderful good sense, a fine timing in her humor and enormous energy. She has been on the front pages of the Australian press for about two weeks and seems always to have exactly the right thing to say. . . . She is a load of fun, and I am sure you and your gang will love her. I know I do.

The Micheners' itinerary included several months of travel prior to meeting Jim's friends in Bucks County, but one magazine assignment after another extended their trip. A month in Australia led to several months in the South Pacific and then more research in Asia—including a tiger hunt in India — before continuing home through Europe. The honeymoon stretched into seven months, and the Micheners did not arrive in Pipersville until late in the spring of 1956. They were home less than three months, however, when *Reader's Digest* sent Michener back to Asia. Mari, who preferred a slower pace of travel than what her husband's itinerary permitted, opted for a pleasure cruise to Europe on her own.

Unlike Vange, Mari regarded marriage as her career and adapted almost immediately to life with Michener. Friends enjoyed watching the interplay between them. They were rarely affectionate in public, but they called each other Cookie, and they liked to tease and argue. If Jim expressed an opinion and Mari disagreed, as she often did, she said so, and a lively debate followed. Of course, Michener was always right, even if Mari let him be right, and some of Michener's friends appreciated that quality in her.

Like every marriage, this one required a period of adjustment. On Thanksgiving day, 1956, Mari wrote to her husband in a reflective mood from Amsterdam where she had been visiting the Hague and reading Boswell:

> We have had our little tiffs, but lovers always do I am told . . . they say the first year is the hardest. You don't beat me every Saturday and I don't nag you every week so the scales balance.
>
> This marriage of ours means everything to me and I'm sure it means something to you, but probably in a different way. This is a new life with all sorts of new adjustments but with a new and deeper meaning in that one shares his life with another. I sometimes am led to believe that is not so with you, but understandably so, for in a way, it's a road you've traveled before.
>
> I can be light hearted about many unimportant things but I cannot be towards anything that I feel deeply. I am a sensitive person, but I try not to be too sensitive. So I hope you will continue to be patient and understanding as you have been. For this I am grateful and appreciative. I am proud being your wife.

A good example of how their relationship worked occurred in the fall of 1956 when Michener, en route home from Asia, met Mari in Amsterdam. He had just arrived when Pearl Buck cabled with some unsettling news from Bucks County. Vange had returned Mark to Welcome House and had waived her rights to his custody. The boy was an orphan again, unless Michener assumed responsibility for him.

How, Michener wondered, could Vange give up a four-year-old child? What had happened? After the divorce, she and Mark had moved to Swarthmore, much to Michener's surprise. She had no family there, and knew only Michener's acquaintances, all of whom were associated with the college. She convinced at least one of her Swarthmore neighbors that her famous ex-husband had abandoned her and Mark. Otherwise, however, she engendered little sympathy from the residents of the college community.

"No one knew why Vange came to Swarthmore, but she wanted to be accepted," said Terry Shane, whose husband had joined the Swarthmore administration after teaching with Michener at George School: "I saw her occasionally at parties, but people tended to ignore her. No one at the college would have anything to do with her. After a while she gave up Mark and moved away."

Stories circulated in Swarthmore that Vange had mistreated Mark—one woman never forgave her for sending him to day school when he was ill—and that she resented him. In general, people thought it would be best if Welcome House found Mark another home. "I have always felt that Vange never, from the very beginning, really loved Mark," Michener's secretary wrote to him in November 1956.

Michener had liked the idea of adopting an orphan, and according to Mari, Mark's welfare was her husband's "first consideration" after hearing about his son's fate from Miss Buck. "Jim was a good father and loved the boy and wanted him from the start," Mari wrote to Miss Buck in late November 1956. Michener regretted that Vange had returned Mark to Welcome House, but the consequences of assuming the child's custody frightened him. "My husband is thoroughly convinced," Mari informed Miss Buck, "that [Vange] will continue to try to make trouble for him and Mark and more so if Mark were with us. This is very painful for Jim knowing as I do how much he feels for the boy and the boy's happiness." Apparently Michener could not bear the thought of Vange possibly upsetting his life in the future. She and her attorney had knocked him to his knees once with a huge settlement, and he intended to block every avenue by which that might occur again. He decided to waive his right to Mark's custody.

Mari agreed with Michener's decision, although she did not fear Vange Nord. "What can she possibly do to you?" Mari asked her husband. "She has divorced you and she has her money. She might try to break up our marriage through devious ways, *but just let her try.* She'll regret it." Mari said her concern was that Michener "not only express but feel the fear of this woman [Vange Nord] and what she can do to you emotionally. Almost anything else is easier to fight than fear."

One of Mari's characteristics was that she occasionally disliked people even without knowing them. She sounded as though she despised Vange Nord. In Mari's opinion, Vange had deliberately used Mark "for her own selfish interest" to obtain a "tremendously large" alimony settlement. She told Miss Buck, "I also have a suspicion that knowing how much Jim wanted the child, [Vange] held on to him . . . as an excuse in the future to harass Jim—probably for more money." Mari admitted this was "a strong indictment against a woman whom I do not know," but nonetheless she told Miss Buck, "we have to deal with a woman who has not only selfish motives, evil intentions but malice in her heart." Based on these conclusions, Mari continued, "it might be wiser in the long run to find a new home for [Mark]. Perhaps there will be less likelihood of Vange Nord's entering the lives of another couple."

Vange Nord may have been a troubled woman, but she was not nearly as malevolent as Mari's portrayal. Once she returned Mark to Welcome House, she disappeared from Michener's life and from the country as well. After

Swarthmore, she moved to Europe, and the Micheners never heard from her again. Happily, Mark was adopted by a college-town couple in Ohio, and at a Welcome House reunion years later, he reportedly appeared to be a well-adjusted, cheerful teenager.

It was never clear how Mari felt about succeeding Vange as Mark's mother, but motherhood itself did not seem important to her. Once, in a letter to Michener, 'she hinted she was pregnant, yet she did not appear to be especially thoughtful of children. Her niece, Lin Sabusawa, attested to that when at age twelve she wrote to "Auntie Mari and Uncle Jim" and pleaded with them to send their godson, Randy, who was Lin's seven-year-old brother, a present, or at least a card for Christmas. "When all of us kids open their presents from godparents," Lin explained, "I know Randy feels left out. I wouldn't blame him if he went to his room to cry." She said she understood that her aunt and uncle were busy, "but even if it will be weeks late, please send Randy something. Please." Apparently, in a life that revolved around a famous husband, Mari had overlooked the significance of such remembrances.

More than anyone before her, with the exception of Mabel Michener, Mari cared about Michener's peace of mind. From the outset of their marriage she was his untiring helpmate, and soon it appeared that his life seemed more important to her than her own. Eventually, as she accepted responsibility for his day-to-day needs, it looked as though his happiness became her fundamental concern. Anyone who hoped to see Jim Michener first had to penetrate his wife's protective wall. He alone decided where to travel and what to write, but the details of almost every arrangement fell to Mari. When she became his wife she also assumed the roles of housekeeper, cook, secretary, travel agent, librarian, valet, hostess, chauffeur, and personal accountant. And at all times she remained charming, self-effacing, and *grateful*. No wonder Michener cherished her. Along with her undying love, Mari freed him to work at his own pace, uninterrupted.

It was Mari who contacted Welcome House to inform Pearl Buck that she should find Mark another home. Michener had already boarded a plane for Austria to carry on with what mattered most to him. *Reader's Digest* had asked him to interrupt his vacation to cover the Hungarian revolution, and while at first he hesitated, weary, perhaps, of war, he accepted the assignment. In a cable to Hobe Lewis he explained that he felt an obligation to write about an event of worldwide significance.

No one really knew how bad Michener felt about Mark because it was his nature to grapple privately with his emotions. He wanted a child, that was certain, but it seemed that he intended to forget Mark, if possible. After many years his memory of Mark's adoption was blurred, or confused. At one point he denied that he had adopted a son: "It would be correct to say we were in the *process* of adopting," he explained in 1971. However, in 1979 he said that he and Vange had adopted Mark, "but in divorce proceedings the court awarded the boy to Mrs. Michener who for reasons I have never understood dissolved the legal proceedings, so that the adoption failed." Perhaps in attempting to forgive himself for what must have seemed like abandoning a child, Michener tried to rationalize that Mark's adoption had not occurred. It *had* occurred, and as a reminder of it, the $10,000 trust fund that Michener had so proudly established in Mark's name in 1953 remained untouched in a Philadelphia bank.

There was never to be a child in Michener's life, and that, he said during a quiet moment of reflection in 1975, was his one regret. He did not dwell on that disappointment, however, nor did he pity himself. Problems that evaded his control he buried therapeutically in research and manuscript pages. For everything else, he depended on Mari.

## CHAPTER ELEVEN

# Teller of Epic Tales

> It is that sense of sharing a universe
> which I'm quite sure Thackeray, for
> example, had in *Vanity Fair*, and Balzac
> had in certain of his Paris novels. I know
> some of the secrets for creating such a
> universe, though I can't do it hurriedly,
> and I can't do it without constant
> reference to the land.
>
> JAMES A. MICHENER, 1975

WHILE IT WAS true that Jim Michener "always felt the urge to write something which may explain Asia and the Pacific to my fellow Americans," he was not so quick to write about events in Europe. "Someone else can do a better job," he informed Hobart Lewis when the *Digest's* editor asked that he cover the Hungarian revolution in the fall of 1956. Michener had never been to Budapest, he did not speak the language, and having just joined Mari on vacation in Amsterdam he was not expecting another big assignment. Besides, as he reminded Lewis, in the last several months he had already written eight long articles (seven for *Reader's Digest* and one for *Holiday*) on topics in Australia, Indonesia, India, and Japan, and he was writing a short book of profiles, *Rascals in Paradise,* with co-author A. Grove Day. He had his fill of writing nonfiction, and as soon as he and Mari completed their pleasure tour and returned to Bucks County he looked forward to beginning a novel. There was no time to cover the uprising in Hungary.

En route to the Folies-Bergère one night with Mari, however, Michener was surprised to see a group of Europeans protesting in front of a communist newspaper office. Trapped by the curiosity that marks every good journalist, he stopped to watch the demonstration. Later he recalled, "I was impressed by the new bitterness and violence of the European revolt against Russia," and on the spot he changed his mind about going to Hungary. The next day, leaving Mari behind, he boarded a plane for Vienna and then drove fifty miles to Andau, a small town along the Austro-Hungarian border where twenty thousand Hungarian refugees were about to escape to freedom. Within moments of his arrival Michener knew why he had come:

> Standing at Andau, watching an endless parade of fugitives crunch over the ice and frost, you knew you were present at one of the big moments of history. You could see newspapermen crying for no apparent reason. You might not know what it all meant, but it got you just the same.

In October the small country of Hungary had thrashed its Russian captors. Angry crowds using homemade bombs, rocks, sticks, and bare hands had destroyed Russian tanks and armored cars. Hungarian patriotism had smashed the foul and brutal communist AVO (secret police), and for several days two million Hungarians enjoyed a lost freedom. The hated hammer and sickle were ripped from the Hungarian flag and replaced with the Kossuth crest. Uncensored newspapers appeared on the streets, and people gathered in Parliament Square to sing their cherished national anthem.

But the Russians were never easily defeated. When the Hungarian hero, Colonel Pal Maleter, met with the Soviets for what he thought would be a discussion of all Soviet troops withdrawing from Hungary, the Russians brushed aside the truce and imprisoned him. In November, 4,000 Soviet tanks, mobile heavy artillery, airplanes, and 140,000 foot soldiers, each with a submachine gun, returned to Hungary and destroyed 8,000 buildings and killed 80,000 people in Budapest. Nearly 200,000 thousand people fled from Hungary, and some 30,000 of them came to the United States.

In Vienna Michener teamed up with Georgette Meyer "Dickey" Chapelle, the daring free-lance photographer who later died in a Vietnam minefield, and risked crossing the border on several occasions to usher refugees to safety. The eerie exodus was almost too incredible and awful to be touching. For one month Michener patrolled the border alongside ministers, rabbis, fellow journalists, and the interpreters who helped him interview refugees as they crossed the rickety wooden footpath over the Einser Canal near Andau. Hundreds of Hungarians who crossed the bridge received a card bearing Michener's address in Vienna, and the promise of a hot meal and a beer in exchange for their stories.

The "soul of a nation" followed Michener into freedom and testified to a nightmare. Families, parts of families, young men and women traveling alone, sat with the probing American stranger and spoke of their terror.

Many of them wept for those they had left behind: their parents, children, countrymen. "They talked in a matter-of-fact way about things that would make your hair stand up," Michener later recalled. "They didn't mention the Russians often, and they didn't seem to think much about them. The people they hated were their own secret police."

The worst stories came from people who had been tortured by the AVO. One broken man of thirty-five told Michener how he had spent three hellish years at Recsk, the notorious prison. He lived in a small room with eighty other men. They had no radio, no books, no newspapers, and they were not permitted visitors. Not even their families knew their whereabouts. They lived "a life of blank terror." From 4:30 A.M. until nightfall the prisoners reduced a granite outcrop to gravel, and each man was required to produce two hand trucks full of gravel a day.

In all of Michener's experiences he had never witnessed an event more brutal than what he saw at Andau. "In my time I have observed many emigrations," he later remarked, "pathetic Indians struggling out of Pakistan, half-dead Korean women dragging down from Communist-held North Korea, Pacific island natives fleeing the Japanese," but from Hungary fled the finest young people of that nation. The communists later insisted that only the elderly and troubled left, but whole groups of people fled Hungary during the revolution. Ballerinas, football players, three Gypsy orchestras, mechanics, engineers, scientists, musicians, artists, writers, professors—all of them packed up their lives and ran. Their average age was twenty-three.

The Hungarian revolution was more than just another fight for freedom, as Michener learned at Andau. This was not a revolt by Western-style democrats seeking a complete break with communism. The communist elite, the young intellectuals whom the Russians had nurtured, led this revolution. Nationalistic Hungarian communists battled Soviet domination once the young intellectuals realized that the promises the Russians had made in the 1940s were never to be fulfilled. One young leader told Michener, "I looked at the life of fear we led and concluded: Life under communism has no hope, no meaning. Yesterday, today and tomorrow are all lost."

For years the effectiveness of communist propaganda in Asia had baffled Michener, but now the evidence of communism rejecting itself in Hungary encouraged him. The Soviets had been defeated intellectually, at least, betrayed by their own army, by police, young people, and peasants. Only force could hold Hungary, and all of the world had seen how Russia behaved. If there was anything right about the Hungarian revolution, Michener knew it was this shattering of the Soviet fable.

Unfortunately, while the horror of Hungary should have made an impact in Asia, the revolution was upstaged by the Suez Canal crisis. For that reason, and also because he had played a vital role in the emigration, Michener was determined to do as much as possible to expose the communists, even if it meant a further delay of his plans to begin a new novel. He wanted to shock Asians and Americans "into a realization of how much communism can corrupt an entire nation," and to demonstrate "what being behind the Iron Curtain really means." The revolution was a turning point in world events, Michener told columnist Sidney Fields in the New York *Daily Mirror,* and "the Communists can no longer peddle all their old lies."

In December, with a partly finished manuscript and a head full of sober impressions, Michener returned to Bucks County and finished writing *The Bridge at Andau.* To tell the story without revealing identities he amalgamated much of the information he had gathered. For example, the hero in the first chapter, "Young Josef Toth," represents the combined experiences of three eighteen-year-old freedom fighters who dared not reveal their real names for fear of endangering the relatives they had left behind. In other chapters, with permission, Michener did reveal true identities to support the authenticity of his reporting. Each chapter told a story so revolting that it deadened the senses. Most alarming, perhaps, was "The AVO Man," in which Michener detailed the sadistic atrocities conducted by some thirty thousand brutal police and secret agents who had terrorized the Hungarian people for ten years.

Even before Hobart Lewis finished reading the manuscript he suggested that Random House publish it in book form because he thought the story deserved as large an audience as possible throughout the world. In March 1957, every edition of the *Digest* carried a condensed version of the story. The European editions each added sixteen pages at a cost of $65,000 just to carry the piece, but "all of us, Wally [DeWitt Wallace] especially, feel it's well worth it," Lewis informed Michener.

At about the same time, Random House rushed into print with *The Bridge at Andau,* postponing the release of *Rascals in Paradise* until June, and setting what must have been a record for book production. Editors Albert Erskine and Bert Krantz polished the manuscript during a chilly weekend in the Random House mansion. A month after Michener delivered the last chapter, the book appeared in bookstores, and before anyone could accuse Random House of profiting from a tragedy, publisher Bennett Cerf announced plans to donate the book's proceeds to Hungarian relief agencies. Following in kind, Michener pledged his royalties to the Academy of Arts in Honolulu, where for several years he had been adding to the collection of Japanese prints.

Prior to publication, Michener doubted the American public's interest in a book about Hungary. Most readers, he said, wanted something "lighter and more diverting." Still, a story of hope, anguish, and drama transcends many boundaries, and while *The Bridge at Andau* was not a best-seller, it sold briskly in bookstores throughout the world. In the United States, where critics hailed the story as "a major weapon against Communism," the book became one of Michener's most widely circulated titles, in part because it told Americans precisely what they were in the mood to hear about communism.

While *The Bridge at Andau* was more than cold war rhetoric, it violently rejected Russian communism and suffered from the ideological presuppositions of its author. Rambling, sentimental, and sometimes superficial, the book was nonetheless a rousing testimonial to mankind's innate desire for freedom. Critics pointed out that the story was obviously written in "white heat," but applauded Michener's "brilliant reporting," "magnificent competence," and "masterly job of narration." A reviewer in *Commonweal* prescribed the book for everyone who imagined there was a chance of humanizing the Iron Curtain countries.

Pausing to analyze the book's success Michener realized that for the first time in his career he had struck a sensitive nerve in the public, reaching many people who had never before read his books. *Andau* was an epic tale, passionate, violent, and heroic, a saga unlike any of his earlier stories. Nothing he had written had ever prompted a more emotional outpouring from readers. This typical letter, written in longhand, came from a Connecticut housewife:

> I started *The Bridge at Andau* yesterday. Diapers are piled in the pail, ironing goes untouched, the kitchen floor goes unwaxed, and the family very nearly goes unfed, for I have not been able to put it down. It is such an heroic account, it is so overpowering, it is so terrifying in the truth that I will not be back to normal for days.

As readers considered Michener's message—"any nation which permits itself to be drawn into Communism's orbit is certain to lose everything it values, including its freedom"—he accomplished his goal with *Andau* and won many new readers as a bonus. More important, the reader response to *Andau* unlocked one of the secrets to his future success. His forceful narrative skills suited the epic story and provided a reading experience that was almost universally attractive. It was a perfect combination, and Michener was fortunate to have found it. Now, more than ever, he was anxious to write fiction, epic fiction, for in that genre he saw the opportunity to write the classic books that would be read "fifty and one hundred years after I am dead."

Instead of delaying his plans to write fiction, Hungary advanced Michener's schedule by one or two books. In 1956 he was still planning to write *The Americans,* the novel that he had outlined earlier about his countrymen traveling through Asia, but in the spring of 1957 he informed Lewis he was moving to Hawaii to write his next novel. He belonged in Hawaii, he said, where he knew the people, their art, literature, and culture. He had served a long apprenticeship in the South Pacific, he explained, and now he was ready to write "seriously" about the territory. Once again he postponed *The Americans.*

"Your plans . . . sound most stimulating," Lewis responded in early 1957. "Hawaii would seem, symbolically at least, to be a fitting place for you to live for a time—at the crossroad between the two worlds." But regardless of where Michener lived, Lewis wanted his name in the *Digest,* and already he had another book-length nonfiction assignment in mind: "there is a great book" to be written about the Strategic Air Command, he told Michener.

"The story has never been properly done . . . because it's almost impossible to convey this marvelous but complex stuff to an uninitiated reader." Michener could accomplish it, Lewis knew. "You said not long ago that a writer had the right to feel that a subject had never been handled until *he* did it. "In more ways than one, you have that right in this instance."

The appeal to Michener's ego worked because SAC had always fascinated him and he wanted to write about the operation. He agreed to produce an in-depth article for the magazine, but he refused to expand it into another nonfiction book. His mind was set on a novel about Hawaii, and he would not depart from that plan. However, he was not about to turn away work when Lewis offered him a dollar a word, up to 15,000 words. With alimony payments to Vange and debts piling up at Fountainhead and Aquaclub, two real estate ventures he had embarked on with Herman Silverman, he needed the money.

The Strategic Air Command had been formed in 1946 as part of the U.S. Army Air Force and charged with deploying the nuclear arsenal. In the mid-1950s, the American public knew less about SAC's striking power than did the rulers of the Soviet Union. Washington intended it that way: if the Kremlin understood the devastating potential of America's nuclear power, its leaders might never order a surprise attack on the West.

It was Lewis's practice to guide a writer's approach to a story, even when the writer was his favorite—Michener. He thought the piece should center on the SAC's "eternal vigilance" and "rattlesnake reputation":

> Esprit de corps is probably the essence of it and that must come from leadership. . . . Perhaps this is the story of [General] Curt LeMay and his boys. . . . As you will learn, SAC never sleeps. . . . The dedication of officers and men to the job is undoubtedly impressive and it might be well to find out how the flight crews live, and where, what hours of duty, what their wives and kids know about their daily missions, how they come and go, how the practice alerts keep them poised. . . . I don't need to say that we count on having plenty of human interest and drama and anecdotes.

Michener postponed his move to Hawaii and planned his research for the SAC article from Pipersville. During the spring of 1957 he visited command bases in different parts of the world and learned as much about SAC as security permitted. He interviewed pilots, crew members, and General LeMay; rode in a B-47 bomber, an astonishing plane that soared to more than 40,000 feet and flew around the world without landing for fuel; and he talked with SAC wives and families, gathering the human interest material requested by his editor. After several weeks he had accumulated enough to write his story, which he completed in midsummer.

In October the *Digest* published "While Others Sleep," Michener's book-length SAC feature. Exactly to order, Michener delivered a fascinating report with more details in it than had ever before been revealed about America's premier security operation. From the pride of the men who flew the B-47s to the loneliness of the wives who knew almost nothing about their husbands' work, and with hardly a flaw or a doubt, Michener captured the essence of America's mighty bombing force. He explained SAC's enormous budget— the new B-52 bombers, with their electronic equipment, cost about ten million dollars each—but the expense was a necessary sacrifice, he said, for the safety and freedom of the United States. "To win our war to prevent war, SAC must be kept super-armed," Michener wrote, "with nuclear weapons, fighting fit, ready to go. For the present there is no other way in which our freedom, and the freedom of our friends through the world, can be preserved."

In the cold war era a majority of Americans shared Michener's views, or accepted them as enlightenment from one of the country's foremost writers, published in the country's most popular magazine. People believed that Michener knew the communists. He had opposed them face to face in several parts of the world, and right or wrong, he believed that power and force remained the most effective means of communication with the Kremlin. He would have preferred coming to terms with any culture through mutual respect and admiration, but that required a two-way road. Brotherhood could not be legislated and expected to succeed. In Michener's opinion, and the *Digest's* as well, Russia had to make choices, and the United States had to be prepared for the worst.

In the spring of 1958, Michener moved to Hawaii and found the islands "a marvelous answer to so many of the tensions of our time, a marvelous refutation of much of the nonsense in our worried world." He and Mari settled into a tiny Waikiki apartment. Another celebrated author might have rented a villa or at least a home with a view, but a thrifty Michener had no interest in luxuries. Besides, Hawaii itself was distraction enough during the next year. There was an epic tale in Hawaii's history, and writing it was the sort of challenge he sought to test his talent in fiction. At age fifty-two, he needed to know the extent of his talent as a novelist if he was ever to feel confident about himself as a writer.

Michener's personal aspirations aside, a book about Hawaii in the late 1950s made perfect sense. The islands were a crossroads between America and Asia, and in spite of conflicts between the two worlds in Japan and North Korea, and the likelihood of a third disruption in Indochina, the leaders on both continents sought a peaceful relationship. A novel about Hawaii could attract attention to America's gateway to Asia, and lead to mutual understanding, believed a didactic Michener.

Another reason, this one political, prompted Michener to write about Hawaii. Along with 65 percent of the American people, Michener favored statehood for the Pacific territory. In the mid-1950s he had begun pressing for statehood among congressional leaders. "If we don't [grant statehood]," he warned, "we will make ourselves as unwelcome as the French and Dutch in

Asia. . . . I will speak out for Hawaiian [and Alaskan] independence [state-hood] wherever I am and wherever I go before we wear our welcome out."

For many reasons the American Congress opposed granting Hawaii state-hood. Race-conscious southern representatives objected because so many of Hawaii's residents were not Caucasians. Many World War II–era con-gressmen shivered at the prospect of serving alongside a Japanese represen-tative. And senators from big states like New York, Pennsylvania, California, and Texas feared a further dilution of their proportional leverage by admitting a thinly populated Hawaii.

But times were changing, and Michener argued that by any social or economic criterion Hawaii merited statehood. Its schools, libraries, and museums compared favorably with those of the mainland. There was little crime. The population out-numbered that of six states and paid more in taxes to the federal government than ten states, including Idaho, the Dakotas, and Vermont. Aesthetically Hawaii was heavenly, spectacularly beautiful year-round. "If we accept Hawaii as a sovereign state we are getting a going concern," Michener persisted. "Hawaii is already a real success."

Of more importance than what Hawaii offered America was what Hawaii meant to Asia. Nearly half a million people lived in Hawaii, and any one of them probably understood Asia better than the average American. Many Hawaiians spoke Asian languages and were well versed in Asian problems. At the same time, these people were profoundly American in sympathy, philosophy, and culture. Most of them were American citizens, and Michener wanted them officially included among his countrymen.

It was not the floral beauty of Hawaii, the great volcanoes, the tropical climate, or the airy, carefree spirit that left Michener starry-eyed. It was the social phenomenon of Hawaii that attracted him. This melting pot of the Pacific "is unusually representative of America in that it recapitulates the history of our extraordinary nation. Like America, Hawaii was settled entirely from without," Michener explained in the *Hawaiian Weekly Magazine* of the Honolulu *Star-Bulletin*. "I appreciate Hawaii because one can see here, postponed by a couple of centuries all the influences and experiences that some generations ago combined to produce America."

What Michener appreciated most about this phenomenon was that Hawaii's people—Polynesians, English, Germans, Portuguese, Japanese, and Chinese—had formed a congenial society. He saw the opportunity to use their success as a major theme in a novel. While he knew that Hawaii was not the "heavenly paradise of brotherhood" that some publicists and residents claimed, and that Michener himself sometimes extolled in moments of weakness, he liked the idea that "legally and in public morality all men are equal here." Typically, social groups in Hawaii tended to discriminate against one another, yet in public life individuals were free from discrimination and segregation. A Japanese woman could become principal of a school, and a Chinese man could become chief of police. Elective offices in the islands were attainable by all qualified citizens. This equality attracted Michener, who described himself as having no racial prejudices. With the islands as his setting, he decided to write about Hawaii's social harmony and hold it up as an example for the rest of the world.

His motive was not entirely altruistic. The problems of immigration, cast in an era of civil rights legislation and social revolution, were timely topics, indeed. Michener denied that marketability factored into his decision to write a particular book, but it was not simply a matter of luck that he wrote *Hawaii* when he did. Like most best-selling writers, Michener knew how to recognize a good story and then present it in a pleasing way for his readers.

While researching the SAC piece, Michener had written in confidence to his one-time co-author A. Grove Day, a professor at the University of Hawaii, and revealed the plans for his next novel. The letter serves as a good example of how Michener structured a book prior to beginning the research:

> For a good many years I have wanted to do a major, long novel on Hawaii and have had it outlined for the last three. It falls into five parts: (1) the coming of the Polynesians to Hawaii; (2) the coming of the haoles to Maui; (3) the coming of the Chinese to Oahu; (4) the coming of the Japanese to Kauai; (5) the coming of the Filipinos generally. The family that we pick up in (1) is seen, through its descendants, through all the subsequent sections, and the haoles whom we meet in (2) produce descendants whom we watch in the later sections; etc. etc.
>
> I would expect each section to run about 50,000 words, or a short novel in itself, and I would hope that we would see, through the successive intrusions of new characters and new peoples the full range of Hawaiian history. In time the novel would range from about 1050 A.D. to 1954. It would be as strong as the events which it covers.

Later, Michener explained how several "family histories" had inspired the structure of his proposed novel. He admired *The History of Rome Hanks and Kindred Matters,* by Joseph Pennell, *The Grandmothers,* by Glenway Wescott, *A Lost Lady,* by Willa Cather, and most of all, *The Timeless Land* by Eleanor Dark. Similar books, Michener told Grove Day, were necessary to help people speculate about their home regions. Dark's book, for example, explores the social evolution of Australia, beginning with the relationship between the aborigines and the first English settlers, and the settlers' accommodations to the land. When he read the book in the navy, Michener thought it showed him a different way of telling a story, and after many years of thinking about the book in relationship to Hawaii, the structure for his novel had gelled.

A parade of writers representing every field from art to zoology had already written about Hawaii. The novelists among this group included Jack London, Somerset Maugham, and John P. Marquand, who liked to think of Hawaii as his personal property. Marquand became indignant when

Michener arrived on the scene. Privately, he called Michener a "journalistic show-off and self promoter" who, "with no credentials or literary qualifications to speak of, had appropriated as his fictional bailiwick a whole quarter of the globe." Marquand thought he knew more than Michener about the South Pacific, and perhaps he did. The difference was that while Marquand complained about his misfortunes, Michener kept his mouth shut and worked.

Understandably, Marquand and other writers envied and resented Michener's sudden rise into the literary limelight. He had been a newcomer, who, perhaps because of a Pulitzer Prize, received more attention and many more attractive offers than other writers, who might have had more talent and worked just as hard. To his credit Michener never boasted about his success, but he knew how to cultivate it. After falling in love with Hawaii in 1949, he became friendly with the islands' top promoters, and frequently sought their help. In turn, they treated him like an important client, one who could bring tourists and revenue to the islands through his travel articles. These people provided research assistance, introduced him to story ideas, and arranged complimentary reservations at the Halekulani, Honolulu's posh hotel. There was nothing unusual about this treatment, even when it clouded Michener's objectivity to a degree that made the promoters blush. For example, after "Hawaii: A State of Happiness," appeared in *Reader's Digest* in August 1953, the public relations director of the Hawaii Visitors Bureau wrote to Michener and said, "Sometimes I wish that Hawaii were as fine as you make it out to be." The article, continued this embarrassed publicist, was "a grand plug . . . it's about all we could ask for." That type of journalism irked Marquand and others, and diminished their respect for Michener's work. But Michener was about to change their opinions as he began the most ambitious novel ever written about Hawaii.

In late April 1958, Michener shoved a desk against a blank wall in his Hawaiian apartment and uncrated a manual typewriter and some reference books. On May 1 he began working, and for six hours each day, seven days a week, he wrote. He rose at 7:00 A.M., drank a glass of fresh pineapple juice, and went directly to his desk. In the afternoons, after a swim at Waikiki, he continued his research. He frequently worked at the Bishop Museum, the Mission Children's Library, and the public library. He consulted with department heads at the University of Hawaii, and also with his research assistant, Clarice B. Taylor, a daily newspaper columnist whom Grove Day recommended to him. In this routine, working almost undisturbed for the next ten months, Michener produced the massive manuscript of *Hawaii*.

Mrs. Taylor was not immediately enamored with Michener, and for the first month of their professional relationship they sparred. She was skeptical about intermingling the lives of the four main racial stocks of Hawaii in a novel, but Michener was not interested in her opinions on that topic. He had already chosen his novel's theme and mapped out its structure, and Mrs. Taylor eventually realized that he was not about to change his mind. "His

Mabel Michener, mother of James Albert
Michener, at age 21.
*(Courtesy of David G. Michener)*

Doylestown High School's championship
basketball team, 1924. Michener appears in
bottom row, left. *(Courtesy of Spruance Library
of the Bucks County Historical Society)*

Lieutenant Michener at about the time he wrote
his Pulitzer Prize winning novel.
*(Library of Congress)*

Michener, 41, and his second wife, Vange Nord, 1948. *(AP/Wide World Photos, Inc.)*

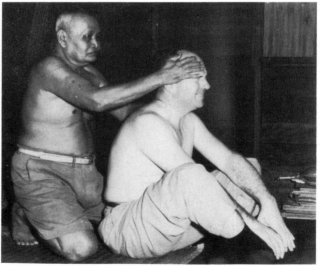

Michener sought and wrote about the treatment of Nai Yok Nuyphakoi, a Siamese doctor, renowned for his ability to cure nervous trouble. *(Library of Congress)*

Michener and his wife, the former Mari Yoriko
Sabusawa, after their wedding in Chicago,
October 23, 1955. *(AP/Wide World Photos, Inc.)*

Michener at work in his den in Pipersville.
*(Temple University Libraries)*

Jim and Mari Michener during his campaign for Congress, Bucks County, 1962. *(Photo from personal files of Don Mattern)*

The Micheners at home with "Java." The paintings are by Michener. *(Temple University Libraries)*

Michener receiving the Medal of Freedom from President Ford, January, 1977. *(AP/Wide World Photos, Inc.)*

terseness was deafening," she reported in a *Star-Bulletin* feature after her work with Michener was completed:

> I tried to read his mind and put into his hands the literature I thought would help him. Since the only good literature on the culture of the peoples of Hawaii is contained in scientific works, I threw these at him by the dozen.
>
> Finally I said to him: "The things you want are not to be found in books. You are breaking new ground. . . . No one has ever successfully recreated the discovery voyage made by Polynesians to these islands. All this material you want has to come out of my head." . . . Each time I said to him, "You are the first" . . . his determination seemed to say, "I am going to do it!"

As soon as Michener met Mrs. Taylor he knew she was the right person for his assignment. Her sense of humor appealed to him. Michener discovered that "this quiet little woman has an absolutely unquenchable love of the ridiculous, the absurd, the pompous-deflating yarn." Later he said, "If I had dared to use half the riotous stuff she told me, both I and my book would have been banned in Boston." Ironically the book was all but banned in Hawaii, and Michener was asked to leave the islands.

Long before Michener moved to Waikiki, he read or reviewed more than two hundred books and journals about Hawaii. Included on his reading list were *Insects of Hawaii, Ancient Tahiti,* written by the granddaughter of an English missionary, and the 1826 diary of Captain James Hunnewell. Now, with Mrs. Taylor's assistance, he consulted "a couple hundred" additional volumes, mainly to establish the historical framework for his story. He recorded few notes, relying instead on a trained memory and on page references jotted inside the back covers of books he planned to consult while writing. Intermingling fact with his own imagination, stimulated by his presence in the islands, he invented characters and scenes.

In the *Star-Bulletin* Mrs. Taylor provided a good account of how this process worked and explained why it later resulted in so many problems for the author. During one of her earliest meetings with Michener, he was puzzled about missionary husbands of earlier times who insisted on delivering their own children. "Why," he wondered, "didn't they use the capable Hawaiian midwives?"

"Don't you know," Mrs. Taylor responded confidently, "that no ethnic group would ever trust its wives to another ethnic group? White men would not trust their wives to the best trained Hawaiian. That was also true of the Chinese . . . the Japanese brought their own midwives as did the Filipinos." She told Michener about her own experience as a public health nurse calling on a new Filipino mother and explaining that babies should be fed at regular intervals. The mother looked at her skeptically and said, "How do you know? You never had a Filipino baby."

Finally she referred Michener to Ethel Damon's *Koamalu*, wherein he discovered the daring adventures of Mary Rice, missionary and mother. During her eighth month of pregnancy in May 1844, Mary Rice walked forty miles across an island just so another missionary could deliver her baby. Both mother and child survived, but there were countless incidents of other women dying at the hands of inexperienced missionary husbands.

Michener intended to show the senselessness of these deaths, many of which could have been prevented had the society been free of racial and religious prejudices. He made his point by creating a scene that paralleled the story of Mary Rice. In his book he sends a young missionary and his pregnant wife forty miles across Maui on foot to find Abner Hale, the missionary hero of his novel. Hale has had no experience delivering babies, but the missionary couple will entrust to him alone the delivery of their child. Before they reach Hale, however, sheer exertion triggers early labor, and the pregnant woman collapses in a trader's shack. Hale is summoned and, his copy of Deland's *Midwifery* underarm, he rushes to the woman's side. Inexperienced and embarrassed about seeing a strange woman without clothing, Hale fumbles.

Outside the shack Michener assembles a group of Hawaiian midwives, "heathens" all, and therefore unfit by missionary standards to deliver a white Christian baby. Like a Greek chorus the midwives tell a crowd of curiosity-seekers what Hale should be doing to deliver the baby and save the mother. She is weak, they announce, and will bleed profusely after birth. For two thousand years, they explain, a special brew of herbs has been used to stop bleeding, and since Hale is ignorant of the concoction and would reject it from their hands, the midwives predict the missionary mother's death. Afterward, when the young mother has bled to death, Michener shows Hale and his bereaved missionary brother embracing and agreeing that the death "was the will of God." The Hawaiians, watching this, say, "How strangely the white men do things."

This is one of many examples showing how Michener mixed fact with fiction in a genre that some critics called "faction." In the late 1950s, although Michener and others, including Norman Mailer and Irving Stone, had previously used the mixture, faction was still a literary anomaly. Mrs. Taylor objected to it and argued that Hawaiian readers would think Michener had made a mockery of their history by using what seemed like historical figures in his own version of Hawaii's settlement. But again, Mrs. Taylor's opinions apparently were of no significance to Michener. On such matters as genre and structure he sought the advice of no one, not even his agent and editors. Even when Mrs. Taylor told him that he could not marry a Punti Cantonese man to a Hakka woman, he ignored her. After all, he was writing a novel.

Through the summer and into the fall Michener composed his story, typing with two fingers. He had never learned to type proficiently, but he was content not knowing how. He liked having time to think while he wrote, and he explained that "if I used all of my fingers, I'd type too fast and leave out too many details of the story." Typing nearly half a million words this way was a slow, tedious process, but when Michener finished the first draft of his novel — more than a thousand pages—he returned to the beginning and started again. He rewrote most parts of the manuscript four or more times.

Critics and readers have surmised that Michener either dictated his stories and hired typists to transcribe them or employed writers to assist him, but neither supposition is true. Writing is a physical and personal process for most writers, and certainly Michener thought so. While writing, he wanted to hear the click of the typewriter pounding his thoughts onto paper—it made him feel that much more a part of the story—and to see each page of his manuscript fall into place. He had no interest in hiring someone to transcribe for him, or to write for him, as either would rob him of the tasks he enjoyed most.

In February 1959, Michener completed his untitled manuscript, and having written and rewritten half a million words, he must have been exhausted. Countless scenes and characters had pulled him in every direction. No previous project had drained him so thoroughly, but this novel represented a huge emotional investment. Day after day Michener directed his story from his typewriter, shaping it, giving it life, taking life from it, and finally depending on the story for his own existence. All of his energy, for most of one year, was expended in moving it steadily toward a conclusion. Now that he was finished, his emotions were mixed. What, if anything, he wondered, had he achieved? That he had completed the book was of itself gratifying, proof to him at least that he was a writer of epics, but would readers buy the book and keep it in print for the next hundred years? There was no way of knowing. The book was nine months from publication, and that was too long a time to sit and wait for something to happen.

Michener's peace of mind depended on forgetting about his manuscript, surrendering its future to his editors, his publisher, and fate. This was the bittersweet moment when he had to separate himself from his manuscript, a moment familiar to many writers. Michener had become attached to his imaginary world, friendly with the people, familiar with their problems, and content in their presence. Breaking away was not easy, and for several days in February he felt empty and alone. Part of him yearned to tell someone that at last he had finished, but without reading his manuscript no one could appreciate his accomplishment. Not even Mrs. Taylor, who had led him through much of the research, or Mari, who had lived with him for the duration, could have understood his feelings. Yet, it was important to confirm that he had finished, and to return to the world beyond his typewriter. Thus he carefully inserted a crumpled piece of paper into his typewriter and wrote this passage:

> On May 1, 1958, I first rolled this piece of paper into my typewriter as backing for the first page of a novel I intended writing on Hawaii.

From that day to this I have sat at this typewriter every morning from 0730 to 1200, excepting only a short trip to California, one to Lahaina and one to Kauai. I worked seven days each week from 0730 till 1200. When I had to see a doctor or a dentist, I worked in the afternoon.

One of the most pleasant experiences of the day came when I reported to work in t-shirt and shorts, wearing zori, and picked up this increasingly frail piece of paper. By the time I reached the end of the novel, and its many rewritings, I had practically beaten the paper to pieces. But it seemed a loyal friend.

Now let it rest.

Sentimentality for anything, least of all a piece of paper, was not like Michener, and before anyone had a chance to read this passage he buried it. The page lies now among the Michener papers, deep in the Library of Congress. Of course, at the time, it was not important that anyone read it. All that mattered then to Michener was that he had finished, and that he could move on.

It was autumn of 1959 before the public knew that Michener's new novel was called *Hawaii,* his twelfth book in as many years, and the first of the family sagas to appear in the post–World War II era. Published in November, the book appeared just in time for Christmas, and on the heels of Hawaii's statehood celebration. But for many islanders the novel was something less than a gift. Hurricanes had swept across the islands with less commotion than the uproar caused by the publication of this novel.

The story of *Hawaii* spans 1,100 years and opens with a ten-thousand-word descriptive essay about the formation of volcanic islands, several million years before the birth of Christ, the creation of soil, and the arrival of birds, plants, and insects in the islands. There are no characters in this long, detailed introduction, and it seemed a most unappealing way to begin a lengthy novel. "No beginning writer would have dared it," said Michener proudly. He considered this almost scholarly piece of work his finest writing to date, and thereafter, when anyone dared suggest that he was merely a "popular writer," he defended himself with this first chapter. The less-than-serious reader, he believed, would have quit reading *Hawaii* after the first few pages. Of course, he had no way of knowing how many readers skipped the first hundred pages of his book, but many did.

As soon as Michener introduced people into *Hawaii* his mixture of fact and fiction created a storm of protests. Mainland readers, who enjoyed Michener's romantic, idealistic portrait of the islands, were amazed by the uproar that occurred when the first copies of the novel arrived in Hawaii. Even Michener, who had anticipated making a few readers angry, was shocked when Hawaiian newspapers carried letters and editorials by readers who insisted he stay out of the islands. Readers of every racial group, but particularly the Caucasians, lambasted him in the daily press and in his mail, shaming him for destroying their sacred ancestries. Thousands of readers objected to his portrayal of missionaries as moralizers, and to several passages of what seemed to them a misinterpretation of the sexual customs of early Hawaii.

"Why do you do it?" cried one woman, who wrote that she had burned her copy of *Hawaii* in her fireplace. "I tell you truly I *grieve* for that book. It could have been such a grand story for young students and readers everywhere but I cannot recommend it to anyone." She had enjoyed the book, she said, until Michener described "the debauching of a 13-year-old boy. . . . Surely that helps no one and does only harm." These stories "are not for the general reader," she continued. "Why do you modern writers mess up your lovely writings with such details?"

What irritated readers most was that Michener had written a "false history" that could supersede the truth about the islands. "What was his motive in calling it *Hawaii* leaving the impression it is a historical book, then calling it fiction?" asked a reader in the Honolulu *Star-Bulletin*. "Why didn't he give it a coined South Sea island name, and it might have left a better taste, for to many it is a deliberate distortion."

Indeed the same complaint had been lodged nearly half a century earlier when Jack London wrote about Hawaii. "You came to Hawaii and absorbed local color enough to give realism to your tales . . . but like the historical novel, worked in so much fact with the fiction, that [the tales] give the impression to the uninitiated that they are more fact than fiction," complained a critic of London. This was a legitimate concern about *Hawaii*, too. People who should have known better referred to Michener's novel as a work of history. "The novel is truly a comprehensive social history of our 50th state," announced S. L. Hopkinson in *Library Journal*.

"It is unfortunate," wrote the Reverend Abraham Akaka, pastor of the historic Kawaiahao, "that a historical novel often passes as the truth. People . . . think about it [and] start believing that's how it really was." This is exactly what Mrs. Taylor had predicted months earlier. In the *Star-Bulletin* five months prior to *Hawaii*'s publication, Mrs. Taylor warned the readers of her column,

> Some of you will scream when you read James Michener's novel. . . . Michener treats all alike—Missionary families, Hawaiians, Chinese and Japanese—and steps on some toes in doing so.
>
> The screams in certain quarters will arise because many of us in Hawaii are accustomed to reading pretty stories about ourselves and our ancestors, stories which make plaster saints out of our leading businessmen and particularly our laborers.
>
> This is not for Michener, who hews to the truth.
>
> In one of his final chapters he says that no one in the Islands is what he appears to be.

Following *Hawaii*'s release, irate readers incessantly telephoned Mrs. Taylor, demanding, "How could you let Michener write this?"

"Isn't it ridiculous," she later wrote to Michener, "how people will think that you got your story from some one book? I find it most difficult to make them believe that your stories came from your own brain."

In response to her interrogators, Mrs. Taylor told them, "Michener was writing fiction. He didn't use historical characters and the events of his book follow a historical outline, not facts."

But nothing that she could have said made a difference; many people were offended. Michener's story rang so nearly true that some readers never considered it a novel, and they never forgave him for writing it. Ironically, while Michener had tried to destroy prejudices, readers clung to their prejudices in defense.

Not all Hawaiians reacted angrily, however. In fact, the majority of readers quietly appreciated *Hawaii* while they followed the ruckus in the press. Those who evaluated "the completed portrait," as one reviewer advised, could see "the whole in relation to the mass of parts" and grasp "the full effect of the author's intention." Having done so, every Hawaiian reader could claim pride in Michener's story.

Certainly the "complete message" was glowing for Hawaii, as Michener's friend, Professor Day, pointed out. "Paradise is not an existing spot at which one may arrive," he explained, "but rather an empty stage to which people of many groups may come, bringing with them their material and cultural assets, by which an Eden may be built."

Arriving when it did, at the end of the dull fifties and on the horizon of a booming tourist trade to Hawaii, Michener's message was enthusiastically received throughout the United States. Even book reviewers who had earlier decided Michener was "a good journalist" but "a weak novelist" acquired a higher level of respect for him. Those who had suggested that Michener was "writing a shade too swiftly for his reputation's sake" by publishing a book almost every year, were impressed just by the sheer volume of *Hawaii*. "Into it," said John K. Hutchins in the New York *Herald Tribune*, "the Pacific's most renowned present-day celebrant has poured what for many a chronicler would be a lifetime of data gathering, of observing, of imagining."

Not every reviewer was willing to concede that *Hawaii* was more novel than "dramatized journalism," as it was called in *Catholic World*. Ronald Bryden in the *Spectator* said Michener had developed "corn-flake-package characters," and *Christian Century*'s reviewer compared Michener's Polynesians to "pasteboard figures." *Time*'s critic said the characters "do not run deep, but they move fast," and Paul West in the *New Statesman* wrote that familiar Michener stereotypes emerge in *Hawaii*, but Michener "goes into them more deeply than usual." A reviewer for the Kirkus syndicate said the book "falls of its own weight."

Only one critic identified the major flaw in Michener's story, the weakness that relegated *Hawaii* to the class of "superior popular novel" when it could have been a "great novel." Maxwell Geismar, in the *New York Times Book Review,* said that *Hawaii* was disappointing because Michener never resolved the central conflict of his story: What price progress? Michener spent so much time enticing readers with Hawaii's qualities and people that he glossed over the crux of the story. He became a missionary of sorts, or an apologist, and never delivered more than an unthinking acceptance of modern American values.

Hardly anyone denied, however, that *Hawaii* was a masterpiece in one way or another. In the *Saturday Review,* Horace Sutton summed up the favorable opinions when he wrote that

> high-domed, long-haired *litterateurs* may argue that Michener's characters are often as paper-thin as the color-ad image in which Hawaii is held by mainland tourists, but *Hawaii* is still a masterful job of research, an absorbing performance of story telling, and a monumental account of the islands from geologic birth to sociological emergence as the newest, and perhaps the most interesting of the United States.

At Random House, Michener's editors and publisher hoped Sutton was right. As soon as *Hawaii* came off the press, a nervous Albert Erskine wrote to Michener and said that four thousand copies of the book were en route to the islands by boat (air freight was too expensive). The dollar amount of those four thousand copies, Erskine explained in late August, nearly doubled the volume of all Random House books in the islands' bookstores the year before, but he thought the risk was reasonable. He expected *Hawaii* to end up in every American home within a year's time, and "I don't mind looking silly if it doesn't work." Bennett Cerf concurred. "I think *Hawaii* will be selling in one edition and another for the next hundred years," he wrote to Michener on August 24. "It is a wonderful book." There were no sweeter words for Michener to hear.

By early fall, however, Erskine and Cerf wondered how costly was their mistake. Hawaiian bookstore managers had to be coaxed into accepting more than a few copies of *Hawaii,* and distributors anticipated slim sales for this fat novel. Opinions changed quickly, though, when the first shipment of books sold in a matter of several days. It was just luck that subsequent copies arrived in time for the Christmas rush. No one could believe the sales figures. In its first week, *Hawaii* set a record by rising to number five on best-seller lists.

"The daily sales figures are nothing short of fantastic," Cerf wrote to Michener in December. "I have never seen anything like it in all the years we have been in the business!" The next month Cerf reported, "Just a line to tell you that *Hawaii* will finally make the number one spot in the *New York Times Book Review* this coming Sunday. [The book had already hit first place on most other lists]. That makes it just about unanimous. The total is now over the 180,000 mark. . . . Happy New Year!"

In just two months, *Hawaii* became the third best-selling novel of 1959, trailing *Doctor Zhivago* and *Exodus,* both published earlier in the year. For twenty months the ten-dollar hardcover edition of *Hawaii* dominated the best-seller lists and remained there even after the paperback edition appeared in bookstores. (Even today, more than twenty-five years after publication, the book remains in print and has sold more than seven million copies in hardcover and paperback.)

As if this excitement were not sufficient, Helen Strauss opened the bidding for *Hawaii*'s film rights at $600,000 and received $750,000, the highest price ever paid for a picture property at that time. In addition, the contract included 10 percent of the film's gross for Michener, an unprecedented figure. *Hawaii* had required four years' planning time and another two years of research and writing, but not even the author imagined that one novel could pay off so handsomely.

The money and the hoopla did not visibly affect Michener. He rarely mentioned the book in his correspondence during 1959 and 1960. Once he wrote to Professor Day that he was not upset by the angry vibrations coming out of Hawaii. In fact, he was depending on the criticism to promote

> what I wanted this novel to accomplish. . . . I wanted people to talk about it in Hawaii in terms of history, sociology, relevancy, politics, vision. Nothing would make me happier than to have the book dissected page by page, for in doing so perhaps Hawaii will grow up artistically. Then maybe we'll get the great books out of the islands that the islands have a right to expect.

It almost seemed that Michener had written *Hawaii* for purely unselfish reasons. He was already buried in other projects, giving people the impression that he had all but forgotten the novel. The sales figures, the reviews, the Hollywood notice, were just reminders of a book in his past.

Behind the nonchalance, however, Michener was deeply satisfied. "With *Hawaii,"* he explained later, "I finally found great faith in myself as a writer. This was critical. Every writer looks for that moment, and I was happy to have had mine." Surprisingly, he was not planning to write another book, at least not for several years. He had proven to himself what he needed to know and received far more for his efforts than he had ever dreamed likely. Now another challenge in another field beckoned, and he planned to meet it.

## CHAPTER TWELVE

# A Nation To Be Won

Through the years I have developed a
profound love of country. America has
been overly generous to me and I remain
a fortunate son of America. I have always
been conscious of the debt that I owe to
this country.

JAMES A. MICHENER, 1961

AT THE END of the 1950s, no writer in America had more options than James A. Michener. *Hawaii* was about to earn him a fortune, and as Bennett Cerf told him, "the fact of the matter is that you can do no wrong these days and can't possibly miss no matter what the direction you take."

From Michener's point of view life was not that simple during the several months prior to the publication of *Hawaii*. Immediately following the completion of the novel he was caught in a web of "overchoice." He never stopped working—he was already writing a television series for ABC—but anything he did now, he did temporarily while he thought about the future. Each afternoon, as he walked five miles from his apartment out to the famous Diamond Head, he reviewed his options.

While completing *Hawaii* he had agreed to write *The Battle of Leyte Gulf* for a 20th Century Fox production, but when Admiral Stump retired, Michener lost interest in the navy and asked Helen Strauss to release him from the movie contract. The producers balked at the notion. Responding on behalf of the company, David Brown told Strauss that "it has always been our dream to make a big Navy picture based on a story by an author of Jim's calibre . . . we are not interested in a divorce and we hope, as Jim himself indicated, that *The Battle of Leyte Gulf* may be his greatest work." Brown suggested that Michener add another six weeks to his deadline for an outline, and he told Strauss, "Please let Jim know that we are depending on this." Strauss then advised Michener, "it is going to be impossible to cancel out the *Leyte Gulf* contract" without 20th Century Fox filing a lawsuit, and she suggested that Michener postpone the deadline and "keep postponing."

At Random House, where Cerf would have happily published *The Battle of Leyte Gulf,* editor Albert Erskine encouraged Michener to write *The Americans,* if for no other reason than "it has been nagging at you for five or six years." And if not a novel, then Erskine hoped Michener might write one of several nonfiction books they had discussed, including a collection of nine stories about the history of Christianity, and a book about Japan. Erskine was less concerned about the subject matter of Michener's next book than he was about the author's contentment. "Write whichever [book] you will be happiest working on," he advised Michener. Considerations of public acceptance and market strategies were now irrelevant, or so they seemed to Erskine.

Hobe Lewis, at *Reader's Digest,* had several projects in mind for Michener, too. He liked the idea of a big book about Christianity, and in his helpful way he recommended chapters about Antioch, Constantinople, Saint Paul, and early Christian Rome. Michener favored this idea, too, and he returned to it often, but he could not commit himself to it in 1959. *Hawaii* had demanded too much of his energy: he was not willing to begin another major project so soon.

Macmillan Publishing Company also had an idea for Michener. Cecil Scott, who had helped edit *Tales of the South Pacific* and then lost Michener to Saxe Commins, wanted the chance to work with him again. He offered Michener a $7,500 advance, which was substantial at the time, to write a book about Honolulu for the booming tourist trade. "I might say that all of us are tremendously enthusiastic. Nothing would please us better to have you again on our list," Scott informed Michener. "I shall never forget the personal happiness I enjoyed when working with you here. I have not had the same pleasure working with any other author." Michener appreciated Scott's letter, but he was now a Random House author and he had no intention of working for anyone else.

Other offers surfaced from beyond the publishing world. A Honolulu businessman was willing to pay Michener $60,000 annually for making cameo appearances in a TV series entitled "James Michener Presents." Michener liked the idea, but he asked for Strauss's advice. She was not impressed. If Michener was interested in such an arrangement she could land him "a better deal," she said.

The Office of Cultural Exchange in Washington, D.C., invited him to tour American embassies throughout Latin America. Twelve of the foreign service posts had submitted requests for him to spend an average of ten days in each country lecturing and teaching during a four-month period. Michener could not resist the opportunity, but he asked to postpone the tour for perhaps a year.

The University of Missouri asked him to inaugurate a writer-in-residence program during 1960. This he could not resist, either. "I feel the necessity to get back in touch with vital young people and to find out what is really happening in the world," he informed the university's administration, and he promised to begin teaching in 1961. (Later, he postponed the visiting lectureship until 1962, and then he bowed out altogether when "something big came up.")

For several weeks Michener bounced from one idea to the next, rejecting or postponing each one, and in the final analysis he committed himself to a field that wiser men might have advised against. He decided to enter politics, not as a candidate, but as a campaigner. This was not, as some people suggested, an antidote to "writer's block," the immobilizing malady that choked off an author's ability to think and write. Michener rarely suffered the affliction, and when he did, it was his practice to jump to another section of his manuscript and work through the problem. He was serious about politics. "Politics is one of our most honorable professions," he explained, "much more so than writing."

When Michener moved to Hawaii in 1958 with plans for making his home in the islands, local politicians realized they had an opportunity to draw a celebrity into their camp. When he spoke up forcefully for statehood, the professional politicians became all the more excited, and the Republicans in particular courted him.

For most of fifty-three years Jim Michener had been a Republican, although not necessarily by choice. Along with most of Doylestown, Pennsylvania, he had inherited the party at birth. As he explained in 1961,

> I grew up without knowing any Democrats. My mother thought there might be some on the edge of town, but she preferred not to speak of them. When I brought my wife home from Chicago, she met my aunts, who had occasion to observe, "We have really never known any Democrats," and when my wife volunteered, "Well, you know one now," there was a painful silence.

Michener relished the childhood memory of his first political campaign, the 1916 contest between Hughes and Wilson. He was nine years old at the time, and later he recalled the event:

> My mother took me into the center of town that Tuesday night while the victorious Republicans paraded with torchlights and a long, horn-honking file of expensive automobiles. We trudged

home content that Charles Evans Hughes would be a great president, and my mother explained how good life was going to be,
now that the Democrat Wilson had been thrown out.

But later that week, biting her lip to control her tears, Mabel Michener
walked her son back into town to watch from the shadows as the Democrats
celebrated their belated victory. What a grubby lot of people they were,
suggested Mabel. "Never forget this night, James," she said mournfully.
"Look at them. There isn't a Buick in the lot."
    In 1928, soon after Michener left his hometown for Swarthmore College,
he campaigned for Al Smith, but out of respect for his mother he remained a
registered Republican in Bucks County. Until 1959, party politics engendered
little enthusiasm from him, and even as an avowed Democrat he viewed
politics in a democracy "as a process of hard fighting to win a nation,
conciliation when the election ends, and generous compromise when the
office is assumed." Apparently, he had much to learn about how the system
really worked.
    While it was true that his party allegiance changed seasonably—from the
Democrats in the 1930s to the Republicans in 1952, back to the Democrats in
1956—Michener had formed his own political philosophy. Largely, his point
of view stemmed from his personal observations and from the ideas
expressed in the books of three liberal European intellectuals: the scholar
James Bryce, who had spoken tirelessly for better Anglo-American understanding; the political philosopher, Montesquieu, who had influenced the
penmen of the United States constitution with his in-depth study of government; and Alexis de Tocqueville, who had written the classic study of the
United States, *Democracy in America.* Many of the social issues that once
aroused these authors—human freedom, creativity, honor, values—have
always concerned Michener.
    Michener might have easily become a dedicated Republican in 1959. He
seemed to prefer the Democrats only because the Republicans had dominated
national office for eight years, and the country needed "a wholly new
administration. It musn't be saddled with old policies and old policy-
makers," he explained. "Therefore it's got to be Democratic." Also, he
sensed the mood of the American public favored Democrats for their state
legislators and governors in 1960, so "at this critical period we ought to have a
Democratic president, too. I don't like divided responsibilities."
    At least some fundamental differences led Michener to the Democratic
party in Hawaii. While Republicans tended to vote against liberal measures
and to work for a balanced budget, Michener approved of the Democrats'
temporarily postponing a balanced budget in favor of moving the country
forward. Furthermore, under President Eisenhower the Republicans had
failed to support many of the social measures that Michener valued. The
President had not backed the Supreme Court decision to integrate American
schools, nor had he sponsored intellectualism. Also, American prestige

abroad had slipped dangerously in the 1950s. The country seemed to be resisting the great changes sweeping the world. As a result, Michener decided that "my interest and my heart and my patriotism and my sense of history inclined me toward the Democratic view." The Democrats represented a coalition of liberals, intellectuals, union people, blacks, Catholics, and Jews, he said, who were united in fighting for a "vigorous new society."

Basically, Michener the optimist was alarmed about America's welfare in the late 1950s, and once he joined the Democrats as a moderate liberal, he assumed a personal responsibility for the country's political and social future. "There is a nation to be won," he said, and he was firmly poised in the battle for victory. If someone asked him why he was involved, he explained, "Because I want my ideas of justice and accomplishment to prevail."

In Hawaii in 1959, the Republicans refused to believe that Michener had turned his back on them. Some said he was "temporarily deranged," the result of a midlife crisis; others blamed Mari Michener, a die-hard Stevenson-ian. "Don't you understand what the Democrats would do to people like you and me?" asked Michener's Republican friends. But when the rumor spread that Michener was planning to run for governor of the new state, and on the Democratic ticket, the Republicans knew they had lost a member.

If there was ever a chance of Michener becoming a candidate in 1959, he dismissed every opportunity when he gave an interview to the Honolulu *Star-Bulletin:*

> A writer never qualifies for elective office. Like a newspaper-man, a minister or an educator. People in these fields have a function from without. Particularly in the case of a writer. He has to remain a free spirit . . . must have a free mind.
>
> No. I just wouldn't qualify. This is the answer I give to at least three persons a week who ask whether I'm planning to run for office.

In a couple of years he regretted having uttered those words, but in 1959 Michener did not consider himself a professional politician. He was a rank-and-file worker who was determined to bolster the party, and in Hawaii's first statewide election this was enough of a challenge. Like their mainland counterparts during the late fifties, island Democrats were divided on many volatile issues including segregation, civil rights, statehood, and land devel-opment. The breach in Hawaii was serious enough to defeat the party, unless a peacemaker acted quickly. At first, Michener thought the natural peace-maker was Hawaii's Democratic delegate to Congress, John A. Burns, and in February he wrote the representative a two-page letter heavy with foreboding.

"The Democratic Party in Hawaii is in very bad shape," Michener began, as he called on Burns to mend the fences. He urged the delegate to enter the campaign as the party's gubernatorial nominee, but most important, Burns had to provide "constructive and conciliatory" leadership immediately. As to what "deals must be made" Michener said he did not know, but by acting promptly "the prospects are bright [for victory]."

Whatever Burns thought of Michener's letter he took little of it to heart. He entered the governor's race but he was a painfully disappointing candidate and an inept peacemaker. Most of what he did was wrong. He waited too long to announce his candidacy, and instead of returning to the islands to campaign, he remained in Washington, D.C., until late in the election year. Even then, he failed to rally the party.

There was, however, one electrifying night when Burns brought to the islands a Washington colleague who had presidential aspirations for 1960, and who ignited the rank and file. A dashing Senator John F. Kennedy said nothing remarkable that evening, but his very presence brought out the best in everyone, including Michener. While listening to Kennedy quote from several works of history and literature, Michener thought to himself, "It would be nice to have in the White House someone who knows books." After the speech, the senator caught Michener's arm in the crowd and whispered, "I hoped you would be here. I've always liked your *Fires of Spring*." Michener nodded politely and silently registered the senator's shrewd technique. Had someone reminded him of the obscure novel, or had he actually enjoyed it? When the senator invited him to get together later in the evening, Michener declined, fearful of the younger man's magnetism. "He knows what to say to people," Michener thought to himself. "And I'm not sure I want to support him for President. Not yet." Besides, there was an election to win in Hawaii, and if necessary Michener planned to win it single-handedly.

He had already written what he hoped would be the outcome of the voting. In the conclusion of his novel-in-progress he described the election of 1954 as one that islanders would never forget. On that day, in the fictional version of Hawaii's history, the Democrats captured the islands and squashed the reign of Republican rule forever. A new coalition of people, spearheaded by a wise breed of youthful politicians, had grown up in the islands to lead Hawaii into the second half of the twentieth century. To this breed Michener gave the name, the golden men, the best of Hawaii's residents. Among them were Harvard lawyers, war heroes, big bankers, entrepreneurs, and even romantic beachboys. They shared one characteristic that their predecessors had failed to cultivate. Without denying their ancestries they could see "both the West and the East" in their state's future.

For several months, Michener stood among those golden men. Right up to election day, and for what some people said was two weeks after Burns himself had given up the campaign and all but conceded the victory, Michener scrambled around the clock to save his party's ticket. But the Democrats lost the governorship by 4,161 votes, and despite Michener's late-inning blitz, the Republicans maintained a tight grip on America's newest state.

Following the election "the penalties of losing" were worse than Michener had anticipated. "Compromise and conciliation" were words that appeared in his definition of a political fight, but not in others'. Friends avoided him now more than ever. "At one dreadful party more than half the guests preferred not to talk with me, and those who did said ugly things," he recalled several years later. Some months earlier he had accepted the chairmanship of a charity fund drive, but now he was advised to resign because he had offended the islands' Grand Old Party, and as it was expressed to him, "everyone with money is a Republican." Early in the summer of 1959 he did resign, and as quickly as possible left Hawaii.

Explaining to Mari that he needed time to think, he joined the crew of a sailboat making a return trip from Honolulu to Los Angeles. For twenty-two days, "with the wind in one's teeth . . . and the rail under water most of the way," he reviewed the last several months, the role he had played, and how it all related to his future. "It was while I stood at the wheel as our boat headed into the storm that I reached several conclusions."

Two of those conclusions were most surprising.

As quickly as possible, he and Mari would pull out of Hawaii and return to Pennsylvania. He intended to be gone by the time *Hawaii* arrived in the islands. Everyone who had read the galleys of his novel had advised him to leave. At first he ignored the warnings, but if the retaliation he suffered as a result of voting Democratic was an indication of the animosity in store for him, he preferred the security of his hilltop home in Bucks County. Even though the central theme of his novel was the enviable process in which Hawaiians had assimilated men and women from many different races, and while he believed that what he had written about the islands represented a beacon light of hope for racial harmony, on a day-to-day basis he and Mari suffered more racial discrimination in Hawaii than they did in eastern Pennsylvania. (Later, when these comments appeared in print, they enraged the same Hawaiians who had also screamed about *Hawaii,* but by then Michener was gone.)

He reached the second decision during a night watch with the strains of Beethoven's Seventh in the background: he would forget about writing another major book now. Instead, he would commit his energy to working diligently on the local level in the 1960 presidential election: "who my candidate would be . . . I did not know," he recalled. But at that moment, choosing a candidate was not important. All he knew was that politics ran through his veins, and there was yet "a nation to be won."

He arrived in Los Angeles and then returned to Hawaii to inform Mari of his decisions. All that kept him on the islands was some unfinished business relating to a television series. From the beginning of his writing career Michener had been interested in the electronic media, and he had been delighted when Helen Strauss presented him with a television contract in February 1959, about a week before he finished writing *Hawaii.* He wrote to Strauss from Waikiki that "somebody back east must have been doing a lot of high-powered salesmanship." She had informed him that ABC wanted to sponsor a series bearing his name. "I am impressed!" he admitted.

For years Michener had tried to develop his own television series, but after several false starts at scriptwriting he all but abandoned the project. His first unsuccessful stint in Hollywood had occurred in 1951 when Paramount Pictures asked him to write an original South Sea love story. Strauss negotiated a $20,000 contract with the studio, and added another $15,000 by selling serialization rights to *McCall's* magazine. Michener collected none of the money, however, for after several frustrating weeks of working with a collaborator, he finally gave up. The collaborator tried to salvage the project, but failed. Contacted by his agent in Singapore, Michener said he was finished with the fiasco and he never planned to sign another Hollywood contract. Strauss was disappointed, but suggested that perhaps her client was not a scriptwriter. Michener agreed. "I didn't like scriptwriting," he later explained. "I discovered that I had little talent for concentrated plotting and dialogue. It was just not something that I could do."

He did believe, though, that his talent was suitable to television writing. Any time a producer mentioned the possibility of a Michener series, he was willing to listen. Bob Mann wanted to create a weekly program from *Tales of the South Pacific,* using Michener as the narrator, but Rodgers and Hammerstein, who owned all dramatic rights to Michener's first novel, refused to give up ownership.

Every so often Michener developed a proposal for a series and sent it to Strauss. He titled one idea "War for the World," and described it as a "highly dramatic show . . . based upon the exploits and adventures of Americans working overseas and engaged in the endless struggle of our people to help new nations find security." A second adventure series, this one untitled, called for a Mediterranean setting "which permits us to visit the southern lands of Europe, the northern borders of Africa, and the western edge of Asia. Each of these areas . . . provides enormous possibilities for strong story, good characters and situations," he explained. None of these proposals snagged the attention of producers, and Michener continued waiting for the right opportunity.

Strauss was sure she had found it in 1959 when the television producer Martin Manulis, who was also represented by the William Morris Agency, suggested a series of romance and adventure set in the South Pacific. Manulis, famous for "Playhouse 90," developed the idea of a free-spirited schooner pilot, Adam Troy, who sailed charter voyages in the Pacific, and Michener loved the idea. Shortly thereafter a contract was struck between the author and producer for "Adventures in Paradise," the first TV series filmed in the fiftieth state. Michener was not to appear in any of the episodes, but he was guaranteed $1,250 per show and commissioned to write four scripts at $3,500 each. In addition, he was appointed story supervisor.

ABC's executives were ecstatic about the Michener-Manulis collaboration, and the network earmarked $3.9 million for thirty-nine hour-long episodes, making "Adventures in Paradise" one of the most expensive ventures in televison's early history. The debut was set for fall 1959, a coup for both Michener and Random House, as *Hawaii* was bound to benefit from ABC's extensive publicity.

That July, in the wake of a disillusioning election, Michener finished the first script for "Adventures in Paradise" and delivered it by boat to Manulis in Los Angeles. Upon arrival, he worked in Hollywood for several days, overseeing the construction of Wheeler's Folly, the man-made lagoon in which Adam Troy, played by Tyrone Power look-alike, Gardner McKay, rode his schooner.

In September, when everyone thought the series was ready for previewing, the network spent thousands of dollars escorting eleven mainland television critics and reporters to Hawaii for five days "to sit in the sun, eat like the rich and spend an hour with writer Michener and producer Manulis." Staying at the lovely Royal Hawaiian, the press corps charged everything to ABC, and after five days began feeling nervous about spending so much money.

Imagine, then, how ABC's executives felt when these very reviewers panned "Adventures in Paradise"! No one at ABC had expected this assembly of eleven writers to sit around in the sun and collectively analyze the series' weaknesses. Yet that is precisely what occurred. While almost everyone enjoyed Gardner McKay's performance and liked many of the scenes—"the feel of the South Pacific came through exactly right," offered one critic—the preview lacked polish. Even Michener agreed with the reviewers. The story line was weak and confusing, little use was made of South Seas music, camera angles were uncreative, and the sound was poor. "Thus the elements that go into a successful story were not fused together in a manner that the audience would enjoy," Michener reported to Oliver Treyz at ABC.

By the time the preview was over Michener was in a fit of rage. He immediately wrote to Strauss and referred to the production as a "catastrophe," a "shambles," and a "massacre."

He was angry for three reasons. First, he felt that the series made him look incompetent, foolish, and money-hungry. "When a story said to have been written by me loomed up with a line like, 'Won't those drums ever cease?' I felt more embarrassed than the critics." Somehow, prior to the previewing and perhaps as an apology, the message was spread among the critics that this first episode was less than appealing. Yet, there was Michener talking to the press as though he thought the series was first rate.

> They must have thought I was an idiot, but I did not know how inept the film was, and I went staggering into an almost ridiculous situation that must have confirmed the critics' suspicion that I had entered this whole deal callously, knowing that the end result would be junk and not caring.

Second, Michener expected the sour reviews to hurt *Hawaii,* copies of which were now arriving on the islands.

Third, he believed his agency had used him. He learned that William Morris personnel had been forewarned about the series' inadequacy. "Yet when I spent over a week right next door to the television lot, nobody warned *me* of what the situation was, and I was left fat, dumb and happy to make a fool of myself." He was not warned, he surmised, to protect Martin Manulis's contract with the agency. No one wanted "[me] to injure the relationship with your other and potentially more productive client," he told Strauss.

As a result, Michener stressed, "I want to be a part of no more package deals," although he quickly excluded the package that Strauss was arranging for *Hawaii*. The television experience "must never be repeated," he said. If he lost money as a result of refusing to work with another William Morris client, he did not care. "I have got to be handled by you alone, as a writer alone. . . . To operate otherwise is fundamentally unsound." In the future, he shared "no possible interests" in Hollywood, and he told Strauss that if she was ever pressured by her agency to override his decisions, "you must say no, or lose one of your oldest clients."

Strauss must have felt relieved that Michener had not terminated their relationship on the spot. She did, however, defend her agency, saying that "we tried to get an easy way for you to have a television series. I suppose in the end nothing is very easy." What happened, in her opinion, was "that ABC and Twentieth [20th Century Fox, headed by Manulis] did too much of a selling job on this series, too far in advance. . . . Between the motion picture and Madison Avenue tactics, I think they all goofed a little." Of course, she noted Michener's demands and promised not to involve him in another package. In fact, she suggested "you should . . . instruct me to keep you out of television and writing for the movies . . . you're happiest in the medium of writing for publication."

When Michener's anger subsided, he told Strauss and Treyz, "I will do everything possible to help" make "Adventures in Paradise" a success. He cared about the artistic quality of the production, and as unlikely as it seemed to critics, he cared less about the money. His reputation concerned him most of all. Harsh criticism for a project that "had started with such high hopes . . . galls me," he informed Treyz, "and I would be less than normal if I didn't admit it." For this reason, he was willing to campaign to save the series.

Actually, there was not much Michener could do—the series required technical expertise that only extra money could provide—and regrettably Michener ended up making himself look all the more foolish. First, he wrote a letter to a critic and explained, unconvincingly, that reviews made little difference to him:

> Many people have asked me how it feels to read a bad review like the one you ran on ["Adventures in Paradise"]. Apparently they think a man wants to go out and cut his throat. Nonsense. If you offer works to the public you expect some bad reviews and

some good ones. Neither kind can be allowed to throw you off your rocker.

If he had stopped at this point the critic might have assumed his intentions were sincere, but he went on to defend his record:

> *Time* magazine originally said that *South Pacific* was a dud. It ran only five years. Reviewers lambasted one of my novels that later sold a million copies. Two magazines slapped *Sayonara* around, but it matured into a modest success.

Then, in a sort of separation from the television project, he added,

> I gave the TV boys a pretty good idea for a series, and I feel quite confident that they will ultimately lick the problem and wind up with a good series. . . . I have never been particularly impressed by good reviews, nor disheartened by bad. The professional in any of the arts takes these things as they come and probably that is why he survives to become a professional.

Next, Michener defended himself in a *TV Guide* "puff piece" that explained how "Adventures in Paradise" evolved. He also wrote a similar piece for national distribution to daily newspapers, in time for publication on October 6, the eve of the series' television debut.

Basically, the newspaper article answered the transparent question, "Why should James Michener, who writes novels, bother with an adventure series on television?" According to Michener, many people had asked him that question and he always answered "quickly and with force." Reading between the lines, he heard people asking him, "Are you so desperate for money that you'd demean yourself in television?" It was that implied criticism that he wanted to defend, and not the television series. The newspaper article, he explained to Treyz, would "at least quash *that* line of argument."

In Michener's words,

> It occurred to me that perhaps the general viewing audience might be curious [about his decision to work in television]. I have had a rollicking good time in the South Pacific . . . a great deal worth noticing goes on in the Pacific . . . [and] it therefore seems to me that the South Pacific is an ideal locale for a television series, and I have had a good deal of fun trying to bring to the screen some of the exuberance of the coral isles I have so deeply enjoyed.

The quality and tone of this writing was less than good journalism, and the editors who ran the article performed a disservice to their readers. However, the "hype" helped sell "Adventures in Paradise." Once the series began, the William Morris Agency collected more than a million and a half dollars in commissions as a result of Michener and others participating in the production, Strauss reported in her memoirs. "The agency's officers "didn't know what to do with it all, so there were snowstorms of Christmas bonus checks falling on every desk."

In spite of everything, what Michener feared most did eventually happen. His reputation fell several notches as a result of the series. Fans accused him of "selling out to television" and "insulting intelligent people," and forever after critics tagged him a "popularizer." Some who had praised his fiction wavered now between condemnation and apology. In the *New Yorker,* John Lardner said Michener had demonstrated how a "practical writer" who

> after he has followed up a self-imposed assignment to certain lengths and written some pleasant things as a result, can allow his ideas on the subject to soften into a bromidic dream, with Maughamesque overtures, and then, with the right kind of help, can translate his dream into a contract for a TV adventure series, probably with residual clauses.

Lardner said it was difficult to believe that Michener ever wrote anything like an "Adventures in Paradise" episode.

However, even if the series failed to live up to Michener's artistic expectations, he acknowledged that, commercially, "Adventures in Paradise" was "a whale of a success." In 1971, perhaps to console himself, Michener noted privately that regardless of the negative comments, the series "ran three years on prime time and seven more in reruns, [and] kept a studio alive for two years. . . . You stay in there and fight," he concluded.

In a gentlemanly way, Michener *was* a fighter, but he always avoided making himself too vulnerable. He could defend "Adventures in Paradise" from behind his editorial byline, for example, but he was not about to remain in Hawaii in the fall of 1959 and defend his novel. What he did not realize, though, was that in running away from Hawaii, driving across the United States with Mari, he was running into a bigger fight at home. It began the moment he told Mari he had some doubts about Adlai Stevenson in 1960.

Mari Michener was not involved in Hawaii's political campaign in 1959, but she had been active nationally as one of Stevenson's avid supporters in 1952 and 1956. She intended to work again for Stevenson in 1960, and she assumed that her husband planned to do the same. "My God!" she demanded from behind the steering wheel. "Who else is there?" Who among the Democrats could possibly top Stevenson? Of all people, she shouted, her husband, perhaps the most traveled man of the century, knew what America really needed: a President with courage and brains; someone the other nations could respect; a man with determination in the field of social legislation. "There's only one man you could possibly support," Mari insisted, and for days she stressed the reasons why Stevenson should become America's next President. Across Nebraska, Iowa, and Illinois her campaign continued, with her husband, a captive audience, watching the land and recalling earlier travels that had endeared him to the country. Across Indiana and Ohio she tried shaming him out of supporting anyone other than Stevenson, but Michener did not bow to the pressure.

"If you had to give me just one reason why I should support Adlai, what would it be?" he asked, close to home.

"Because the people sense that he's big enough to do the job," Mari replied.

"Do you think he can get elected?"

"This time, yes," she was sure.

But when the car reached Pipersville, Michener remained undecided, as he later explained in *Report of the County Chairman*. After settling in at home, he secluded himself for one November week to think about America's political future. From his den he watched the autumn transformation occur on his hilltop, and eventually he saw that America required a similar change, a "wholly new administration" free of "old policies and old policy-makers." There was no doubt in his mind that it had to be Democratic, and that each of the Democratic contenders was a better man than Richard Nixon, the obvious Republican nominee. But victory hinged on one critical question: "Who should be the Democratic nominee?" In the waning days of 1959, Michener grappled with that question.

# CHAPTER THIRTEEN

# *Barnstorming*

I am a liberal now, tomorrow and for the
rest of my life because I believe that
liberal views are essential to any society.
JAMES A. MICHENER
*THE WASHINGTON POST*, 1980

IN *REPORT OF the County Chairman*, a short anecdotal book that Michener wrote following his role in the 1960 presidential campaign, he explains in detail how he arrived at the choice of John F. Kennedy for the presidency. He considered six men in all, Stevenson first among them, of course, but he decided that only Kennedy could bring back to the Democrats the labor, black, suburban, and Jewish voters who had left the party to support General Eisenhower in 1956 and who were needed in 1960 for a Democratic victory. As good as they were, the other presidential hopefuls—Symington, Humphrey, Williams, and Johnson—could not build a coalition. As for Stevenson, Michener thought he could make an excellent President, but he had lost two previous elections and, in Michener's opinion, stood a good chance of losing this one, also. The obvious choice was Kennedy. The more Michener studied the senator, "the more convinced I became that he had the makings of a superb political leader with the social conscience of a Franklin Delano Roosevelt, the intellectual capacity of a Woodrow Wilson, and the

down-to-earth political know-how of a Harry Truman . . . he has the makings of a great man."

Once confident about Kennedy, Michener visited Johnny Welsh, an old
friend in Doylestown, and the boss of the Democratic party in Bucks County
for many years. Michener found Welsh at his real estate office where he "sat
like a gray eagle surveying everything with cold caution." Real estate supported Welsh's wife and six sons, but everyone knew that his heart was in
politics full-time.

"Johnny," Michener said, "if Senator Kennedy wins the nomination, I
want to work for his election."

"I thought you were a Republican," snapped the wiry, well-preserved
Welsh. "What's a Republican doing working for Kennedy? You're not a
Catholic."

"I think the country needs him," Michener responded, much to Welsh's
satisfaction.

"If anything turns up later on, I'll let you know."

Months passed before Michener knew if he had a candidate to support, and
during this time, while following the primaries, he returned to traveling and
writing. *Reader's Digest* sent him to Mexico where he nervously awaited the
results of the Wisconsin primary with U.S. Ambassador Robert C. Hill and a
Republican entourage. He had astonished Hill's friends by announcing that
Kennedy was going to be America's next President, and they all played along
with him when he bet that the senator was about to topple Humphrey in the
latter's own state primary. Kennedy did win, but narrowly, and the ambassador's team had a lot of fun at Michener's expense.

Then the West Virginia primary guaranteed Kennedy the nomination, and
Michener savored that victory. He was in Guatemala at the time with a group
of American military personnel, and on the eve of the primary he predicted a
Kennedy victory by at least 54 percent of the votes. Everyone laughed until
Kennedy won by 69 percent. Then the biggest smile spread across Michener's
face. Now, he thought, if only the Republicans nominated Nixon, and not
Rockefeller, Kennedy would spend the next four years in the White House.

The summer of 1960 was one of the most leisurely in Michener's life. He
played "Mich the Witch" at the local fair, played tennis daily, and entertained
friends on the hill during weekends. It all ended once the Democrats met in
Los Angeles and nominated the presidential ticket of John F. Kennedy and
Lyndon B. Johnson. Johnny Welsh called soon thereafter and asked Michener
to head a committee of independents and Republicans to work for Kennedy
in Bucks County.

"I'm neither an independent nor a Republican," Michener objected, until
Welsh explained that the Kennedy strategists planned to establish these
committees in every county of America. At that point, Michener became
county chairman of Citizens for Kennedy. The national committee would
contact him in the near future, but meanwhile, he was to establish headquarters, build a team of volunteers, and raise funds.

In mid-August Michener went to work, and he never quit until November 8. From the first of September until election day he delivered at least three speeches daily and toured Bucks County from end to end. He worked as hard as any candidate and thrived on the activity.

Prior to 1955 there was not the slightest chance of a Democrat winning an election in Bucks County. Since the turn of the century, the county had bowed to the wishes of GOP boss Joseph R. Grundy, one of America's most successful lobbyists, and according to his biographer, "one of the most maligned figures in Pennsylvania and national politics." Grundy had supposedly raised more money for a political party than any man in U.S. history. He was a "king maker" of hand-picked Pennsylvania governors and one U.S. President, Warren G. Harding, dark horse of the 1920 GOP campaign. In Michener's mind, "he was an arch-Republican, one of the greatest party politicians, and he tyrannized our county."

Powerfully built and blessed with political savvy, Grundy opposed all forms of social legislation and vowed to smash progressive ideas that, in his opinion, led only to "socialism and communism." As a mill owner and principal stockholder in the Farmers National Bank, an institution founded by his great-great-grandfather, Grundy had inherited a fortune, and he used his family's bankroll to finance his personal interests. Michener recalled in 1961,

> I can see him now, marching from our newspaper offices (which he owned) over to the courthouse, where every man who worked did so solely because Mr. Grundy had assigned him to the job. I suspect that even the judges were judges because Mr. Grundy had selected them. His word was absolute law, and the two things he hated were Democrats and disloyalty.

Grundy's prime political aim was to protect industry in Pennsylvania. He fought for low statewide taxes and a high national tariff, and he boosted the candidacies of politicians who shared his interests. For Calvin Coolidge, Grundy raised $800,000, two-thirds of it his own money. He could not, however, prevent the social legislation that Congress passed in the 1930s, and he was no match for Franklin Delano Roosevelt. In 1932, Pennsylvania voted Democratic for the first time since 1890, and even Grundy's hometown favored FDR. During the 1930s, as increasing tax burdens forced some of Pennsylvania's big business, including steel and textiles, to move westward and southward, "Uncle Joe" Grundy watched with disdain. Still, he never lost control of Bucks County until shortly before his death in 1961 at the grand age of ninety-eight. A bachelor, he left millions of dollars to charity.

Grundy's diminution of power coincided with a recent social phenomenon in Bucks County's southern end and breathed life into the Democratic ranks. From the time of Michener's childhood and until 1952, southern Bucks remained rural. Its most famous citizen was the benevolent Joe Grundy, who lived in Bristol. But in 1952, United States Steel opted to build the world's largest continuous-flow steel mill along the Delaware River; to house the mill's workmen the New York builder Levitt began construction of 17,000 homes on the unused meadowland of southern Bucks. The community was called Levittown.

The appalling disruptions caused by this combination of steel and suburbia remade the face of Bucks County, explains Michener in *Report of the County Chairman*:

> Land speculators acquired fortunes overnight. A hundred service industries suddenly sprang up and some prospered fantastically. Restaurants, stores, schools, newspapers, insurance offices exploded all over the place, and 70,000 new people crowded into the area in the space of a few years.

Many of the newcomers belonged to labor unions, and of course, many were Democrats. From 1900 to 1950 the county's population had doubled in a slow, orderly, conservative fashion, but in just six years, between 1954 and 1960, the population more than doubled again. Shock waves spread throughout the central and northern regions of the county. "They tell us that most of the people who are moving in are either Jews or Italians," said one of Michener's former neighbors in Doylestown. "Bucks County will just never be the same."

Boss Grundy planned to keep it the same, though. When his control of the county began to slip, he allegedly barged into a Republican central committee meeting and shouted, "You, you and you are fired." When someone asked why, Grundy said, "Because your places are going to be taken by the three best young Republicans in Levittown." And when someone else said there were no Republicans in Levittown, Grundy snapped, "Find them, and we'll meet here again tomorrow. Now go home."

The tactic worked, for less than 50 percent of Levittowners supported Stevenson in 1956. But by 1960, Michener was encouraged by the fact that wherever he campaigned in suburbia, people were willing to reconsider what they had lost by joining the Republican party.

Suburbia represented Michener's only hope of helping Kennedy become the thirty-fifth President of the United States. Short of a major blunder by Nixon, Kennedy could not win Bucks County, but by uniting Levittown's voters, Michener's committee could cut Nixon's margin of victory from 17,000 to 2,000 votes. If all else went as planned across the state, Democratic majorities in Philadelphia and Pittsburgh would capture Pennsylvania's thirty-two electoral votes for Kennedy. It was an interesting theory, but when Welsh heard it he shook his head gravely. "I wish I knew what the up-county religious are going to do," he said.

The up-county religious were the Mennonites and Amish whose women had not voted in a presidential election since 1928 when their churches demanded the defeat of the Catholic Al Smith. Welsh expected the women to turn out again against Kennedy, and as he watched the county's Republican registration swell, his fears were confirmed.

But Michener plunged ahead relentlessly, determined to win the sparse liberal pockets that also existed up-county. His merry-go-round of activity began at dawn seven days a week and continued through dusk as he met the people of Bucks County, assuring them, sometimes in a raspy whisper, that "John Kennedy will be president of all the people . . . his only ambition will be to give the nation the responsible leadership it deserves."

No one spoke more eloquently for a candidate than Jim Michener, but unfortunately, "Gentleman Jim" was too kind for politics. Any voter who had not chosen a candidate prior to hearing Michener speak, walked away still undecided and perhaps even confused about whom Michener really preferred. Yes, Michener was chairman of Citizens for Kennedy, yet he also liked Richard Nixon, and he frequently let that be known. When Michener could say that "Richard Nixon is a pretty good candidate, and if he wins . . . the nation will be in fairly good hands," Bucks County Republicans felt no urgency about changing their voting habits. Ardent Democrats urged Michener to attack the opposition. However, he was afraid of alienating his audiences. It was easier, he said, to keep people attentive and open-minded without inveighing against their candidate. Then, like a teacher or writer, he had a chance of educating them about *his* candidate. Sadly, Michener was slow to discover that his approach failed.

Given the circumstances, however, few campaigners could have fared better in Bucks County. Two twists of the campaign dimmed Kennedy's hopes in Pennsylvania, and neither had anything to do with Michener's personality. The first problem—a split in the local Democratic party— paralleled events in Hawaii. The old guard felt threatened by a young, upcoming constituency whose members objected to traditional politics. Levittowners said the old guard was suspicious of Jews and union men, and the traditionalists, led by Welsh, said the upstarts alienated themselves because they were unwilling to labor in the vineyards.

Similar skirmishes occurred across America and hurt the Democratic party in 1960. In Bucks County, Michener made "a dozen overtures to both sides to see if my independent committee could be the mediating force," but instead of mending fences, he widened the gap. Levittowners said he was a stooge for Welsh, and Welsh said the southern end of the county was not for John Kennedy. In the end, Michener accomplished nothing.

Worse yet was the second twist. From the beginning of the campaign Michener suspected the problem existed, but until his mailbox bulged with hate mail, beginning immediately after he accepted the county chairmanship, he had not expected such a surge of bigotry in response to Kennedy's religion. "I will not be able to forget the deluge of anti-Catholic mail that I received," he noted after the campaign.

Much of the literature was disseminated by churches and originated from both ends of the county—in the north, where the German sects opposed the

Roman Catholic church, and in the south, where one preacher warned his congregation that if Kennedy won the election, Protestants would be crucified in Levittown shopping center. Michener and Welsh knew the anti-Catholic propaganda spelled disaster, but they were not in a position to fight it. Therefore, reflecting the opinions of Kennedy's national advisers, Michener advised his committee that

> Religious intolerance has already gained for the other side all the votes it's going to deliver and I don't think that anything you or I say will win back a single one of those votes, so don't worry about them. Argue with nobody. . . . A little more of this anti-Catholic smear stuff and a lot of uncommitted people . . . are going to vote for us. Such filth fights right back by itself.

In time, Michener expected the Catholic-haters to trip up the Republicans, but ultimately the smear campaign helped the GOP more than it aided the Democrats. In Bucks County alone, Michener figured that religious prejudice cost Kennedy 9,000 votes.

Michener was quick to admit that the religious issue, the party breach, and even his own amateur committee limited progress for Kennedy in Bucks County. However, Kennedy's national advisers considered Michener an asset to the campaign, and during the waning days of the election they asked him to join a group of celebrities and tour eight states to stump for the Democratic nominee.

Thus an impressive "galaxy of stars" gathered at the Washington airport one rainy morning to board a private plane bound for the Midwest, where Kennedy needed help. There was Angie Dickinson, blond and beautiful, and there was Harvard historian Arthur M. Schlesinger, Jr., whose two books, *The Politics of Upheaval* and *Kennedy or Nixon: Does It Make Any Difference,* were current best-sellers. Other members of the troupe included "Stan the Man" Musial, Jeff Chandler, the handsome movie star, and the Kennedy women, slim, beautiful, and effective campaigners. Greeting them was the dignified James A. Michener.

With Angie Dickinson curling her golden hair and calling Professor Schlesinger "Artie," this lively band descended upon Republican strongholds to give voters one last reason to support Kennedy. At every stop it was the same show. Chandler spoke first to break the tension, then Dickinson appeared—"absolutely delicious," said Michener—followed by Musial, "handsome as a young god," and Schlesinger, who appealed to the intellectuals. Michener talked about patriotism, and the Kennedy women "wound up the show with a bang." Everyone then climbed into convertibles for a fast ride to the airport and a hurried flight to the next town. It was as grueling a tour as could have been devised, Michener was certain, but how much it accomplished was anyone's guess.

By election day, Michener was confident but not cocky about Kennedy's chances. He toured the five Kennedy headquarters in Bucks County, and then awaited the election results. As soon as he heard that Connecticut had given Kennedy an astonishing majority of 90,000 votes, he knew the senator had won the presidency. The rest of that evening he drank beer with his friends and wound down a surprising campaign. Of course, he expected his candidate to lose Bucks County. Nixon won there by 10,000 votes, but that figure was only half the size of President Eisenhower's majority in 1956. Michener was pleased. By reversing the Republican trend in Bucks County, Michener's committee had bolstered up Senator Kennedy's majorities in the state's big cities, and the Democrats carried Pennsylvania, a key state in a presidential year. For the first time in weeks Michener went to bed without thinking of defeat.

The next morning, after analyzing the votes, Michener thought of himself as the Typhoid Mary of the Kennedy campaign: everywhere he had appeared, Kennedy had lost. "Of the eight states in which I campaigned with the barnstormers and the four where I spoke alone, every district . . . went Republican." Still, he thought the election was a "tremendous moral victory" over religious bigotry. It was then that he decided he had not really worked for John F. Kennedy, a man he had never gotten to know personally, but for himself, and for his vision of what the United States might one day become.

When the election was over, Michener began writing *Report of the County Chairman,* and by the end of December, with interruptions to speak at Swarthmore College and the University of Oregon, he completed the book. In Chapter One, he explained why he had written it:

> Since it seems likely that the 1960 Presidential election will long remain a matter of speculation for historians, I think it might be of interest to have a factual record of the reflections of a citizen who found himself involved in the campaign at the precinct level.

Many people expressed a dim view of this breezy memoir. Prior to publication, Johnny Welsh, to whom the book was dedicated, read the first several chapters and said they contained "many stretches of truth." Michener quickly grabbed the manuscript and told Welsh the story had to read that way to make it interesting. Some readers found the book a tedious recital of Michener's shrewd postures and rebuttals during the campaign. Too often Michener called attention to himself, as though *he* were the candidate. He had traveled everywhere in and out of his country; he better than anyone knew his county; his state. Twice he reminded readers that he had taught economics (as a social studies teacher). After a while, the text caused embarrassment if not disdain. Michener was always "gasping" at a comment by Senator Kennedy; "waiting in fear" for Vice-President Nixon to seize the victory; "bellowing" at straw votes; "guffawing" with Angie Dickinson; and whispering to himself each night late in the campaign, "Thank God we got through another day." At one point, while considering the value of the federally supported theater project in Colorado, which had inspired him as a young man, he estimated that his novels, and the plays and movies resulting from them, had produced at least $30 million in federal taxes. That, he stressed, was a handsome return to the government for a $100,000 investment. It was, but readers wondered if there was no end to Michener's ego. One critic in the *Saturday Review* summed up the views of many readers when he stated his hope that Michener had purged himself of compulsive narration and would now "sit down and write for us another engrossing novel."

No one understood, however, that Michener was serious about politics—which he called "the most honorable of professions"—and might never have written another novel if he had landed a satisfactory job in the Kennedy administration. It almost happened when he was asked to go to Korea as the new American ambassador, a generous offer in return for his role in the campaign. Michener considered it seriously, but because Mari was Japanese, he thought better of it; relations between the two nationalities had been tense since the Japanese occupation of Korea. He wondered, though, could he have Afghanistan, the wild country that excited him more than any other? Or if not Afghanistan, then Indonesia? No, both were already promised, but perhaps there was some other post for him. Michener thought not, and finally it was decided that he should serve as an "informal adviser," someone whom the administration could call upon for special favors. Meanwhile, he started thinking about another novel.

The year 1961 was the most uneventful of Michener's life, and yet circumstances made it the most personally gratifying. It began with a snowstorm that forced him and Mari to remain indoors for nearly a week, isolated from the rest of the world. Most of that year, except for a short trip to Spain and a vacation in London, he remained in Pipersville. He spent the time writing a novel and a few articles, and attending to personal matters: adding to his financial portfolio, considering several investments (including land in Hawaii and dressmaking in the Carolinas), transplanting trees on his property, planting a vegetable garden, and playing "red-hot" tennis with three neighbors. He also expanded his collection of modern art, a hobby that he and Mari had begun in the fifties, and he painted self-portraits and assembled a collage. He spoke at several universities where he was granted honorary degrees; he visited the statehouse in Harrisburg where the Pennsylvania House of Representatives honored him for "outstanding literary achievements . . . dedicated public service and exemplary citizenship"; and he posed under a covered bridge for an industrial development advertisement aimed at bringing families and business to Bucks County. Weekends he kept free for friends, especially the Silvermans, with whom he and Mari drove to Atlantic City for a stroll on the boardwalk. He wrote every day, too, if only long letters to fans who had enjoyed *Hawaii*.

This was a new, relaxed Michener. Suddenly it was as though he had discovered himself and liked what he found. He was fifty-four years old, healthy, financially secure, happily married, and at the top of the popular fiction market in the United States. He seemed to have surrendered the sense of urgency that had preceded him everywhere in the last ten years. He was willing to be more reflective now, and almost introspective about his life. His letters mirrored this change. Two women wrote to him wondering if he felt motivated or inhibited by an "aesthetic sense," and a man inquired about the meaning of success. To the women he replied,

> I feel that my life fifteen or twenty years from now should have added up to something reasonable, that it should have an inner logic of its own and that the essential characteristic of that logic would be derived from aesthetic principles.

At first he thought aesthetic sense inhibited him because its principal purpose was to block behavior that contradicted an otherwise acceptable aesthetic pattern, but as he thought more about it he decided that aesthetic quality actually motivated him, as religion did many others:

> I must say that I feel this drive most acutely and my whole judgment of success and failure in life is focussed upon or derives from the extent to which what I do conforms to this sense of a logical and permissable [sic] life. . . . I feel increasingly content to allow this aesthetic sense to guide me in a good deal of what I do.

As for the meaning of success, Michener replied that

> everybody has within him a capacity quotient consisting of his raw ability, his ambitions, his ideals, his hopes and his likelihood of accomplishing what he sets out to do . . . success is determined by the degree to which in his life one achieves the capacities with which he is endowed.

Income, fame, the judgment of his contemporaries, self-satisfaction with a job well done, were secondary concerns, Michener believed. Rising above his heredity made man the greatest success of all, he said.

It was in this reflective mood that Michener wrote "Report from the 'Frenzied Fifties'" for the *New York Times Magazine.* He had read a medical report about the "dreadful things" that happened to 50 percent of American executives and professional men as they passed from their forties into the "frenzied fifties." Hypochondria, alcoholism, suicide, even murder were among the maladies, and they seemingly struck men who had failed to confine their aspirations within the contours of their limitations. A man in his fifties, doctors reported, could no longer hide from himself that he had "squandered his reserves of emotional, intellectual and physical strength" and he was likely to feel depressed when he discovered that he lacked "what it takes to do everything he wants and needs to do."

In Michener's neighborhood, the "frenzied fifties syndrome" had struck three men who had surrendered to the "luxury of melancholy" and then committed suicide. A fourth was overtaken by hypochondria. Men in their fifties were lucky if they stumbled onto some means of maintaining their sanity, Michener reported in the *Times,* in a tone that underlined his fear.

Fortunately for himself, he continued, he had experienced a sobering moment on his forty-fourth birthday. He was out walking on a country road when suddenly the inner voice that had once convinced him he was a writer now told him, "Michener, you're as good a man today as you will ever be. From here on out everything is down hill." He never thought of himself in quite the same way after that walk. With each year he anticipated feeling less energetic, less physically capable, less desirous sexually, and knowing this he was prepared for the future. Not long after his birthday, he began taking better care of his health. He napped daily, he dieted and exercised, and he climbed into bed each night by eleven.

Still he worried about what doctors called climacteric because he had seen it destroy lives. He was sure his odds were greater for surviving the fifties than most men he knew, but he was not smug about it. "If in American society a man can live to age 65 without ending up in jail or the boobyhatch, he should consider himself a real success," he told the *Times Magazine*'s readers. He said he had about ten years to go, and while he was not sure he could make it, he planned to give it "the good old college try." This left him with goals, and perhaps as much as anything, goals determined the difference between men who survived their fifties and those who did not.

One of Michener's goals in 1961 lay in the area of politics. Therefore, that fall, when he was rested and looking fit, his color pink and youthful, his stamina intact, he was interested when the Bucks County Democratic Committee appealed to him to run for the U.S. Congress in 1962. Late in January of that year, a Philadelphia *Evening Bulletin* headline reported "Author Michener Reluctant on Bid to Run for Congress," but he was considering the offer seriously. Three objections gave him pause. First, the county Democrats still had not resolved their differences, and in a district where Democrats never won, he knew he could not win unless he had a united front on his side. Second, Lehigh County, which along with Bucks County composed the eighth district, had not expressed support for his candidacy. Third, and the most unyielding of the objections, Mari Michener had informed her husband that he was not to run under *any* circumstances.

If these three objections could be overturned, Michener explained, and if he thought his candidacy was for the good of the party, he might change his mind.

That said, Michener returned to his novel. Meanwhile, John C. Mulligan, who had succeeded an unhappy Johnny Welsh as party chairman, went looking for Michener supporters in Lehigh County. And State Democratic Chairman Otis B. Morse, intrigued by the thought of a best-selling American novelist running for Congress, promised to unite the local party, beginning with a truce between Mulligan and Welsh, who had been feuding since the 1960 campaign. Sometime before the spring primary, everyone hoped to negate Michener's objections and mount a James A. Michener campaign for Congress.

The writer who had said that men in their fifties must learn to face their limitations was about to contradict himself. Politics, in its roughest form, was not Jim Michener's game, however. If he had learned anything in Hawaii in 1959 and again in Bucks County in 1960, it should have been that he was not a politician. Furthermore, as a Democrat and a poor boy from Doylestown, he must have known that he could not win his district's seat for Congress. For twenty-five years, the eighth district had sent only Republicans to Congress.

But as always, idealism speaks first to the heart and then to the head, and in 1962, in spite of the obstacles, Michener dreamed about serving his home-town and his district in the U.S. capital. He envisioned himself proposing legislation, catering to his constituents, *caring* about issues and the posture of his country. "The big decisions today are made in politics," he said, and he wanted to be a part of that scene. In light of that, no one blamed him for trying, and while the Democratic leaders tackled his first two objections, he subtly approached the third.

From the first mention of a Michener for Congress campaign, Mari Michener had said no. Michener reported that when the local committee formally broached the topic, Mari warned the members that she would campaign for the Republicans if her husband's name appeared on the local ticket. And if by some chance he won the election and moved to Washington, she said she would return to Hawaii! The committee was impressed, but any member who knew the Micheners understood that if Jim Michener decided he wanted the nomination, then he was running for Congress, and Mari would support him as though he were kin to Adlai Stevenson. It happened exactly that way. Mari never rescinded her objection. "I talked against the campaign until I was blue in the face," she wrote to a friend in the spring of 1962, "but he made up his mind and we've been in it together." Once the local Democrats pledged their unified support, and industrial Lehigh County promised its support, Michener, with Mari next to him, announced his candidacy in mid-February.

In a speech that reminded some people of Richard M. Nixon talking to the Boy Scouts of America, James A. Michener became a candidate for the Eighty-eighth Congress. "As a boy I lived in dire poverty and was rescued by scholarships, fellowships and the generosity of our nation," he told a gather-ing of friends at a Bucks County restaurant. "I owe a debt to America which I want to repay. Serving my government is one method of repayment." Before he finished he added, "The odds against my victory are overwhelming, but this is going to be the fight of the century."

From the beginning of the campaign, Michener was out to convince voters that he could serve them better than his opponent, the incumbent seeking a fourth term. In spite of an almost dull record, the incumbent had been the district's overwhelming favorite for years. He was the hand-picked candidate of Boss Grundy and had previously served as Bucks County's district attorney. In 1956 in his district, he won more votes than Eisenhower did, and in 1960 he ran 27,000 votes ahead of the Democratic nominee. Congressman

Willard S. Curtin was secure in his job, and when he heard that Michener was challenging him, he said: "I think Jim Michener is a fine author. I'm sure that after this election is over he will continue to find many new literary fields to conquer. I look forward to reading his books for many years to come." Curtin had that haughty air that so frequently reduced humble opponents and carried lesser candidates to victory. Michener was no match for him, but no Democrat was.

Beginning in the spring of 1962, as promised, Jim Michener launched the "fight of the century." In the May primary, Curtin won 10,000 more votes than did Michener in Bucks County alone, but the numbers merely said to Michener that he must campaign more vigorously. He knew from his two previous campaigns that candidates won by going directly to the people, and in the back of his mind he could not help thinking that if Eisenhower, Rockefeller, or Nixon had spent just one more day in Philadelphia, Jack Kennedy might not have entered the White House in 1961. Thus, he devoted his energy to the election, and never worked harder in his life.

In April he wrote to a colleague,

> My new novel has, as you can well surmise, been postponed by the fact that I am dabbling in politics a bit more deeply than previously. I do not think that there is any great risk that literature will lose one of its minor lights because my opponent starts off with an advantage of 28,000 votes and this is pretty hard to overcome. On the other hand, Jack Kennedy's reaction to the steel business was one of the most exciting things anybody around here has seen for a long, long time and it is going to help all of us.

To another friend that month he wrote,

> The campaign goes well and the word is that I have a very good chance . . . but the local papers refuse to admit I'm around. They're really scared. My opponent is a real coward in every public matter, but the other day the local rags carried big editorials regarding one of the most fearless, forthright, noble men in Congress, and we want all of you to vote for him!

Privately Michener spoke harshly about his opponent, but publicly he ignored personalities in favor of issues. He believed in Medicare through Social Security; a $600 income tax exemption for parents of college students; a revision of the tax structure; federal aid to medical and dental schools; and the creation of a Department of Urban Affairs. Curtin's voting record showed that he tended to support the reactionary, militarily dependent policies of Barry Goldwater. But as an election strategy, he purposely avoided addressing important issues. When Michener said he supported the United Nations, for example, Curtin joked about Michener being a writer. When

Michener talked about education, Curtin made cracks about Michener writing plays, a reference to the author's collaboration to produce the Broadway show, *Tahiti*.

Out of frustration, Michener finally responded,

> I tell my opponent this, "You are not running for district attorney in some small western county. You are running for the Congress of the United States, one of the world's great deliberative bodies. Behave accordingly. Don't be a cheap comedian. Discuss the great issues that face our nation. I shall, because after November 6, I am going to be a Congressman, and I hold that office in great respect."

When the local press further incensed Michener by ignoring his candidacy, he turned to the national media for help. "Why I Am Running for Congress," by James A. Michener, appeared in the May 5, 1962, edition of the *Saturday Evening Post,* and the November issue of *Reader's Digest.* Michener informed the country that he was running for one of the 435 most important jobs in the United States, and that he was angry because people were asking him, "Why would a man like you get mixed up in politics?" He said it was insulting for anyone to think he was above politics, and from around the country wellwishers wrote to encourage him. Walter Winchell praised the article and said, "Michener will make patriotism popular again."

Locally, however, by reminding voters that he *was* a renowned author, the article hurt his candidacy more than it helped. With Curtin's prodding, the issue of the campaign suddenly became Michener's intentions. People began asking, "Is it true that you are committed to doing some writing early next year for Franco in Spain? Is it accurate that you will write four articles next year for *Reader's Digest* regardless of the outcome of the election? Could a millionaire who has spent much of his life abroad really be interested in serving the eighth district?"

Senator Hugh Scott answered that last question when he called Michener an "adventurer in politics" whose only interest was research for another book.

Ignoring the senator's remark, Michener wrote to a fan, "I am now engaged in a vigorous campaign for a seat in the United States Congress. I hope I win and if I do I will be turning my writing skills to use in another field."

In June, Michener informed a friend in Hawaii that he had cut Curtin's lead by 10,000 votes and "we feel confident that by the time the voting rolls around we will be practically even with the other side. . . . Prospects do look exciting." In August, a headline in the *New York Times* read, "Michener Buoyed in Congress Race." "'Splendid receptions everywhere' have convinced James A. Michener that the margin against him in his seven-day-a-week battle for a seat in Congress is growing smaller every day."

It was true that huge audiences followed Michener, and based on numbers Curtin might have been scared, but he probably noticed that these audiences were composed of Michener fans first, and voters second. People who had always pictured Michener pecking away at a typewriter on some remote Pacific island showed up at his speeches with two and three copies of his books tucked under their arms. They listened to him say, "I am Jim Mich-en-er, and I am running for Congress. I tend toward the liberal Democratic point of view, but in my private life I am more of a rock-ribbed individual than the most conservative Republican." Then, after polite applause, the people would crowd around him for what they had really come to get—his autograph. Michener was not flattered; he was worried. These people were more interested in his next novel than in his opinions about the state of the Union.

In October Drew Pearson tried to help Michener by reporting in his national newspaper column that Curtin—"the Pennsylvania Republican whose chief legislative accomplishment is introducing a bill to make the marigold the national flower"—used his congressional office to expand his law firm. While Curtin denied the charge, the local press made little mention of it.

Michener tried everything to attract attention, but nothing worked. Still, he never quit. He promised that if he won in 1962, he planned to run for reelection in 1964 "and as often thereafter as the people of this district will have me."

On election night Michener joined his party's faithful at headquarters in Doylestown, and while the mood there was raucous and optimistic early in the evening, it quickly died down as the results were posted. Johnny Welsh recalled what happened:

> We could see from the trend that Jim did not have a big enough margin to win. By 10 or 11 we were all glum, and Jim felt betrayed by the people. He thought he was going to win. He had attracted such big crowds, but when the votes were counted and he saw the results he was amazed that people said one thing and did another. They said they were going to elect him. He was very down-hearted. He had especially wanted to win his own home county.

The complete vote tally showed that Curtin had beat Michener by 17,800 votes, several thousand fewer than his earlier victories, but still a solid margin. Michener accepted the defeat gracefully, and in a letter to his "Fellow Democrats" he said, "I got clobbered but I have no regrets. . . . I'm sorry I lost, but I blame nobody but myself."

As Herman Silverman explained,

> Jim just did not come across. People did not trust him. They were afraid they could not control him. He was too independent and too rich and even the Democrats doubted him. He was not a good politician because he *didn't* need the job. He *didn't* belong in Congress. Jim is a born writer and a loner. He said he was going to

Washington for the rest of his life, but I didn't believe it. He would have been bored after two or three years.

Congressman Curtin interpreted the victory as the choice between a man who had lived continuously in the district and served it, and one who had a famous name but who spent little time in Bucks County.

Johnny Welsh agreed with that summation:

> Michener made no mistakes. He campaigned harder than any previous candidate in Bucks County. He spent $50,000 of his own money and he worked seven days a week. . . . But he could not convince people that he could give up his worldwide reputation to represent them in Congress.

Apparently, voters thought the House of Representatives was a step down for an accomplished writer. In Europe a writer could be an intellectual, a diplomat, or a cabinet minister, but in America a writer was a writer, much to Michener's disappointment. On November 7, whiling away the time, he assembled a collage, including in it a note of condolence from Vice-President and Mrs. Lyndon B. Johnson, and similar messages that arrived in his mail. Outside the county, people were shocked that he had lost, and Michener himself remained stunned. He recalled the line he had written in *Report of the County Chairman*. "How much easier it is to crash into political activity than to crash out again." He was a long time getting over the defeat, and for many weeks he visited his old friend Johnny Welsh to hash over what had gone wrong. But nothing had.

## CHAPTER FOURTEEN

# Writing Again

> I'm a man who works in a very exciting
> field. I have all the intellectual and social
> excitement and activity a man would
> want. . . . Why would a man give that
> up and go into politics? I can only say
> that I love politics. . . . If I am elected to
> Congress I will probably accomplish
> more there than I would in equal time as
> a novelist.
>
> JAMES A. MICHENER, 1962

JIM MICHENER'S GREATEST disappointment in life was his political defeat in 1962. Almost twenty years after the fact he wrote,

> It galls me that I lost. I would have tried to be a good Con-
> gressman. I would have found great fulfillment in such service,
> and I would have gladly surrendered my books if I could have
> been of real service in Washington . . . the 1962 run was not a flash
> in the pan.

Yet while Michener felt betrayed by the people of his district, his political intentions were not altogether clear in 1962. He had promised to work full-time as a congressman, but in the middle of his campaign he signed a contract, with an advance of $500,000, to write four novels for Random House. The first book, entitled *Mexico,* was due April 1, 1963, just five months after the election! Not a word of this had leaked publicly, but apparently Michener had doubted his chances for victory, and he had protected himself.

Once the election was history, he immediately returned to publishing to restore his "shaky family finances." Hobe Lewis at *Reader's Digest* was among several editors who sighed with relief when the votes were counted in Pennsylvania's eighth district and Michener had lost. Lewis sent his regrets on November 7, but he happily welcomed one of America's most popular writers back to the business. "It is grand to know you are going to be thinking in our terms again," he wrote to Michener, offering a choice of several assignments, including an in-depth piece about the Middle East, a tenth anniversary article about Korea, a series of articles about GIs who had remained in the South Pacific after the war, and an article about the Japanese emperor.

Michener chose the Middle East and arranged to join newspaper columnist Leonard Lyons and celebrity Harpo Marx on a junket to Israel in April 1963. First, however, he was scheduled to visit Vietnam on a fact-finding mission for the Kennedy administration, and then he had to deliver *Mexico* to Random House.

Albert Erskine must have been surprised to hear that instead of delivering *Mexico* in April, Michener was turning in a short, documentarylike novel about Afghanistan. Right after the 1962 campaign Michener had abandoned the book about Mexico and returned to an uncompleted manuscript about Afghanistan, the world's most inaccessible country, and a kingdom whose affection was sought by both America and Russia. He called the book *Caravans;* it was a story about one-fifth the length of *Hawaii* and every bit as readable. While the book's implied purpose is to underscore the importance of protecting the world from the communists, the plot centers on a young American diplomat's search for a romantic runaway woman who has decided to marry an Afghan. In the summer of 1963, *Caravans* sold briskly, but in the long run it was one of Michener's less popular titles, perhaps because it was not the sort of epic that his readers expected of him.

By the time *Caravans* appeared, Michener was working on another epic, this one set in the Middle East. He had not considered writing about Israel until the idea was pressed on him while he was exploring a castle along the shore of the Mediterranean during his April junket. As he later explained,

> While we were there, three men, including the mayor-to-be of Jerusalem, all got me in a corner and said that in view of *Hawaii,* I could write a similar book about Israel. I remember saying it should not be written by a gentile, that I was not capable of doing it—that they had good people in Israel who could do it—but I outlined the whole book for them.
>
> I then went home and got a letter from the mayor-to-be who said he could not find anyone to write the book. No one who was interested or capable. So I said I would do it if they would give me

bibliographic help. They did and [in May] I moved to Israel for a year of research.

This project was to become Michener's epic story of modern Israel, birthplace of three great religions: Islam, Judaism, and Christianity. The original outline of *The Source* focused on Istanbul and Islam, but during his research, Michener decided to frame the story within the story of an archaelogical dig; he transferred the setting to Israel and a fictional place called Makor, meaning "source."

News of Michener's arrival, with Mari, spread quickly throughout Israel, and—except for those scholars who said it was arrogant and improper for a popular American author to attempt such a book—readers throughout the world waited impatiently for the finished work. Members of the press followed Michener everywhere in Israel, hoping to get some inkling of his plot, but he refrained from saying anything more than "I'm writing about a mixed marriage, an American who comes to live in a kibbutz, a romance between an Arab and a Jew, and the irrigation of a field."

Traveling throughout Israel, Michener toted a typewriter, a translation of the Torah, and various interpretations of Jewish history and religion. Following the same work schedule that he had established in Hawaii, he arrived at his desk by 7:30 A.M., wrote until lunch time, napped in the afternoon, then visited libraries, museums, and schools and participated in numerous archaelogical trips to Galilee and other points including the famous Megiddo.

This time he stayed out of local politics, but he kept track of events at home, where he had pledged to help bring victory to the Democratic party in 1964. "You were the first to say what I've been fearing about the forthcoming election," he wrote to Herman Silverman in October. "If Goldwater runs, the wormy ones will really come creeping out of the woodwork, hoping that he might make it. It will be a hideous election." Typically, he added, "I suspect that if he did win he would make a fairly decent president and most of the crap he's talking about now would be forgotten. . . . But I for one could not stand aside and see Kennedy defeated. . . . I'll be home."

Working seven days a week, he planned to deliver *The Source* to Random House in January and spend the remainder of 1964 in the States campaigning for Kennedy. But when an assassin's bullet stopped the President in Dallas, Michener appeared to lose interest in everything political. The news about Kennedy reached Michener in Haifa. He and Mari had been invited by a Jewish family to their Friday seder, and after the meal, the host informed them that Kennedy had been shot. Although the radio was not supposed to be played after sundown on Fridays in Orthodox homes, the family made an exception in this instance. Tuning in to a station in Egypt, the Micheners learned that the President was dead. Mari began to cry, Michener later informed Jim Bishop, who wrote a book about the assassination. Returning to their apartment overlooking the Mediterranean, the Micheners sat for a while to digest the news. After Mari went to bed, Michener sat alone in the darkness for a long time. Along with most Americans, he had loved John Kennedy even without knowing him well. He had believed in Kennedy as a symbol of aspiration for America, and he was sure the President had been gunned down as part of a conspiracy to elect a conservative leader. With so many miles between him and home, he felt sick. Instead of returning to the States, he extended his stay abroad and buried his sorrow in his work. It seemed he hardly noticed a letter from Johnny Welsh asking him to run again for Congress from the eighth district. The Democratic leadership had decided Michener was the best man for the candidacy, and wanted him to think about running for the Senate in 1968. But Michener was not planning to be home.

*The Source* was all that mattered to him now. By April 1964, he had completed the first draft. Six weeks later, in Jerusalem, he finished a second draft. When Helen Strauss visited him, he gave her the only copy of the manuscript to carry back to New York, where she delivered it to Erskine and then began submitting it for a movie contract. She had sold *Caravans* to Hollywood for half a million dollars without even trying, she said, and she expected a windfall for *The Source*. "It should be fascinating," quipped one columnist upon hearing that *The Source* was nearly completed, "this novel written in Israel by a Doylestown Quaker married to a Nisei who is Presbyterian."

*Hawaii* numbered 937 pages; *The Source* fell a few pages short at 909, but *Hawaii* was less of a challenge both for the author and the reader. In this new book, no one could doubt Michener's appetite for research, his courage as a writer, and his overall power of assimilation in a field far removed from his previous work. Michener was proud of his accomplishment, and had every right to be.

The focal point of *The Source* is the fictional village of Makor, located not far from the Mediterranean port of Akko, and about fifteen miles northeast of Haifa. In 1964, John Cullinane, an Irish-American Catholic—note the convenience of his initials—Jemail Tabari, an Arab Mohammedan, and Ilan Eliav, an Israeli Jew, successfully excavate fifteen layers of civilization in the Tell Makor, "a barren elliptical mound . . . the patiently accumulated residue of one abandoned settlement after another."

The story begins with the family of Ur in 9831 Before the Common Era (BCE). Ur, his wife, and their offspring are the first humans to move out of the cave and into the plateau of Makor, where a hidden spring attracts habitation. Soon Ur's wife discovers a way to cultivate wild wheat, and shortly thereafter she persuades her family to give thanks to whatever force is responsible for protecting their crops and their lives. This is the beginning of an informal religion, and from it develops the workshop of a monolith god, and in turn the worship of many gods.

Gradually, Makor evolves into a city, complete with a wall, a temple, houses, and farms. Through the ages Michener traces the progression of modern theological ideas as they are manifested in his characters who work in modern Israel. Religion becomes formalized and often horribly brutal.

For continuity in what is a novel of many stories, Michener ingeniously relied on the excavation of 1964, returning to it between each exhaustive chapter of successive civilization. Around the archaeological "finds," amplified by scriptural and historical passages, the author juxtaposed the philosophies of the three religions practiced by his main characters. In this way, he presented his personal opinions about life, people, religion, and Israel, and provided sporadic relief to the reader. He analyzed such intricate problems as Arab-Israeli relations, marriage and divorce laws in Israel, the grievances of the Sephardi Jews, the state of mind of the American Jew vis-a-vis Israel, and the unrequited love of an American gentile for a worldly but nationalistic Israeli-born woman who is committed to marrying only a Jew.

It seemed unlikely that a gentile, particularly one who said his views about religion were irrelevant, could carry any depth of emotion into a book like *The Source*. But in his epic mind, Michener thought "Something was going on [in Israel] that the history books did not tell." Through religion, he saw an opportunity to reach millions of readers and to spread his message of brotherhood and goodwill among people. As a result, many critics said *The Source* was his most important contribution to literature.

With Erskine editing *The Source* in New York and Michener planning to return to the States in the fall to polish the manuscript, Hobe Lewis seized the opportunity to assign Michener several articles. Lewis met Michener in Istanbul to discuss the assignments, which included a series of travel pieces on places between Java and Japan. He also tried convincing Michener to begin researching the history of Christianity, for the book they had discussed earlier, but all of this overwhelmed Michener. He was tired. He appreciated Lewis's confidence, but he was no longer capable of chasing magazine articles around the globe and writing books, too. He told Lewis he could not possibly accept all the assignments the *Digest* planned for him, and furthermore, he had written everything he had to say about Asia, at least for the moment. He advised his editor to seek out younger writers who could offer the *Digest* a fresh perspective. He was, however, amenable to writing about the Hermitage in Russia, and accepting three or four other short assignments related to art and museums in Europe, but only if the *Digest* provided research assistance. In the meantime, he promised to think about the Christianity book.

By September, Michener completed "Hermitage: Russia's Fabulous Art Palace," and he conducted some research in Finland for another article before returning to the King David Hotel in Jerusalem where he made preparations for his trip home. Mari was waiting for him in Paris, and on the tenth of the month he wrote to tell her that he was about to forget Israel forever. "Two dreadful things have happened since we were last here," he teased. "Super Sol [a market] no longer carries figs and it has begun to distribute Green Stamps!" In an aside, he commented on the upcoming election in the States. "I'm satisfied that Johnson chose Humphrey but would have preferred McNamara. Have a real conservative-liberal party with the Demo's pulling over to their side the liberal Republicans" (with whom Michener was most comfortable). He hoped Mari was enjoying herself, and he told her to find "a shop that sells Smyrna figs."

The next day, Michener wrote to Elie Mizrachi, a researcher who had helped him with *The Source*. Ever since meeting Lewis in Istanbul, Michener had been thinking about the Christianity book, and with Mizrachi's assistance, perhaps as co-author, he planned to write the story in the next couple of years. He had "another big novel" in mind first, he told Mizrachi, but meanwhile he was interested in reading more about Jerusalem, Antioch, Alexandria, and Petra, and he wanted Mizrachi to collect the information.

He then sent an outline for the Christianity book to Lewis and said it "excites my imagination more each day I work on it." As Michener explained,

> The book is personal, travel, reflection but always archae-ologically correct and . . . biographically interesting. It's not like anything else I've done and I don't know what the final results will be, but I know it'll be interesting.

With his work completed and his plans laid, Michener returned to the States and spent the next several months honing *The Source* with Erskine and his copy editor, Bert Krantz. By now, Erskine had read the manuscript twice. In July he had written to Michener to compliment him:

> If I had a hat on, I would take it off. The construction is so clever and the balance of narrative material with other elements so neatly done that I believe readers who wouldn't have thought they would be interested, will be in spite of themselves. It is really a magnificent job.

When Michener arrived in New York, Erskine had earmarked dozens of questions that surfaced in his second reading of the manuscript. Several examples show the detail of Erskine's work:

> Crusader, both as adjective and as noun, is usually lower case in manuscript. Dictionary allows this, but I find a slight preference for a CAP C, since this indicates immediately that something specific rather than something general is intended.
> Manuscript uses frequently Lake Galilee, which may be all right. On maps, ancient and modern, it is given as Sea of Galilee.
> Gentile, noun and adjective, is both CAP and lower case in manuscript. It seems to me that a CAP is better.

Michener filled a notebook with these queries and challenges and returned to Bucks County to rewrite portions of the manuscript. He finished late in

February 1965, just months before publication. Reporting to Mizrachi, he said,

> The text reads well . . . heavy and at places awkward or too
> compressed, but very powerful. Working on it every waking hour
> as I do, I frequently feel that it is hopelessly complicated and that
> no one will take the trouble to read it. I hope I'm being only
> traditionally pessimistic at this stage.

He *was* being pessimistic. Published in June, *The Source* climbed immediately to number one on best-seller lists across the country and remained in that position for seventy weeks. The book sold a quarter of a million copies by the end of 1965, an average of seven thousand copies a week! It was the best-selling novel of the year, surpassing Bel Kaufman's popular book, *Up the Down Staircase,* which had dominated best-seller lists for twenty-four weeks. Michener could not have been more surprised: "although I knew that I was writing a book which would be read for many years, because there was nothing else like it, I did not think that the initial reception would be what it has been," he confided to a friend in Israel.

As expected, critics said *The Source* was difficult reading, shallow, uninspiring, and full of mediocrity. Helen Strauss had warned Michener that "the reviews are going to be . . . strange. *Time* and *Newsweek* are again reviewing how much money you're going to make, and I think this is also true of the *New York Times.*"

In Israel, there were no outbursts like those that occurred in Hawaii. In fact, the most thoughtful reviews of *The Source* came unexpectedly from Jewish scholars. In portions of the book they regretted the author's combination of fact and fiction, but they applauded him nonetheless for bringing Jewish history into the foreground. The harshest criticism was leveled by an Arab who said a "money hungry" Michener had been used by "the corrupting Jews." Incensed by the comments, Michener responded to the Arab in a three-page letter. "You have it all wrong," he told Omar Azouni, a member of the Palestine Arab Delegation. Instead of the Jews paying him to write about them, he had used the Jews to advance his own ideas, and in the process had spent more than $20,000 working in Israel. Furthermore, he wanted Azouni to know that before leaving Israel, he had contributed several thousand dollars to a project in Jerusaelm designed to promote creative enterprise between Jews and Arabs.

There was little time for arguing over *The Source,* however, for Michener was already involved in other projects. During the spring and summer of 1965 he returned to Spain to gather research for a *Digest* article about the Prado Museum. Then, all of a sudden it occurred to him that instead of writing another novel immediately, he wanted to write about the 900-day siege of Leningrad. He had never mentioned the topic before, but it was one of countless ideas that fascinated him, and in thinking about it one day he saw exactly how to approach the book. "Thus," he wrote to Lewis, " . . . I have a majestic problem before me. . . . I want to see Germany and America, the conflict between the commissar and the general, the contrasting claims of Holy Russia and the Communist Party." To write the story, he planned to spend a month in Manchester, England, another month in Germany, and the winter of 1966 in Leningrad. If the *Digest* shared his interest, he needed experts in the three countries to assist with his research. Lewis responded favorably and gave the *Digest's* pledge to pay for all research and travel expenses associated with the book.

In early September Michener arranged to move to Manchester. Before departing late in that month from Pipersville, he planned to tour the United States to raise money for the American–Israel Cultural Foundation. But at 5:00 A.M. on September 10, 1965, a Friday, a massive heart attack struck the fifty-eight-year-old author.

It had been bound to happen sooner or later. Michener's doctors had warned him in 1957 to slow down his pace of work and travel. He believed that hard work hurt no one, though, and he thought he was protecting himself by not smoking, not drinking, and exercising vigorously several times weekly. Unfortunately he overlooked the fact that he worked under constant stress and tension, some of it imposed by deadlines and itineraries, and much of it by his own desires, and on that September morning it overpowered him.

For most of 1966, under the care of his local physician and Boston heart specialist Dr. Paul Dudley White, who had successfully treated Presidents Eisenhower and Nixon, Michener was confined to bed rest in Pipersville. "I had a very near call," he wrote to friends in Spain, and "[I am] following the doctors' orders to the hilt." Still, he announced that he planned to move abroad in the spring, and, teasing Mari, he said he intended to climb Mount Everest just to prove he was well. His doctors, however, advised him not to travel before midyear, and instead to spend his days writing letters, reading, painting, and building hi-fi sets, a hobby he had begun years earlier.

Nothing was more tedious than recuperation for a man who had been so active, but through these various interests Michener remained in good spirits. He spent much of his time furthering his interests in art. Few people knew that Michener subsidized the publication of three volumes about Japanese art in the 1950s, and in 1962 he produced a fourth book, *The Modern Japanese Print,* donating all proceeds to the artists who had contributed to the volume. Ever since college, when he had posed as a steel worker to gain entrance to the exclusive Barnes collection in Merion, Pennsylvania, he had wanted to collect art. When they could, he and Mari, who adored the work of Hans Hofmann, channeled much of their spare income into a collection of Japanese prints, and a larger collection of modern American art that represented the accomplishments of painters who worked between 1900 and 1960.

In 1961, the Micheners had organized a foundation to support and circulate the American collection and to donate the Japanese prints to the Honolulu Academy of Arts. The Allentown Art Museum, not far from Michener's home, became caretaker for the American collection. In 1968, Michener donated the paintings, valued at $3 million, to the University of Texas, much to the annoyance of people in Bucks County.

While Michener was recuperating in 1966 he assembled a scrapbook about the foundation to show how it functioned during one year. He explained that he and Mari collected art as "a study in the creative process" to see how "the end product fitted into the artist's personal development and the intellectual history of our times." Many of the Micheners' paintings were of considerable importance. They were reproduced in textbooks and referred to in works of art history. Three of the most cherished pieces were Max Weber's *Repose 2,* 1950; Raymond Parker's *Number 15;* and John Mitchell's *Rock Bottom.* About half of the 250 paintings were abstract. Part of the collection frequently toured the United States, and the first comprehensive showing was organized in Allentown in 1963. (Ironically, due to some "bad press" by the Allentown newspaper during the previous year's congressional campaign, Michener refused to attend the black tie affair.)

As his recuperation progressed, Michener felt well enough in April to outline his next book and lay some plans for the research he intended to begin that summer. He had since abandoned the Leningrad project—it was too ambitious now—and decided instead to write a manuscript to be titled *A Year in Spain.* "It will be a series of twelve extended essays on twelve different cities in Spain," he informed his editors and several friends. "Taken together, [the essays] should convey to the reader a sense of what Spain—her history, her culture and her current mode of living—is like." He had already gathered most of the research during previous trips to Spain, and recently he had contacted two men who could help him collect the research that remained. He planned to complete the manuscript in 1966, for publication in 1967. At the end of June, with Dr. White's permission, he and Mari left for Madrid.

What words, what scenes, could Michener possibly write that had not already been contributed to the literature about Spain by Morton in *A Stranger in Spain,* or Brenan in *The Face of Spain,* or Hemingway in his essays and books? Michener thought there were none, or few. "I learned in my first week in Spain during 1932 everything that I was going to learn about the country," he confessed, but he proceeded to write about Spain because he was a writer with a passion for the country. "There's not much phoniness in Spain," he explained. "It's a rugged, to-hell-with-you-country—a first-rate country that makes little concession to the artist. That's why the artist has always liked it . . . certain men just vibrate to certain environments." Thus Michener was responding to Spain. By his own estimation he had become Spain's most frequent American visitor. Ever since he first journeyed into the country through the port of Burriana, he thought he belonged to Spain, like a Titian painting in the Prado Museum. This was "a man's country," he said— melodramatic, violent at times, wild and panoramic, full of mystics and heroes, chivalry, romance, and Don Quixotes, and Michener arrived one more time to honor it.

Upon arrival in Madrid, barely showing any signs of fatigue, he arranged a string of interviews about music, bullfighting, *zarzuela, quinillas,* and so forth, and examined each topic in terms of Spanish history and mores. What troubled Michener about Spain were several queries that triggered his decision to write a book about the country. Why was Spain not altogether a part of Europe? Why had the country reversed its earlier ethnic tolerance? Why did the Spanish people seek major solutions in dictatorial forms of government? Why were they prone to self-impoverishment? And how could the earthy Spaniard, so outgoing and in love with life—much like himself—be at the same time withdrawn and inwardly mystical?

For three months, accompanied by a researcher, a photographer, and a cautious Mari monitoring his health, Michener searched for answers between Madrid and Teruel, then Valencia and Pamplona (in time for the *feria),* across the top of Spain to Santiago de Compostela, to Galicia, Cordoba, and Badajoz. All the while he was writing, and by January, he had put together the rough draft of a twelve-chapter book, far from complete, and mailed it to Random House. "It certainly tells you more about Spain than you want to know," he informed Erskine. "I would describe it as a 19th century travel book in the same tradition, filled with very personal opinions . . . told in a very leisurely and narrative manner."

While Erskine edited the manuscript, Michener continued redrafting it, and when they were finished they sent the book for a review by Professor Kenneth Vanderford, who in Michener's opinion possessed "an encyclopedic knowledge of Spain." With a savage eye for detail, Vanderford picked apart the manuscript and sent Michener nearly seventy pages of single-spaced questions and objections. During three weeks in Spain, working with Vanderford from 8:00 A.M. until 11:00 P.M., with time out for a bullfight each afternoon, Michener then rewrote the manuscript a final time. In the end, he titled it *Iberia.*

He seemed never to have enjoyed writing more than during these three weeks with Vanderford; "we hacked away at every crazy idea we had," Michener explained in his private notes filed with his manuscript in the Library of Congress. "Some were brilliantly good . . . some were the result of [Vanderford's] phobia on this or that; and on several of the big ideas Van was glamorously wrong and delightfully pig-headed about it. On these points we argued bitterly, and sometimes for days."

One of their trivial arguments was about the translation of a Spanish name, and its repetition now demonstrates the depth of Michener's research, and the kind of fun he enjoyed while writing a book. He and Vanderford debated the translation of Santo dos Croques, the statue in Santiago. As Michener explained,

> Is this to be translated Saint of the bumps (who has bumps on his head) or Saint whom you bump (your head against his for good luck). What a hassle we had on that one, and how much fun

it was, arguing points of scholarship like this. Van held that the Spanish language was such that the construction "saint of the bumps" meant that the bumps must have belonged *to* the saint and were *of* his essence.

I argued pragmatically that people did bump their heads against the stone head, but I had to admit that Van did have an intellectual point. However, when I found the English translation of the Rosalia poem on the matter, I found that Os Santo dos Croques had been translated properly as "Saint they bump their heads against," and this quite staggered Van. Finally he developed that theory that the translator of the poem . . . and I were . . . horses' asses.

When *Iberia* was published in the spring of 1968, it received less fanfare than his blockbusters, *Hawaii* and *The Source,* but it outsold any of his previous nonfiction titles and rose high on best-seller lists everywhere, including Spain where it was originally banned. Once Spanish officials saw thousands of people arriving with the thick copy of *Iberia* tucked under their arms, they released their own censored version of the book. Curiously the purging occurred with Michener's permission, which he kept confidential, no doubt to avoid claims that he had sacrificed his book's vitality in order to sell more copies.

In mixed reviews, critics called *Iberia* "unfailingly interesting," a "mish-mash of history," and "a noble pilgrimage." Many who read the book as a travelogue decided it was neither coherent nor analytical, but a bubbling potpourri of Spain, informative in historical background, vividly descriptive and perceptive. Others said it was the ideal companion, stunning and memorable. Another group of reviewers questioned Michener's lenient attitude toward Franco's dictatorship, and his matter-of-fact reporting about the Spanish Civil War. They said Michener wrote of a country far removed from the Spain of Goya and Hemingway, and portrayed a bourgeois Spain, perfectly valid, but often irrelevant.

Surprisingly, reviewers found factual errors in the text. For example, Michener fondly described the fountains on the Avenido José Antonio, but from Madrid came a review that asked, *"What* fountains?" The reviewer pointed out several other errors and half-truths until he finally decided "it would be unkind to pursue the list further."

If Michener responded to this reviewer, as he did on occasions when double-guessings annoyed him, he left no evidence of it, but a Fairleigh Dickinson professor, who pointed out an error in *Iberia,* riled him into a fit of sarcasm. After explaining how he had eagerly anticipated reading *Iberia,* the professor said he stopped on page seventeen when Michener set Mont Blanc in Switzerland instead of its correct location in France. In fact, the professor pointed out, Mont Blanc was "part in France and part in Italy" and he continued that "if the rest of *Iberia* is as accurate as the statement about Mt. Blanc, the book should be set aside as far as my or my classes reading it."

Responding through his secretary, Michener said that upon reading the professor's letter he was so deeply disturbed he burst into tears. The secretary continued,

> You are probably aware that [Mr. Michener] has written over 4,000,000 words and this is the first error that anyone ever discovered in anything he has written, and it is humiliating. He especially wanted you to know that under no circumstances should you let any of your classes see *Iberia,* or for that matter *Hawaii* or *The Source* either, because if an error crept into *Iberia,* there is a possibility (not a very great one to be sure) that an error might have crept into the other two books.

The balance of Michener's fan mail about *Iberia,* and receipts from the sales, made it easier for him to ignore the critical comments. A typical letter arrived from a woman in the Midwest who said she was reading and rereading *Iberia* as "a reliving of my own experiences there." And a woman from New York explained in the spring of 1968 that she and thirty-nine traveling companions studied *Iberia* en route to Spain. As Michener's publisher pointed out, there was an endless market awaiting *Iberia.* In hardcover it sold more than 128,000 copies, a modest number compared to Michener's fiction, but satisfying nonetheless.

Michener had made a wise choice writing *Iberia* when he did. The book was timely, as well as convenient for his cautious return to publishing. But in 1967 he was ready for something more challenging, and undoubtedly another book of fiction. However, in the midst of reviving his plans to move abroad and begin the Leningrad novel, politics snagged his attention once more, if even halfheartedly.

Upon returning from Spain in the summer, he learned that Pennsylvanians had scheduled a Constitutional Convention to begin in December. It had been almost one hundred years since Pennsylvanians updated their constitution, and the charter badly needed twentieth-century revisions, to which Michener thought he could contribute. After some thought about what to do, he contacted Johnny Welsh and expressed interest in campaigning for election to the convention as Bucks County's Democratic representative. He doubted that he could win, but he looked forward to the opportunity.

Each Pennsylvania district could nominate four candidates, two Republicans and two Democrats, and send three representatives to the convention, thus ensuring minority representation. In the eighth district, the Democrats nominated Michener and Charlotte Gantz, an attorney who had participated in New York's civic reform movement under Mayor Fiorello La Guardia. Because Gantz had written a book about constitutional reform, she seemed destined, along with the eighth district's two Republican nominees, for a trip to Harrisburg, where the three-month convention would convene.

In this political bid, Michener resurrected little of the excitement that had marked his congressional campaign, but as he reported to Dr. White, "I tire much more quickly and I do not feel that I have the reserve that I once had." He campaigned slowly, preserving his energy for the novel he was about to undertake, and never denied that Gantz was the better candidate. In fact, he gave up just two weeks before the election. The more he thought about his novel, the more anxious he was to begin, and finally he departed Bucks County to do research in Bangkok and Singapore, and then Russia; "you don't earn many votes in Republican Bucks County from campaigning in Tashkent," he wrote to a friend in October. But how surprised he was when the news reached him that he had won, and not Gantz.

At last, Michener emerged politically victorious, and returning home immediately from abroad he planned to make the most of it. No one could convince him that the three-month job was going to be a disappointment. Hobe Lewis tried to persuade him to forget the convention and write a book about the Soviet Secret Service with "the full and exclusive story" supplied by the CIA, but Michener wanted to hear nothing of it. "What we do [in Harrisburg] will have great bearing on the commercial lives of everyone," he announced to the press in December. He was among the optimists who anticipated great reforms within the convention. He was so enthusiastic about the job that he and Mari, who had just recovered from a devastating bout with cancer, moved into a rented town house in Harrisburg, a ninety-minute drive from Bucks County. Most delegates commuted to the convention, and all of them went home for weekends, but not Michener. He wanted to live "right in the heart of things," he explained, where he could savor every moment of his political glory.

When the convention opened on December 1, no delegate was better informed than Michener. Upon his victory he began studying the experiences of similar conventions in New York, Michigan, Maryland, and Rhode Island, and he read *Miracle at Philadelphia* and *The Federalist Papers*. He was prepared to prevent his own convention from making any serious blunders.

On the opening day, the delegates, impressed by the best-selling author in their ranks, elected Michener secretary of the convention, a choice that pleased him to no end. "This will be the most important writing job I've ever done," he told newsmen who wondered if he was serious. He was. The position of secretary elevated Michener to the second most powerful post at the convention. He became an ex officio member of every committee, and it was his responsibility to assist the president in trying to "see that this great enterprise keeps moving ahead." Thus, he had the advantage of considering all proceedings before they reached the convention floor.

Each afternoon during the convention the Micheners opened their apartment for cocktails and socializing, and in this cigar-chomping, back-slapping environment, Michener made friends with every delegate. He enjoyed telling his new acquaintances that he loved politics and just dabbled in writing, but he was quick to point out how much money he was losing by working in

Harrisburg. He measured that loss as proof of his commitment and idealism. It was important, he said, to keep the democratic system at the operating level of citizenship. A strong government depended on the involvement of grass roots people, he said. Not a delegate disagreed with him, at least not in his living room, where the martinis flowed freely, and at his expense.

It was a major task, the rewriting of a state constitution, and on many occasions the delegates had to pass judgment in a few hours on matters that might have reasonably required weeks of thought and debate. As proposals were amended and withdrawn, even the most informed delegates, many of them members of the legislature, lost track of the proceedings. Some found the convention so confusing that they decided the best vote was for the status quo.

Michener fared well, but at times even he admitted he was in over his head. Due to his position as secretary, and his professional reputation, the delegates looked up to him, at least during the first two months of the convention. By the third month, his "end of the world speeches" had become melodramatic, complained one delegate. "Several times he predicted the convention would live or die on a certain vote and after a while the device bored the delegates. He also made more appeals to conscience than the average delegate cared to hear." By the convention's end, Michener's reputation had worn thin, and instead of James A. Michener the famous writer, he was simply Jim Michener, another delegate who had learned to accept defeat as a member of the liberal minority.

When the convention ended on February 29—nonpartisan politeness having given way several times to hot tempers—the delegates had a new document to place before the electorate in April. However, few of the delegates believed the convention had met its basic expectations. The most revolutionary changes concerned local government. Pennsylvanians were about to win broad powers to govern themselves. Heated debates had surrounded the issues of legislative apportionment, and in the end the delegates brought the state's constitution into alignment with the 1962 U.S. Supreme Court decision of "one man–one vote." Under the judiciary, the delegates approved some minor reforms, the most important of which provided a unified judicial system to be administered by the Supreme Court.

Michener left the convention "in a blaze of confused glory," he confessed to a friend in Hawaii, where preparations were under way for similar deliberations. "Those of us who wanted a fully modern document had to settle for somewhat less than we had hoped for." Disappointed, Michener flew to Venezuela on a cultural mission for the U.S. government.

When he returned from Venezuela, where rioting students burned down the library at Maracaibo three hours before he was scheduled to speak, sending him home bewildered about youth, he admitted he was depressed about the convention and politics in general. "I've found so many people who are so damned afraid of the twenty-first century," he protested in the *Saturday*

*Review.* "But I guess I really become frightened now and then myself. . . . We're becoming self-contained when we should be expanding."

He expressed deeper bewilderment to his longtime friend William Vitarelli, to whom he wrote, "if you think people are conservative in your branch of U.S. government you should have been with me [in Harrisburg]. I think I lost 103 straight votes in little things we were trying to do to bring the convention up-to-date. I felt I was with cave men, politically speaking."

One of the reforms Michener favored would have reduced the Pennsylvania legislature by at least one hundred members, but the numerous legislators participating as delegates in the convention defeated that measure. He had also fought for a better system of electing judges, but the conservatives who controlled the convention favored the old-fashioned system of promoting party hacks into judgeships. "This was how the average politician made his money," Michener surmised. "Hope to become a judge one day."

In spite of his unhappiness, which he kept private, Michener was not about to see the electorate reject his work. Overall, he thought the revised constitution was an improvement. "We got some great things through thanks to the work of some utterly splendid middle-of-the-road Republican business men whom I came to admire more than any of the other delegates," he informed Vitarelli. Like Michener, "they were intuitively conservative but they were ready to vote for the really good things that a state needs." As a result, when other delegates and members of the media clamored for defeat of the constitution, Michener resumed his "end of the world" speechmaking to warn voters that "failure to approve these Constitutional changes would be a dreadful mistake, and a lost opportunity." He urged people to vote yes for their own good and for the good of their children.

He was playing the politician, however, for he intended to vote against several of the reforms. Privately, he confessed he was dissatisfied with at least a fourth of the new charter. Nonetheless, Pennsylvania's voters approved the constitution on April 23. Following the vote, Michener addressed his fellow delegates by letter a final time:

> No delegate could have been more pleased than I was with the outcome of the voting . . . We have done a good job for Pennsylvania, one whose major merits will be appreciated only with the passing decades. . . . Hooray! Hooray! Hooray!

Long after the doubts and disenchantment had passed, Michener rated his three-month job in Harrisburg as "the most important political role" of his life. "I certainly am as proud of [the job] as I am of any book I've written," he said in 1973. During those three months in Harrisburg he lost some of his naiveté about politics. At last he realized what it meant to be a professional politician. "Some of them don't believe in anything and some of them bore me very much because they tend to be men without any dedication or conscience," he admitted. Still, he was filled with admiration for the politician who "gets kicked in the teeth year after year and comes back and finally sees his view prevail." By now, though, Michener probably realized he could not become one of them.

In the spring of 1968 there was much speculation in Bucks County about a James A. Michener campaign for Congress. "I'm sure he'd love to erase that blot on his record," his former campaign manager told the media. After Harrisburg, however, Michener appeared to have lost most of his desire to work in politics full-time. The professional politicians could depend on his cooperation and financial support. He was willing to represent the government abroad, as he did for the Kennedy and Nixon administrations; to write a campaign biography, as he did for Hubert Humphrey in 1968; to work on almost any important committee, as he did after President Nixon appointed him to the USIA and then to the nation's Bicentennial Committee; to testify before Congress, as he did against pornography, and in favor of NASA; and to campaign on the national and local levels. But otherwise he was out of politics for good. He never mounted another political campaign, even though he was tempted to run for the U.S. Senate in 1982.

At the end of the 1960s, Jim Michener was a man with one less option, but still many interests, and he decided to devote the remainder of his life to writing books.

## CHAPTER FIFTEEN

# Youth, Rebellion, and Michener

People ask me if I believe in young
people? It's silly not to. One day we're
going to turn the world over to them.
JAMES A. MICHENER, 1970

AFTER ENTERTAINING 163 delegates and staff for three months in Harrisburg, Michener explained he had "run up some pretty big bills," but they were almost insignificant compared to the income awaiting him in Bucks County. *Reader's Digest* had sent him nearly $100,000, including $10,000 for "GMRX: An Alternative to Movie Censorship," in which he "longed for the simpler days when Rhett Butler grabbed Scarlett O'Hara in his arms and carried her upstairs. That was real sex!" he said. And then there were semiannual royalty statements, the most startling of which was nearly $40,000 of income from *Tales of the South Pacific*. "It's amazing," said Michener. "Twenty-one years after it was published I get a check so large that I called my publisher to make sure it was right. And it was most welcome, too!" Most of the payment resulted not from the novel, but from performances of *South Pacific* by high school and community theater groups in the United States and abroad.

The Internal Revenue Service curtailed whatever pleasure Michener derived from these large figures in the late 1960s, however. "Michener Owes U.S. $390,103 in Taxes," announced an unwelcome headline in the *Philadelphia Inquirer* in December 1967. According to IRS officials, Michener owed the money against his $600,000 sale of *Hawaii* for motion picture and television adaptations. The press reported that Michener argued he received the income in 1959, and not 1960, the year for which the IRS listed its charges. Furthermore, the press reported that the money was paid to his corporation, Marjay Productions, Inc., as a bona fide capital contribution. He and Mari had formed Marjay in 1959 specifically to receive proceeds from sales of his television, radio, motion picture, and theatrical properties. Since *Hawaii,* Marjay's total income was $1.7 million, and the company paid Michener $60,000 annually. Marjay had contracted with 20th Century Fox for "Adventures in Paradise," which grossed $13 million in the early 1960s. The company sold *Caravans* to Metro-Goldwyn-Mayer for half a million dollars, and *The Source* to the Book of the Month Club for a $60,000 minimum and paperback rights for a $700,000 minimum. The IRS alleged that Michener used Marjay as an unauthorized conduit and that instead of a reported income totaling $32,214 in 1960, he had actually earned $496,338, including $7,314 in unsubstantiated business deductions. For several years Michener's representatives fought the claim; the final disposition was never publicized.

The IRS was the least of Michener's worries in the late 1960s. So much was happening so fast across America that like most people he stumbled trying to keep in step with the country. There was much to be troubled about—race relations, inflation, assassinations, the decay of the inner cities, the alienation of youth—and the overwhelming problem of the painful and seemingly endless war in Southeast Asia.

Everyone knew that the war being fought six thousand miles away was destroying the United States at home. From the outset, most of America's intellectual community opposed involvement in South Vietnam, but Michener supported Washington's official position. "President Eisenhower was dead right to give support short of military intervention," he claimed, and later added, "almost without qualification I support President Johnson and the Administration [in Vietnam]." Once Johnson committed troops to Southeast Asia, Michener expected the war to end "quietly and painlessly."

Because he was a Quaker, a writer, and a liberal, Michener's defense of the war confused many people. On numerous occasions assorted professors, pacifists, and "peaceniks" asked him to denounce the U.S. actions in Vietnam, but emphatically, though politely, Michener turned his back on the anti–Vietnam War movement. Basing his position on twenty years' experience in Asia, he subscribed to the domino theory. He warned that if the communists won South Vietnam, in time they would take all of Southeast Asia, Australia, and New Zealand. He thought it "craven" for the United States even to consider withdrawing from the war, and when 534 writers, led by Catherine Drinker Bowen, Joseph Heller, and John Hersey, petitioned the

White House for a cease-fire and a halt to the bombing of North Vietnam in 1968, Michener refused to join them.

Not until 1970—when the buildup of American personnel in Vietnam became greater than what seemed warranted, and the majority of people at home opposed the war—did Michener reverse his opinion and support an immediate withdrawal. He still insisted the war was necessary, however. "Every justification for our being there in the days of Eisenhower still exists," he maintained in *The Quality of Life,* a short book commissioned in 1969 by a Philadelphia bank for its annual report to stockholders. America's mistake was entering a full-scale war without declaring war. By doing so, we "neither spelled out our moral position nor enlisted public support, and every evil consequence that has followed grew out of those first wrong steps," he explained. He suggested that we "get out as quickly as possible and start repairing our fences here at home." But by then the damage had been done. American soldiers had died fighting an undeclared war, and at Kent State University in Ohio and Jackson State College in Mississippi, students had died protesting that war. Across the country people were dismayed and angry.

In the mid-1960s Michener knew America was in trouble socially and politically. An alarming despair was spreading, even though more people than ever before enjoyed the dream of owning a home in the suburbs, a second car, a color TV, a swimming pool. At the same time, the poor grew angry because they had so little, and young people from the middle class were outraged because they had so much. Both were susceptible to anti-American points of view.

Politically, it looked as though a shadow had begun stretching across the country. Traditional party lines were nearly obliterated. Late in the decade the President emerged as the champion of the military-industrial-labor complex, the old guard GOP, and had forsaken the progressive, liberal, intellectual coalition. The deception left moderate Democrats stranded and leaderless to grapple with an impossible contradiction. America's age of consensus was over, and men and women like Michener suffered through a disturbing period of pondering America's soul.

While searching for answers during this intense social revolution, Michener served as a stabilizing force among Middle Americans. The nation was being held immobile by "our own fears and diffidence," he told students at Penn State University, and "unless we can encourage a new spirit, I am afraid the old spirit will turn rancid." Students thought it already had.

Michener believed that America's discontent stemmed from an erosion of traditional values, and in his attempt to help make sense of the country he wrote "The Revolution in Middle-Class Values" for the *New York Times Magazine* in 1968. (The essay was later published in book form as *America vs. America: The Revolution in Middle-Class Values.*) The thesis of Michener's thoughtful essay was a re-validation of the Protestant ethic. "Cleansed a bit,"

he advised, the useful old values—work, morals, education, ethics, competence, responsibility, and optimism—"ought to prove valuable for generations to come."

In one hurrah for revolution, Michener admonished his own generation
for society's "fundamental cause of disaffection": the contradiction "between
what the middle class says it believes and what it does." All of society's
appurtenances, especially television, "indoctrinate us with the creed of
accumulation," he explained, "but we discover that this brings neither happiness nor stability." He stressed that the revolt of youth against these false
values was all to the good.

However, even while admitting this was "dreadfully middle-class," he
asked young people to work within the system. He wanted to support the
younger generation, but not at the expense of his generation's meaningful
values. He could not accept youth's "new life style" because it was based on
"unproved ideas" and was predisposed toward dictatorship. Later, writing
about this same topic in the *Reader's Digest,* he guessed that 90 percent of
Americans subscribed to the "old life style" and that given a fair test, it was
flexible enough to accommodate everyone.

Young people hardly thought of Michener as a friend for having said this,
but a percentage of his own generation sided with him. In countless letters
following the publication of his essays in the *Times* and *Reader's Digest,*
parents wrote to Michener and pleaded with him to "talk sense" to their
children.

Michener thought the country needed a leader to "talk sense" to everyone.
At least twice during his lifetime, in periods of crisis, Americans had elected a
charismatic President to bail out the country. Now he looked for another
Roosevelt or Kennedy. Young people responded favorably to Senator Eugene
McCarthy, and Michener preferred him, too, but he disagreed with the
senator on one subject: the war in Vietnam. McCarthy opposed that war, so
Michener pledged his support to Hubert H. Humphrey, the loquacious and
ebullient vice-president. As proof of his support he wrote "Hubert H.
Humphrey: Portrait of a President" for the Democratic National Commit-
tee's *Fact Book*. Nevertheless, Michener seemed to doubt that Humphrey
could unite the nation. As the country's preference for a change of regimes in
Washington became obvious, Michener's enthusiasm for his party's candidate
dimmed. Instead of campaigning vigorously on the national level, he devoted
most of his time to local and state politics. He served as chairman of the
Committee to Reelect Senator Joe Clark in Pennsylvania, and co-chairman of
Pennsylvania's Committee for Legislative Modernization.

All during the presidential campaign Michener was distracted by Governor George Wallace's power play to single-handedly select the next President
of the United States. Wallace knew he had a slim chance of winning the White
House by a popular vote, but if he could snag the electoral votes needed to
force the election in the Electoral College, he planned to bargain and throw
the election to whichever party offered him the best deal. The plan was legal,

and frightening in its possible consequences, and it kept Michener awake nights scheming to beat Wallace at his own game.

If Nixon failed to capture the required 270 electoral votes, which he was expected to win, and the election then became vulnerable to Wallace's manipulation, Michener had prepared an appeal to the Electoral College to give the election to either Nixon or Humphrey in spite of Wallace. Most likely, this would have occurred without Michener's interference, but the drama underscored his desire to be involved in national politics. It also provided an opportunity to write about a topic of interest to him. After the election, which left Wallace empty-handed, Michener served in Pennsylvania's Electoral College, and then wrote *Presidential Lottery,* a short attack on America's electoral system. The book is an unusual mixture of history, personal reminiscence, local color, and politics, and the author makes his point that the antiquated Electoral College had once served a purpose but should now be abolished. "This time we were lucky," he wrote, referring to the failure of Wallace's power play. "Next time we might not be. Next time we could wreck our country."

*Presidential Lottery* appeared with little notice, in spite of Michener's name. "People don't care enough until something happens," he said, angry that his book's message had been ignored. "Refusal to revise the Electoral College system is major proof of our stupidity . . . sometime within this century [it will] explode with dire consequences," he predicted. "In retrospect one day they'll remember Michener was right."

As concerned as he was about the electoral process, the great social problems on America's horizon haunted Michener in the late 1960s and led him in another direction by the time *Presidential Lottery* appeared in bookstores. One of the problems worrying him most was the alienation of young people. The issue had never been made more shocking to him than when he had met three Australian girls on tour in Europe while he was writing *Iberia.*

> They were scarred by the knowledge that in Tangiers they had come upon an English girl who was in dreadful shape [suffering from hepatitis]. They asked me to take up a collection to fly her back to England. In Amsterdam or Antwerp or Copenhagen, there is always some American girl in the gutter, and the community by and large rallies around, gets her some money, and sends her home. . . . Now we were going to do this. But when the Australian girls and I got to Tangiers, [the English girl] was already dead.

Returning to America, where there was an increasing number of deaths by "drugs and disillusion," Michener could not forget the English girl's tragedy. He expected someone to write a book explaining to his generation what malady afflicted these youth who so stubbornly and foolishly destroyed their lives, but no such book appeared. Everywhere in the late sixties parents sought answers, and many searched for their runaway children. Intrigued by both problems, Michener returned to Spain in March 1969 to write the book himself.

With drugs flowing in and out of Spain, Torremolinos had become a Mediterranean haven for European and American dropouts, a trap for debauchery and death. In this international city Michener rented an apartment to research and write a book that he first called *The Wanderers,* and later retitled *The Drifters.* He arrived with only a sketchy outline in mind, and for several weeks he gathered his thoughts among the young people who hung out in the bars of Torremolinos. At sixty-two, with thin gray hair cropped short and an air of detachment, he looked like an American tourist, but when the young people heard that the author of *Iberia* was about to research a book about *them,* they welcomed him into their private circles with beer, which he accepted, and marijuana, which he refused, although he had experimented with the drug once or twice. Each time he was introduced to a different group he fielded a litany of questions about *Iberia,* which was popular among travelers of all ages, and then gradually turned the conversation to politics or drugs or sex or war or music or parents. For hours each day, and often in his apartment at night, he listened to the young people talk about their revolution. By April he had outlined his plot and characters and sent the proposal to Erskine in New York.

Six sensitive youngsters under the age of twenty-one, all of them running away from another part of the world, dominate the novel. They include a draft evader from California, the daughter of a Norwegian functionary, a folksinger from a proper Boston family, an Israeli hero of the Six Day War, a self-indulgent British girl in search of thrills, and a virile, intelligent American black on the lam from the Philadelphia police.

The hopes and dreams of these six bring them together in Torremolinos where their varied backgrounds provide bountiful discussions about the six-day Israeli-Arab war, black anti-Semitism, ecology, occultism, *Les Enfants du Paradis,* Bob Dylan, the 1968 Democratic convention, slave trade, Janis Joplin, African game sanctuaries, Greek shipowners, Islam, the drug culture, the assassination of Bobby Kennedy, television, *King Kong* and Muesli, a Swiss breakfast food. They become companions—a couple of them are lovers—and travel from one exotic spot to the next throughout Europe. Their mode of transportation is a yellow Volkswagen "pop top." With countless side trips along the way, they drift to Portugal, to Mozambique, to Marrakech. They arrive in Pamplona in time for the San Fermín *feria.*

Two adults complete the cast of characters. One is Harvey Halt—forty-four, divorced, at odds with the world, living on memories of World War II and Korea—who finds himself working abroad installing radar equipment at airfields. He meets the six young characters but is at a loss to understand them. The second adult is the story's narrator. At sixty-one, George Fairbanks, international investor, becomes a sort of global den father. Desperately clinging to yesteryear, he keeps an open mind and feels "the need of comprehending . . . the youth of this age." He is the adult David Harper, the alter ego of James Michener.

No real problems were to be solved in *The Drifters,* but Michener aimed his message at his readers in Middle America. The message read, The revolution will not go away by itself. It will sweep on, gathering its own momentum, and you must try to understand it.

"Wow," Erskine responded to the outline. "You've cut out quite a piece of work for yourself . . . don't stop working; it's too nice to know you're back at it."

Michener's research continued through the spring and summer, and the highlight, notwithstanding Mari's objection, was a daring run with the bulls at Pamplona, where he was almost gored. A free-lance photographer captured the near-fatal scene for *Esquire,* which then commissioned Michener to write about the escapade. In explaining why he ran, Michener said

> I have always had a commitment to knowing exactly what I was writing about, and when the time came to deal with Pamplona in a novel, I discovered what I had often observed before: knowing a subject from the nonfiction point of view bears little relation to knowing it well enough to use it in fiction. I knew Pamplona, but not as a novelist.

In the fall and winter, allowing interruptions for several *Digest* articles, Michener wrote *The Drifters.* He returned to Pipersville with the novel in rough draft, and while polishing the manuscript that spring, preparing it for early fall publication, a blast of gunfire in Kent, Ohio, on May 4 disrupted his schedule. In the most senseless tragedy ever to occur on an American campus, the social revolution exploded that day at Kent State University. National Guardsmen, determined to squelch an anti-war protest, had turned on a group of demonstrators, leveled their rifles, and fired. They mortally wounded four students and injured several others. What struck Michener was that any one of the young protesters could have been a character in his new novel, and in the aftermath of the tragedy he wanted to know more about how it had happened. Oddly enough, Hobe Lewis called one morning and asked Michener to explain the Kent State debacle in a book to be co-published by Random House and the Reader's Digest Press.

Once again, Michener was attracted to the role of reporter-at-large. It was his duty to explain Kent State, he said, because he knew "the structure [of the revolution] as well as anybody of my age could. I was an expert at it as a result of having worked at the novel." That summer, therefore, he moved to Ohio where a team of *Digest* researchers had been investigating the story since early May.

The news of rioting, and then death, at Kent State University, spread rapidly throughout the world. On Friday, May 1, the first warm weekend night after a long, cold winter, a larger than normal group of young people gathered downtown in the bar district of the college town. It was as though someone had organized a celebration for the arrival of spring. The atmosphere was noisy and good-natured, although many angry words were spoken about Nixon and Cambodia and bombs. Tensions mounted, and as sometimes happens in a college town where cheap beer flows almost endlessly, the crowd turned rough and abusive. Someone set off a string of firecrackers; a group of rowdies stopped traffic and rocked an old sedan with an elderly man and his wife inside; others emptied trash cans in the middle of the street and set the contents afire; and still others threw beer bottles at storefronts and began the most destructive act of malicious mischief ever to occur in the history of this typical middle-class community. Police arrived in riot gear to end the disruption by forcing the crowd toward the campus, which was within walking distance of town. Along the way, dissidents stormed several more storefronts and caused considerable damage, which in turn agitated the city's merchants and residents. Before the night was over, police used teargas and arrested many of the troublemakers.

On Saturday night, in what was clearly an anti-war protest, dissidents fire-bombed the campus ROTC building and watched it burn to the ground in a glorious blaze. On Sunday, May 3, the governor sent National Guardsmen to restore order on the campus and in the town, but that night several hundred protesters started agitating again. Chanting anti-war slogans, the protesters headed downtown until they were stopped at the edge of the campus by a group of city police, strengthened by a contingent of National Guardsmen, with bayonets affixed to their rifles. A second company of Guardsmen lined up behind the demonstrators, but permitted them to move back onto the campus. For the next ninety minutes confusion reigned in an eerie scene. A Guard helicopter illuminated the night with a searchlight from the sky. Fifty or so young people sat in the street; others taunted the Guardsmen, who answered in kind. Soon, three self-appointed leaders of the protest announced that the crowd would not disperse until the president of the university and the mayor of the city appeared to hear their demands, which were being hastily written on a sheet of paper. First among the demands was removal of the ROTC program from the campus; second, total amnesty for all persons charged with burning the ROTC building the night before. Few protesters seemed to know they were violating a curfew, although this knowledge may have made no difference. At one point a young protester led the crowd to believe that the president and the mayor were on their way to meet with the demonstrators, but this was never true. Suddenly, around 11:00 P.M. the scene exploded when the two sides clashed. The Guard fired teargas into the crowd, which responded by throwing a barrage of rocks and bottles. Using gun butts and bayonets to clear their way, the Guardsmen marched across the campus, rounded up many of the protesters, and hauled them off to jail. The weekend fling was over.

On Monday morning the university awoke to its normal peace and quiet, although the presence of the Guard on campus prolonged the tensions of the night before. Shortly before noon, just as morning classes were ending, protesters, perhaps not all of whom were students, began ringing the campus victory bell, which was housed at the bottom of "Blanket Hill" at the edge of the Commons. Again, it was not generally known that this act defied the law. A state of emergency had been declared in Kent, and that presumably meant that all demonstrations were banned. The din of the bell attracted a hundred or so young people who were greeted with more anti-war, anti-Nixon, anti–National Guard chants. Across the Commons, in full view of the bell and with gas masks at hand, Guardsmen watched a gathering that they were certain was illegal. Behind the troops lay the smoldering ruins of the ROTC building. For a while protesters merely chanted; then the Guard ordered the swelling crowd to disperse. When the dissidents held their ground and chanted louder, the Guard launched several canisters of teargas and swept across the Commons toward the bell. There were now several hundred to a thousand demonstrators and two to three thousand more people watching from the top of "Blanket Hill" outside Taylor Hall, home of the campus newspaper and the School of Journalism. One hundred five Guardsmen, some of them Kent State students, and all of them tense and tired after spending a weekend in the campus gymnasium, intended to break up what a week before would have been considered just another campus demonstration.

Foolishly and fearlessly the protesters jeered at the Guard and rang the victory bell in defiance. Some picked up spent teargas canisters and lobbed them back at the troops. As the Guardsmen approached the bell, bayonets extended at chest level and gas masks covering their faces, the demonstrators dispersed in two directions around Taylor Hall. The Guard split its ranks and pursued the dissidents in hope of trapping them in front of Taylor Hall where arrests could be made, but before this happened, one contingent of the Guard did something so foolish that it could not be satisfactorily explained. Supposedly under orders, the Guardsmen walked onto a partly fenced athletic field and trapped themselves in one corner. Angry agitators closed off the contingent's only escape path, but bayonets and rifles kept them at a safe distance. More embarrassed than endangered, seventeen Guardsmen knelt on one knee and seemed ready to fire into the crowd, which had come prepared with rocks and other objects. If the Guardsmen had fired, they would have hit at least twenty-two demonstrators. They did not fire at this point, but one of them discharged a revolver into the air, as a show of force, perhaps, and the rest of the men backed away. Several Guardsmen huddled for a moment— scared and confused no doubt—and then the contingent retreated toward the front of Taylor Hall, with the dissidents fanning out to give them space. Whatever was discussed in that huddle might have explained what was to occur a few moments later when these men reached the Pagoda outside Taylor Hall. It was then that several Guardsmen wheeled around; some aimed their rifles and fired. There was a single shot, a period of silence, a prolonged fusillade lasting about eight seconds, more silence, and then two final pops. Twenty-eight Guardsmen fired, and several dozen young people hit the ground, thirteen of them wounded, four of them dead almost instantly. One of the dead had been innocently crossing the campus between classes and had not participated in the demonstration.

Why did the Guardsmen fire? When Michener arrived on the scene this remained the mystery of Kent State. Investigators had already ruled out the possibility that a sniper had fired the first shot. They now believed that one of three situations had developed. One possibility was that the Guardsmen panicked and fired mindlessly into the crowd. The second possibility was that while they huddled on the athletic field they conspired to shoot the agitators. The third possibility was that someone ordered the Guard to open fire, but this seemed unlikely.

That summer and into the fall, assisted by two *Digest* employees and a half-dozen student interviewers hired through Kent's School of Journalism, Michener researched and wrote the book concurrently. Using a motel room as his headquarters, he interviewed dozens of people—students and professors, business executives and housewives—all with facts to offer or opinions to share. Some arrived late at night so as not to be seen by local authorities. Others preferred that Michener visit them at the university or at their homes. The Guardsmen involved in the shootings spurned his attempts to interview them. "The Guard has imposed almost a blood oath of secrecy," he informed Andrew Jones, a *Digest* senior editor who had collected the preliminary research for the project. Jones had arranged for Michener to interview several Guard officers, but none of the men who had fired a rifle. By this time, the Guardsmen feared the possibility of civil suits and criminal proceedings. I. F. Stone and others, who had written what Jones called "quickie books" about Kent, had already accused the Guardsmen of murder.

Few people told Michener anything that was not also discovered by the federal commission investigating the shootings, or by the FBI, whose agents made themselves unpopular, tracking students across the country to ask questions about the May riots. Michener kept hoping that one of the Guardsmen would come forward to unravel the mystery, but none did. The most startling bit of information came to Michener one afternoon from a young man who said he had heard an order for the Guard to fire and that he could identify the officer who gave the order. Subtly, being careful not to scare the interviewee by pointing to the significance of his testimony, Michener probed for more details. But under pressure the informant backed off, taking with him Michener's hope of solving the mystery. Later, not knowing how to assess the interview, and having decided not to use the information in his book, Michener gave the young man's name to the Justice Department for further investigation.

Contrary to what people believed, Michener did not share his research with the FBI during his investigation. He tried, but was turned away. "The FBI did not want to get mixed up with a guy like me . . . and this inhibited us a bit," Michener later explained. However, some people thought Michener was a front man for the Nixon administration or the FBI, and because of this they avoided him. Many others, noting that he was writing for the conservative *Reader's Digest,* surmised that he could not write an accurate report of what had happened at Kent State. Michener, they argued, was a novelist who did not even take notes during an interview. Cynics cracked that he had come to Kent to exploit a tragedy. "For him and the *Digest,* it's just another bestseller," they remarked.

Very few people knew that before Michener set foot in Kent he had donated $100,000 to the university, twice the amount he expected to earn from the book (his advance was $31,500). He gave the money to protect himself from the accusation that he was taking advantage of a tragedy. People also did not know that Michener prided himself on a "Germanic memory"; like Truman Capote, he rarely made notes during interviews. He believed in the journalist's theory that notetaking frightened sources; the journalist with total recall was smarter to wait until after the interview to record what had been said. This explains why Michener conducted interviews in his motel room. Once the interviewee left him alone, he sat at his typewriter and "unloaded the interview verbatim." Michener seemed never to doubt his memory; since his finished report contained factual errors, however, critics said his work was suspect.

There were traces of Michener the novelist at work in Kent, and it became obvious in March 1971, when the *Reader's Digest* released the first installment of his two-part report, later published in book form as *Kent State—What Happened and Why.* Michener implied that Kent State was a hotbed of revolutionary activity, full of young radicals working toward the destruction of the status quo. *He guessed* that 80 percent of the student body had tried marijuana. Every so often a nationally known revolutionary—Mark Rudd, Bernardine Dohrn, or Weatherman Terry Robbins—passed through town to stir up trouble. Michener wrote "for the first time in its history the stolid university rang to cries of student demonstrations." His report lent support to those who blamed Kent's students for everything that happened on May 4.

In truth, few of Kent's 21,000 students had attended the sporadic political rallies sponsored by the Students for a Democratic Society (SDS) and similar organizations. As Michener himself pointed out, Kent was a conservative university, known by some as Apathy U. Yippie Jerry Rubin once attracted two thousand students to a peaceable rally, but he was an exception. No more than fifty students gathered to hear Mark Rudd. Kent State students kept abreast of current events and protested bitterly against the war, but they were less interested in revolution than they were in the opposite sex, weekends, sports, part-time jobs, and even their studies.

Michener suggested that the whole Kent incident had been planned and inspired by outside agitators, but both the FBI and the President's Commission on Campus Unrest, which had conducted extensive hearings had attributed the "primary cause" of the weekend eruptions to President Nixon's announcement that he had ordered the bombing of Cambodia. "The reaction of some Kent State University students and faculty members was immediate," said the FBI. Michener reported it this way:

> The great majority saw the disturbance as merely another spring frolic and were activated by nothing more serious than a desire for fun. There was, however, a hard-core of radical activists — abetted by a few revolutionaries, not necessarily from the university—who grasped at the disturbance as a means of advancing their own well-defined aims. President Nixon's Cambodian speech had minimal effect upon the first group, but a profound one upon the radicals, who would have approved nothing he proposed.

Numerous other misleading or mistaken notions appeared in the report. Two Kent State speech professors tested Michener's work for accuracy by distributing two hundred questionnaires to people named or quoted in the book. The conclusion was that *Kent State—What Happened and Why* contained "inexcusable errors of form and substance. . . . The vast majority of the inaccuracies consisted of Michener having people describe things they did not witness, of Michener having them use language which is not characteristic of them, and of Michener embellishing and or distorting what people did say or do."

Most of all, readers in Kent objected to Michener's conclusions. As anyone who knew Michener's politics might have guessed, he explained the events of May 4 as an accident, partly the result of the current clash between old and new life-styles in America. It was "deplorable and tragic," he said, although "some kind of major incident had become inevitable. . . . That it happened at Kent State was pure accident, but the confrontation was not." Who was to blame? Conveniently, Michener blamed everyone—the Guardsmen, students, demonstrators, faculty, college administrators, the community, local police authorities, and the governor. In a nutshell, American society was responsible for the tragedy at Kent State.

If Michener had arrived only at these conclusions, he might have been spared the wrath of many readers. Several of his other conclusions prompted doubts about the balance of his report, and the implications of these conclusions were alarming.

For example, when an unknown student used a bullhorn to spread information that he knew to be false, Michener charged the student with "a malicious act which had far-reaching consequences." He was not nearly so critical of Ohio's lame-duck governor, who was desperately fighting to survive in a primary campaign for the U.S. Senate, and inflamed the community with his remarks when he arrived in Kent to take control of matters. Michener concluded that this was "in the flamboyant tradition of American political leadership and cannot be unduly faulted for that."

Furthermore, after characterizing National Guard Commander General Canterbury as an insensitive man, Michener said, "One cannot help but feel sympathy for Canterbury . . . given the circumstances he conducted himself rather sensibly." Yet, just moments after Canterbury's men had shot and killed four students, the commander general had to be coaxed out of sending his troops into action a second time.

Michener's most devastating conclusions were these, however:

> It seems likely . . . that on the football field when the students were being obnoxious and stones were drifting in, that some of the troops agreed among themselves, "We've taken about enough of this crap. If they don't stop pretty soon we're going to let them have it." It was in this mood that they retreated up the hill—hot, dusty, sweating, and cut off from the rational world by their gas masks.

Continuing this theory of "conspiracy," a few pages later Michener wrote, "There is no acceptable proof of collusion on the part of officers or men to account for that sudden and dramatic turn of 135 degrees before firing, but it seems likely that some kind of rough verbal agreement had been reached among the troops when they clustered on the [football] field."

How, then, could Michener justify spreading the blame? If he believed the Guard had conspired to shoot the demonstrators in cold blood, then had he not indicted the Guard? Many of his readers thought so. Yet, in an about-face, Michener concluded there was death at Kent State, "but not murder."

Author Peter Davies was among the outraged readers who rebutted Michener's statements. In *The Truth about Kent State,* which followed Michener's book, Davies wrote that "If some [of the Guardsmen] agreed among themselves to shoot, then it was no accident. It was, as James Ahern, a member of the [President's] Commission said, simply a question of murder or manslaughter." Several times Davies asked Michener to reverse his illogical conclusions. He asked Michener to say straight out that there had been a conspiracy and to help him and others build a case against the National Guardsmen. Michener refused. The question of conspiracy, he said, was "a highly technical legal point. I have no doubt at all that some kind of agreement was reached at the playing field. Whether it constituted a bonafide conspiracy or not is for others to decide."

But strangely, Michener worked against any attempts to convene a federal grand jury, the most logical body to charge with deciding whether or not a conspiracy existed. "Common sense tells me," Michener said in his address before Kent State's graduating class in the winter of 1970, just prior to his book's release, "that if a federal grand jury did indict the Guard, jurors would then feel obligated to bring in a handful of indictments of students and professors just to prove they were even-handed." Later, he said that as someone who knew "more about the inside of the case than almost anyone else," he was sure the Guard itself would be exculpated and that civilians would have to bear the burden of publicity, court trials, and probable damage to their reputations and careers. This he deemed "a bad bargain." Society would not be well served by such an investigation, he said. Making this same point in the spring of 1971 to Arthur S. Krause, father of Allison, one of the four students who died at Kent, Michener said, "Nothing was served by forcing the Nuremberg Trials in 1946 and the Yamashita Trial in 1947 except the opening of wounds that will haunt us for years." Krause, who pleaded for justice in the case of his slain daughter, must have found Michener's historical parallels difficult to accept. Michener never changed his mind about a federal grand jury investigation. In May 1973, when there was pressure on the White House to reopen the case, he wrote to Leonard Garment, then a member of the Nixon administration, and said "I remain . . . quite convinced that a federal grand jury would do more harm than good. . . . I have always testified to this position and still adhere to it."

Yet, the Kent State tragedy deeply disturbed Michener. He did not want to simply forget what had happened if the truth could be known "with none of the potential unwanted consequences" that he predicted. Therefore, he favored a congressional inquiry into the case, like the one Senator Sam Ervin was conducting to investigate the Watergate scandal. This committee approach "would uncover facts," Michener told Garment, but without indictments. "It would put the National Guard on the stand where it should have been a long time ago. And it might dissipate feelings that the government did not care [about the miscarriage of justice that had occurred]." However, Congress had no constitutional right to investigate the Kent State tragedy, where murder may have been committed, and many people believed that justice could be served only by a federal grand jury probe. But the probe never occurred.

Michener's thesis about old versus new life-styles, his assumptions about right and wrong, and his unwillingness to examine certain events in history — a reluctance that is typical of his generation—blocked any attempt he might have made to accept the logic of his conclusions about the events that had occurred on May 4. Ultimately, this sabotaged the even-handedness of his own report. In what seemed like a desperate attempt to exempt the Guard from punishment for shooting the students, Michener quoted Ohio law, which deemed law enforcement officers guiltless for killing anyone "in suppression of a riot." But even Michener had argued there was no riot at Kent State on May 4. Furthermore, the law said guilt was absolved only if the use of force was "necessary and proper." Michener had already conclusively proved this was not the case: the National Guard was in control at all times; there was no sniper; the Guard was in no mortal danger at the time of the firing; no student performed any act on May 4 for which he deserved to be shot. Still, Michener seemed to be saying that no one should be punished. All he mustered was this dispassionate admonition:

> The United States cannot allow young people to be shot down
> in its streets, for if this were to become common, a revulsion
> would result of such dimension as to sweep away our forms of

government. Young people who brazenly defy soldiers, daring them to shoot, commit more than suicide; they commit a grave crime against organized society. And soldiers or policemen who fire without ultimate provocation run the grave risk of alienating the support which sustains them.

Frighteningly, Middle America agreed with Michener. Many of his readers were so concerned about "our forms of government," "organized society," and "the support which sustains" military force that they lost sight of what really happened at Kent State. Some of them mocked any attempt to understand youth and youth's rebellion. As Tom Wicker asked in the *New York Times,* "What price are we going to pay in this country to maintain not just law and order, but the old life style?"

Michener bristled when people in Kent attacked his report, and before long he entered the public debate. He appeared on the "Today Show" with I. F. Stone and two others who had written books about the tragedy. Stone, who said off the air that *Kent State—What Happened and Why* was "bullshit, right down Nixon's alley," started to read a statement on the air from the Kent Student Senate branding Michener's work a "fiction."

"Now, wait a minute, I know that statement," Michener interrupted.

"Now, let me speak," Stone went on. "You smeared those kids."

"I won't let you read that," Michener cut in, and by then the program had run out of time. But Stone had made his point.

Then, when the two speech professors offered their findings, for publication, Michener prepared a lengthy rebuttal and said their questionnaire was "loaded"—specially designed to elicit desired answers. He said he could support everything in his book and that in due time he would deposit his working papers and notes in a public archive where scholars could prove that he had written the truth. However, he also said that the dialogue in his book "is as accurate as memory and sometimes sketchy notes will permit." His papers and notes—which included newspaper clippings, scribbled messages, notebooks, photographs, research reports, interview transcripts, and manuscripts—were deposited at the Library of Congress, a safe distance from Kent, but their disarray made it difficult to substantiate selected passages and dialogue in his book.

In spite of the confusion, *Kent State—What Happened and Why* received widespread favorable reviews. Some critics objected to Michener's magisterial, pontificating tone, but most national reviewers found the book valuable. *Time* magazine praised Michener for placing the tragedy in perspective: "Now we know there *were* outside agitators at Kent." And Tom Wicker, while admonishing Michener for adhering too rigidly to his own standards, said that Michener had produced "the definitive account of what happened at Kent State" a "detailed, painstaking, fair-minded, skillful, often illuminating book." Indeed it was that, and of the dozen books written about the tragedy,

Michener's was the most thorough and revealing. It was just not always accurate.

It was also not a best-seller, but it served as a prelude to everything Michener would later say about youth and rebellion in *The Drifters*. That novel appeared on the heels of the Kent report and was quickly devoured by thousands of curious and often distressed parents. Michener's six young characters in *The Drifters* are the spiritual descendants of Henry David Thoreau. They had "dropped out" temporarily to "study the facts," but in the end, each one (except one who died) realizes that nothing productive comes from running away, using drugs, and "sleeping around." Thus, they slowly accept almost traditional life-styles and return to the mainstream of life.

Critics and young people, however, scoffed at *The Drifters* because they regarded it as a somewhat preposterous story marked by words and descriptions that belonged to an "old life style" writer. For example, Michener still called women "chicks" and blacks "cats." As one reviewer complained, "Michener is feeling his age and showing it. [He] has created six young people, not as young people really are, but as he wishes they had been when he was young." A college reviewer said Michener "accomplished what no other American has ever done with a single book—he has turned off an entire generation." A writer for *Book World* called the story "interminable . . . it all comes across like the numbing torture of being subjected to a weekend of colored slides by dull acquaintances just back from a world tour."

Who could accept the idea of six drifters under the age of twenty-one maneuvering through Europe and Africa "inspecting their dreams" uninterrupted by family problems, the need for money, or run-ins with authorities? And who could accept the "old fart" Uncle George Fairbanks just happening to appear everywhere in the story and knowing in detail each drifter's family history?

Droves of readers could, and did, if only because they wanted to believe what Michener had written. Young people, Michener was sure, could drift until the age of twenty-five or even thirty without coming to harm. "If they can get their ideas straightened out, and if they can return unimpaired," he explained, "they will make notable contributions to our society."

In the early 1970s, when *The Drifters* sold 100,000 copies, Michener's theory sounded farfetched. But early in the next decade, after members of the radical generation had disappeared temporarily and then resurfaced to assume responsible jobs on Wall Street, in law firms and banks, and on university faculties, critics looked again at *The Drifters*. Ironically, they decided that even while stubbornly conservative and middle class, Michener's novel was close to the mark. The turning point in youth's rebellion was the spring of 1970. As Michener later explained,

> a lot of us saw then that the United States must not go down
> this course [of destruction]. It was too dangerous, too terrify-
> ing. . . . I think the whole nation reviewed its posture after Kent

State and I'm quite proud of the way we handled it . . . young people looked the thing over and saw what was acceptable and what was not. . . . I think Americans behaved superbly [after May 4].

But in the early 1970s, with the future an unknown, there was still much that troubled Michener about America. The Vietnam War rumbled on, inflation weakened the economy, and the Watergate affair monopolized the headlines. "The United States had better beware," Michener warned in *The Quality of Life*. "We have junked our old beliefs without having evolved new ones, and if we remain adrift for even one generation we could decline into our own brand of barbarism."

He never doubted the country's resourcefulness, or its ability to survive, but now he thought it was time for him to look even more closely at what was happening and, if possible, to help inspire "a new spiritual agreement," a new set of national goals, a new consensus for America.

CHAPTER SIXTEEN

# A Gift for America

I honestly believe that a nation remains
strong only so long as it remains idealist.
JAMES A. MICHENER, 1972

JIM MICHENER RECEIVED thousands of fan letters every year, and through
the mid-1970s dozens of these letters began with the same request: "When are
you going to write about America? . . . Isn't it time you did for your own
country what *Hawaii* did for Hawaii and *The Source* did for Israel?"

By the late 1960s, the pressure for a Michener book about America was
formidable. Helen Strauss, now retired from the William Morris Agency and
working in films, and Hobart Lewis, who thought of Michener as America's
greatest living storyteller, each contributed to the prodding. Strauss urged
Michener to write about California in the style of *Iberia.* "I think it would be
fascinating," she explained. "Geographically, California is unique with the
great bald mountains in the south, the lush forests in the north, the deserts,
the anything but pacific Pacific Ocean." She was sure the book could be sold
to *Reader's Digest,* and she foresaw film possibilities, too.

And Lewis, who seemed never at a loss for ideas, awakened at 2:30 one morning with what he thought was the perfect Michener story, a broad sweep across this continent resulting in a book to be called *America*:

> Into such a novel you could weave all of the important national strains that go to make up the American character and experience. You could follow a New England family, a Southern family, obviously a Negro family and of course other nationalities too, and somehow with the Michener magic weave the whole thing into a book. . . .
>
> I know it is a monumental undertaking and I don't have the faintest idea how to go about it, but you are the only person in the country who could do it, and I think it is exactly the right time for such a book to be written.

At the culmination of these various influences in the spring of 1970, Michener decided it *was* time that he wrote about America. And Lewis had showed him exactly how to do it. Strauss's idea was not without merit, but California did not inspire him. Ever since *Hawaii* he had been besieged with requests to write about other states, especially Alaska and California, but he showed no interest in them now. Lewis's idea, on the other hand, was a story of vision, one to inspire readers as well as entertain them. It was much to Michener's liking, and in a modified form, it became the nucleus of a book set in America.

Early on April 7, 1970, several months after receiving Lewis's letter, Michener awoke and walked directly from his bed to his desk. He sat down, rolled a piece of paper into his typewriter, and wrote this passage:

> This morning I woke up with a complete novel outlined. I had not thought of its subject since 1937, but now it stood forth in complete detail.
>
> The background, I suppose, is that many people have been after me to write about the United States, Helen Strauss and Hobart Lewis, among my immediate friends, scores of my correspondents.
>
> Also, the Centennial Commission has been having some private meetings with me on the subject of our nation's two hundredth birthday, and I've been poring over the secret report to the President, helping to draft certain sections.
>
> The word Centennial must have reminded me of the Centennial State, and of an imaginary plains town of that name which has lived with me since 1937 when I first saw the Platte, nighty [sic] and grubby river.

Without correcting errors—it was the Bicentennial Commission, not the Centennial; and the Platte was a mighty river—Michener ripped the page from his typewriter, neatly trimmed the edges and pasted the passage inside the front of a ruled, 8½-by-11 notebook. It was a dramatic moment, typically Michener, and it did not end on April 7. Two days later he added a second page to the notebook, this one listing twelve chapter headings, dubbed The Big Chunks:

1. Land
2. Occupants
3. Old Beaver
4. Fort Brill
5. The Wagon
6. The Massacre—Buffalo
7. The Cowboy
8. The Smell of Sheep
9. The Railroad
10. The Lamberts
11. Sugar Beets
12. The Depression

This was the conception of *Centennial,* the novel that Michener delivered to his readers in the decade of this nation's two hundredth birthday. It was intended as a gift for America, and it was also likely to be Michener's last book, because by the time of its publication he would be sixty-seven, and he had implied that he was thinking about retiring. Therefore, the production of *Centennial* became a special event in Michener's life, and to preserve what he called "the gravity" of his work, he planned to keep an *aide-mémoire* to record how he had created the novel. In a notebook he scribbled information about geography and geologic periods, listed names of professionals to consult, and preserved newspaper clippings about farming, recipes for souse (a pickled food), and a postcard picture of a dinosaur. He also recorded tentative names of characters, complete with fictional genealogies. Keeping the notebook, which required at least weekly and sometimes daily attention, made the production of *Centennial* all the more meaningful, and even dramatic.

An aura of gravity—indeed, solemnity—surrounded the genesis of Michener's novel. Along with the many letters that had prompted it, the book was also a result of brooding about America's future in the late 1960s, when the nation was torn by riots and war. Never was Michener's discontent more painful than when he witnessed the collapse of the American Revolution Bicentennial Commission, an impressive body of dedicated Americans, to which he and Hobart Lewis had been appointed by President Nixon. The goal of the commission was to help forge a national commitment, a new spiritual agreement to carry the United States into the twenty-first century. As a member of this esteemed commission, Michener was responsible for summarizing the group's wealth of ideas in literary form for presentation to the Congress, which had to approve the plans for the festivities. However, lacking bipartisan leadership, the commission became a grab bag for what Michener called "influential and ill-intentioned" politicians "who ridiculed every intelligent proposal, scuttled every promising possibility and reduced the [celebration] to one half-baked fair in the city of Philadelphia." As a result, he complained, "Instead of a feast of the imagination, we shall have a hastily contrived picnic with plastic hamburgers."

Lewis recalled that the commission failed because "The Democrats did not want the Republicans to have the Bicentennial as a feather in their cap, and there were too many plans that did not gel. The only good thing we did was approve the Bicentennial emblem."

Michener was too polite to choose sides—"I don't know which party behaved worse," he said—but the grand design for a celebration was thwarted, and as he explained, he wept. As he walked alone among the pines and snowdrifts on the hill in Pipersville, his frustration stirred deep memories about America. He must have felt then like his soon-to-be created character, Paul Garrett, whose life was carefully tailored to epitomize the history of the West. In the thought-provoking final chapter of *Centennial*, Garrett becomes chairman of Colorado's statewide committee to plan not only the Bicentennial celebration in 1976, but also Colorado's centennial celebration that same year. Troubled by events that are destroying his state, Garrett searches for peace of mind in the far nothern land of his ranch. "The fact that he had sought the company of turkeys and prairie dogs reminded him of how deeply he was afflicted by the permanent American illness. A deep depression attacked him, which he could identify but not explain, the awful malaise of loneliness."

Michener's disappointment was easy to understand. Here was a man whose life and career had become a testimonial to the reality of the American dream and to the value of hard work, loyalty, and honesty. To thwart the noble plans for America's two hundredth birthday was to reject James A. Michener himself. So at that point when Americans lost every chance of enjoying a nationwide celebration in 1976, Michener decided it was each citizen's responsibility to honor America's historical rite of passage. "Each of us must confirm his own commitment to the future," he said, and not allow 1976 to pass in silence. Michener celebrated the event by writing *Centennial*. It was to be a panoramic saga, full of history, people, and challenge, a sociohistoric epic in which he hoped to capture the faith in and spirit of the American dream.

When on April 7, 1970, Michener awakened with the outline for a story in mind, he had completed the initial phase in his process of producing a novel. As he explained,

> The idea comes first, and I usually fool around with four or five ideas at a time. I pursue them all until I settle on "the big idea" and its place in the universe of my thoughts and ambitions. . . .
>
> I tend to have great difficulty reaching a commitment as to what I want to do next. Once I reach it, I work with great

directness and diligence, but I have a very anxious time trying to decide what to do.

Once I think an idea might be right, I may spend several years reading widely and talking, building up a pretty good background without much focus. Then I commit myself, and I go back and really zero in.

The gestation period for *Hawaii* was seven years, the average length for one of his big novels, but *Centennial* required much longer. Subconsciously, at least, he had begun thinking about this book in the mid-1930s as he explored the Colorado landscape with Floyd Merrill, the newspaper editor who had befriended him when he was a young teacher in Greeley. During many field trips with Merrill, Michener had photographed animals, wildflowers, rivers, and mountains, and through the years his slides served to remind him of the story that awaited him in the Centennial state. It was the story that Floyd Merrill said he hoped to read, the story that he repeatedly urged Michener to write, particularly after the success of *Hawaii*.

In 1950, Michener had spent several weeks drafting the outline for a novel about the American West to be called *Jefferson,* the name of an imaginary state that resembled Colorado, with a range of mountains along its western border, and with plains in the east. Michener had written about one hundred pages of the book before abandoning it, but he intended to resurrect it someday. *Jefferson* was going to be "a splendid portrait of a young woman in the west," according to Michener. His heroine was the teacher Betty Benson, born in 1917, the daughter of a carpenter who had killed a man and had spent twenty years in prison for his crime. At nineteen, Betty Benson was five feet six inches tall and weighed 126 pounds, with brown hair and brown eyes. "Hair to shoulders," Michener described her in a brief character sketch. "Trim neck. Rounded shoulders. Arms thicker than usual. Thin wrists and ankles. Full breasts. Wide hips. Strong, lovely face: small, straight nose; rounded chin with dimple; eyes deepset and wide." Neither Betty Benson nor Jefferson were brought fictionally to life in 1950, but a quarter of a century later many of their characteristics surfaced in the people and events of *Centennial*. In comparing the two ideas Michener later revealed,

> The books would have covered roughly the same terrain and many of the emotional contents were similar. *Jefferson* would have stressed not the glamorous mountains but the prairie drylands. It would have contained many of the characters, sometimes in different guise, and at least a dozen of the specific dramatic scenes that appeared in *Centennial*.

Lacking the expertise to structure an epic story in 1950, Michener abandoned *Jefferson*. Developing a structure was the second phase of Michener's novel-writing process, and as he testified many times, it was the most perplexing task of all to accomplish satisfactorily:

> I could think up six or seven great books a year, no doubt about
> it, but it would take me six or seven months with each one to find
> the right structure, and until I find it I am lost. . . . I must be able
> to identify the end product as a total work in which every item has
> its proper and subordinate place . . . [and] if I have not identified
> this appropriate structure, I waste my time if I try to write, for I
> will produce nothing.

In spite of this, structuring a story was Michener's forte in the art of
storytelling. With each novel he attempted to create what he called "a little
universe in which the reader can live for a couple of weeks and from which he
will get an overwhelming sense of reality." Verisimilitude was one secret of
his success, for every time he published a book a multitude of readers
responded that they had found his story so real they never wanted it to end.
*Huckleberry Finn, Vanity Fair,* and *The Idiot* had appealed similarly to
Michener as a youngster, so as a writer of popular novels he decided it was
more important to create "a little universe" than to provide anything else.
Structure was more important than either the plot or characterization, two
elements of fiction that Michener never mastered. "They don't interest me at
all," he admitted. "And the fact that my books have been so very widely read
proves that at least in certain respects I wasn't wrong."

In three of his earlier novels—*Tales of the South Pacific, Return to Paradise,*
and *The Source*—Michener had developed what he considered "ideal structures." Each one helped him complete "what otherwise would have been an
impossible task."

In *Tales of the South Pacific* he used an unconventional structure whereby no
one concept, character, or setting assumed priority in a loose collection of
interrelated stories. *Return to Paradise* opened with a lively essay about an
island, and then continued with a story about the island. His most challenging structure, however, was the invention of The Tell in *The Source*. An
extensive time period presented a serious problem in this novel. Michener
was afraid of losing readers to a long narrative, but by threading a contemporary story through each of fifteen episodic stories he made his structure
enticing.

In writing *Centennial*, which posed a problem similar to that of *The Source,*
Michener developed a new narrative technique. His proposed western saga
stretched from prehistoric times to the Watergate era and presented a variety
of incidents involving more than seventy characters over a huge geographical
area. To bind the tale together he created Dr. Lewis Vernor, a history professor in the style of James A. Michener. The editors of *"US"*—a magazine
Michener invented—send Dr. Vernor to Colorado in 1973 to file a detailed
"report on the scene" three years before the state's centennial celebration; thus
the professor becomes the vehicle for moving the novel forward. After
establishing Vernor's role in a lively first chapter, Michener could then write
the succeeding chapters as Vernor's reports to his editors in New York.

Vernor's narrative, which reflects the historical development of Colorado, including the movement of people into the state, leads to a final summing up called November Elegy, Michener's plea for social progress in America. True to Michener's craftsmanship, the novel's structure is excellent, albeit contrived.

In the third phase of Michener's work he plotted the story. He had devised a basic outline of the plot during the idea phase of his project; once he had structured the story he began to refine the plot. He had developed the technique of anchoring the plot to a half-dozen "pillars" around which the story evolved. He selected these pillars only after reading widely about the historical background of his novel, and he liked to make use of topics basic to life. For example, transportation, irrigation, and ecology were three of the pillars he used in *Centennial*.

At this point it was essential for Michener to become emotionally involved in his story, and he could do so only by visiting or moving to the scene of his novel. He was not prepared to reveal any specific plans. As always he remained evasive about his project until publication, but on May 10, 1970, several weeks before he accepted the assignment to write about Kent State, he did inform Floyd Merrill that he planned an excursion to the Centennial state:

> My wife and I are coming to Colorado to do a little exploring regarding some writing I may want to do. We expect to be in Greeley sometime around Tuesday, May 27. We are interested in much of Colorado history and wonder if you have from the schools a good history of the state that we could purchase? We are also much interested in a history of Weld County, any account of buffalo, beaver, Herefords, sheep and Folsom man.

He also wrote, in a most unassuming manner, to the curator of the Meeker Museum in Greeley:

> First, let me introduce myself: I am a writer of serious books who will be visiting your museum sometime in the latter part of May. At that time I would like to have the name of someone on your staff with whom I could discuss a few questions relating to the history of the west.

He directed a similar letter to the superintendent at the Fort Laramie national monument in Wyoming:

> My interests are rather general at this time, but I am concerned to know what Indians inhabited the area between the two Plattes, where the beavers lived in this area, where the buffalo flourished, and of course the general details of exploration and trail movement up to the building of the railroads. I could be much more specific but I am in that condition in which I don't know what I am looking for until I find it!

Of course, "a writer of serious books," as Michener described himself, or a scholar, as he sometimes referred to himself, should immerse himself in reading material prior to contacting experts and professionals for interviews. But Michener's worldwide reputation influenced many museum curators, college professors, scientists, librarians, and other professionals to overlook his informal research methods and make it easier for him to find what he was after.

On May 17, having already sent *The Drifters* to Random House, the Micheners packed their station wagon and headed for Colorado to conduct a "protracted exploration." Allowing time for frequent stops along the way to study the lay of the land, imagining what it must have been like a hundred years earlier when the pioneers crossed the country in wagons, they arrived in Colorado late in the month. Almost immediately Michener met two men who impressed him with their knowledge of the West.

The first was eighty-year-old Herman Werner, who had homesteaded a small property and was now dean of Wyoming ranchers, owning more than a million acres. He and Michener spent several hours talking about Herefords and ranching.

The second was Otto Unfug of Sterling, Colorado, a tall maverick of a man, as Michener described him, and one who had worked in numerous occupations. Unfug was dying of cancer, but he was eager to pass along all that he knew about the West to Michener, and to introduce the author to a host of other men who could talk about "what made the West tick." For the next several weeks Michener relied on Unfug to organize small discussion groups to talk about irrigation, homesteading, real estate, sheep, banking, and anything else that interested him. Michener sat listening for hours at a time, studying each of the curious men who gathered around, wondering what motivated them, and plotting his grand story of the West.

At the end of three weeks Michener was ready to go home to read and think some more about his idea, but first he stopped in Greeley to visit Floyd Merrill, "an old man now, hard hit by various attacks." For memory's sake they walked together on the prairie, and later in the day they relaxed in Merrill's study, crammed full of assorted books. For several hours they talked until at last Michener assured Merrill that he was going to write the novel of the West. Pleased, the old man smiled and nodded. But by the time Michener returned to Pipersville, Merrill had died.

Michener found a message in Floyd Merrill's death. It was the same message that Alex Haley's aunt had bequeathed to him when she died just as he was preparing to write *Roots*. At home in Tennessee, Haley's aunt had often lectured him about their forebear, the "old African," and in her final years she lamented that her memory of their ancestor would vanish with her unless Haley recorded the story. Shortly thereafter, at the precise moment of Haley's arrival in Africa to begin researching his ancestry, his aunt died in Tennessee, just as if she knew her wish had been granted. Through many difficult years spent struggling with the research and the writing of *Roots*,

Haley never forgot his aunt's strange sign of trust, and without her he could not have completed his book. Similarly, without Merrill, Michener might not have produced *Centennial*. It was Merrill who had first ignited his enthusiasm for the lore and myth of the American West and who then encouraged him through the years to write about the events that were so vital a part of the American experience. Now, Michener discovered, Floyd Merrill was as influential in death as he had been in life.

Shortly after returning to Bucks County, carrying home several histories of the West, plus technical volumes such as *Survey of Neoglaciation in the Front Range of Colorado,* and *A Guide to the Geology of Rocky Mountain National Park,* Michener was summoned by Hobe Lewis to write *Kent State—What Happened and Why.* Considering the excitement he had already generated by starting to research and write *Centennial,* it was difficult to imagine that he could suddenly shift to a nonfiction book. That he did so proved the sincerity of his attempt to understand and report the plight of young people in America. In midsummer, setting aside the notebook relating to his western novel, he packed his bags and headed for Ohio.

It was November 25, 1970, before the Kent State book went into production at Random House, and he was again free to consider the novel. He studied "The Big Chunks" he had listed in his notebook and switched the order of the sheep chapter with the railroad chapter, then jotted in the margin of his notebook, "This still looks workable after a long hiatus." Several magazine articles, a trip abroad, and pressing commitments in Washington, D.C., where President Nixon had appointed him to the U.S. Information Agency (USIA), delayed his full-time commitment to the research. During the next eighteen months he continued thinking about the novel, however, and he and Mari drove west several times more to trace the Oregon Trail from St. Joseph, Missouri, to South Pass, Wyoming. Finally, on June 28, 1972, he printed "WORKABLE" under his notation of November 25, 1970, and now there was no turning back. He immediately made plans to move to Denver that fall for a year of intensive research and writing.

Meanwhile, he resumed his research by mail, a method he frequently used during the preliminary stages of collecting information for a novel. Earlier, he had written a curious appeal to the mayors of Laramie and Denver. Not knowing either mayor's name, he simply began one letter with "Dear Mayor" and the other with "Dear Sir." Both times he introduced himself as "a writer who has done quite a few books of a serious nature," and then he asked for help "on a peculiar problem which I cannot solve by myself." He needed to know the names and locations of "the great dance halls" in which the big bands performed in Wyoming and Denver before World War II. "I don't want you to waste your own valuable time on this," he explained to the mayors, "but you probably have/someone on your staff who would remember and I would deeply appreciate a letter from them." The mayor of Laramie may not have had the slightest knowledge about the ballrooms, but he passed Michener's query on to a superior court judge who had been a musician prior to World War II, and then sent the information to Michener. However, a question remained as to the accuracy of such research.

Another letter by Michener, this one more professional, was addressed to Dr. Merrill J. Mattes, a scholar who had written about the Platte River. Michener advised Mattes that he was writing a novel about the development of a small town along the South Platte, and having read Mattes's "fine volume on the North Platte," he was now ready to ask a few questions "whose answers will be simple to you but somewhat obscure to me." He asked, for example, "What was the earliest appearance of cholera? What was the earliest epidemic? When was the elephant first discussed at campfires? When was the first mammoth excavated, in part or whole, in the Nebraska region? When was the earliest covered wagon caravan along the South Platte? . . ." and so forth. His single-spaced letter covered an entire page, and in closing Michener said, "I have asked too many questions, but you probably have all the answers at your finger tips. I would appreciate any guidance you could give me." He signed his letter, "Most warmly, James A. Michener." Mattes apparently responded enthusiastically, no doubt pleased to oblige a famous author. Later, when Michener had finished writing his novel, he relied on Mattes to read sections of the manuscript for accuracy.

All through the summer Michener continued his search for information, reviewing "three hundred to four hundred" books about the West. It was his practice to send a raft of questions to an expert and then, after receiving a reply, quickly draft the portion of his manuscript that related to the material at hand. For example, in August he wrote to a museum curator in Lancaster, Pennsylvania, seeking answers to several questions. "What did Lancaster look like in 1840? How did butchers conduct their business in that period? Who were the principal wagon makers of the period? What were horses worth in this period? Was there an orphanage in Lancaster at this time?" No doubt he could have found all the details he needed in a history of Lancaster from a Philadelphia library, but it was easier and less time-consuming to rely on a professional researcher. When the curator responded, Michener then drafted The Wagon and the Elephant, Chapter Six of his novel, and the introduction of Levi Zendt, who trekked by Conestoga from Lancaster to Colorado.

In September, having accomplished more than he expected from Pipersville, Michener packed his station wagon again, this time loading it with reference materials, research, old photographs, and parts of several chapters in rough form. He and Mari left Bucks County and traced for the fifth time each mile of the Oregon Trail. Late that month they moved into a Denver high-rise apartment, whereupon they wrote a community letter to their friends back east. They addressed the letter to several couples and individuals, including Albert Erskine, Hobart Lewis, and Owen Laster, who had succeeded Helen Strauss as Michener's agent, and imposed upon one of the recipients to reproduce the letter and mail copies to the others on the list. The Micheners frequently corresponded this way, and apparently thought nothing of the inconvenience it caused their friends. In this letter they wrote to "Mary and Ham, Sue and Joe, Pete and Adelaide . . ." and a dozen others.

We hope that Mary Place [a neighbor in Bucks County] will xerox this letter and send copies to the above. Nadia [Michener's secretary in Bucks County] can provide addresses and postage.

Mari did a great job of finding an apartment. . . . The place is stunning, with a large room, a good kitchen, two bedrooms, and a balcony. It is just a little larger than we wanted and somewhat more expensive. . . .

Near the apartment house is a superb Chinese restaurant and a great cafeteria with many salads. A stunning Sunday dinner for two today cost, total, $3.62. We may never come home.

. . . the big reason we took this apartment is that it has a fine gymnasium, with eight different exercise machines. They bore me to distraction, but the swift jumping from one to the other does lend variety, and it makes you feel great.

Mari then continued the letter, explaining that

My job as social and appointments secretary, cook, house-keeper, maid and chief messenger keeps me busy. Tomorrow I have to go to City Hall to pay a fine for JAM who parked in front of a store while he was buying a typewriter, desk and office supplies.

In signing off, Michener added, "Hobart: We are all at work." Lewis had no reason to assume anything less, but since the *Reader's Digest* was under-writing a chunk of Michener's research expenses—which made his penny-pinching comments all the more amusing—Michener felt obliged to assure the editor that the project was progressing.

Through Lewis, Michener met John Kings, an Englishman who had ranched in Wyoming, and Tessa Dalton, a professional wildlife pho-tographer, and these two, plus Leslie Laird, a former *Digest* employee who had worked with Michener in Kent, formed his research team. In ten months they traveled approximately 25,000 miles with Michener, visiting fourteen states in search of material for *Centennial*. Along with companionship, the researchers provided answers to endless strings of questions: "How long do potatoes take to grow? How many sheep were there in Wyoming in 1933–1953–1973? 'When It's Springtime in the Rockies' [sic], who wrote it? When? Still alive?" Before arriving at the end of the trail, each of the researchers had filled several notebooks with assorted facts, figures, and opinions, and each discovered how difficult it was to compile a Michener novel.

Mari was the fourth member of the research team. Her contribution was not always apparent, but without her Michener would have been at a consid-erable loss. Occasionally Mari went along on field trips, and in her role as caretaker she was forever advising Michener about what he should or should not have done. This idiosyncrasy soon earned her the title "Prime Minister of Shoulda."

Actually, Michener loved Mari's attention as much as she enjoyed sparring with him. They called each other Cookie and they enjoyed each other immensely. He teased Mari about her weakness for buying gimcracks on each research trip. Michener himself collected souvenirs, but discriminately. On his desk in Denver, for example, he kept an ashtray that he had rescued from the debris of a bombed pub while in Belfast along with twenty other media representatives. But Mari possessed "an insatiable desire to collect nonsense items," observed her husband, who was powerless to do anything about it. "The result," he informed the librarians at the University of Northern Colorado, where he deposited his *Centennial* papers, "is this box full of junk." Among the items were statues, bones, seashells, and miniature models of dinosaurs and beavers. As for Mari, she just went on collecting.

Once Michener settled in Colorado, he began earning the praise that fans and critics often said he deserved as a researcher. Ironically, he thought that complimenting him for doing research was like "praising a bus driver for knowing how to shift gears." As he explained, "I went to a fine college and six or seven great graduate schools, and if I didn't learn something I ought to be arrested." He did his best work during the research phase of producing a novel, when he interviewed experts: "I can't tell you how delightful it is to find material that you're looking for. When I have it all down on paper and realize the story is viable because of the research, I sometimes get a feeling of real power." With *Centennial,* the excitement began forty-eight hours after his arrival in Denver.

Lauren Wright, a geologist whose specialty was the Rocky Mountains, spent most of one morning in the mountains sharing his vast knowledge with Michener. In the afternoon they drove to the prairielands east of Denver to explore the geologic development of two remote buttes that Michener planned to include in his story. Later that day they rode to nearby Keota, a ghost town whose people Michener remembered from the thirties as "men and women of hope" who had lived in the belief "that they could make the barren wastes of the American desert bloom." Now the town was gone—the railroad platform, the bank, the grain elevator, the hotel—all blown away, with little left save an ancient post office and a wispy postmaster named Clyde Stanley. He was a former homesteader, editor of the town newspaper, and land commissioner, and he had witnessed the rise and fall of Keota, prototype of many western towns. Michener knew immediately that Stanley was a researcher's treasure, and time and again, while writing *Centennial,* he returned to Keota to pump the postmaster for information.

"Now Mr. Stanley," Michener later reported he began on countless occasions, "I'd like to review that first day. The would-be farmers would arrive at Greeley on the Union Pacific. The real estate people would be waiting for them in rented cars. They'd drive out here, and they could either homestead

320 acres from the government, or they could pay the real estate people cash for a whole section. Did any families do both?"

Then Michener sat back and enjoyed the old man's version of how the West was settled. There was little, it seemed, that Stanley could not recall, and Michener checked the accuracy of the old man's memory by asking him the same questions over and again, weeks or months apart. The two men talked endlessly, and Stanley was the last person Michener visited before completing *Centennial*. "Government's closing down the post office next week," he said sadly to Michener. "When it goes, the town's officially dead." Not long afterward, Stanley was dead, too. But in *Centennial* he survived as the prototype for the land commissioner, Walter Bellamy.

Not all of Michener's field trips were as rewarding as those to Keota, but each was exciting. Recorded in his notebook, his 1972–1973 itinerary included trips to:

- Utah to inspect dinosaur sites.
- Fort Laramie, Wyoming, to inspect military and Indian conditions [sites]. This trip was repeated four times from different angles.
- Texas, Oklahoma, and New Mexico, to study, under field conditions, the old cattle trails.
- Old Mexico, New Mexico, and southern Colorado, to determine from where and how Mexicans immigrated into the beet fields.
- Lincoln, Nebraska, to inspect natural history museum and to talk with experts in that field.
- Wyoming, Utah, Montana, Idaho, to check the sites and conditions of the fur trappers' rendezvous.
- St. Louis and Lincoln, Nebraska, to review materials on the fur trade and on animal life in the region.
- Wyoming to inspect Indian reservations and to visit several cattle ranches.
- Utah, California, University of Arizona, University of Nebraska, various digs in the Nebraska area, to study animal remains from the prehistoric period.

The only interruptions of Michener's year in Colorado were several business and personal commitments. They included monthly USIA meetings in Washington, D.C.; trips to Finland, Norway, and Iceland for the USIA; a vacation in Haiti with "our permanent travel group, the [Walter] Cronkites, the [Bob] Considines, the [Art] Buchwalds and the [Neil] Morgans"; and a long holiday weekend at Thanksgiving to join former President and Mrs. Lyndon B. Johnson for a football game at the University of Texas. (Afterward the Micheners visited their American art collection, housed on the Austin campus in a new humanities building.) At one point Michener wrote to his editor and secretary and said "I find myself under very heavy pressure to do a lot of things in all parts of the world, and I must ask your help in keeping them to a minimum." In late April he planned to fly back to New York to receive an award, and then shortly after his return to Denver he intended to go to Greeley to help inaugurate a new library. Then he would fly to Alaska to deliver a commencement address. "If alluring invitations reach you for *anything,*" he advised, "the answer must be no." In a woman's handwriting was this postscript: "Unless it's interesting for MM [i.e., Mari Michener]!"

Between the research and the travel, Michener isolated himself in his Denver apartment for "the hardest work of all," the final phase of his project: writing the novel.

> It's a lot of nonsense about writers needing special surround-
> ings for their work. A writer should be able to work anywhere. I
> have written all my good books on a door, laying it across two
> filing cases or piles of bricks to make a desk top.

*Centennial* was not written on a door, however. Instead, Michener used a sturdy oak desk, purchased at a secondhand shop in Denver, and a manual typewriter, circa 1950, set on top of a rickety stand. On his desk along with other reference materials he kept a dictionary, a speller, maps, Crabbe's *English Synonyms,* a Bible, notebooks, and a small, cracked globe; he kept a tarnished, spiral-armed reading lamp taped to the top of a Texsun unsweetened orange juice can to give it added height. There was also an ashtray (although he never smoked), a magnifying glass for studying maps and photographs, and two cube puzzles that he enjoyed taking apart and reassembling. Showering light on his typing table was a domed floor lamp. Typically, Michener's work environment was modest. Even in Bucks County his den consisted of an old wooden desk, several metal filing cabinets, a manual typewriter, and one wall lined with books, record albums, and research materials.

His day in Denver began at 5:30 A.M., earlier than with previous books. He poured himself a glass of unsweetened juice—he thought breakfast was the "ugliest" word in the English language—and went immediately to his typewriter. He wrote a manuscript in three stages. First he drafted the narrative, which flowed almost spontaneously if he had spent a couple of years thinking about the story and reading background material. For *Centennial,* most of the narrative was on paper by the time he arrived in Denver. It was typed "on an as-if basis"—that is, written as if he had all the research at his fingertips. Later, when the research was completed, he returned to the narrative during stage two and filled in the gaps, frequently returning to his collection of photographs from the 1930s to remind him of what he saw and how he had felt about a place or object. Michener thought his only unique artistic talent was the ability to write a striking narrative:

> Writing is hard for me, but I do know how a story ought to
> unfold and I have a great feeling when it's going the wrong way.

Character, dialogue, plot—all of that I leave to others. The average person has no conception of how carefully worked out my books are, how sound they tend to be. Narration requires a reverence for beginning, middle and end.

By this time the novel was half completed, but the challenge remained in stage three: the rewriting. Now Michener refined what he called the architecture of his prose. Unlike Hemingway's works, in which he created beautifully honed sentences that conjured up distinct images, Michener concentrated on the selection of individual words, often agonizing over his options. As he explained one evening at the Academia de la Lengua,

> At almost every point in writing a sentence I face a choice. Shall I use a Romance-derived word or an Anglo-Saxon one? That is, shall I use a longer word with a fancier meaning, or a shorter word with a more brutal meaning?
>      . . . because of my long association with Romance languages I intuitively first choose the Romance word, then go back in my rewriting and editing and substitute the shorter Anglo-Saxon word. Thus I almost always write on my typewriter *obtain*, which is the same as *obtener*, but usually I change it in longhand to *get*, which comes from the German, I suppose. It is this constant choosing between words . . . that makes the writing of English so difficult and its end product so strong.

Michener rewrote a novel at least twice before sending it to his editors, after which he rewrote parts of the manuscript several more times. For a book the length of *Hawaii* or *Centennial*, this meant he typed about two million words—using two fingers.

> I have never thought of myself as a good writer. Anyone who wants reassurance of that should read one of my first drafts. But I'm one of the world's great rewriters. The only competence I have . . . is that I feel reasonably sure I could do a good job of describing that table over there. Like all writers, I know damn well I can write as well as the average novelist. Without that vanity, I wouldn't be able to see it through.

Michener typed his drafts with narrow margins, thereby delaying the continuous interruption of changing paper. His first drafts were sloppy. He crossed out large portions of the manuscript in green ink and printed substitute phrases or words between the lines of double-spaced text. While rewriting a manuscript, he pasted additions to each draft page so that he retained his original page numbering system. This was the outgrowth of "a tremendous kinesthetic sense" generated while creating the narrative flow. His mind's eye knew exactly how a given page looked and how it related to the other pages in a chapter, so in retyping, he was careful not to lose that perspective.

On a good day, Michener wrote two thousand words, working until noon and, with luck, stopping at a high point.

> Hemingway said a long time ago—and I subscribe to it—that a smart writer quits for the day when he's really steaming, when he knows it's good and knows where it's going. If you can do that, you've fought half the next day's battle.

He was not always lucky, though. On more than one occasion, after a difficult morning at his typewriter, he wrote to one of his correspondents, "How it goes I don't know. Sometimes I think there aren't a dozen people in the United States who want to read a novel about the Platte River." Michener was not without insecurity. He explained,

> Invariably when I am half-way through a very long task which will occupy me for three years I wonder if anyone will want to plough through this involved material I'm creating, and I reach the point at which I deem it all futile. For to write the kind of novel I do is an act of supreme arrogance: Who would want to waste time reading it? Why do you think that your view is worth attention? What makes you think there's a waiting audience?

The only consolation he had at such times was that he had found readers before, and soon the doubts disappeared and he was profitably at work again.

After lunch he napped, taking advantage of his ability to fall asleep quickly and awaken refreshed. Through late afternoon he conducted field trips and interviews. At 5:30, if he was home, he went to the apartment house gymnasium to work off tension. Following a light dinner he spent evenings reading, answering mail, and entertaining himself by assembling a wall collage of the envelopes and postcards that arrived in his daily mail. In this routine, working seven days a week, Michener wrote *Centennial*. At times he was lost in the project. Invariably he knew what he wanted to write, but occasionally he was stumped. He had "loused things up," he recorded in his notebook, or was "not in good health," or he "worked too hard and hadn't slept well," and on those days he fumbled to get back in the groove. As he explained,

> Writing is a lonely business, and even for me there's much insecurity. No one can give you a clue about your writing, not your wife, or your editor or agent. You have to hold on to the idea that what you're writing is something somebody will want to read.

Once Michener completed a chapter, or section of a chapter, he mailed it to his secretary in Bucks County for clean typing. He logged the chapter and date in his notebook and then worried until he received notice by return mail that the pages had been safely delivered. Foolishly, Michener did not keep copies of his work, and this imposed the worst sort of suffering because he "felt almost sick" each time he had to send a chapter "so carefully edited and so almost irreplacable." Within several weeks of his arrival in Denver, he sent his secretary the first seventeen pages of Chapter 2. In November he added twelve more pages of that chapter, plus fifty-eight pages of Chapter 3, fifty-four pages of Chapter 4, and a twenty-five-page article, "The Red Kimono," which he had somehow managed to write for the *New York Times Magazine*. The next month he mailed twenty pages of Chapter 1, forty-five pages of 5, and fifty-nine pages of 4. The practice of jumping from one chapter to another might have distracted another writer, but once Michener knew the structure of a novel he held the book's pattern in mind and could pick up the narrative at any point.

By January 1973, he had completed the first five chapters of *Centennial*. When he finished the next three, he sent all eight to Albert Erskine at Random House for a quick reading. "It was pleasurable, like curling up with a good book," the editor responded in late March. "I want to know how it *turns out; so* keep at it." During the first six months of 1973 Michener spent only about one hundred days writing—he devoted the remaining days to field trips and travel—but drafted seven chapters and polished the first five. At one point he sent Erskine a frightening yet prudent note: "Because I have so much travel facing me I thought I ought to outline the last two chapters of the novel. Then, if anything hits me, the book could be finished." Happily, nothing stopped him from writing the chapters himself, which he did with incredible speed before the end of summer. By August, the novel was completed and ready for the final editing in New York.

While experts and Michener's researchers reviewed sections of the *Centennial* manuscript for accuracy, his perceptive secretary, Nadia Orapchuck, had the earliest opportunities to comment about the story. Aside from her enthusiasm for her boss's work, Nadia was a stickler for spelling and forms of words. "After proof-reading I looked up half-breed and find that both my dictionaries show it hyphenated for both noun and adjective," she reported. She also discovered that "sugar beet" was two words, as was "sugar cane," but "roundup" was one. As soon as Nadia finished typing and proofing a chapter she sent the original to Erskine, and a copy to Michener, who then rewrote portions of the manuscript and airmailed his edited versions to Erskine for safekeeping. As John Kings noted in a slim volume entitled *In Search of Centennial,* between January and July 1973, Michener's "attention was continually split between writing, revising and doing further research, all within the same time frame." While writing first drafts of some chapters he was reworking earlier chapters, updating them with additional research and changes recommended by experts who had reviewed the manuscript. "This complex assortment of activities required skillful orchestration," said Kings, and Michener explained how it was managed:

When one has a manuscript as long as this one, as intricate, and as closely interlocked in its parts, the loss of even one page can be devastating. I have therefore always followed the practice of allowing not one page to be removed without making a note of where it has gone.

I do this on slip sheets of cheap yellow paper and insert them to represent the missing pages. I cannot relate how helpful this has been and how confused and mixed up I would often have been without them.

Sometimes, in the preparation of the manuscript, I had segments of it (1) with Erskine, (2) on the way to Erskine, (3) with Nadia being typed, (4) on the way to Nadia to be typed, (5) on the way from Nadia to Erskine, (6) with Kings or Dalton or Laird to be edited, (7) with any of a dozen experts to be read for accuracy. Only the most careful mothering of this flock of papers enabled me to hold them together in some form or other.

This jigsaw, as Kings reported, appealed to Michener's love of intricate detail, but it was also part of the underlying drama that Michener had created while producing *Centennial*. More interesting, perhaps, was the fact that he took the time to record all of this information—a sign that he believed in his importance and his own destiny.

In the summer of 1973, his work in the West completed, Michener noted that in addition to his staff's salaries, which were paid by *Reader's Digest,* he had spent more than $50,000 for research—a sum that would prohibit most other writers from attempting such a book. Before fall he returned to Pipersville and awaited the final editing of his novel in New York.

Meanwhile, he attended to other projects, including work for the government in Washington, D.C., and an unusual request from his publisher to write a short book called *About Centennial*. The book was published in a limited edition to publicize the release of his novel.

Current political events made this an emotional time for Michener, as evidenced by letters that he wrote to correspondents who reacted in anger to articles that he published about Watergate. The first of these articles was lengthy and it appeared in June in the *New York Times Magazine* under the heading "Is America Burning?" Here, with much optimism, Michener wrote sympathetically of President Nixon and concluded that both the nation and the political system would survive Watergate and be stronger as a result of it. As for the President, Michener concluded he would remain in the White House, "a chastened but not a crippled leader."

But by fall, when matters worsened and Nixon gave only the most evasive explanations for his connections to Watergate, Michener changed his mind. In a short opinion piece for the Sunday *Times* in November, he said,

I was wrong. . . . When I wrote in June, I did so prayerfully, hoping that Mr. Nixon would rise to the cruel realities which

confronted him. I was deceived. Mr. Nixon never intended conciliation. He does not know how to bind a nation together, and it
is folly to continue hoping that he will learn. He must be neu-
tralized.

Leaving no doubt about what he thought must be done, Michener called
for the President's resignation, and failing that, his impeachment.

The flood of mail that arrived in Pipersville after this second article was
overwhelming, both in quantity and content. "Here we are forty seven
million voters for Nixon and you want to wrest our mandate for president
from us! Is this democracy?" cried a woman from York, Pennsylvania. And
from Saugerties, New York, a man said he had enjoyed reading many of
Michener's books: "They were delightful." But this opinion of President
Nixon "will lose you countless thousands who might have been readers of
your future writing."

In his polite responses to the letters, Michener said that Nixon had
accomplished "many admirable things" as President, "but I do not believe this
gives him license to alter our constitutional form of government." He also
noted that many people agreed with his opinions, as indeed they did, and he
predicted that Nixon would be out of office by April or May. He was only a
few months shy of the actual resignation date in August.

By early winter 1974, *Centennial* returned to Michener's center of focus
and he wrote to his three researchers:

> I'm working three days a week in New York with Bert Krantz
> and her eagle-eyed assistant. Five queries a page on a manuscript
> of 1,300 pages is 6,500 separate questions. They're wonderful
> . . . they know absolutely nothing about anything west of the
> Hudson River, so they are especially helpful in checking things I
> take for granted. . . .
> We're cutting a lot. The dynamiting of the rattlesnakes: out.
> Those glorious paragraphs from the local paper on the wreck of
> the circus train: out. The soldiers hunting bison north of Fort
> Laramie: out. Two of Lame Beaver's exploits: out. And lots of
> small paragraphs that added but did not illuminate: out.

By spring, four years after Michener had awakened with an outline for a
novel in mind, his gift for America was in production, and that September, in
909 pages covering 136 million years of history, *Centennial* was published.
Immediately the book became a runaway best seller with 300,000 copies in
print prior to its official publication date. Michener was amazed. *Centennial,*
he predicted, was going to be read by twenty million people. He was closer
now than ever to immortality.

## CHAPTER SEVENTEEN

# A Place in the World

A lifetime is a very short thing, sir.
We have so much to do and so few days
to do it in.

JAMES A. MICHENER, 1973

AMERICA'S LITERARY COMMUNITY was not impressed by Jim Michener's message in *Centennial,* perhaps because it was several years ahead of its time. Critics noted that Michener wrote the book to celebrate America's bicentennial, and most thought that was laudatory, but many focused on what one called the "shower of gold" that resulted from the novel, dropping more than two million dollars into Michener's hands. No one mentioned November Elegy, *Centennial's* crowning chapter, with its plethora of details about environmental issues and the author's striking social commentary. The moral tone of that final chapter was prophetic, not so much in the era of Watergate, but later, when a crippling energy crisis nearly stopped the nation in the summer of 1979. That July, in a nationally televised speech, President Jimmy Carter called for the restoration of America's values. It was time, said the President, to "join hands in America," to give the country a new sense of purpose and direction, to heal the wounds of the past and to march forward in the grand American tradition. It was as though he had just read November

Elegy and its message that an erosion of traditional values in America could only destroy the country.

The problem with such a message was that it was obvious, and as one Michener acquaintance pointed out, "It irritates the educated to have the obvious over-explained, especially in a 'Gee whiz, look what I have just discovered' fashion." But in continuing an elitist and exaggerated line of argument, this acquaintance, who was also a writer, legitimized James A. Michener's career. "I think that his most devoted admirers have read very little about *anything;* and if everyone who goes out and buys his opuses actually manages to read them, then millions of people are learning a lot of things that the populace *ought* to know."

Therein lay the Michener rub. Blinded by its own prejudices, the literary community missed the thrust of Michener's work, be it *Centennial,* or any one of his major novels. While the literati sometimes admitted that Michener's career was meaningful, most regretted that he did not write good literature for literature's sake, or good history for history's sake. But good literature and good history seemed to mean less to Michener than enlightening millions of people throughout the world. As George J. Becker pointed out in a short scholarly treatment of Michener's work in 1983, "He seeks to bring understanding and renewed zeal to a not-so-muddled majority, made up of us who are middle-class, middle-brow Middle America." To accomplish this, Michener created his own didactic narrative style, devoid of sex, violence, and sensationalism. Admittedly he was neither a great stylist nor a first-class social historian:

> I'm a realist about myself. I'm moderately good at what I do. I've written some books that have been enormously successful, but I'm not known for my style and I don't pretend to be an expert in anything. Simplicity is my virtue. . . . I don't really write well. I'm weak on floss. . . . I'm still learning, and I'm painfully aware that there are half a dozen people out there who write better than I do."

But like the nineteenth-century novelists whom he admired, Michener channeled enormous effort into structuring his epic tales so that he wrote with more scope and perspective than any contemporary American author in the twentieth century. Becker thought that "What Michener seems to have done is to take the examples of Balzac, Zola and Dos Passos and stretch them to panoramic histories covering three or four hundred years, or in the case of *The Source* several thousand years." Believing that art was serviceable, Michener used social observations, obstructed at times by a neo-conservative bent, to advocate progress and change in the status quo. As a result, he distinguished himself as America's most popular *serious* novelist, a consensus novelist who forecast mainstream America's public attitudes and shifting moods.

President Gerald R. Ford confirmed the significance of Michener's career in 1977 during a ceremony at the White House. Along with General Omar N. Bradley, Joe DiMaggio, Lady Bird Johnson, Vice-President Nelson A. Rockefeller, Norman Rockwell, and other distinguished Americans, Michener received the Medal of Freedom in the year following the nation's bicentennial celebration. As the President explained, "Author, teacher and popular historian, James Michener has entranced a generation with his compelling essays and novels. . . . The prolific writings of this master story-teller have expanded the knowledge and enriched the lives of millions." Later, Ford added privately, "I, like thousands of others, identify with Michener and feel he has left an indelible mark on our literature of this period."

Members of the literary community disagreed with Ford's assessment. "It seems to me that it's been a long time since Michener stirred the heart," said John Leonard, former editor of the *New York Times Book Review*. "He did it in *Tales of the South Pacific* and *The Fires of Spring,* but when he started writing doorstoppers he got away from that." *Washington Post* book critic Jonathan Yardley said flatly, "To suggest that Michener has any place in American 'literature' is preposterous on its face."

On a bad day, this sort of castigation tortured Michener. It was unfair, and it was beneath him. "Damn it," he told reporters, his high forehead wrinkled with frustration, "when you've done ten or twelve books in a row and they've all been enormous best sellers, you at least know *something*. . . . I get twenty or thirty letters every day, all year round, because the reading experience has touched someone's life." Even if there were not that many letters every day, there were enough of them to balance what the critics said, and always enough to make Michener want to continue writing, if even in spite of the critics. As he explained,

> I deem critics absolutely essential to good writing . . . and I would deplore any lessening of critical fervor. Perceptive criticism got me started; it was critics who gave me the Pulitzer Prize; it is critics who have selected my books for the wide readership they have enjoyed. . . .
>
> My books do not circulate in tremendous numbers because everyone says they're bad; they are read because the general society has come to know that I will do a reasonably decent job. This kind of acceptance is not only invaluable; it is to be cherished.

What startled Michener more than anything late in his career was that while the critics pounded him, the reading public's response to *Centennial* was overwhelming. He had enjoyed blockbusters before, but while *Centennial* climbed to the number one best-selling book of fiction in 1974, its price also broke the record for a hardcover novel. After bookstores sold 175,000 copies of the book at $10.95, Random House raised the price to $12.50, and during the last four months of the year the novel sold 330,289 copies. Upon reflection, Michener decided *Centennial* was going to endure for hundreds of years. "I suppose I feel this way," he explained to a reporter, "because I told a story that needed to be told."

There were other stories that needed to be told, he concluded, and as soon as he completed a nonfiction tribute to America's favorite pastime, which he titled *Sports in America,* he moved to Maryland's eastern shore to produce *Chesapeake,* an encore to his western saga, in 1978. The novel sold 250,000 copies the moment it was released and made publishing history by becoming the nation's number one best-seller in advance of its official publication date. He followed *Chesapeake* in 1980 with *The Covenant,* a story about South Africa, published in an unprecedented first printing of 300,000 copies. Incredibly, Michener's novel accounted for 25 percent of all fiction sales during the week before Christmas, and it snatched a record $1.75 million book club advance from the Literary Guild. Total earnings for this novel easily exceeded $3 million. Two years later, Michener produced *Space,* an exploration of "the new frontier," with a first printing so large that no warehouse in the country could stock all the copies. *Poland,* released late in the summer of 1983, sold three-quarters of a million copies in just four months to become the second best-selling book of fiction that year. Meanwhile, at the grand age of seventy-five, showing some signs of slowing down—he walked with a limp, the result of a deteriorating hip, and he was in constant pain from a herniated disc—Michener had moved to the Southwest to begin researching a book that would honor the Lone Star state's sesquicentennial in 1986. Even before the book was finished ABC optioned it for a ten-episode mini-series, certain that the story—presumably to be called *Texas*—"should be irresistible." When he completed his work in Texas, Michener had other ideas in mind: -

> I keep working pretty much along the lines that I dimly envisaged when I was in college. I remain a social studies person at heart, I suppose, with a great love of English, and this combination has been a most fruitful experience for me. I always have a half dozen ideas in mind that I'm ready to begin exploring.

Before starting another book, however, he planned to return to his native Bucks County, where he had been noticeably absent since the publication of *Centennial.*

The historian and novelist Paul Horgan once said, "One is where one lives, where one writes." Such was the case with Michener. At home one day in Pipersville, he explained,

> I can't turn my back on the place of which I come. . . . I'm in love with this part of my heritage, and I'd feel impoverished without it. I carry with me a full memory of my childhood, and feel lucky to bring it into comparison with the whole world. I

don't want to forget, I want to be reminded only because as a boy I knew what it meant to be dispossessed and I wanted no part of this for myself or anyone.

Between books Michener had always fortified himself on the hill in Pipersville, where during long walks he carried a stick and cut a winding path across his land, thinking all the while about his next project. "Out there, walking," he said, "is where I really do my writing."

For ten years, however, he had not gone home—except in 1976 to vote for Jimmy Carter—and it seemed he had practically lost the desire to return. Even the wildlife had disappeared from his land for a while. Hunters, in defiance of the trespassing laws, had penetrated the sanctuary, and once a bullet had ricocheted through the center of Michener's picture window. Fortunately, he was not home at the time.

Michener's problems in Bucks County had changed through the years, from prejudice in childhood to jealousy during a celebrated career, but the level of ridicule and resentment remained severe in parts of the county, and he always seemed unprepared for it. Sometimes it surfaced unexpectedly and in unusual ways. For example, in 1965 the local Quaker Meeting, to which he had belonged for twenty-five years, asked that he reexamine his priorities and participate in the Meeting. At the least it was suggested that he contribute financially. As one who had supported Quaker education, and who was about to give $100,000 to his Quaker alma mater, Swarthmore College, Michener must have been insulted. In a polite, but pointed letter to the clerk of overseers, he made known his intentions. "Dear Friend," he began,

> It would be logical . . . for you to drop me from your rolls. I will never be an active member in the strict sense of this word and it would be illogical for me to be carried on your books as one.
>
> It is, of course, obvious that I shall continue to adhere to the social teachings of your church and that my removal from your rolls will modify my behavior in no way. I shall proceed with my plans to help support Quaker education and I would hope that my public and private deportment will not bring too great disfavor on the movement of which I was once a passive part.

In closing he explained that when he had taught in Greeley, Colorado, teachers were required to state publicly their religion, and he recalled that the chairman of his department, one of the most Christian men he knew, had announced that he was a Home Baptist. "I suppose I am congenitally a Home Quaker," Michener added. "I acknowledge that an organized church must be built of what one might call Meeting Quakers, but this I cannot be."

The Quaker incident irritated him less than what happened in 1972, at about the time he departed Bucks County for a year in the West. It was a petty but ugly matter, and it deeply hurt Michener. "If anyone wants to see how a man's community thinks of a writer while he is alive he could profitably look into the files of this classic bit of revelry," Michener noted in his private papers while he was in Colorado. "It was ridiculous but also highly instructive."

The episode began when a county library committee, without consulting Michener, decided to name the new Quakertown branch library in his honor. Almost immediately the Quakertown community, situated several miles north of Doylestown and adjacent to Pipersville, protested most vehemently. Friends of the Library said there were political implications behind naming a library after Michener, an active Democrat who had recently helped his party gain control of the county, and organized in opposition to the proposal. Spearheading the movement was Nancy Larrick Crosby, president of the Friends, who argued that Michener was better known to the Doylestown area than to Quakertown, and that the people of her community preferred to include the words "Upper Bucks" in the library's name. "We've been snubbed by the other end of the county," she explained, "and we resent it."

When Michener's secretary in Bucks County wrote to him in Denver and explained what was happening, he was amused at first. "I have grown to think of Nancy Larrick Crosby as one of my favorite people in the whole world because she is so *real,*" he responded to Nadia Orapchuck, "and I want nothing done that would disturb her in any way or curb her energies. We need gals like that. They remind us what we're fighting for." Mari noted in the margin of the letter: "I certainly don't agree!" Michener did, however, ask to be kept informed of the incident "for reasons which may become clearer later."

The protest quickly lost all humor for him when Friends of the Library collected 750 signatures in opposition to placing his name above the door of their library. They had circulated petitions throughout the shopping district of their community, and at the local high school, too. Now Michener was perturbed. As he later explained,

> When the community enlisted 10-year-old students in the fight against me, and when they wrote full page editorials against me in letter after letter to the editor to the effect that I was contaminating their community, I thought things got most unpleasant. I wonder what those school children who signed the petition against me will think of the affair when they are old enough to read.

In a rare mood he seemed to want vengeance, so much so that he allowed this trivial event to steal precious time from his research and writing schedule while he planned a counterattack. On January 3, 1973, he made his intentions known to his secretary, who also became part of his scheme:

> This letter is sent to you in the severest confidence and you may not discuss it with your husband or anyone else. . . . the news will probably break in the immediate future, but let it come from

[Colorado]. It is something that only pointy-headed people like you and me, with an evil sense of humor, will appreciate.

It so happened that while "the little one room library in Quakertown was raising bloody hell about having its sacred precincts named after me," the University of Northern Colorado, originally Colorado State College when Michener had taught there in the thirties, was building "one of the great research libraries in the west, a stupendous affair, and as handsome a building as I've seen in recent years, a real winner." When the five-million dollar library and media resource center was about completed, with a small percentage of the money coming from Michener, the university announced that it wanted to name the library after their most famous alumnus and former faculty member. In addition, on the top floor of the building, the university planned to include the James A. Michener room, complete with the author's desk, typewriter, books, research, and correspondence from the period during which he wrote *Centennial*.

Teasing about a "dreadful pain" in his side from laughing too much, Michener continued to his secretary:

> Now that you have stopped ricochetting around the kitchen walls you will understand why it was imperative that I make no comment about the ultra sad events at Quakertown. . . . I will, of course, withdraw my name with full apologies to the people of Quakertown for any embarrassment they may have been under. I will send you a carefully worded letter for you to hand personally to the commissioners and later to the two newspapers. In it I shall apologize for having been so busy out here that I could not attend properly to the affairs in Bucks County.

As soon as the local press printed the news from Colorado, Michener planned to have his secretary wait two days and then hand-deliver his letters. He gave her precise instructions as to how to go about it. At 11:00 A.M. she was to appear at the commissioners' offices in the Doylestown courthouse. "If all or any of the commissioners are absent, merely deliver the letters to their secretaries." Then "have lunch on me and at one or two o'clock hand deliver a copy [of the letter] to the [Doylestown] *Intelligencer*." That completed, she was to "drive to Quakertown and hand-deliver [a copy of the letter] to the editor of the *Free Press*." However, with the exception of typing his "carefully worded" letter, she was to do nothing until she heard from him again.

In the interim, Michener had written a long, sorrowful letter to his friend of many years, Pearl Buck, who had lived in Bucks County and had since moved to Vermont. He began,

> I have been thinking of you very much these days . . . a recent occurrence in your old community has served to bring you to mind. It is one you would appreciate. Indeed, it is a kind of

recapitulation of what you went through at various times. It is a tragedy which seems inescapable, and I am somewhat amused—if this is the right word—to find that in your absence as a favorite kicking-ball, the community has resorted to me.

In two and a half single-spaced pages he relayed the lamentable story.

I am bewildered as to why people behave this way. . . . I wonder if the people of this county would have found greater pleasure in me if I had remained a problem child, destined for reform school and jail instead of a man struggling with the full range of contemporary problems. I have considerable evidence that had I made a complete mess of my life, my neighbors would have felt a little more at ease. . . .

For the bulk of my public life, whenever I have done anything commendable, a gentleman who lives somewhere in the Philadelphia area sends me an anonymous letter of the vilest contents, pointing out that whereas I may have fooled the others, he knows better. And he proceeds to list with relish every whisper he has ever heard against me, every reminiscence of possible ill doing. He has been a powerful force in my life, a most salutary one. Not only does he deflate me at time of possible arrogance, but he also gives me a target against which to judge my actions. . . . I wish I knew his name so that I could inform him of how invaluable he has been in my life. . . .

Well, it's a mystery why people behave in this way. Is it a fear of talent? Is it no more than raw envy expressed in strange ways? . . . I am distressed that such behavior should be common in Bucks County, of all places, because it continues to pride itself as being a refuge of the arts . . . but not of artists. Some well intentioned people came to visit us . . . to assure us that "when Mr. Michener is dead, we feel sure the county will name something after him," as if I had sought that empty honor. My wife summarized our feelings rather nicely, I thought, when she replied, "If this county ever names any building after my husband, I will dynamite it out of the ground by nightfall." We promise to do the same for you. . . .

It's a marvelous world, Pearl. You set us all an example for graceful acceptance of those inescapable insanities, and we love you for it. Get well . . . we need you.

From a hospital bed in Vermont, where she was recovering from gallbladder surgery, Miss Buck responded sensitively on October 16:

After thinking it over, my feeling is that you are too big a person to pay any attention to these people who are harassing you. If I were you, I would ignore the whole situation and all those concerned. I am sure that what you say about the Bucks County people is true and yet, who cares? There is so much else to enjoy there. . . .

What I am trying to say is that people like us . . . cannot ever expect understanding from people less successful. . . . In other words, my friend, I beg you to ignore the whole local petty situation. You are a man of the world . . . in the very youthful and immature nation, the United States. Laugh at the whole situation. It is not important. What is important is that you see your place in the world. The approval or disapproval of little local people is nothing. Continue to do your kindnesses, not because of the people, but because that is the person you are. Do not descend into the miasma of small people. Expect nothing from them, ask nothing, want nothing.

Michener knew that Miss Buck was right, and he decided not to bait the people of Bucks County with his "carefully worded" letter. It helped that ardent leaders on the library board, along with the county commissioners, refused to back down to Crosby's committee. The recent protest, said the library board's president, was not representative of Upper Bucks County's sentiments, and the library board proceeded with its plans to dedicate the James A. Michener Branch of the Bucks County Free Library in early 1973, hoping that Michener would be the guest of honor.

"I was robbed," Nadia wrote to her boss when he stopped her from hand-delivering his letters, "no lunch . . . no beer . . . no pony express deliveries. . . . Curses, I'm foiled." She had looked forward to getting even, but she dropped the matter. "To have shared this tête-à-tête with you was delightful and still brings forth a private silly grin from time to time," she concluded.

Michener was not grinning, not yet, anyway. He thought the incident was one of the "saddest" experiences of his writing career. He could never understand why people in his own community felt compelled to attack him, when thousands, perhaps millions, of people in the world thought he was one of the century's greatest writers Years after the library dedication ceremony, at which Michener graciously appeared and delivered a short address, Nancy Larrick Crosby still resented the presence of Michener's name on her community's library. As for the pain and humiliation that her campaign caused Michener, she was not apologetic. "I don't feel sorry for Michener," she said. "He came off well in dollars and cents and fame."

Indeed he did, but the respect of his community meant something to him, too. Shortly after that respect was bestowed on him in what Nadia Orapchuck called a "bass-ackward" way, he moved out of the county, thinking that someday he might return to retire on the hill.

There was little chance of Michener retiring, though. As Pearl Buck revealed, James A. Michener was a man of the world: he belonged to no one place; to no one people. He seemed to understand this, too, when on Easter Sunday 1969, from Seville, Spain, he wrote to eight of his friends and explained that if he died while abroad or away from home, he wished to be buried where he died, and in the simplest manner. He felt this way, he said, because he had lived in many parts of the world and found them all congenial. He had been at home with people of all colors and creeds, and he would be content buried among whatever people he happened to be visiting at the moment in death. Furthermore, he could be buried "in any kind of cemetery which local custom provides, under the auspices of any church or religion that will tend to the matter, and under any circumstances that might arise." He could be cremated, buried at sea, "or anything else."

Death was of little concern to Michener, but, barring poor health, only death would stop him from writing. He worked every day as though he still had something to prove. In the early 1980s, when interviewers asked him if he had thought any more about retirement, he shook his head and replied:

> I think about Tolstoy, Flaubert and Dickens, and I'm jealous of what those authors accomplished. Because I am jealous, I am a writer now. I remain jealous and this gives me a guide to what I might accomplish. Without that sense of jealousy, of greatness, I doubt that I would have amounted to much.

Reminded that it was Hokusai, the great Japanese printmaker, who said, "At 90 I shall penetrate the mystery of things, at 110 everything I do will be alive," Michener responded, "That is my commitment, yes. Not fatuously, either. I really have some things to say."

# Notes

The notes have been keyed to the text by page number and catch phrase. The following abbreviations have been used:

| | |
|---|---|
| GB | George P. Brett, Jr. |
| PB | Pearl Buck |
| BC | Bennett Cerf |
| AGD | A. Grove Day |
| AE | Albert R. Erskine |
| HL | Hobart Lewis |
| JAM | James A. Michener |
| MM | Mari Michener |
| VNM | Vange Nord Michener |
| OM | Osmond Molarsky |
| WM | Wilbur Murra |
| CS | Cecil Scott |
| TS | Theresa (Mrs. Joseph) Shane |
| AS | Ann Silverman |
| HS | Herman Silverman |
| RS | Robert E. Spiller |
| HMS | Helen M. Strauss |
| LT | W. Lester Trauch |
| WV | William V. Vitarelli |
| DW | DeWitt Wallace |
| JW | John T. Welsh |
| JH | John P. Hayes |
| COR | Correspondence (in the possession of the person to whom the letter was written, unless otherwise noted, in which case it is in LOC or UNC collections) |
| LOC | Library of Congress (the Manuscript Reading Room houses most of the Michener collection of papers and manuscripts. The collection includes 220 containers, occupies 75 linear feet of shelf space, and includes approximately 54,600 items) |

NYT     The *New York Times*
PI       The *Philadelphia Inquirer*
UNC     University of Northern Colorado (the Michener Library houses
         that portion of the Michener collection which pertains to the
         research and writing of *Centennial)*
SC       Swarthmore College (the library is the repository for all of
         Michener's published works; also houses a collection of papers
         relating to the research and writing of *The Covenant;* and the alumni
         office keeps a large biographical file)
RD       *Reader's Digest*


# CHAPTER ONE

1. "Men are not": JAM, *The Fires of Spring* (New York: Random
   House, 1949; reprint, Bantam, 1951), pp. 413–14.
1. "Gentlemen": JAM COR to *Newsweek,* undated (c. 1950), LOC.
2. Living national treasures: Respondents to the *Family Weekly* survey in
   1983 also elected Walter Cronkite, Hank Aaron, Dr. Jonas Salk, and
   Martha Graham.
2. "Where do": JH attended the autograph party on November 17,
   1978, at John Wanamaker, Philadelphia.
2. "A fundamental fact": JAM to JH, December 15, 1971, and November 17, 1978.
3. "I've worked too hard": John DeGroot to JH, December 29, 1981.
4. "My best advice": Jack Beatty, review of *Chesapeake, Newsweek,* July
   24, 1978, p. 82.
4. "Years later": JAM to JH, December 15, 1971.
4. "It's not fair": Larry Swindell, "All Those Readers Are His Grand
   Jury," PI, undated clipping in LOC.
4. "It bothers Jimbo": Edward J. Piszek, Sr., to JH, October 29, 1981.
   The film series was titled "The World of James Michener" and
   included nine programs broadcast on educational television.
4. "I am more academic": JAM COR to JH, November 16, 1977; and
   Steve Neal, "Michener: Last Stand in Bucks," PI, January 14, 1974, p.
   1.
5. Own count: JAM COR to JH, November 16, 1977; JAM to JH, May
   1980.
5. "One of the": UNC.
5. "I have a form letter": Lawrence Grobel, "Playboy Interview: James
   A. Michener," *Playboy,* September 1981, pp. 65–92; JAM to JH, May
   1980.
5. Guiding spirit: JAM to JH, September 1975.
6. An essay: Untitled, container 128, LOC.
6. "Hell of a good pro": JAM to JH, October 1975.
6. "There is a great deal": *Playboy,* p.76; and "Good Morning America"

TV interview, September 8, 1983.

7. "Jim has money": DeGroot, 1981.
7. "Jim is strange": HS to JH, May 26, 1982; May 2, 1984.
7. "Not interested": AS to JH, May 26, 1982; May 2, 1984.
7. Vietnam: AS.
7. Great Society: AS.
8. "Jim's closest friends": HS.
8. Has given away: Bruce Beans, "The Source," *Philadelphia,* June 1981, p.126; William Ecenbarger, "James Michener in Space," *Today,* PI, October 10, 1982, pp. 35–36.
8. "Everybody who works": JAM to JH, December 15, 1971.
8. "Jim takes no advantage": HS.
8. Incident in Frankfurt: Piszek.
9. "Pineapple juice": *Playboy,* p. 68.
9. "A depression Quaker": JAM to JH, September 1975; and "Good Morning America," 1983.
9. Coat, gloves: Source requested anonymity.
9. "Aware of issues": AS.
10. "I'm amazed": JAM to JH, November 17, 1978.

## CHAPTER TWO

11. Never knew his parents: JAM to JH, December 15, 1971. With permission of JAM, JH searched for JAM's birth certificate in Pennsylvania and New York. Neither state could produce the document.
11. Evidence suggests: The best single piece of evidence regarding JAM's birth is Robert Michener's letter as quoted on p. 13. Most members of the Michener family, and lifelong residents of Doylestown, who said JAM was born to Mabel Michener, asked not to be identified. David G. Michener, son of Robert, in COR to JH, June 21, 1983, said "There has never been any question to anyone within the family that James was Dad's brother. . . . Physically it would be silly to even consider any other alternative." David also pointed out that Mabel Michener's last will and testament left all her possessions to her two sons, Robert E. and James A. Michener.
12. "Adopted": JAM to JH, December 15, 1971; September 1975.
12. "To hell with it": JAM to JH, October 1975.
13. "Has bred": William W. H. Davis, *History of Bucks County* (Lewis Publishing, 1905), p. 585.
13. Forced off the farm: Robert Michener COR to Kenneth A. Moe, September 14, 1976.
13. "Strange how vivid": Robert Michener.
13. Alienated her: "Straight from the Source: Michener Talks Back," *Philadelphia,* August 1981. In Bruce Beans's article about JAM in *Philadelphia,* June 1981, p. 120, he said Mabel Michener was "scorned

by her late husband's noted Quaker family for subsisting with a
sweatshop and an orphanage." In responding to that statement, JAM
wrote in his letter to the editor, as cited above, "Totally accurate, and
much worse than Beans indicates."

13. "Weekly crises": JAM to JH, September 1975.
14. "On many nights": JAM to JH.
14. "I made up": JAM to JH.
16. "A strict mother": Eleanor Van Sant to JH, October 26, 1980.
17. Birthdays: JAM to JH, September 1975.
17. "I was surprised": JAM, "Six Children and a Tree," PI *Book Review,*
    December 5, 1948, p. 1.
18. "I expected you": PI *Book Review,* December 5, 1948, p. 1.
18. "Only eight": Van Sant.
19. "They fed him": JAM to JH, September 1975.


# CHAPTER THREE

20. To sneak through: JAM to JH, September 1975.
21. "River families": Donald Knox, producer and director, "James
    Michener's Home Country," KYW-TV, Philadelphia, 1968.
21. Shortchanging: *Playboy,* p. 75. JAM said, "We played that amuse-
    ment park like an accordion, finagling the turnstiles, stealing the
    bloody place blind. I very quickly learned all the tricks of the
    trade. . . . When I go to the theater now and pass in money, I watch.
    They're using every trick we used. It's still flourishing."
21. "People who owned": JAM to JH, September 1975.
22. "I am indebted": JAM to JH, October 1975.
22. "As a result": George C. Murray Memorial, Inc., reunion program,
    1957, Bucks County Historical Society.
22. United Boys' Brigade: Robert McNealy to JH, April 9, 1977.
23. Parents forbade: Ed Twining to JH, February 26, 1977.
23. "Present": McNealy to JH.
23. A brawl: McNealy to JH.
24. "The baskets": JAM, *Sports in America* (New York: Random House,
    1976), p. 4.
24. Waving away: Twining to JH.
24. "Obsessed with basketball": LT to JH, February 26, 1977.
24. B class: JAM to JH, September 1975.
25. "One thing we knew": LT.
25. "To be a bright": JAM to JH, September 1975.
25. "Most sadistic treatment": LOC, 1963.
26. "Silly sentimentalities": LT. JAM's satire, "Silly Sentimentalities,"
    appeared in *The Torch,* January 1924, p. 2.
27. "Son of a bitch": JAM to JH, May 1980.
27. "An Old, Old Theme": JAM, *The Torch,* May 1925, pp. 10–11.

28. "Surrogate father": *Sports,* p. 5.
28. "Psychological costs": JAM to JH, October 1975.
29. "A field goal": J. Van Pelt, "Athletics," *The Torch,* December 1923, pp. 14–15.
29. Victory triggered: Ed Twining to JH, February 26, 1977.
29. "Last moments": *Sports,* p. 6.
29. "In our little world": *Sports,* p. 6; and JAM to JH, December 15, 1971; and October 1975.
30. "A terrible thing": JAM to JH, September 1975.


## CHAPTER FOUR
31. "For this is": JAM, *The Fires of Spring* (New York: Random House, 1949; reprint, Bantam, 1951), p. 430.
32. "Guarded education": John M. Moore, "A Centennial Tribute and a Question," Baccalaureate Address, SC, June 3, 1973, p. 11.
32. "Service to society": Homer D. Babbidge, Jr., "The Pursuit of Truth in a Quaker College," *Friends Journal,* June 1, 1964, p. 245.
32. "Flee the contamination": JAM COR to Marion Hall, June 13, 1976.
32. "He just moved in": RS to JH, November 4, 1981.
33. Awarded surreptitiously: Evaristo Murray is dead. Information provided by former college classmate who requested anonymity. When Michener was told of Murray's story, he wrote to JH on November 4, 1981: "I cannot conceivably understand how the business association had anything at all to do with obtaining me a sports scholarship. I know of no recommendation even that they submitted. I assumed it was my school record and my interview which sealed the matter, but if they say so, I wish you would say so also. Makes things more interesting."
33. In 1976: JAM, *Sports,* p. 5.
33. "Full scholarship": Paul F. Levy, "Hard Work Got Me Out of the Poorhouse, Says Millionaire Author James Michener," *National Enquirer,* September 8, 1981, p. 13.
33. "Open scholarships": JAM COR to JH, January 10, 1982.
34. "Intramural basketball": JAM COR to JH, January 10, 1982.
34. "The college game": *Fires,* p. 213.
34. "At the Palestra": Charles P. Larkin, Jr., telephone interview with JH, January 12, 1982.
34. "Got no money": *Fires,* p. 162.
34. "I saw them as doomed": Quoted in Michael J. Bandler, "Elder-Author Shares Youth's Malaise," Baltimore *Morning Sun,* July 4, 1971, p. 1.
35. "Everyone knew Jim": H. Thomas Hallowell,Jr., telephone interview with JH, January 7, 1982.
35. Storm the dormitories: *Fires,* p. 178.

35. Ice cubes: Horace Sutton, "The Strange Case of James Michener," *Paradise of the Pacific,* September–October 1963, pp. 21–64.

36. "Elizabethan blank verse": JAM to JH, December 15, 1971.

36. "Brainwashing their offspring": Source requested anonymity.

37. "What we got": JAM to JH, October 1975; and JAM COR to JH, February 9, 1979.

37. "A productive life": JAM, "When Does Education Stop?" RD, December 1962, pp. 153–56.

37. "Without discipline": JAM to JH, December 15, 1971, and September 1975.

38. In public service: JAM COR to Hall, 1976.

38. "If you carry": *Fires,* p. 191.

39. Psychological exercise: RS.

39. "Gee whiz": Source requested anonymity.

39. "Spring Virtue": JAM, *The Portfolio,* March 1928, pp. 10–12.

40. Sir Galahad: OM COR to JH, September 1, 1983.

40. "My own principal impression": OM COR to JH, May 15, 1984.

41. "Michener was rejected": OM to Kenneth A. Moe, undated tape-recorded message.

41. "College landmark": Source requested anonymity.

41. "A poor steelworker": "Michener, Dr. Barnes in Stormy Feud over Art and Life on the Main Line," PI, April 5, 1950, p. 11. Supposedly, when JAM attended SC, he heard "of a very wealthy man who had a hidden collection of art. I outsmarted him by sending him a letter postmarked in Pittsburgh and stating I was a poor steelworker who would like to see his nice pictures." The ruse worked, and Michener visited the famous Barnes Museum for a private viewing of the collection, which included works by Picasso, Renoir, Cezanne, and others. Barnes never liked Michener, once the latter began publishing books and articles. In the PI, Barnes said Michener "glamorized ordinary people" and catered to "the smug complacency of snobs."

41. "Plain people": Joseph Miller, "Barnes Wanted 'Plain People' Admitted Free to Art Gallery," PI, April 5, 1962.

41. Haircut: Barbara Pearson Lange Godfrey to JH, October 7, 1981.

42. "The hazard of attending": Source requested anonymity.

42. "Respect religious teachings": JAM COR to Betty W. Morehouse, clerk of overseers, Doylestown Monthly Meeting, August 12, 1965, LOC.

42. "When one has sat": JAM, "Some Practical Applications," in *Through a Quaker Archway,* ed. Horace M. Lippincott (New York: Yoseloff, 1959), pp. 61–75.

43. "That the fate": Robert O. Byrd, *Quaker Ways in Foreign Policy* (Toronto: University of Toronto Press, 1960), p. 17.

43. Chautauqua Assembly: *Academic American Encyclopedia,* (Danbury, Conn.: Grolier, 1982), Vol. 4, p. 305.

43.     "The Swarthmore Chautauqua": Barbara Pearson Lange Godfrey.
44.     "A poorhouse crum": *Fires,* p. 272.


# CHAPTER FIVE

45.     "I doubt that": JAM, "On Wasting Time," *Campus Colloquy,* Winter 1974, pp. 6–7.
45.     "Secret of happiness": "Ivy Orator Expresses New Valuation of College Life," JAM Baccalaureate Address SC, *The Phoenix,* June 3, 1929, p. 7.
46.     "We really did believe": JAM to JH, May 1980.
46.     "Posing": JAM, "Michener Remembers," *Hill,* (Hill School *Bulletin),* September 1981, pp. 12–13.
46.     "For half a year": *Hill,* pp. 12–13.
46.     "Kept me indoors": *Hill,* p. 13.
47.     Toogood: JAM to JH, May 1980.
47.     "It came along": JAM to JH.
47.     "Herr Wagner": JAM to JH, September 1975.
47.     "Luckily": JAM to JH.
48.     "I am settled here": JAM COR to RS, July 20, 1932.
48.     Studying the novel form: JAM COR to RS, 1932.
48.     Rounding out his interests: JAM COR to RS, 1932.
49.     "It was a formative": JAM to JH, December 15, 1971.
49.     "Knocking around Europe": JAM to JH, September 1975.
49.     "Brightness of vision": JAM, "Idealism Today," speech delivered in Chicago; and published in *High Points,* May 1949, pp. 13–21; condensed, *Education Digest,* December 1949, pp. 44–47. Reprinted in E. R. Davis and W. C. Hummel, eds., *Reading for Opinion* (Englewood Cliffs, N.J.: Prentice-Hall, 1960), pp. 252–54.
50.     "He was brilliant": James H. Taylor COR to JH, August 1, 1981.
50.     "Jim had two habits": TS to JH, July 22, 1981.
50.     "I liked seeing": JAM to JH, May 1980.
51.     "Keen competitive spirit": WV COR to JH, September 18, 1980; and November 16, 1980.
51.     "One night a group": TS.
51.     "Patti was actually": TS.
51.     "Moderately large classes": "Idealism Today," p. 1.
52.     "With practically no regrets": "Idealism Today," p. 2.
52.     "Accumulation of knowledge": William L. Wrinkle, assisted by members of the staff of the Secondary School, *The New High School in the Making* (New York: American Book Company, 1938), Introduction.
52.     "Some special calling": *New High School,* Introduction.
53.     "The social studies teacher": *New High School,* pp. 65, 76.
53.     "He stimulated youth": Edith M. Selberg COR to JH, July 1, 1979.

53. "Constructive thinking": "Idealism Today," p. 5.
54. "In the social studies": JAM, "Bach and Sugar Beets," *Music Educators Journal,* September 1938, pp. 29, 43.
54. "I believe that social studies": *Music Educators Journal,* p. 43.
55. "A great philosopher": Mayre Kagohara COR to JH, July 1, 1979.
55. Angell's Club: JAM to Educational Television Staff of UNC, May 1, 1973, transcript at UNC.
55. "Cicerone to Colorado": JAM, *About Centennial* (New York: Random House, 1974), p. 1.
56. "At least three times": *About Centennial,* p. 2.
56. "They knocked some sense": JAM to JH, May 1980.
57. "I find myself": JAM COR to RS, September 3, 1949.
57. His departure: JAM, "The Mature Social Studies Teacher," *Social Education,* November 1970, pp. 762–63.
57. "He didn't need me": JAM to JH, December 15, 1971.
58. "Too much talent": Robert T. Porter, MD to JH, August 1979.
58. "If I had listened": JAM to JH, September 1975.

## CHAPTER SIX

60. "What Are We Fighting For?": *Progressive Education,* November 1941, pp. 342–48.
60. "Draft board": JAM to JH, September 1975.
60. Knowlton: WM COR to Kenneth A. Moe, October 2, 1976.
60. "After war broke out": WM COR to Moe, 1976.
60. "What I saw": JAM to JH, May 1980.
60. Persuading Patti: WM COR to Moe, 1976.
61. Petitioned his superiors: Navy file, LOC.
61. "Good woman secretary": JAM to JH, December 15, 1971.
62. "On most of my assignments": JAM to JH, May 1980.
62. Mother Margaret: JAM, "Perfect Teacher," *Coronet,* June 1951, pp. 21–24.
63. "As close to paradise": JAM, "James Michener's Return to Bali Hai," *The Sunday Bulletin,* Philadelphia, November 22, 1970, pp. B1, 6.
64. Reading list: JAM COR to RS, December 15, 1944.
64. "The literary fare": JAM COR to RS, December 15, 1944.
65. The question stunned him: JAM, "When Does Education Stop?" RD, December 1962, pp. 153–56.
65. Plane crash: This was one of three plane crashes in which JAM experienced a brush with death. The most widely publicized of the three occurred in 1957, the day *Sputnik* was launched. "That was a pretty frightening thing," JAM said in *Playboy,* p. 72. "I was the oldest person there. Christ, we were in deep waves and the plane disintegrated in three minutes. We were in the water, in rafts, for about 18 hours before planes got to us and radioed a Japanese fishing boat." In the crash, JAM lost an entire book manuscript about the Japanese artist, Hokusai, as well as the outline for *Hawaii.*

65.   "That discovery": *Fires,* p. 277.
65.   "I was as good": JAM COR to Leslie Laird, January 31, 1973.
65.   "One Sunday": Porter to JH, August 1979.
66.   In one corner: JAM to JH, December 15, 1971; and AGD, *James A. Michener* (New York: Twayne, 1964; 1977), p. 22.
66.   "One was a brilliant": JAM COR to RH, 1946, LOC; and JAM to JH, December 15, 1971.
66.   "I wanted them": JAM COR to RH, 1946, LOC; and JAM to JH, December 15, 1971.
67.   "I wish I could tell": JAM, *Tales of the South Pacific* (New York: Macmillan, 1947), p. 1.
67.   "Each man": *Tales,* p. 72.
68.   "Now, I know": GB COR to JAM, January 28, 1944, LOC.
68.   "You know well": JAM COR to GB, January 31, 1944, LOC.
69.   "Long experience": GB COR to JAM, May 17, 1945, LOC.
69.   "All in all": JAM COR, Navy file, 1946, LOC.
69.   "Long after I'm dead": AGD, *James A. Michener,* p. 22.
69.   "A lot of work": GB COR to JAM, June 7, 1945, LOC.
69.   "The writer's own attitude": GB COR to JAM, June 7, 1945, LOC.
70.   "All of us agree": Harold Latham COR to JAM, July, 1945, LOC.
70.   "My recent experiences": JAM COR to Latham, November 23, 1945, LOC.
70.   "We need you": GB COR to JAM, October 8, 1945, LOC.


## CHAPTER SEVEN
73.   "I figured costs": JAM to JH, December 15, 1971.
73.   Wedding band: WM COR to Kenneth A. Moe, October 2, 1976.
73.   Never saw her: JAM to JH, December 15, 1971; May 1980.
73.   "Jim was secure": OM COR to JH, May 15, 1984.
74.   "You have no doubt": JAM COR to Latham, undated, LOC.
74.   "I wonder": Fan mail, LOC.
74.   "The rare first edition": AGD, *James A. Michener,* p. 23.
75.   "Isn't going to create": JAM COR, undated, LOC.
75.   "This long book": Orville Prescott, "Books of the Times," NYT, February 3, 1947, p. 17.
75.   "My dear Mr. Michener": Fan mail, LOC.
76.   "Michener's trash": Fan mail, LOC.
76.   "I jumped on the telephone": JAM COR, 1947, LOC.
76.   "When I got home": JAM to JH, September 1975.
77.   $500 against royalties: Dorothy Dunbar Bromley, "Writer Resists Fame," New York *Herald Tribune,* May 29, 1949, p. 1.
77.   "I flinch": Orville Prescott COR to JAM, April 8, 1947, LOC.
78.   The average novelist: Doylestown *Daily Intelligencer,* April 28, 1949.
78.    "After your first book": LT, "Pulitzer Prize Winner Talks of Books,

Authors," Doylestown *Daily Intelligencer,* October 21, 1949.

78.   "One of the worst": JAM to GB, March 16, 1948, LOC.

78.   "Dear Jim Michener": GB COR to JAM, March 18, 1948, LOC.

79.   "I feel a": JAM COR to CS, March 31, 1948, LOC.

80.   "Any advance?": Saxe Commins COR to JAM, March 9, 1948, LOC.

80.   May 3, 1948: Horace Sutton, "The Strange Case of James Michener," *Paradise of the Pacific,* September–October 1963, p. 22.

81.   "With the deepest": JAM COR, May 4, 1948, LOC.

82.   "Forcefully relayed": Peter Eihss, "Hemingway Lost Pulitzer in 1941," NYT, April 20, 1966, p.41; and Robert Bendiner, "Truth about the Pulitzer Prize Awards," *McCall's,* May 1966, pp. 82–83.

82.   "That prize initiated": John Hohenberg, *The Pulitzer Prizes* (New York: Columbia University Press, 1974), p. 201; and Pulitzer Prize jury transcript, 1947, Columbia University.

82.   No great significance: John P. Marquand, review of *Return to Paradise,* by JAM, *Book of the Month Club News,* April 1951, p. 1.

82.   "I know I don't belong": James Atlas, "Life with Mailer," NYT *Magazine,* September 9, 1979, p. 53.

82.   "There was a flurry": JAM to JH, December 15, 1971; and Joanna Pagson, "Bucks County Portrait," *Bucks County Life,* undated, p. 21, JAM Branch of the Bucks County Free Library, Quakertown, Pa.

83.   "Somewhat autobiographical": "Pulitzer Boy," *New Yorker,* undated, LOC; and *Current Biography* 1948, p. 450.

83.   Two reporters: Bromley, p.1; and Sidney Fields, "Only Human," c. 1951, publication unknown, LOC.

84.   "If I had written": "James Michener's Tribute to Unknown Friend," *Horizons,* Haverford College, Fall 1965, p. 20.

84.   "When I read": JAM to JH, May 1972.

84.   $4,500: Don Ross, "'South Pacific' Actor: Michener," New York *Herald Tribune,* July 31, 1960, Section 4, p. 1.

85.   "The whole tenor": JAM COR to HS, undated.

85.   Shot full of novocain: "James Michener Finds a New 'South Pacific' in a Jungle Village," PI, August 31, 1972, p. 23.

86.   Performed . . . once a week: Herbert Mitgang, "Why Michener Never Misses," *Saturday Review,* November 1980, p. 23.

86.   "It never amounts": JAM to JH, December 15, 1971.

86.   "In many ways": JAM to JH, September 1975.

86.   One of her tenants: HMS, *A Talent for Luck* (New York: Random House, 1979), p. 97.

86.   "I've never really": *Talent,* p. 99.

87.   "Handball": *Talent,* p. 100.

87.   "One must always": *Talent,* p. 99.

87.   Spin-offs: HMS tried many times to get back the rights but could not.

87.   "He looked at me": *Talent,* p. 102.

88.		"It's a major": JAM to JH, May 1972.
88.		"You can make it": JAM to JH, September 1975.


CHAPTER EIGHT
90.		"About August 7": Doylestown *Daily Intelligencer,* August 9, 1949.
90.		"Some time ago": JAM COR to Walter Winchell, July 7, 1949, LOC.
91.		"A hankering suspicion": JAM, *The Voice of Asia* (New York: Random House, 1951), p. 4.
91.		"A monomania": *Voice,* p. 4.
91.		"The destiny": *Voice,* p. 5.
91.		"There is only one": JAM, *Return to Paradise* (New York: Random House, 1951; reprinted Fawcett Crest, 1974), p. 416.
92.		"More intensive exchange": Loy W. Henderson, "The United States and Asia," *Vital Speeches,* May 15, 1950, p. 461.
92.		"Imagine": JAM, "Fiji," *Holiday,* June 1950, pp. 60–63.
92.		"Today": JAM, "Australia," *Holiday,* November 1950, pp. 98–109.
92.		"The relationship": JAM, "New Zealand," *Holiday,* January 1951, pp. 44–47.
93.		"The essays are superb": Walter Havighurst, "Michener of the South Pacific," *The English Journal,* October 1952, p. 401.
93.		"Resolutely determined": *Voice,* pp. 8, 53.
93.		"Whether or not": JAM, "Blunt Truths about Asia," *Life,* June 4, 1951, pp. 96–123.
94.		"Understand the Asiatic": Introduction, "Teller of Tales," New York *Herald Tribune,* May 8, 1951, p. 1.
94.		"Intellectually honorable": *Return,* p. 7.
95.		"America has": *Voice,* p. 327.
95.		"Fighting for": *Voice,* p. 329.
95.		"In this sweeping": *Voice,* p. 333.
95.		"For the life of us": HMS COR to JAM, February 26, 1951, LOC.
96.		"I'm sure that we": DW COR to JAM, June 10, 1952, LOC.
96.		$2,500: HL to JH, July 1980.
96.		"100% Educational *Interest*": DeWitt Wallace, quoted in James Playsted Wood, *Of Lasting Interest, The Story of Reader's Digest* (New York: Doubleday, 1958), p. 28.
97.		"Ultra-sophisticated": HL to JH, July 1980.
98.		"A Better America": John Tebbel, *The American Magazine* (New York: Hawthorn, 1969), p. 223.
98.		"Burning desire to write": HL to JH, July 1980.
99.		"For some reason: JAM to JH, December 15, 1971; and JAM, *A Michener Miscellany: 1950–1970* (Connecticut: Fawcett, 1975), p.14.
99.		Kill fee: HL COR to JAM, June 24, 1952, LOC.
99.		"Your picture": HL COR to JAM, September 30, 1952, LOC.
99.		"Your classic": DW COR to JAM, November 3, 1952, LOC.

100.    "You can go anywhere": JAM related this information on many
        occasions, and HL verified it to JH, July 1980.
100.    "Middle America demanded": HL to JH, July 1980.
100.    "Cutters": *Miscellany,* p. 13.
100.    "Once a piece": JAM to JH, May 1980.
101.    "Many scars": JAM to JH, December 15, 1971.
101.    Annoyed him: JAM COR to Miss Bailey, W. Colston Leigh, Inc.,
        October 4, 1950, LOC.
101.    "Mr. Michener": JAM to JH, December 15, 1971.
102.    One reporter: "Man Who Wrote *Tales of the South Pacific* Will Never
        Be Mistaken for Ezio Pinza," unsigned, undated newspaper clipping,
        LOC. Includes published photo of reporter with JAM.
102.    "Up in smoke": JAM COR to Miss Bailey, W. Colston Leigh, Inc.,
        October 4, 1950, LOC.
102.    "I must seriously": JAM COR to W. Colston Leigh, November 29,
        1952, LOC.
103.    "Foregone conclusion": WM to JAM, July 20, 1966.
103.    "He had that ability": HL to JH, July 1980.


## CHAPTER NINE

105.    "The luckiest": JAM, *Selected Writings of James A. Michener* (New
        York: Random House, 1957), Foreword.
105.    "Don't let me": JAM COR to HS, March 9, 1952 and "Michener's
        New Tales of Asia Start Wednesday," PI, 1953, LOC.
106.    "Brave Men": "Michener Tells Story of Famed 'Bald Eagle,'" New
        York *World-Telegram and Sun,* February 26, 1952, p. 3, LOC.
106.    "Here was complete": *World-Telegram and Sun,* 1952.
107.    "Theme is admirable": Review of *The Bridges at Toko-ri, New Yorker,*
        August 1, 1953, p. 59.
107.    "I wrote it": JAM to JH, May 1980.
108.    "I think they did not": HL COR to JAM, October 9, 1952, LOC.
108.    "The war has been": JAM, "Way It Is in Korea," RD, January 1953,
        pp.1–6, 139–44.
109.    Citizens for Free Asia: Preamble, Asia Foundation, LOC.
109.    "The foundation was": JAM to JH, May 1980.
110.    Observations in 1955: Michener's report to the Asia Foundation,
        undated, LOC. In 1953 Michener devoted time and energy to the Asia
        Institute, the only graduate school in the United States exclusively
        concentrating on scholarship in Asian affairs. He served as president
        for a short term but resigned when the financially failing school was
        about to close its doors for good. In another goodwill effort in 1954,
        he helped found the Fund for Asia, a national organization that
        provided technical assistance to Asia through private agencies in the
        United States. Many of the fund's activities were underwritten by

Michener's book royalties. The Fund for Asia, with Michener as president, operated through 1956.

110. "Most solid contributions": Speech of Daniel K. Inouye of Hawaii in the U.S. House of Representatives, *Congressional Record*, September 17, 1962. pp.1–2.

111. "Went into a nation": *Voice*, p. 9.

111. Riots: JAM COR to HS, July 20, 1955; also see *Playboy*, p. 72.

112. *Afghanistan:* JAM, "Afghanistan: Domain of the Fierce and the Free," RD, November 1955, pp. 161–72.

112. *Nehru:* JAM, "The Riddle of Pandit Nehru," RD, July 1956, pp. 96–102.

112. *Japan:* JAM, "Why I Like Japan," RD, August 1956, pp. 182–86.

113. *Wild West:* JAM, "Today's Wild West: The Great Australian North," RD, April 1956, pp. 63–70.

113. "Tough stand": JAM, "Pakistan: Divided It Stands," November 1954, pp. 136–47; and "Indonesia: Islands of Beauty and Turmoil," September 1955, pp. 30–44, both RD.

113. "It is great": JAM, "Afghanistan: Domain of the Fierce and the Free," RD, November 1955, pp. 161–72.

113. "Throughout Asia": JAM, "Madame Butterfly in Bobby Sox," RD, October 1956, pp. 21–27.

113. "I really believe": JAM, "This I Believe," RD, July 1954, pp. 143–44.

114. "Young enough to feel": Peter Lewis, *The Fifties* (Philadelphia: Lippincott, 1978), p. 7.

114. "I do not believe": "This I Believe," p. 144.

114. A brief synopsis: JAM COR to David O. Selznick, December 13, 1952, LOC.

115. "Generous offer": Selznick to JAM, September 8, 1953, LOC.

116. "Jim Michener received": *Talent*, p. 112.

116. "The pattern is more than": Saxe Commins COR to JAM, June 15, 1951, LOC.

117. "Very upsetting": *Talent*, p. 109.

117. "I needed an educated man": JAM to JH, September 1975.

117. "Palace revolution": *Talent*, p. 109.

117. "Editorial help": *Talent*, p. 109.

118. "Writes as a man": Review of *Sayonara*, Book of the Month Club *Bulletin*, 1954, LOC.

# CHAPTER TEN

119. "Mich the Witch": *Playboy*, p. 86. JAM had learned a system for fortune telling in Egypt and thought it was "quite extraordinary." It was fraudulent, he admitted, and he gave it up because "I would hit so close that it really became quite frightening." He wrote an account of his experiences and his relationship with the woman who taught him

the system, but is withholding it from publication until after his death because it is "a little undignified."

120. "You'd be a dope": JAM to JH, October 1975; and Doylestown *Daily Intelligencer,* May 5, 1972.

120. $5,000: Doylestown *Daily Intelligencer,* January 30, 1970.

121. "Money is a factor": JAM to JH, December 15, 1971, and May 1980; and William Ecenbarger, "Tales of James Michener, From Bali Ha'i to Chesapeake Bay," *Today,* PI, November 27, 1977, p. 33.

121. Donated $4 million: Ecenbarger, p. 33.

122. McCarthy hysteria: WV COR to JH, September 18, 1980.

122. "You marked the last": JAM COR to WV, December 8, 1959.

122. "Batik": VNM COR to HS, October 29, 1951.

122. "Obedient mama-san": VNM COR to HS, December 13, 1951.

123. "Travel can be hard work": JAM COR to HS, February 14, 1952.

123. "Dearest Dear": VNM COR to JAM, October 10, 1950, LOC.

123. "Superficial": Sources requested anonymity.

124. Maiden name: LT to JH, February 26, 1977.

124. Savage case of mumps: JAM to JH, October 1975; *Playboy,* p. 74.

124. "No finer thing": Floyd Merrill COR to JAM, August 30, 1953.

124. "Vange wanted a career": AS to JH, May 26, 1982.

124. For a while: After the Micheners adopted Mark, they received many letters of congratulations from friends and associates. News about the first adoption, and then the second, also appeared in newspaper columns, including The Lyons Den by Leonard Lyons. All COR and clippings in LOC.

124. Trust fund: JAM COR, LOC; Harriet M. Mims to JH, February 11, 1984.

125. "My own affairs": JAM COR to WV, February 19, 1954.

125. "War played": JAM to JH, December 15, 1971.

125. "Wonderful as they are": JAM COR to HS, March 9, 1952.

126. Neighbors called: JAM, "Pursuit of Happiness by a GI and a Japanese," *Life,* February 21, 1955, pp. 124–40.

126. Mari was born: JAM COR to his aunts, Hannah Pollock and Laura Haddock, December 12, 1955, LOC.

126. "Picture bride": This was a phenomenon of the period. When a man who had immigrated to the United States wanted to marry a woman of his own nationality, he wrote home to his family or friends and requested that he be sent an eligible woman. The woman's arrival in the United States was frequently preceded by her photograph.

127. Not a Michener fan: JAM to JH, December 15, 1971.

127. "Jap": *Playboy,* p. 74.

127. "Experience shows": "Mixed Marriages, A Noted U.S. Author Discusses Their Wisdom," undated article in Australian newspaper, LOC.

128. "People need": J. Whitbread, "The Private Life of James *(Hawaii)*

Michener," *Good Housekeeping,* February 1960, pp. 28–30.

128. She did not intend: Whitbread, p. 30.

128. "My lady": JAM COR to HS, undated.

128. Tiger hunt: JAM COR to HS, January 24, 1956. JAM said, "Mari wrangled us an invitation . . . to a fabulous tiger hunt put on by a maharaja. . . . Our party got a huge tiger and scouted several others-."

129. "We have had our little tiffs": MM COR to JAM, Thanksgiving day 1956, LOC.

129. "I saw her occasionally": TS to JH, July 22, 1981.

130. "I have always felt": Evelyn Shoemaker COR to JAM, November 22, 1956, LOC.

130. "Good father": MM COR to Pearl Buck, November 22, 1956, LOC.

130. "What can she": MM COR to JAM, November 19, 1956, LOC.

130. "Have a suspicion": MM COR to Pearl Buck, November 22, 1956, LOC.

131. Hinted she was pregnant: MM COR to JAM, November 19, 1956, LOC. MM wrote, "I'm beginning to have a sneaking suspicion that this female [Vange Nord] may have . . . heard that we were expecting a child and knowing how much you had wanted to take care of Mark decided that this would be the most opportune time to bring up the problem. A pregnant woman can easily lose her child through undue worry or concern—even the strongest. The double emotional and physical aspects of preparing for a new baby and another entirely new baby [meaning Mark] would be quite a strain indeed. If this was her intent, that is unforgivable. I would hate to think that there would be such a hateful woman who would do that to another woman. Let's hope that I am entirely wrong."

131. "When all of us": Lin Sabusawa COR to MM and JAM, undated, LOC.

131. "It would be correct": JAM to JH, December 15, 1971.

131. "Dissolved the legal proceedings": JAM COR to JH, May 29, 1979.

132. Trust fund: When questioned by JH in 1982, JAM would not clarify the status of the unclaimed trust, but according to a source who requested anonymity, the trust has collected interest for more than thirty years and amounts to more than $100,000.

## CHAPTER ELEVEN

134. "I was impressed": AGD, *James A. Michener,* p. 97.

134. "Standing at Andau": Undated clipping, LOC.

134. Free-lance photographer: One night, against Michener's advice, Chapelle slipped across the border alone and did not return. She was captured and imprisoned for six months.

135. "They talked": JAM to JH, May 1972.

135.   "Blank terror": JAM, *The Bridge at Andau* (New York: Random House, 1957; reprint, Fawcett Crest, 1957), p. 102.

135.   "In my time": "Michener Saw Hungarians Escape," Greeley, Colorado *Tribune,* February 16, 1957, p. 6.

135.   "I looked at": *Andau,* p. 32.

136.   Turning point: Sidney Fields, New York *Daily Mirror,* February 17, 1957, LOC.

136.   "All of us": HL COR to JAM, undated, LOC.

137.   "I started": Fan mail, LOC.

137.   Belonged in Hawaii: JAM COR to HL, undated, LOC.

137.   Strategic Air Command: HL COR to JAM, March 23, 1957.

138.   "Esprit de corps": HL, March 23, 1957.

138.   "While Others Sleep": RD, October 1957, pp. 68–75.

139.   Statehood: JAM, "Hawaii," *Holiday,* May 1953, pp. 34–35; excerpts in RD, August 1953, pp. 102–7.

140.   "If we accept": *Holiday,* pp. 34–35.

141.   "For a good many years": JAM COR to AGD, March 22, 1957, LOC.

141.   Home regions: AGD, *James A. Michener,* p. 115.

142.   Marquand complained: Stephen Birmingham, *The Late John Marquand* (Philadelphia: Lippincott, 1972), pp. 172–73. Marquand also referred to Michener as a lousy writer and a literary exhibitionist, according to Millicent Bell in *Marquand* (Boston: Little, Brown, 1979), pp. 406–07.

142.   "Sometimes I wish": COR to JAM, 1953, LOC.

143.   "I tried to read": Clarice B. Taylor, Honolulu *Star-Bulletin,* undated clipping, LOC.

143.   "If I had dared": AGD, *James A. Michener,* p. 116.

144.   "If I used": JAM to JH, December 15, 1971.

146.   Twelfth book: In addition to the books already cited in the text, JAM had written three books about art: *The Floating World* (New York: Random House, 1954); *The Hokusai Sketchbooks* (Tokyo: Charles E. Tuttle, 1958); and *Japanese Prints* (Tokyo: Charles E. Tuttle, 1959).

146.   Family sagas: George J. Becker, in *James A. Michener* (New York: Ungar, 1983), pointed out that JAM was the first to use the historical novel to represent and sum up a span of centuries.

146.   But many did: JH discovered that readers of JAM's novels frequently could be classified in one of two groups: those who enjoyed JAM's detailed research, and those who enjoyed his stories. Members of the latter group almost always said they skipped the first chapter or two of a JAM novel because they found it "too complicated," "dry," or "too technical." However, members of both groups frequently said they did not want the novels to end.

147.   "Why do you": Fan mail, LOC.

147.   "False history": Letter quoted by Leonard Lyons in his newspaper

column, "The Lyons Den," February 18, 1960, LOC.

147. "It is unfortunate": The Reverend Abraham Akaka, *All About Hawaii* (Honolulu: Star-Bulletin, 1967), Charles E. Frankel, editor, p. 227.

147. "Some of you will": Clarice B. Taylor, "A Preface to a Novel," Honolulu *Star-Bulletin,* June 5, 1960, Women's Section, p. 8.

148. "Isn't it ridiculous": Clarice B. Taylor COR to JAM, LOC.

149. "High-domed": Horace Sutton, review of *Hawaii, Saturday Review,* November 21, 1959, p. 40.

149. "The daily sales" and "Just a line": BC COR to JAM, LOC.

150. In just two months: See Alice Payne Hackett and James Henry Burke, *80 Years of Best Sellers 1895–1975* (New York: R. R. Bowker, 1977), p. 178; and *Publishers Weekly* for 1959 and 1960.

150. Film rights: *Talent,* p. 119.

150. "What I wanted this novel": JAM COR to AGD, undated, LOC.

150. "Great faith": JAM to JH, December 15, 1971; also see *Playboy,* p. 68.

## CHAPTER TWELVE

151. "The fact of the matter": BC COR to JAM, May 24, 1959, LOC.

152. *"Leyte Gulf":* David Brown COR to HMS, September 11, 1959, LOC.

152. "Keep postponing": HMS COR to JAM, September 14, 1959, LOC.

152. "Write whichever": AE COR to JAM, August 25, 1959, LOC.

152. "I might say that": CS COR to JAM, April 1959, LOC.

153. University of Missouri: JAM COR, July 10, 1960, LOC.

153. "I grew up": JAM, *Report of the County Chairman* (New York: Random House, 1961), p. 47.

153. "My mother": *Report,* p. 51.

154. "As a process of hard": *Report,* p. 213.

154. "A wholly new administration": *Report,* p. 213.

155. "Vigorous new society": *Report,* pp. 4, 203.

155. "A nation to be won": *Report,* p. 8.

155. "Don't you understand": *Report,* p. 3.

155. "A writer never qualifies": Honolulu *Star-Bulletin,* April 14, 1954, p. 38.

155. "The Democratic Party": JAM COR to John A. Burns, February 1959, LOC.

156. "He knows what to say": *Report,* p. 1.

156. The golden men: JAM, *Hawaii* (New York: Random House, 1959; reprint, Bantam, 1961), p. 1130.

157. He did resign: *Report,* p. 3.

157. "Several conclusions": *Report,* p. 5.

157. "Somebody back east": JAM COR to HMS, 1959, LOC.

158. "Scriptwriting": JAM to JH, December 15, 1971.

158. "War for the World": Several proposed scripts are filed in LOC.

159.  Press corps: News clipping, September 29, 1959, no source, LOC.
159.  "Thus the elements": JAM COR to Oliver Treyz, September 11, 1959, LOC.
159.  "They must have thought": JAM COR to HMS, September 12, 1959, LOC.
160.  "We tried to get": HMS COR to JAM, September 14, 1959, LOC.
160.  "Many people have asked": JAM COR, October 1959, LOC.
161.  "It occurred to me": "Michener Tells Why He Turned Pen to TV Efforts," *Los Angeles Times*, October 6, 1959, p. B1.
162.  "Snowstorms": *Talent*, p. 120.
162.  "Practical writer": John Lardner, review of "Adventures in Paradise," *New Yorker*, October 24, 1959, pp. 165–69.
162.  Noted privately: 1971, LOC.
162.  "My God." *Report*, p. 9.


## CHAPTER THIRTEEN

165.  "Makings of a great man": *Report*, pp. 89–90.
165.  Johnny Welsh: *Report*, p. 46.
166.  "One of the most maligned": Ann Hawks Hutton, *The Pennsylvanian: Joseph R. Grundy* (Philadelphia: Dorrance, 1962), p. 241.
166.  "Arch-Republican": JAM to JH, May 1980.
166.  "I can see him now": *Report*, p. 51.
167.  "Land speculators": *Report*, p. 57.
167.  "They tell us": *Report*, p. 58.
167.  "You, you and you": *Report*, p. 59.
167.  "I wish I knew": *Report*, p. 60.
168.  "John Kennedy will be": *Report*, p. 214.
168.  "Richard Nixon": *Report*, p. 54.
169.  "Religious intolerance": *Report*, pp. 67, 185.
170.  "Of the eight states": *Report*, p. 183.
170.  For his vision: *Report*, p. 206.
170.  "Since it seems": *Report*, p. 1.
170.  Quickly grabbed the manuscript: JW to JH, October 21, 1980.
171.  $100,000 investment: In September 1981 JAM estimated the $30 million return had increased to $70 million, *Playboy*, p. 72.
172.  His letters: JAM COR, November 14, 1960, LOC.
172.  "Report from the 'Frenzied Fifties'": NYT *Magazine*, August 13, 1961, p. 15.
173.  Three objections: "Author Michener Reluctant on Bid to Run for Congress," Philadelphia *Evening Bulletin*, January 24, 1962, p. B22.
174.  Mari warned the members: JAM COR to friends, January 1962, LOC.
174.  "As a boy": JAM news conference at Conti's Cross Keys Restaurant, February 17, 1962.

175. "I think Jim Michener": Undated newspaper clipping, LOC.

175. Spring of 1962: Complete collection of JAM campaign papers, 1962, container 138, LOC.

175. "My new novel has": Campaign papers, LOC. U.S. Steel had announced a $6-a-ton price increase, and it was rolled back by President Kennedy's pressure.

176. "I tell my opponent": Campaign papers, LOC.

176. "Why I Am Running For Congress": JAM, *Saturday Evening Post,* May 5, 1962, p. 8.

177. In October: Drew Pearson, "Washington Merry-Go-Round," October 1962, LOC.

177. "We could see": JW to JH, October 21, 1980.

177. Vote tally: "Curtin Defeats Michener in Bucks County House Race," NYT, November 9, 1962, p. 61.

177. "Jim just did not": HS to JH, May 13, 1982.

178. Curtin interpreted: NYT, 1962, p. 61.

178. "Michener made no mistakes": JW to JH, October 21, 1980.


## CHAPTER FOURTEEN

179. "It galls me": JAM COR to JH, February 9, 1979.

180. "It is grand": HL COR to JAM, March 21, 1963, LOC.

180. "While we were there": JAM to JH, May 1980.

181. "I'm writing about": Philadelphia *Bulletin Magazine,* December 22, 1963, p. 6.

181. "You were the first": JAM COR to HS, October 28, 1963.

181. Mari began to cry: JAM COR to Jim Bishop, June 26, 1973, LOC.

182. "It should be": Undated newspaper clipping, LOC.

184. "Smyrna figs": JAM COR to MM, September 10, 1964, LOC.

184. "The book is personal": JAM COR to HL, September 14, 1964, LOC.

184. "If I had a hat on": AE COR to JAM, July 21, 1964, LOC.

185. "The text reads well": JAM COR to Elie Mizrachi, February 2, 1965, LOC.

185. "Although I knew": JAM COR to friend in Israel, undated, LOC.

185. "The reviews": HMS COR to JAM, undated, LOC.

185. "You have it": JAM COR to Omar Azouni, July 27, 1967, LOC.

186. "Majestic problem": JAM COR to HL, undated, LOC.

186. Boston heart specialist: Paul Dudley White, M.D., COR to MM, September 13, 1965, LOC.

186. Barnes collection: See note "A poor steelworker": p. 41.

187. University of Texas: He tried to keep the paintings closer to his home, but during a thorough investigation of several museums and universities that expressed interest in housing and caring for his collection, he was most impressed by the University of Texas.

187.  *A Year in Spain:* JAM COR, April 29, 1966, LOC.
187.  "A man's country": JAM to JH, December 15, 1971.
188.  "It certainly tells": JAM COR to AE, undated, LOC.
188.  Three weeks with Vanderford: JAM notes, June 11, 1967, LOC.
188.  Santos dos Croques: Notes, 1967, LOC.
189.  *"What* fountains?": Peter Besas, review of *Iberia, Guidepost,* October 25, 1968, p. 35.
190.  "You are probably aware": JAM COR, November 22, 1968, LOC.
191.  "I tire much more": JAM COR to Paul Dudley White, M.D., August 31, 1967, LOC.
191.  "You don't earn": JAM COR, undated, LOC.
191.  "What we do": Rose DeWolf, "A Novel Job for Michener," PI, December 26, 1977, p. C1.
192.  "End of the world speeches": Bernard McCormick, "Portrait of the Artist as an Elder Statesman," *Philadelphia,* April 1968, pp. 74–77, 113–19.
192.  "Blaze of confused glory": JAM COR, undated, LOC.
192.  "I've found so many": Phyllis Meras, "A Desire to Inform," *Saturday Review,* May 4, 1968, p. 29.
193.  "If you think people": JAM COR to WV, March 8, 1968, LOC.
193.  "This was how": JAM to JH, October 1975.
193.  "Intuitively conservative": JAM COR to WV, 1968, LOC.
193.  Vote yes: JAM report to constituents, undated, LOC.
193.  Intended to vote against: JAM COR to friend in Hawaii, May 29, 1968, LOC.
193.  "No delegate": JAM COR to fellow delegates, May 1, 1968, LOC.
193.  "I certainly am as proud": David Barnett, Jr., "Michener's views reflect novelist's eye for detail," Bucks County *Courier Times,* November 25, 1973, p. 3.
193.  "Some of them don't believe": Barnett, p. 3.
194.  "I'm sure he'd love": *Philadelphia,* p. 119.

## CHAPTER FIFTEEN
195.  "GMRX: An Alternative to Movie Censorship": RD, January 1969.
195.  "Twenty-one years": JAM to JH, September 1975.
196.  Internal Revenue Service: Jerome S. Cahill, "Michener Owes U.S. $390,103 in Taxes, IRS Officials Claim," PI, December 26, 1967, pp.1, 37; and "Michener Fights U.S. Tax Claim," publication unknown, April 4, 1967, LOC.
196.  "President Eisenhower": JAM to JH, September and October 1975; and Joseph C. Goulden, "Interview with Author James Michener," PI, November 21, 1965, p. 1.
196.  534 writers: "Writers Bid U.S. End Bombings; Urge Cease-Fire," NYT, August 12, 1968, p. 53.

197. "Every justification": JAM, *The Quality of Life* (Philadelphia: Lippincott, 1970; reprint, Fawcett, 1971), p. 111.

197. "Encourage a new spirit": "J. Michener on THE Desire To Explore," Penn State University *Collegian,* March 4, 1966, p. 1.

197. "The Revolution in Middle-Class Values,": NYT *Magazine,* August 18, 1968, p. 87; *America vs. America: The Revolution in Middle-Class Values* (New York: New American Library, 1969).

198. "Talk sense": Fan mail, LOC.

199. "We were lucky": JAM, *Presidential Lottery* (New York: Fawcett, 1969), p. 7.

199. "Michener was right": JAM to JH, October 1975.

199. "They were scarred": JAM, "Michener, Off the Cuff," *Swarthmore College Bulletin,* April 1975, p. 7.

200. Experimented with the drug: *Playboy,* p. 84.

201. "Wow": AE COR to JAM, April 21, 1969, LOC.

201. "I have always had": JAM, "Seven theories why *anyone,* including a sixty-two-year-old writer with a history of heart trouble, seeks fulfillment running with the bulls in the streets of Pamplona," *Esquire,* December 1970, p. 183.

201. "I was an expert": JAM to JH, October 1975.

204. "The FBI did not want": JAM to JH, May 1980.

205. *He guessed:* JAM COR to Leslie Laird, October 24, 1970, LOC. In a note to Miss Laird, who was his research assistant and a RD employee, Michener requested, "I wish you would bend all your efforts in getting me a reasonable estimate of the percentage of KSY [sic] students who have experimented with marijuana at least once. . . . Please ask among a wide circle of your acquaintances for their best educated guesses."

205. "For the first time": JAM, "Kent State—Campus under Fire," RD, March 1971, pp. 244–46.

206. "The great majority": JAM, *Kent State—What Happened and Why* (New York: Random House, 1971), p. 135.

206. "Inexcusable errors": JH, "Michener Rejects Survey Results," Kent-Ravenna *Record Courier,* January 27, 1972, p. 36.

206. "Deplorable and tragic": *Kent State,* p. 412.

206. "A malicious act": *Kent State,* p. 295.

206. "One cannot help": *Kent State,* p. 326.

207. "It seems likely": *Kent State,* p. 361.

207. "There is no acceptable proof": *Kent State,* pp. 409–10.

207. "Murder or manslaughter": Peter Davies, *The Truth about Kent State* (New York: Farrar, Straus & Giroux, 1973), pp. 41–42.

207. "Bonafide conspiracy": JAM to JH, September 1975 and May 1980; and JAM COR to Melvin B. Yoken, Southeastern Massachusetts University, August 27, 1973, LOC.

207. "Common sense": Baccalaureate address by JAM, Kent State Uni-

versity, December 1970.

207.   "Bad bargain": JAM COR to Leonard Garment, May 17, 1973, LOC.

208.   This same point: JAM COR to Arthur S. Krause, April 23, 1971, LOC.

208.   "More harm than good": JAM COR to Leonard Garment.

208.   "The United States": *Kent State,* p. 412.

209.   "What price": Tom Wicker, review of *Kent State—What Happened and Why,* NYT *Book Review,* June 6, 1971, p. 31.

209.   "Today Show": Joe Eszterhas and Michael Roberts, "James Michener's Kent State, A Study in Distortion," *The Progressive,* September 1971, pp. 35–40.

209.   "Loaded": "Kent State Study Scores Michener," NYT, January 15, 1972, p. L76.

209.   His working papers and notes: JAM's collection of papers relating to the Kent State incident is filed in more than two dozen containers in LOC.

210.   "If they can get": *Quality of Life,* p. 69.

210.   "A lot of us saw": JAM to Educational Television Staff at UNC, 1973, transcript at UNC.

211.   "Had better beware": *Quality of Life,* Introduction.


## CHAPTER SIXTEEN

212.   "I think it would be": HMS COR to JAM, January 5, 1970, LOC.

213.   "Into such a novel": HL COR to JAM, November 18, 1969, LOC.

213.   "This morning I": UNC; John Kings, *In Search of Centennial* (New York: Visual Books, 1978), p. 17.

214.   Thinking about retiring: On several occasions JAM said to JH, "After this next book, I see one or two more and then I'll be finished writing. I've always thought I might return to the university to teach."

215.   "Half-baked fair": JAM, *About Centennial* (New York: Random House, 1974), p. 5.

215.   "Plastic hamburgers": Ron Javers, review of *Centennial,* PI, September 8, 1974, p. B10.

215.   "The Democrats did not": HL to JH, July 1980.

215.   "The fact that": JAM, *Centennial* (New York: Random House, 1974), pp. 852–53.

215.   "Each of us": JAM to JH, October 1975.

215.   "The idea comes first": JAM to JH, December 15, 1971; JAM COR to JH, May 29, 1979; and *Today,* PI, p. 33.

216.   "The books": JAM to JH, September 1975; *About Centennial,* p. 4.

217.   "I could think up": JAM to JH, December 15, 1971, and October 1975; and *About Centennial,* p. 11.

217.   "They don't interest me": JAM to JH, December 15, 1971.

218. "My wife and I": JAM COR to Floyd Merrill, May 10, 1970, UNC.
218. "First, let me": JAM COR, April 23, 1970, UNC.
218. "My interests are": JAM COR, April 23, 1970, UNC.
219. Haley: Alex Haley, "Alex Haley Tells the Story of the Search for *Roots*," spoken recording, (Burbank: Warner Brothers, 1977).
220. Mayors of Laramie and Denver: JAM COR, both letters, November 10, 1969, UNC.
221. "I have asked too many": JAM COR to Merrill J. Mattes, July 4, 1970, UNC.
222. "We hope that": JAM COR, undated, UNC.
223. "Insatiable desire": JAM COR, "Materials in the Library at the University of Northern Colorado," undated, UNC.
223. "Bus driver": JAM COR to JH, November 16, 1977.
223. "I can't tell you": JAM to JH, May 1980.
223. "Now Mr. Stanley": *About Centennial*, p. 9.
224. Walter Bellamy: *In Search of Centennial*, p. 74.
225. "It's a lot of": JAM to JH, December 15, 1971.
225. "Writing is hard": JAM to JH, October 1975.
226. "At almost every": JAM, address before Academia de la Lengua, undated, LOC.
226. "I have never": AGD, *James A. Michener*, p. 135.
227. "Hemingway said": JAM to JH, September 1975.
227. "Invariably": JAM COR to JH, May 13, 1978.
227. "Writing is a lonely": JAM to JH, September 1975.
228. "It was pleasurable": AE to JAM, March 27, 1973, UNC.
228. "Because I have": JAM COR to AE, undated, LOC.
229. "When one has": JAM notes, UNC.
229. $50,000 for research: Michener's out-of-pocket expenses for *Hawaii* were estimated at $34,000; for *Chesapeake*, $40,000; and for *The Covenant*, $40,000. RD also paid $82,000 for research assistance for *The Covenant*, according to JAM.
229. Opinion piece: JAM, "When the 'Mandate of Heaven' Has Been Lost . . ." NYT, November 11, 1973.
230. "I'm working three days": JAM COR, February 2, 1974, UNC.

## CHAPTER SEVENTEEN

232. "It irritates the": Source requested anonymity.
232. "He seeks": George J. Becker, *James A. Michener* (New York: Ungar, 1983), p. 186.
232. Admittedly: *Playboy*, p. 68. JAM said he knew his deficiencies better than most of the critics. "I am not very good at dialog. I don't use words as well as Roth. . . . I don't use social structures as well as Joyce Carol Oates. I don't have the quality of touch that Robert Penn Warren has. I do not begin to project myself into the life of another to

the degree of . . . Norman Mailer or Truman Capote. . . . I am not very competent in dealing with sexuality. . . . I am not very good at plotting."

232.  "I'm a realist": JAM to JH, December 15, 1971; and Steve Neal, "Michener: Last Stand in Bucks," PI, January 14, 1974, pp. 1, 5.

232.  "What Michener seems": Becker, *James A. Michener,* p. 168.

232.  *Serious* novelist: Herbert Mitgang first used this description of JAM in "Why Michener Never Misses," *Saturday Review,* November 1980, pp. 20–24.

233.  "Author, teacher": White House press release, January 10, 1977.

233.  "I, like thousands": Gerald R. Ford COR to JH, October 8, 1979.

233.  "It seems to me": John Leonard as quoted by Bruce Beans, "The Source," *Philadelphia,* June 1981, p. 130.

233.  "To suggest that": Jonathan Yardley COR to JH, March 5, 1984.

233.  "Damn it": Jan Herman, "A Michener Review of His Epic Success," PI, January 1, 1981, p. 9; and Adam Smith II, "The Last 'Author' in America," *New York,* June 7, 1971, pp. 95–96.

233.  "I deem critics": JAM COR to JH, November 16, 1977.

233.  Raised the price: Alice Payne Hackett and James Henry Burke, *80 Years of Best Sellers 1895–1975* (New York: Bowker, 1977), p. 216.

234.  "I suppose I feel": *Trenton Times,* undated clipping, LOC.

234.  *Chesapeake:* Random House publicity department. Also see Daisy Maryles, "The Year's Bestselling Books," *Publishers Weekly,* March 13, 1981, p. 31.

234.  *The Covenant:* Beans, *Philadelphia,* p. 128. Also see Herbert Mitgang, "Why Michener Never Misses," *Saturday Review,* November 1980, pp. 21–24; *Publishers Weekly,* p. 31.

234.  *Space:* Random House publicity department.

234.  *Poland:* Random House publicity department.

234.  ABC optioned: *USA Today,* March 16, 1984.

234.  "I keep working": JAM to JH, May 1980.

234.  "I can't turn my back": Donald Knox, producer and director, "James Michener's Home Country," KYW-TV, Philadelphia, 1968.

235.  "Dear Friend": JAM COR to Betty W. Morehouse, clerk of overseers, Doylestown Monthly Meeting, August 12, 1965, LOC.

236.  "Bit of revelry": JAM notes, UNC.

236.  Protested most vehemently: "Michener Name Opposed by 750," Quakertown *Free Press,* October 10, 1972. "Library Wants Michener Name for New Quakertown Branch," Allentown *Call-Chronicle,* January 2, 1973.

236.  "We've been snubbed": Nancy Larrick Crosby telephone interview with JH, August 31, 1979.

236.  "I have grown": JAM COR, December 7, 1972, UNC.

236.  "When the community": Beans, *Philadelphia,* p. 136; JAM notes, UNC; JAM COR to Nadia Orapchuck, January 3, 1973, UNC.

236. "This letter is sent": JAM COR to Nadia Orapchuck, January 3, 1973, UNC.
237. "I have been thinking": JAM COR to Pearl Buck, October 4, 1972, UNC.
238. "After thinking it over": Pearl Buck COR to JAM, October 16, 1972, UNC.
239. "I was robbed": Nadia Orapchuck COR to JAM, undated, UNC.
239. "I don't feel sorry": Crosby, 1979.
239. "Bass-ackward": Orapchuck, undated, UNC.
240. From Seville, Spain: JAM COR to Nadia Orapchuck, HS, Graham Place, Evelyn Shoemaker, AE, Harry Sabusawa, Hiram Bruner, Virginia Trumbull, Easter Sunday 1969, LOC.
240. "I think about": *Playboy,* p. 78; and JAM to JH, May 1980.

# Index

ABC television series, 157-62, 234
*About Centennial,* 229
Academia de la Lengua, 226
Academics, opinions of Michener, 4-5.
   *See also* Critics
Acheson, Lila Bell, 97
Ackerman, Dean Carl, 81
Adabi, Mansor, 94
Adoption of sons, 124
"Adventures in Paradise" (TV), 158-62,
   196
*Afghanistan: Domain of the Fierce and the
   Free* (article), 112, 113
Agents, literary, 76, 87-88. *See also*
   Strauss, Helen
Ahern, James, 207
Akaka, Abraham, 147
Alienation of youth, 199-211
Allentown Art Museum, 186-87
Ambassadorship offer, 171
American Baptist Home Mission Soci-
   ety, 126-27
American Book Award, 5
American Revolution Bicentennial
   Commission, 194, 213, 214-15
*Americans, The,* 137, 152
*American Tragedy, An* (Dreiser), 46
*America vs. America: The Revolution in
   Middle-Class Values,* 197
Anake, Par, 94
Angell's Club, 55
"Appointment in Asia" (TV), 109
Art
   collection, 171, 186-87
   interest in, 41
Asia
   interest in, 91-96
   works about, 105-18
Asia Foundation, 109-10
*Atlantic* (magazine), 83
Australia
   article about, 92
   honeymoon with Mari in, 128

Awards, *pl. 10,* 5-6, 80-82, 233
Aydelotte, Frank, 33, 37
Azouni, Omar, 185

"Bach and Sugar Beets" (article), 54
Balzac, Honoré, 22
Barnes, Albert C., 41
Barra (island), 48-49
Basketball team, *pl. 2,* 27-30, 33-34
*Battle of Leyte Gulf, The,* 151-52
Baxter, George, 22, 23
Becker, George J., 232
"Beginning Teacher, The" (essay), 56
Bellow, Saul, 81
Bendiner, Robert, 81
Bertogna, Felix, 106
Bicentennial Commission, 194, 213,
   214-15
Bigley, Harry, 28
*Big Sky, The* (Guthrie), 80
Bishop, Jim, 181
Book of the Month Club, 196
*Book World* (magazine), 210
Bora-Bora (island), 63
Bowen, Catherine Drinker, 196
Boys' Brigade, 22-23, 120
Bradford, Andrew, 97
Brett, George P., Jr., 68-71, 77, 78-79, 84
*Bridge at Andau, The,* 136-37
*Bridges at Toko-ri, The,* 6, 106-8, 118
British Merchant Marine, 48
Broomhead, Norman, 106
Brown, David, 152
Brown, John Mason, 88
Bryce, James, 154
Bryden, Ronald, 148
Buchwald, Art, 7, 224
Buck, Pearl, 89, 91, 118, 124, 129, 237-39
Bureau of Aeronautics, 61
Burns, J.H., 83
Burns, James A., 155-56
Butcher, Fanny, 118

Campaigns, political
  Congressional, *pl. 8*, 173–78
  Humphrey, 198–99
  Kennedy, 164–69
Canterbury, General, 206–7
*Caravans*, 180, 182, 196
Carter, Jimmy, 231–32
Cather, Willa, 6, 141
*Catholic World* (magazine), 83, 148
"Cave, The" (from *Tales of the South Pacific*), 67–68
Citizens for Free Asia, 109–10
"Cemetery at Hoga Point, A" (from *Tales of the South Pacific*), 68
*Centennial*, 213–30
  conception of, 213–16
  critics on, 231–32
  narrative technique, 217–18
  publication of, 230
  public response to, 233–34
  research on, 220–21, 222
Central Intelligence Agency (CIA), 110
Cerf, Bennett, 80, 87–88, 117, 120, 136, 149, 151–52
Ceylon, observations of, 110
Chamberlain, John R., 82
Chandler, Jeff, 169
Chandler, Raymond, 107
Chapelle, Georgette Meyer "Dickey," 134
Chautauqua, 41, 43–44
Chautauqua Assembly, 43
*Chesapeake*, 234
*Christian Century* (magazine), 148
CIA, 110
Citizenship, good, 8–10
Clark, Joe, 198
*Clearing House* (magazine), 56
Cold war, 136, 139
College experience. *See* Swarthmore College
*Collier's* (magazine), 93
Colorado, writing *Centennial* in, 219–29
Colorado State College of Education in Greeley, 52–58, 237
Columbia University, 81, 121–22
*Comédie Humaine* (Balzac), 22
Commins, Saxe, 78, 79–80, 116–17
Communism
  in Asia, 113
  *Bridge at Andau* and rejection of, 136–37
  in Hungarian revolution, 135–36
  interest in, 47–48
Congressional campaign, *pl. 8*, 173–78

Conrad, Joseph, 66
Considine, Bob, 224
Constitutional Convention, Pennsylvania, 190–94
Coolidge, Calvin, 166
Cooper, Gary, 94
*Covenant, The*, 234
Cozzens, James Gould, 89
Critics
  on *Bridge at Andau*, 137
  on *Bridges at Toko-ri*, 107
  on *Centennial*, 231–32
  on *Drifters*, 210
  on *Fires of Spring*, 83–84
  on *Hawaii*, 148–49
  on *Iberia*, 189–90
  impact of, 3–4
  on *Kent State—What Happened and Why*, 209–10
  Pulitzer Prize controversy, 81–82
  on *Report of the County Chairman*, 171
  on *Return to Paradise*, 94
  on *Sayonara*, 117–18
  on *Source*, 183, 185
  on *South Pacific*, 85–86
  on *Tales of the South Pacific*, 75–76
  on *Voice of Asia*, 95
Cronkite, Walter, 7, 224
Crosby, Nancy Larrick, 236, 239
Cuornos, John, 75
Curtin, Willard S., 175–78

*Daily Intelligencer* (newspaper), 12, 24, 120
*Daily Mirror* (newspaper), 136
Dalton, Tessa, 222
Damon, Ethel, 144
Dark, Eleanor, 141
Davies, Peter, 207
Davis, William W.H., 13
Day, A. Grove, 74, 103, 133, 141, 148, 150
Degrees, honorary, 5. *See also* Education
DeGroot, John, 3, 7
*Delight Makers, The*, 56
*Democracy in America* (de Tocqueville), 154
Dempsey, David, 75
De Tocqueville, Alexis, 154
Dickens, Charles, 17
Dickinson, Angie, 169
Divorce
  from Patti Koon, 83
  from Vange Nord, 124–25
Domino theory, 196

"Dos Sabios" (poem), 39
Doubleday Publishing Company, 88
Doyle, William, 15
Doylestown, Pennsylvania
  history of, 15
  youth in, 13–20, 22–30
Doylestown High School, 25, 27
Drafts, writing, 226–27
Dreiser, Theodore, 46
*Drifters, The,* 200–201, 210, 219
DuBois, William, 83
*Duke, The* (Guedalla), 64

Earnings, 77, 103, 195, 233–34
Education, 24–44
  college, 31–44
  high school, 24–30
Eisenhower, Dwight D., 154
Eliot, T.S., 38–39
"Empty Room, The" (short story), 77
Environment, work, 225–26
Epic fiction, appeal of, 137
Erskine, Albert, 117, 136, 149, 152, 182,
    184, 221, 228
Ervin, Sam, 208
Espíritu Santo (island), 61, 64, 65
*Esquire* (magazine), 93
*Essex* (ship), 106
Ethic, Protestant, 9, 197
Extemporaneous Speaking Contest,
    41–42

"Faction" style of writing, 81, 144
Failure, fear of, 31
Faulkner, William, 116
FBI, Kent State investigation and, 204–5
Fields, Sidney, 136
*Fields of Troy, The. See Fires of Spring, The*
Fiji Islands, observations of, 92
*Fires of Spring, The*
  autobiographical aspects of, 31, 32, 34,
      35, 38, 41, 65
  critics on, 83–84
  original titles, 76, 77
  popular response to, 84
  publication of, 79–80, 83
  sales, 118
Flynn, Errol, 59
Fonda, Henry, 77
Fonthill (estate), 21
Ford, Gerald R., *pl. 10,* 5, 233
Fort Laramie national monument, 218
Foundation for art collection, 186–87
Franklin, Benjamin, 97

Fraternities, 33–34
*Free Press* (newspaper), 237
"Frenzied fifties syndrome," 172
Friede, Donald, 76
Friends of the Library incident, 236–39
*Future of the Social Studies, The,* 56

*Gang's All Here, The* (Smith), 64
Gantz, Charlotte, 190, 191
Gardy, Allen, 28
Garment, Leonard, 208
Geismar, Maxwell, 82, 149
George School, teaching at, 49–52
*Getting the Most Out of Farming* (Reader's
    Digest), 96
"GMRX: An Alternative to Movie Cen-
    sorship" (article), 195
Goetz, William, 115, 116
"Gold" (play), 39
*Good Housekeeping* (magazine), 128
*Grandmothers, The* (Wescott), 141
Great Depression, 45–46, 47
Grey, Zane, 6
Grundy, Joseph R., 166, 174
Guadalcanal, naval duty in, 61
Gunther, John, 91
Guthrie, A.B., Jr., 81

Haas, Victor P., 81
Haddock, Arthur (uncle), 13
Haddock, Hannah (aunt), 13
Haddock, Kate (grandmother), 12, 13
Haddock, Laura (aunt), 21
Haddock, Robert (grandfather), 12, 13
Haley, Alex, 219–20
Hallowell, Thomas, 35
Hammerstein, Oscar II, 77, 82, 84–85,
    87, 89, 158
Hammett, Dashiell, 107
Harding, Warren G., 166
Hart, Moss, 89
Harvard University, School of Educa-
    tion, 57
Harvard University Press, 56
Hawaii
  move to, 139–50
  statehood issue, 139–40
*Hawaii,* 4, 141–50
  "Adventures in Paradise" publicity
      and, 159
  critical response to, 148–49
  popular response to, 146–48
  publication of, 146

"Hawaii: A State of Happiness" (article), 142
Hawaiian Weekly magazine, 140
Hearst, William Randolph, 96, 127
Heart attack, 186
Heggen, Tom, 75, 86, 104
Heller, Joseph, 196
Hemingway, Ernest, 6, 46, 48, 64, 107-8
Herbert, Victor, 21
"Hermitage: Russia's Fabulous Art Palace" (article), 183
Hersey, John, 196
Hicks, Granville, 73
Hicksites, 42
High school, pl. 2, 24-30
Hill, Robert C., 165
Hill School, teaching experience at, 46-47
History of Rome Hanks and Kindred Matters, The (Pennell), 141
Hofmann, Hans, 186
Hohenberg, John, 82
Hokusai, 240
Holden, William, 107
Holiday (magazine), 90, 92-93, 95-96
Holmes, Jesse "Ducky," 36
Homeward Journey, The. See Fires of Spring, The
Honorary degrees, 5
Hoover, Herbert, 42
Hopkinson, S.L., 147
Horgan, Paul, 234
"Hubert H. Humphrey: Portrait of a President," 198
Humphrey, Hubert, 194, 198
Hungarian revolution, coverage of, 131, 133-36
Hunnewell, James, 143
Huntsman in the Sky (Toogood), 47
Hutchins, John K., 148

Iberia, 9, 188-90
Image, self-, 6-7, 10, 35-36
Indonesia, observations of, 110
Inouye, Daniel K., 110
In Search of Centennial (Kings), 228
Insecurity over writing, 227
Intelligencer (newspaper), 237
Internal Revenue Service, 196
"Is America Burning?" (article), 229
Israel, travels in, 180-84

Jackson, Ruth, 41, 51
Jackson State College, 197

James, Henry, 6
Jefferson, 216
Johnson, Lyndon B., 165, 224
John Wanamaker's (department store), 2
Jones, Andrew, 204
Jones, Jennifer, 114
Joshua Lippincott Fellowship, 47
Julius Lefkowitz and Company, 103

Kagohara, Mayre, 54-55
Kain, George Hay, 32
Kant, Immanuel, 5-6
Kaufman, Bel, 185
Kelley, James, 107
Kennedy, John F
  assassination, 181-82
  campaign, 164-69
  in Hawaii, 156
Kennedy or Nixon: Does It Make Any Difference (Schlesinger), 169
Kent State University debacle, 197, 201-11
Kent State—What Happened and Why, 205-6, 209-10, 220
Kings, John, 222, 228
Knock on Any Door (Motley), 81
Knowlton, P.A., 57, 60, 77, 80
Koamalu (Damon), 144
Koon, Patti (first wife), 51-52, 55, 60, 73, 83
Korea, ambassadorship offer to, 171
Korean war, 99, 105-8
Krantz, Bert, 117, 136, 184, 230
Krause, Arthur S., 208
Krock, Arthur, 81-82

Ladies' Home Journal (magazine), 77
La Follette, Robert M., Sr., 43
Laird, Leslie, 222
Lardner, John, 162
Larkin, Charles P., Jr., 34
Laster, Owen, 221
Late George Apley, The (Marquand), 64
Latham, Harold, 69, 70, 74
Lecture circuit, 101-2
Leigh, W. Colston, 101
LeMay, Curt, 138
Leonard, John, 233
Levittown, 167
Lewis, Hobart
  advice on Bridge at Andau, 136
  assignments from, 108, 131, 133, 137, 183, 201
  Christianity book idea, 152

Lewis, Hobart—cont.
  editor-in-chief of *Reader's Digest*, 100
  encouragement for book on U.S.,
    212-13
  introduction to, 98, 99
  letters to, 221-22
  on Michener's personality, 103
  Michener's political activity and, 180,
    191
  on *Reader's Digest* audience, 97
Lewis, Peter, 114
*Library Journal*, 83, 147
*Life* (magazine), 93, 107, 125-26
Literary agents, 76, 87-88. *See also*
    Strauss, Helen
Literary community, feelings toward
    Michener, 231-33
Literary critics. *See* Critics
Lockridge, Ross, 86, 104
Logan, Joshua, 77, 115-16
London, Jack, 141, 147
Longworth, Alice Roosevelt, 81, 82
*Lost Lady, A* (Cather), 141
Lyons, Leonard, 180

MacArthur, Douglas, 91, 93, 113
*McCall's* (magazine), 81, 117
McCarthy, Eugene, 198
McCarthy, Joseph, 121, 122
McDonald, G.D., 83-84
McKay, Douglas, 122
McKay, Gardner, 159
Macmillan Publishing Company
  initial job offer, 57
  publication of *Tales of the South Pacific*,
    73-74
  Scott's offer from, 152
  working at, 59, 71, 73-88
McNealy, Bob, 24, 28
Mailer, Norman, 82, 144
Malekula (island), 65
Maleter, Pal, 134
Mann, Bob, 158
Manulis, Martin, 158-60
March, Frederic, 107
Marjay Productions, Inc., 196
Marquand, John P., 64, 72, 141-42
Marriages
  to Mari Sabusawa, 126-32
  to Patti Koon, 51-52, 55, 60, 73, 83
  to Vange Nord, 82-83, 89, 90, 111, 119,
    122-25
Martin, Mary, 85
Marx, Harpo, 180

Mattes, Merrill J., 221
Maugham, W. Somerset, 66, 141
Mead, Margaret, 25
Medal of Freedom, *pl. 10*, 5, 233
Meeker Museum, 218
Melinda Cox Library, 25
Melville, Herman, 66
*Men at War* (Hemingway), 64
Mercer, Henry, 21
Merrill, Floyd, 55-56, 58, 216, 218,
    219-20
Metcalf, John, 118
Metro-Goldwyn-Mayer, 76, 77, 115, 116,
    196
*Mexico*, 179
Mexico, assignment in, 165
Michener, Edwin (father), 11-12
Michener, Ezra (grandfather), 12-13
Michener, Isaiah (great, great grand-
    father), 12
Michener, James Albert
  adoption of Mark and Brook, 124
  awards, *pl. 10*, 5-6, 80-82, 233
  birth, 11, 13
  in Colorado for *Centennial*, 7, 219-29
  critics' impact on, 3-4
  education, 24-44
    college, 31-44
    high school, *pl. 2*, 24-30
  in Europe on fellowship, 47-49
  first novel, 65-71
  friends, 7-8
  "good citizenship," 8-10
  in Hawaii, 139-50
  heart attack, 186
  insulated life of, 6-7
  interest in Asia, 91-96
  lecture circuit, 101-2
  literary agent, 87
  at Macmillan, 59, 71, 73-88
  marriages
    to Mari Sabusawa, 126-32
    to Patti Koon, 51-52, 55, 60, 73, 83
    to Vange Nord, 82-83, 89, 90, 111,
      119, 122-25
  mother, 11-19
  move back to Bucks County, 89-90
  in navy, *pl. 3*, 61-71
  paintings by, *pl. 9*
  personality, 6-8, 103
  philanthropic work, 8, 120-22
  politics
    Congressional campaign, *pl. 8*,
      173-78

Michener, James Albert—cont.
  politics
    interest in, 153-57, 162-63
    Kennedy campaign, 164-69
    Nixon-Humphrey election, 198-99
    Pennsylvania Constitutional Con-
      vention, 190-94
    philosophy, 154
  public response to, 2, 3
  religion, 8-9, 42-43
  in South Pacific, 61-71, 90-93
  in Spain, 187-90, 200-201
  social revolution, dealing with, 197-211
    Kent State, 201-11
  State Department interest in, 108-11
  teaching experience, 46-47, 49-58
  values, 9-10
  in Venezuela, 192
  work environment, 225-26
  writers contemporary with, 2-3
  writing style, 81, 118, 226-28
  youth, 11-30
    basketball, *pl. 2*, 24, 27-30
    in Doylestown, 13-20, 22-30
    travels, 20-22
Michener, John (ancestor), 12
Michener, Louis (uncle), 12, 40
Michener, Mabel (mother), 11-19
  boardinghouse, 16, 17-18
  illnesses, 14
  photograph, *pl. 1*
  political opinions, 154
  status in Doylestown, 15-16, 18-19
Michener, Mari (third wife)
  Congressional campaign and, 173, 174
  illness, 191
  marriage, 126-32
  photograph, *pl. 6, 8*
  politics of, 155, 162-63
  role of, 222-23
  travels, 181, 183
Michener, Mark (adopted son), 124,
  129-31
Michener, Mary (ancestor), 12
Michener, Patti Koon (first wife), 51-52,
  55, 60, 73, 83
Michener, Robert (brother), 11-12, 13, 19
Michener, Vange Nord (second wife)
  after divorce, 129-31
  marriage, 82-83, 89, 90, 111, 119,
    122-25
  photograph, *pl. 4*
Middle America, Michener's appeal to, 3
Middle East, writing in, 180-84

Mielziner, Joe, 77
Mims, Harriet, 125
Missouri, University of, 153
*Mister Roberts* (Heggen), 75, 86
Mitchell, John, 187
Mitscher, Marc A., 61
Mizrachi, Elie, 184, 185
*Modern Japanese Print, The*, 186
Molarsky, Osmond, 40, 41, 73
Morgan, Neil, 224
Morkawa, Jitsuo, 127
Morse, Otis B., 173
Mother Margaret, 62-63
Motley, Willard, 81
Mulligan, John C., 173
Murra, Wilbur, 60-61, 102-3
Murray, Evaristo de Montalvo, 33, 40
Murray, George C., 22-24, 120
Musial, "Stan the Man," 169

Nai Tok Nuyphakoi, *pl. 5*
*Naked and the Dead, The* (Mailer), 82
National Council of Social Studies, 56,
  60
National Council of Teachers, 49
National Father's Day Committee, 76
*National Geographic* (magazine), 25
National Guardsmen, Kent State
  debacle and, 201-4, 206-8
National Institute of Arts and Letters, 5
National Medal for Literature, 5-6
Navy career, *pl. 3*, 61-71
Navy Gold Cross, 5
New Caledonia, plane crash on, 65
New Deal, 72
*New High School in the Making, The*, 53
*New Republic* (magazine), 107
*New Statesman* (magazine), 148
*Newsweek* (magazine), 1
*New Yorker* (magazine), 107, 162
*New York Herald Tribune* (newspaper), 93,
  94, 117, 148
*New York Times* (newspaper), 4, 75, 83,
  107, 117, 176, 209
*New York Times Book Review*, 149, 233
*New York Times Magazine*, 172, 173, 197,
  228, 229
New Zealand, analysis of life in, 92-93
Nixon, Richard, 163, 170, 174, 194,
  205-6, 229-30
Nord, Vange. *See* Michener, Vange Nord
  (second wife)
Northern Colorado, University of,
  52-58, 237

Novels. *See* specific titles
Nowdoworski, Evangeline. *See* Michener, Vange Nord (second wife)
*Number 15* (Parker), 187

Office of Cultural Exchange, 152-53
O'Hara, John, 116
*Oil* (Sinclair), 48
Orapchuck, Nadia, 228, 236, 239

*Pacific, The* (Resinberg), 64
Paige, Janis, 125
Paintings, *pl. 9,* 171
Pamplona, running with bulls at, 201
Parker, Raymond, 187
*Passage to Vyborg,* 48
Payne, Robert, 94, 107
Pearson, Barbara, 43
Pearson, Drew, 43, 177
Pearson, Paul, 43
Pennell, Joseph, 141
Penn State University, speech at, 197
Pennsylvania Constitutional Convention, 190-94
Perelman, S.J., 89
Pfeiffer, Frank, 125-26
Phi Delta Theta, 34
*Philadelphia Inquirer* (newspaper), 4, 196
Philanthropy, 8, 120-22
Pickett, Clarence, 126
Pinza, Mario, 85
Pipersville, Pennsylvania, 89-90, 119-20, 163, 171, 235
Piszek, Edward, 8
Plane crash on New Caledonia, 65
Pocket Books, 77, 81
*Poland,* 234
Politics
    Congressional campaign, 173-78
    Humphrey campaign, 198-99
    interest in, 153-57, 162-63
    Kennedy campaign, 164-69
    Pennsylvania Constitutional Convention, 190-94
    philosophy, 154
*Politics of Upheaval, The* (Schlesinger), 169
Pollock, Hannah, 14
Porter, Robert, 58, 64-65
Porter, Sylvia, 103
*Portfolio* (magazine), 39
Prado Museum article, 185
Prejudice, religious, 168-69
Prescott, Orville, 75, 77-78, 82
*Presidential Lottery,* 199

President's Commission on Campus Unrest, 205
*Progressive Education* (journal), 59-60
Protestant ethic, 9, 197
Pulitzer Prize
    for *South Pacific,* 86
    for *Tales of the South Pacific,* 5, 80-82
*Pulitzer Prize Novels, The* (Stuckey), 81
*Pulitzer Prizes, The* (Hohenberg), 82

Quaker incident, 235
Quaker values, 8-9, 42-43
*Quality of Life, The,* 197, 211

*Raintree County* (Lockridge), 86
Random House, 9
    changing editors at, 116-17
    contract for four novels, 179-80
    publications
        *Bridge at Andau,* 136
        *Bridges of Toko-ri,* 107
        *Caravans,* 180
        *Centennial,* 230
        *Fires of Spring,* 79-80
        *Hawaii,* 149
        *Iberia,* 189
        *Return to Paradise,* 94
        *Sayonara,* 117
        *Source,* 185
        *Voice of Asia,* 94-95
Rascals in Paradise (Michener and Day), 133, 136
*Reader's Digest* (magazine), 96-101
    assignments
        in Asia, 112-14
        Congressional campaign article, 176
        in Hawaii, 142
        during honeymoon with Mari, 128, 129
        Hungarian revolution, 131, 133-36
        Kent State report, 201-5
        Korean War, 105, 108
        in Mexico, 165
        in Middle East, 180
        Strategic Air Command, 138-39
    development of, 96-98
    short stories, 93
"Red Kimono, The" (article), 228
Religion, 8-9, 42-43
Religious prejudice in politics, 168-69
"Report from the 'Frenzied Fifties'" (article), 172
*Report of the County Chairman,* 163, 164, 167, 170, 171, 178

*Repose 2* (Weber), 187
Research
 on *Centennial,* 220-21, 222
 on Kent State, 204-5
 by mail, 220
*Return to Paradise,* 93, 94, 118, 217
"Return to Paradise" (movie), 94
Reviews, literary, 3-4. *See also* Critics
"Revolution in Middle-Class Values,
 The" (article), 197-98
Rewriting, 226
Rice, Bill, 40
*Riddle of Pandit Nehru, The* (article), 112,
 113
*Rock Bottom* (Mitchell), 187
Rodgers, Richard, 77, 84-85, 87, 158
Rolo, C.J., 83
Roosevelt, Franklin D., 50, 59, 166
*Roots* (Haley), 219-20
Ross, Carmon, 24, 25-26, 30
Royalties, 77, 195
Rubin, Jerry, 205
Rudd, Mark, 205
Russians in Hungary, 134-36

Sabusawa, Lin, 131
Sabusawa, Mari Yoriko. *See* Michener,
 Mari (third wife)
Saigon, observations of, 111-12
Sarnoff, Dorothy, 125
*Saturday Evening Post* (newspaper), 67,
 · 74, 76, 176
*Saturday Review of Literature* (magazine),
 75, 83, 94, 107, 149, 171, 192-93
*Sayonara,* 114-18
Schlesinger, Arthur M., Jr., 169
Scholarship to Swarthmore, 30, 33
Schulberg, Budd, 89
Scott, Cecil, 79, 152
Scott, Hugh, 176
Sekiyas, Sachiko, 125-26
Selberg, Edith M., 53, 54
Self-image, 6-7, 10, 35-36
Selznick, David O., 114
Shane, Terry, 50, 51, 129
Shores, Nancy, 83, 86
Silverman, Ann, 7-8, 9, 124, 128, 171
Silverman, Herman
 building Bucks County home, 90
 on Congressional campaign, 177-78
 friendship of, 7-8, 171
 letters to, 105-6, 111, 122, 123, 128, 181
 real estate ventures, 138
Sinclair, Upton, 48

Smith, Al, 42, 154
Smith, Bradford, 117
Smith, Harvey, 64
Smith, Mary, 76
Sneider, Vern, 117
Social revolution, dealing with, 197-211
Society of Friends, 42-43
Solomon Islands, 61
*Source, The,* 181-85, 196, 217, 232
Sousa, John Philip, 21
South Pacific
 navy duty in, 61-71
 return to, 90-93
*South Pacific* (musical), 83, 84-86, 98, 195
*Space,* 234
*Spectator* (magazine), 118, 148
Spiller, Robert
 letters to, 48, 57, 64
 at Swarthmore, 36, 38-40
*Sports in America,* 234
"Spring Virtue" (poem), 39-40
St. Andrews University (Scotland), 47
St. Leonard's School for Girls, 63
Stanley, Clyde, 223-24
*Star-Bulletin* (newspaper), 143, 155
Stevenson, Adlai, 162, 164
Stevenson, Robert Louis, 66
Stillwell, Red, 106
Stoddard, Charles Warren, 66
Stone, I.F, 204, 209
Stone, Irving, 144
Strategic Air Command article, 137-39
Strauss, Helen
 Asia assignments, 93
 contract for *Voice of Asia,* 94
 encouragement of, 83, 95, 212
 introduction to, 86-88
 *Leyte Gulf* contract, 151-52
 *Reader's Digest* negotiations, 100
 return trip to South Pacific, 90
 *Sayonara* bids, 115-17
 *Source* movie contract, 182
 *Source* reviews, warnings about, 185
 television contract, 157-62
Structure of writing, 216-18
Stuckey, W.J., 81
Students for a Democratic Society
 (SDS), 205
Stump, Admiral, 151
Suburbia, Kennedy campaign in, 167
Suez Canal crisis, 135
Sutton, Horace, 149
Swarthmore, Vange Nord in, 129-30

Swarthmore College
  experience, 31-44
    Chautauqua, 41, 43-44
    fraternities, 33-34
    Honors program, 37-38
    Professor Holmes, 36
    Professor Spiller, 36, 38-40
    social life, 40-41
    Society of Friends membership,
      42-43
    troublemaker image, 35-36
    Woolman House, 32-33
    writing at, 39-40
  scholarship to, 30, 33
  Joshua Lippincott Fellowship award, 47

*Talent for Luck, A* (Strauss), 86
"Tales of South Asia" (articles), 94
*Tales of the South Pacific,* 65-71
  attempted TV series based on, 158
  original version, 90-91
  publication of, 2, 73-74
  Pulitzer Prize for, 5, 80-82
  response to, 74-76
  rewriting, 73
  Rodger's and Hammerstein's interest
    in, 77
  royalties on, 195
  sales, 118
  structure, 217
Taylor, Clarice B., 142-45, 147-48
Taylor, James H., 50
Teaching
  at Colorado State College of Educa-
    tion, 52-58
  at George School, 49-52
  at Harvard's School of Education, 57
  at Hill School, 46-47
Television series, 157-62, 234
*Texas* (TV), 234
Thomas, Norman, 36
Thoreau, Henry David, 210
*Time* (magazine), 4, 117, 148, 209
*Timeless Land, The* (Dark), 141
"Today Show" (TV), 209
*Today's Wild West: The Great Australian
  North* (article), 113
*Today's Woman* (magazine), 93
Tomlinson, "Doc," 28, 29
Toogood, Granville E., 47
*Torch, The* (school magazine), 25, 26, 27
"Tradition and the Individual Talent"
  (Spiller), 38
Trauch, Lester, 24, 25, 85

Treyz, Oliver, 159-61
*Tribune* (Chicago) (newspaper), 118
*Tribune* (Greeley) (newspaper), 55
Truman, Harry S, 72
*Truth about Kent State, The* (Davies), 207
Tulagi (island), 63
*TV Guide* (magazine), 161
Twain, Mark, 6, 17
Twentieth Century Fox, 115, 116, 151-52,
  196
Twining, Ed, 24, 28

U.S. Defense Department, 108
U.S. Information Agency (USIA), 194,
  220, 224
U.S.S. *Kwajalein* (ship), 71
U.S. State Department, 108-11
U.S. Supreme Court, 122
Unfug, Otto, 219
Union League, 36
United Boys' Brigade of America, 22-23,
  120
United Nations, 72
United States Steel, 166-67
*Unit in the Social Studies, The,* 56
"Until They Sail" (movie), 94
*Up the Down Staircase* (Kaufman), 185
USIA, 194, 220, 224

*Vale of Tears, The* (Stalling), 64
*Valley Forge* (ship), 106
Values, 8-10, 42-43
Vanderford, Kenneth, 188-89
Van Pelt, Joseph, 29
Van Sant, Eleanor, 16, 18
*Variety* (newspaper), 115
Venezuela, cultural mission to, 192
*Victim, The* (Bellow), 81
Vietnam War, 7, 196-97
Virginia, University of, 51
Vitarelli, William, 50-51, 90, 121-22, 124,
  193
*Voice of Asia, The,* 94-95, 116, 118

Waddington, Jack, 28
Wallace, DeWitt, 96, 136
Wallace, George, 198-99
Wallace, Irving, 91
*Wanderers, The. See Drifters, The*
Warner Brothers, 116
*Washington Post* (newspaper), 233
Watergate scandal, 229-30
Weber, Max, 187
Webster, H.C., 107

Welcome House, 124, 129-30
Welsh, Johnny, 165, 167-68, 170, 173, 177,
    178, 182, 190
Werner, Herman, 219
Wescott, Glenway, 141
West, Paul, 148
Wexley, John, 89
"What Are We Fighting For?" (article), 60
"While Others Sleep" (article), 138-39
White, Paul Dudley, 186
Whitman, Walt, 6
"Who Is Virgil T. Fry?" (short story), 56
*Who's Who In America,* 11
"Why I Am Running for Congress"
    (article), 176
*Why I Like Japan* (article), 112, 113
Whyte, C.A., 75
Wicker, Tom, 209
Wilbur, Brayton, 109
William Morris Agency, 87, 158, 160,
    161-62

Willow Grove Amusement Park, 21
Winchell, Walter, 90, 176
Woolman, John, 32
Woolman House, 32-33
Work environment, 225-26
Wouk, Herman, 107
Wright, Lauren, 223
Wrinkle, William, 52
Writing, *See also* specific titles
    structure, 216-18
    style, 81, 118, 226-28
    at Swarthmore, 39-40

"Yancy and the Blue Fish" (short story),
    77
Yardley, Jonathan, 233
Youth, alienation of, 199-211
Youth, Michener's, 11-30
    basketball, *pl. 2,* 24, 27-30
    in Doylestown, 13-20, 22-30
    travels, 20-22